THE WAVELESS PLAIN

THE
WAVELESS PLAIN

An Italian Autobiography

by WALTER STARKIE, Litt.D.

LONDON
JOHN MURRAY, ALBEMARLE STREET, W.

First Edition . . . *1938*

Made and Printed in Great Britain by Butler & Tanner Ltd., Frome and London

To
THE CHILDREN
AND
GRANDCHILDREN
OF
DON ALBERTO
AND
DONNA DELFINA

CONTENTS

vii

CONTENTS

CONTENTS

ACKNOWLEDGEMENTS

IN preparing this book I wish to express my indebtedness to the following : T. E. Lawrence, *The Seven Pillars of Wisdom* (London, Jonathan Cape) ; Dr. E. J. Dillon, *The Peace Conference* (London, 1919) ; John Ruskin, *Verona and Other Lectures* (London, 1894) ; G. Gissing, *By the Ionian Sea* (London, 1905). I wish also to express my gratitude to : Professor Cesare Foligno, of Oxford University, for his humanistic work on Padua ; Luigi Villari, for his works on the Fascist Revolution and Italian Expansion ; Professor Camillo Pellizzi, of University College, London, for his works on the aristocracy of Fascism and contemporary Italian Literature ; G. Pitré, for his collections of proverbs, stories, folk legends of Sicily and South Italy ; and many others.

Finally, I wish to thank Professor W. A. Goligher, Vice-Provost of Trinity College, Dublin, and John Grey Murray, for much kind advice.

April 2, 1938.

Many a green isle needs must be
In the deep wide sea of Misery,
Or the mariner, worn and wan,
Never thus could voyage on . . .
. . . .

Ay, many flowering islands lie,
In the waters of wide Agony :
To such a one this morn was led,
My bark by soft winds piloted :
'Mid the mountains Euganean
I stood listening to the Pæan
With which the legioned rooks did hail,
The sun's uprise majestical. . . .
. . . . . .

Lo ! the sun floats up the sky,
Like thought-wingèd Liberty,
Till the universal light
Seems to level plain and height ; . . .
. . . . . .

Noon descends around me now :
'Tis the noon of Autumn's glow,
When a soft and purple mist
Like a vaporous amethyst,
Or an air-dissolvèd star
Mingling light and fragrance, far
From the curved horizon's bound
To the point of Heaven's profound,
Fills the overflowing sky . . .
. . . . . .

And the red and golden vines,
Piercing with their trellised lines
The rough, dark-skirted wilderness;
The dun and bladed grass no less,
Pointing from this hoary tower
In the windless air; the flower
Glimmering at my feet; the line
Of the olive-sandalled Apennine
In the south dimly islanded;
And the Alps, whose snows are spread
High between the clouds and sun . . .

.   .   .   .   .

Noon descends, and after noon
Autumn's evening meets me soon
Leading the infantine moon,
And that one star, which to her
Almost seems to minister,
Half the crimson light she brings
From the sunset's radiant springs . . .

.   .   .   .   .

. . . some calm and blooming cove
Where for me, and those I love,
May a windless bower be built,
Far from passion, pain and guilt . . .

.   .   .   .   .

We may live so happy there
That the Spirits of the Air
Envying us, may even entice
To our healing Paradise
The polluting multitude;
But their rage would be subdued,
By that clime divine and calm,
And the winds whose wings rain balm

On the uplifted soul, and leaves
Under which the bright sea heaves;
While each breathless interval
In their whisperings musical
The inspired soul supplies,
With its own deep melodies;
And, the love which heals all strife,
Circling, like the breath of life,
All things in that sweet abode
With its own mild brotherhood.

. . . . . .

[From Shelley's *Lines*
written among the Euganean Hills.]

PROLOGUE

Lo ! the sun upsprings behind,
Broad, red, radiant, half-reclined.
On the level quivering line,
Of the waters crystalline :
And before that chasm of light
As within a furnace bright,
Column, tower, and dome, and spire
Shine like obelisks of fire.

ONE day, when I was fourteen years of age, I
happened to read Shelley's poem written
among the Euganean hills and all of a sudden
a flash of sunlight entered my soul, revealing the infinite
beauty of Italy, the land of countless memories. I never
forgot the poem ; its rhythms and its swift visions of
history conjured up by a Titanic spirit gifted with the
wings of Ariel would steal into my mind at certain
moments of solitude like a melody of Mozart. When I
visited the Waveless Plain in my early twenties I repeated
those lines as I stood before the house in the mountain
village of Arquà where Petrarch lived and died. Their
music took on a mellower harmony some years later
when my life was linked to Italy by stronger bonds.
And again, after passing some distance down the half-
way road of life through the dark wood, those lines took
on an added meaning when I gazed back at Rome, the
eternal city, with its towers and domes and spires, shining like obelisks of fire in the setting sun. Italy had

become for me, as for many of my countrymen in the past, a flowering isle creating in my mind deep melodies and the love which heals all strife. The only excuse for writing this chapter in the story of my life is a wish to share the thoughts, observations and rhythms which had accumulated over the space of twenty years in the mind of a humble wanderer, whose one restless wish was to get his earful as well as his eyeful on the road of life.

CHAPTER I

THE THREE WAR SONGS

A VISITOR to Milan in the early days of 1915 would have seen huge processions of young men marching through the streets with arms linked together, chanting rhythmically a marching song. Gradually the chorus would swell in volume as the crowds in the streets, the cafés, and the shops took up the refrain. The procession was mainly composed of youths, but they came from every stratum of society. There were pale students, bespectacled clerks of Government offices, brawny athletes, thick-set manual workers, brown-skinned peasants. An eager, excited crowd they were, and their voices were discordant, for their speech was a medley of a hundred dialects. From every region of the country they came; Venetians cheek by jowl with Sardinians, Milanese and Roman arm-in-arm with Calabrian and Sicilian. Such was the crowd that sang, in May 1915, the Song of Intervention whose refrain was:

> Abbasso l'Austria
> E la Germania
> Con la Turchia
> In compagnia!

Here and there dozens of newsboys darted like quicksilver in and out of the crowd, up and down the steps of palaces, through the cafés selling papers, and their harsh reiterated cries of " *Popolo d'Italia !* " sounded as a

kind of counterpoint to the immense chorus. There
was as much wild vigour of youth in the headlines
sprawled across that newspaper as in the crowd itself.
The *Popolo d'Italia* contained the words for the music
they were singing. The words had been composed
by Benito Mussolini, *enfant terrible* of Socialism, ex-
editor of Socialism's mouthpiece, the *Avanti*. The
Popolo d'Italia roused the New Italy. It was Mussolini's
first and favourite sword, as doughty a weapon for him
as Orlando's. The first flaming article in it was headed
" Audacity," and its two mottoes were, " He who has
a sword has bread," and " Revolution is an idea that
has found bayonets for its needs."

The scene changes to a rocky headland in Genoa, the
Rock of Quarto whence Garibaldi in 1860 had set sail
for the conquest of the South and United Italy. It is
the 5th of May 1915, the anniversary of the greatest
Condottiere. Italy's national bard stands alone on the
rock and harangues the crowd. His words rise and
fall like soft, sensuous music, but the venom seethes
through the veins of the mob, rousing them to passionate outburst. Again the Song of Intervention
surges through the air and can be heard by the hosts of
fishermen in their little boats moored off the coast.
And so Italy abandoned the Triple Alliance and declared
war. The creator of the New Italy wrote in his paper :

To-day the nation has been called to arms. Henceforth there
are but Italians. To-day, when steel is striking against steel,
only one cry bursts from us : Evviva Italia. We have never felt
so strongly as at this moment that we have a Fatherland ; we have
never felt so strongly as now that Italy is an historical personality,
that Italy is something embodied, living and immortal.

Then followed the ceaseless sound of tramping soldiers
in the streets of the cities. Good-bye Italy of Boccaccio and Botticelli, Petrarch and Poliziano. Farewell

museums and churches with façades hidden behind piled-up sand-bags. Henceforth the thoughts of the whole nation turned to the Northern frontier high above the Venetian plain on ice-ledges where soldiers had to possess as much of the pioneer and polar explorer as the fighter in their nature. It was now that the prophecy of Marinetti, the leader of the Futurists, was accomplished—Marinetti, who aroused the amused curiosity of Londoners when they visited his exhibition of Futurism before the War. When we read his poetry we little thought that he was to become a European seer. *La Conquête des Étoiles* (1902) and *La Ville Charnelle* (1908) when they appeared aroused but little comment, for their pounding and jagged rhythms, their strident onomatopœia made no appeal to a world at peace; but as soon as war broke out Marinetti swept into our ken with his battle-cry:

" Holla-hé ! Holla-ho ! Stridionla Stridionla Stridionlaire ! " Nature became transformed by the wildness of his poetic imagery. The sea with its battle-cruisers and submarines became, as he had said, the Reservoir of Death with its " Petrified bodies, bodies of steel, embers and gold, furnace of stars, those who died after stoking within their blood the fire of the Idea, the great flame of the Absolute that encompassed them."

Farewell Petrarch, crowned with Virgil's laurel. Henceforth the Vates of Italy will sing no more of Laura. His mistress will be the machine wherewith Man will conquer the stars. The poet will become absorbed by the scientific universe and will portray Man as a dynamo. The author of *Le démon de la vitesse* explains the soul underlying the kaleidoscopic transformations of Italy with its vital impetus and its Nietzschean motto that " Life is to be mounted and

not to be descended. The whole of life is in the strain-
ing upwards."

And so the inferno raged, up in the snowy Alps and
down upon the parched ridges of the Carso near the
Gulf of Trieste—a summer and a winter war simultaneously. We need only read the war diary of Sergeant
Benito Mussolini of the Bersaglieri to capture the spirit
of those days and life in the front-line trenches of the
Alto Isonzo in 1915.

Pale sunshine [he writes in one place]. The scene is a mountain
trench under a terribly heavy fire. Nothing to do. Wounded
men passing, one by one. Donadonibus, the Bersagliere, is having
a glimpse of the sun. Cavalry to right of us, cavalry to left of us.

Another entry :

The life of the trenches is a natural life—primitive and a bit
monotonous. Everyone gets sleep when he likes. During the
day we do nothing. One may go and search for one's friends in
the other Companies at the risk and peril of being hit by an impec-
cable cecchino (the picked snipers of the Austrian army). We
play sette e mezzo, and, when cards are lacking, testa e croce.
When the cannon are firing we count the shots. The distribution
of food and drink are the only diversions of the day.

A last entry :

We are among the rocks. It is not cold. The night is starry.
Silence. We have reached the heights ! The heights ! There is
the smoke of the cannon upon them !

Such was the cry of modern Europe's greatest
Nietzschean.

I hear another song sounding faintly through a thick
snowdrift. It is a song of the Alpini—" quel mazzolin
di fiori " (that bunch of flowers from the mountain).
The wind blows on the heights but the outposts stand
ready with their hand grenades. Suddenly a song
awakens response from a neighbouring peak, a slow,

plaintive sound of a harmonica. Down in the valley the hidden torrent murmurs. The opposing outposts listen to the music, a vision of tenderness, far-off homes, a farmhouse in the Venetian plain, a wattle hut out on the Puszta, far-off women who have been waiting a long time, the scent of May in the distant furrows.

The music ceases.

" Bona note, porci taliani ! "

" Bona note, fioi di cani ! "

Such was the daily scene on which the Alpini played their part—a scene which lives in the epic pages of Paolo Monelli, chronicler of the Alpini.[1] A rapid procession of heroes passes before my inner eye when I hum the melody of that Alpine song—heroes of battles on the Isonzo and of the capture of Gorizia. Captain Bosio with his detachment clambering up a peak in the Dolomites in the snow, roped together ready to attack the enemy garrison : Captain Menotti Garibaldi fighting like a demon with his band on the heights of Pizzo Serauta. Then I see a small force advancing to rush the Sabotino, under the leadership of Colonel Badoglio, the future Field-Marshal. The procession continues. In one place I see a General Commander of a division who, though wounded and ill, led his troops to the attack and was carried into action on a chair. Near him is an old Roman of the people, Enrico Toti by name, hobbling into action on a crutch. Crutch and age did not prevent him from becoming a Bersagliere and he was the first to hobble out of his trench towards the enemy. Twice wounded he was before he fell, and with his dying strength he hurled his crutch into the enemy lines.

The procession advances. From the mountain heights we descend to the Carso Plateau with its caverns, wire

[1] P. Monelli, *Le Scarpe al Sole*, 4th ed., Milano, 1928.

entanglements, and trenches embedded in the rocks. I then begin to hear the third song—" Le Campane di San Giusto " (The Bells of San Giusto). Whenever the Italian soldiers crawling through the inferno of that plateau sang the song they fancied they heard the church bells of San Giusto booming in response. The bells of San Giusto were the Fata Morgana, or mirage, to many a man as he lay gasping in agony on that rocky waste. When finally the triumphant army gathered in Trieste after its capture, a chorus of soldiers singing the song on the piazza outside the Venerable Church made it into a hymn of victory.

CHAPTER II

NO. 1 RED CROSS

"STARKIE," said the chief, " get ready for a spot of work : we're going to lend you to-day to the Italian Red Cross."

" A pledge of Anglo-Italian friendship, I suppose : I'm complimented."

" Yes, fetch that fiddle of yours and go off to the Red Cross Hospital No. 1 ; there's a celebration this afternoon in honour of the battle of Vittorio Veneto. Play them all your highbrow stuff, but don't forget to add in some English, Scottish, and Irish tunes in honour of the occasion."

" Where are you off to ? " said my room-mate inquisitively, as he watched me setting out. For answer I whistled a few bars of " O Sole Mio."

" The devil rides the fiddle-bow," said he with a grin ; " mind your step with the signorinas."

The streets of Genoa were crowded, and the Piazza de Ferrari was ablaze with the flags of the Allies. Small, ragged urchins dashed in and out of the clusters of people shouting the latest news in shrill voices. The sounds of the traffic rose and fell in ceaseless tide, and the flapping bunting of many colours seemed to be the personification of the crowd's excitement. On the bridge over the diminutive river Bisagno, myriads of twittering swallows were perched in shrill conclave ; even they halted to celebrate the victory before speeding away on their winter journey to the South.

7

The Red Cross Hospital was situated in a building that had been a primary school—a dilapidated barrack, full of dark passages. The great central courtyard was decorated with Italian flags, paper garlands, and bright lights of different colours. Here I found row after row of wounded soldiers dressed in the white hospital uniform. Against the wall were the bed cases, and in the centre, in serried mass, sat the others, with here and there groups of Red Cross nurses. When I had recovered from the all-pervading smell of iodoform I began to distinguish the various types. There were fair-haired youths from the mountain districts of Piemonte, alert Alpini and Bersaglieri together with swarthy, bronzed Sicilians and solemn-looking Sardinians. The room became for me a blurred outline of coloured lights, through which I saw visions of bandaged legs, arms, and heads. Amidst the ceaseless buzz of the conversation, the intermittent sound of crutches and iron-tipped sticks against the stone floor came as a jagged, nerve-racking reminder. On the stage, which was draped in the Italian Tricolor, the musical and dramatic performance was given. There were songs, there were short dramatic sketches, and there were speeches. The grey-haired Colonel thrilled me by his characteristic style of oratory. It was not necessary to follow even the meaning of his speech when one was hypnotized by the rhythm and melody of his language. When it was my turn to play, the Colonel introduced me with some charming words in honour of " our noble Allies, the British, who shared in the final and greatest victory of the War."

After playing the usual selection of pieces with a hop, skip, and a jump in them, such as the " Zigeunerweisen " of Sarasate and the " Hejre Kati " of Hubay, I went on to our own war tunes and played them one

after another, introducing them with a few Italian words
of comment—first of all " Tipperary," then " Pack up
your troubles," " Hold your hand out, naughty boy,"
and " The long, long trail." When I had told them
how those tunes had resounded on every British battle-
field and in every hospital, there was a roar of applause,
and the Italian soldiers began to hum their own tunes.
Then some of them called out : " Signorina Italia !
Signorina Italia ! " A young Red Cross nurse came
on to the stage and sat down at the piano. After
preluding for a moment she began to sing, in a beautiful
high soprano voice, the " Canzone dell' Alpino." She
was a lovely girl with pink and white complexion and
golden hair that glittered in the lights of the hall. As
she sang, her voice, which at first had faltered nervously,
began to swell in volume, and her face became fixed
in a mask of sadness. There was a strange quality of
pathos about her singing, which brought tears to the
eyes of those soldiers. Dressed in a white uniform, with
the blood-red cross on her veil, she was like a spirit
flitting above this world of suffering. She was, during
the instant of her singing, the personification of the
spirit of womanhood, because she became for every
lonely soldier in that throng, gifted with the magic
power of reminding him of mother, sister, wife, and
daughter.

After the song of the Alpine soldier she sang
the " Canzone del Grappa " with its memories of
the victory the year before. And then she sang " Le
Campane di San Giusto," the song of redeemed Trieste.
Her clear voice resounded through the silent hall, but
every few moments it would be answered by the rugged,
full-throated chorus of the soldiers. The wounded
soldier next to me whispered : " She is a mother to us
—not a day passes without her coming into the wards

and singing to us the songs we need. She makes us weep when she sings us the tunes we used to hear in the village. She is indeed a mother to all of us." As I listened to her I realized what a deep part patriotic songs play in Italian history. Not an event has taken place in the past 100 years but has found its minstrel to record it in songs which are still remembered by the unlettered folk. The soldiers who fought on the Isonzo and the Piave sang, in their dug-outs, of Oberdan, the ill-fated youth, who was executed by the Austrians in 1882, and they repeated in chorus the old Garibaldian hymns no less than the modern songs of the Great War.

As the girl sang on I thought of Dante's lovely line to Beatrice in the *Vita Nuova*—

" Amore e'l cor gentil sono una cosa."

I then understood the meaning of that beautiful Italian quality of *gentilezza* which we find among all classes of the people, that graciousness towards the sick which springs from innate courtesy of heart. Her singing was youthful in its freshness, but its deep appeal sprang from an inherited tradition of centuries. No matter how modern and commonplace the idiom of those songs might be, there was yet in her singing that sense of cultivated primitiveness which made me, in the flash of a moment, see a whole galaxy of Italian womanhood stretching back in pale, tenuous line to the three eternal heroines, Beatrice, Laura, Fiammetta. I also remembered how Castiglione had said that beauty was the result of emotional struggle in past lives. And it was necessary that all the sufferings and agonized memories of those wounded soldiers should project and dissolve themselves in the singing of that golden-haired girl.

CAMP-FOLLOWER

In the concluding months of the War I found myself
a camp-follower in Italy. Although I had volunteered
for military service on the 4th of August 1914, and at
intervals, I had never succeeded in being passed fit for
active service on account of chronic asthma, from which
I had suffered all my life. C3 I was born and C3 I
would have to remain. I had lived all through that
tragically exalted period of 1914, when the first hundred
thousand had set out, full of the glorious wish to make
a world fit for heroes. Anglo-Irish I was born and
Anglo-Irish I wish to be, for was it not a fact that the
Anglo-Irish have always been the salt of the British
Empire? Nowadays it is the fashion to make us
dwindle into West Britons, flitting pathetically in a
vague Limbo between Gael and Anglo-Saxon ; but like
all other Anglo-Irish I was deeply conscious of my
Irish nationality : for what is nationality but the earth
one springs from and the sky above? The Irish made
me deeply conscious of the region whence I sprang, but
to that was added a sense of universality due to the
English traditions of my family. I had been educated
at Shrewsbury School, and had learnt to love all that
was purest and best in England :

> " This land of such dear souls, this dear, dear land—
> Dear for her reputation through the world."

One may well pity the Anglo-Irish because they find it
difficult to reach perfect equilibrium, pulled, as they
are, aside by the tensions caused by two mother-races
in opposition.

When 1914 came, I was eager to join my old Shrewsbury companions or those from Trinity College who set
out for Flanders, but it was my misfortune to be left at

home eating my heart out, and falling gradually into that neurotic condition of inferiority. Then when 1916 came, and Irish youths I had known joined up in the desperate movement to liberate Ireland, I had the same sense of frustration as I looked with detachment on those agonizing scenes of slaughter and burning. My intimate tragedy was due to the feeling of loneliness. In common with all the rest of that generation I longed to be associated in some great movement, but it was my destiny to be a lonely individual gazing with detachment on a world in flames. In those days I used to console myself in music : I always had vague ideas of the magic of music, and nothing would have pleased me more than to live from hand to mouth as a fiddler in fairs. A minstrel is a pariah : he belongs to no party ; he is mocked and jeered at except when he has caught the ear of the people ; but he possesses the gift of freedom, and he can win his way through the world by his wizardry.

After a period of clerical work in the Colonial Office, I volunteered for service with the Y.M.C.A. abroad. That organization did wonderful work throughout the War in establishing canteens, huts, and relief of every description, for the soldiers in the trenches and behind the lines. In addition to hut-work, it collaborated with the army authorities in carrying out a huge army education scheme, whereby soldiers could prepare themselves for their re-entry into civil life after the War. The Y.M.C.A. was my salvation, for it gave me a purpose in life at a moment when I was sunk in despondency. " We'll send you to Italy," said the chief, " and we'll use you as a hut-worker, teacher of languages, lecturer, and above all, fiddler." " Call me camp-follower, sir," said I, " and there's no title I'd rather have."

The Y.M.C.A. abroad was an amazing collection of

varied types. The army standardizes men and turns them all out identical in externals. The Y.M.C.A. was a collection of individuals making use of their special little talents for the benefit of the troops. Their duty was to soften the routine and discipline by their efforts. Men and women of every nationality within the Empire were to be found in the ranks of the organization. In my billet in Italy there were Canadians, Australians, South Africans, as well as English, Irish, Scotch, and Welsh. Some were discharged soldiers, who had fought two years in the trenches in France and wore the silver GR badge. Others were rabid Pacifists, who were ready to go to jail rather than fire a shot, but were ever eager to tend the wounded and carry stretchers from the firing line.

Although the organization belonged to the Protestant Church there were many Catholics, like myself, eager to co-operate. During all the time I worked in the Y.M.C.A. I never heard an intolerant word, although we were a veritable babel of religions. The toleration we had in those days is best described by a little anecdote : a Jewish padre I knew was one day going up the line, and it was noticed that he was carrying a small crucifix. " What are you doing with that crucifix ? " said the fellows in surprise. " You never know," said the Jew, " what may happen in an advance ; I always keep the crucifix with me in case I see some poor Christian lying out in No-man's land."

Men there were of all sizes and shapes. One friend of mine, a devoted hut-worker, who weighed twenty-three stone, was one of the fattest men I have ever seen. Another was a hunchback, a bright-eyed Scotsman, with whom I used to feel quite embarrassed when in Naples, because the girls would insist on touching his hump to bring them luck in the lottery. Every profession of civil life was represented in our ranks, and those varied talents were always of use in the pioneer work of running huts and canteens in mountain warfare. No matter how individual a man's profession had been, there was always a chance for him in the Y.M.C.A. If he had been an acrobat, conjurer, or comic artist of the music-halls, he found glory and fame in the huts and camp theatres all over North Italy. One man I knew had a strange record : he had dressed in jersey and shorts and worn an iron mask over his face, and wheeled a perambulator around the world. " What did you do that for ? " said I. " It was a bet of £10,000 made by two English lords. I made my way by selling picture post cards of myself in every town I came to. When the War broke out I had done most of the journey, and luckily the bet was paid up."

Do not imagine that the duties of the Y.M.C.A. worker were limited to the British troops—a great deal of our time was devoted to making friendly relations with the natives of the foreign country. In a country like Italy, with which the British were unfamiliar, it was necessary to interpret our mentality to the Italians and the Italian mentality to the British. In those days English people possessed many mistaken views concerning continental relations. As a result of being an island nation, we have been inclined to look upon the continentals in the same way as the Romans looked upon the barbarians. But four years' trench warfare together had broken down many of the barriers.

In Italy the task of fostering good relations between British and Italian troops was more difficult, because in England there has always been a tendency to look upon the Italian as a stagy, unreal character. Right from the moment of my arrival in Italy I realized that the stage-Italian was a greater curse even to his

country than the stage-Irishman was to my own. The
stage-Irishman sprang up at a period in Irish history
when the fires of nationality burnt low. He was the
product of a superiority-complex in the English and an
inferiority-complex in the Irish. It took the full battery
of George Bernard Shaw's satire to blow the stage-
Irishman sky-high, and shatter the complacency of
people who failed to realize that while they were creating
a comic Irishman in fiction, they were creating a tragic
Irishman in fact. If Ireland, which is only separated
from England by a thin strip of channel, has always been
misunderstood, what shall we say of Italy, with its
Mediterranean soul so contrary to the Nordic? The
trouble with Italy is that we have never allowed its
inhabitants to leave the stage. Italian has to be the
language of rhetorical superlatives—a language full of
exaggerated gestures. Italy taught Europe how to act
and how to sing in opera. Consequently, every Italian
is a *primo tenore* who advances to the footlights and
tickles the ears of the groundlings by his florid voice ;
or else he is always some poor devil of a Harlequin
playing for ever the part of the clown.

Among the British troops there were few who
thought of the Italians except as Dago, mandoline
player, or ice-cream vendor. Originally the word
' Dago ' was applied indiscriminately to Portuguese,
Spaniard or Italian, but during the War it was used by
the Tommy, with a certain affectionate contempt, when
speaking of his Italian allies. " Don't get into a quarrel
with any o' them Dagos," said a corporal friend of mine,
" for they'll do the dirty on you. They won't stand
up to you and box ; they prefer to pull out a dagger and
knife you in the back." Fortunately, mutual ignorance
of the language prevented many a bloody quarrel.
When the troops got to know one another, they were

amazed to find that the Italian was more or less the same individual as a British Tommy. He did not sell ice-cream, play barrel-organs, or sing " O Sole Mio " all day. After a short time in Italy one discovered that the stage-Italian was a false creature invented in order to bamboozle the stranger. Whenever the Italian is not serious he becomes an actor, or an opera-singer, but it is a dangerous thing to mistake this external flam-boyancy for the soul of a country which has always been distinguished by its sober seriousness. Every country has a real or imaginary type in which it incar-nates its own qualities. Ulysses was the symbol of ancient Greece ; Don Quixote was the symbol of Spain. When we come to Italy we have only to gaze at the fur-rowed, ascetic brow of Dante to discover the traditional seriousness of the Italian, who, in the words of Giambat-tista Vico, cultivates " a kind of divinity in his mind."

The titanic form of Dante still stands out upon the medieval background of Italy, to point the way along which Italian history was to travel, by those magnificent individuals of the Renaissance. When the blight set in and literature lost its soul, only to become a game of trickery for yawning courtiers, there arose Vico, who continued Dante's serious message and proclaimed the religious conscience of Italy. Then, at the end of the eighteenth century, came Vittorio Alfieri (another Italian who does not laugh, as Gentile calls him), to proclaim, in a louder voice, the gospel of will and character. Alfieri created the model hero in whose image the great men of the Risorgimento modelled themselves, when they set out on their task of unifying their country.

Without that serious, tenacious Dante-Vico-Alfieri-Risorgimento spirit we could not explain the immense war-effort of Italy ; for we should not forget that out of her total population of 36,120,000 Italy mobilized

5,230,000 men, equal to 14.48 per cent. (Of the allied powers, France alone mobilized a higher percentage of her population,—20.08 per cent.[1]) It was all the more surprising that after the terrible defeat of Caporetto in 1917, when, as a result of the Russian Revolution the seeds of discord had been sown in the country, and anti-military propaganda had undermined the morale of the troops, so far from giving way to despair, the spirit of Italy revealed itself in all its strength in the days that culminated in the glorious victory of Vittorio Veneto. It was natural that the five British divisions and six French divisions who arrived in Italy in December, 1917, should look upon themselves as saviours of the country, but before they arrived the Italians had already turned at bay and stopped the enemy advance. They welcomed the arrival of the Allies with joy. The troop trains were received with bands and singing, and bouquets were showered upon them. The consequence was that the soldiers who had come from the grim, shell-swept trenches of France to the fertile land of the Piave, were inclined to minimize the difficulties of the Italian campaign. They had not witnessed the amazing scenes of mountain-campaigning in the Alps ; they were unaware of the terrible conflict on the pitiless, rocky escarpments of the Carso, or the eleven battles of the Isonzo. What could they know of the sufferings endured by Neapolitans, Calabrians, and Sicilians, who were obliged to fight in the glaciers and snows of the Alps after lives spent in the tropical climate of the South ?

Before I had been many weeks in Italy I realized the truth of the old adage : *" L'Italiano farà da se " (the Italian will do the job himself). Too long through her history had Italy watched the foreign soldiers map out

[1] L. Villari, *The War on the Italian Front*, London, 1932, p. 294.

her destiny. Vittorio Veneto was the beginning of the New Italy. On the 3rd of November, when the Italian armistice was signed, the *Popolo d'Italia* published the following paragraph :

It is the great hour of divine joy, when the tumult of emotion suspends the beating of hearts and gives us a lump in the throat. The long passion, crowned at last by triumph, draws tears even from eyes which have seen much and wept much.

We are at Udine. We are at Trieste. We are at Trento. Who is the Italian worthy of the name, who does not grasp the immense historic significance of what has been accomplished in these days by our heroic armies ?

Let a rending shout arouse the *piazze* and the streets from the Alps to Sicily :

"Viva, Viva, Viva l'Italia !"

The article was signed : " Mussolini." [1]

[1] L. Villari, *The War on the Italian Front*, London, 1932, p. 274.

CHAPTER III

WITCHES' SABBATH

EARLY on the 11th of November 1918, the sirens of the ships in Genoa harbour announced that the World War was over! Genoa went as wild as London, Rome or Paris. For three days and three nights the people surged through the streets singing songs, shouting, and all life became one huge Kermesse. Up the line when the greatest War history has ever known ended, the peace was welcomed with more solemnity, more dignity, for men thought of the pals who had gone for ever and jubilation was tinged with sadness. But among the great masses of the cities instinct drove men wild, and those who shouted themselves hoarse and rose to the dizziest heights of jingoism were not always those who had lived the life of the trenches. As for me, the 11th of November remains a day of sad memories in spite of all its orgies. I had gone early in the afternoon to the British Army hospital situated in the Grand Hotel Miramare—a mighty caravanserai perched on a slope overlooking the port of Genoa. One of my friends, a young Irish officer in the Flying Corps, had fallen victim to the terrible Spanish influenza, which raged among the troops with the ferocity of the Black Death. My friend had crashed on the Piave front in the previous month and had been sent to recuperate in Genoa. While in the hospital he had contracted influenza which culminated in pneumonia.

When I reached the hospital the sister told me that he had died at 11.30, just after the sirens had announced the end of the War. " He did not want to die," said the sister tearfully. " He was murmuring all the time through his delirium of the Armistice. He would pray incoherently, begging God not to take him away after three years' gruelling service as a pilot on the French and Italian fronts." As she spoke to me I heard a ceaseless hammering near by.

" What is that row ? " said I.

" They are hammering at coffins out in the yard. The men are dying like flies in here. The undertakers in Genoa have more than enough to do and they say there is not enough wood for the coffins. They are burying the poor in any old packing-case."

The hospital was full to overflowing with patients : many of the wards I passed had sinister screens around some of the beds and I saw priests flit by like phantoms. Even the corridors were crowded with patients in every stage of illness : some lay in a stupor with eyes closed, others sat up and tried feebly to celebrate the occasion by waving tiny allied flags at me as I passed. One of the strange peculiarities of the human heart is that it puts up a stubborn resistance against sadness. My conscience told me to leave the hospital and return to my billet to spend the rest of the day in silent meditation on the departure of my friend. After all, why should we spend the Armistice Day in jollification ? Surely it is the day of memory when we should call up the ghosts of friends who have died in the War. It is they who stand beside us murmuring *memento mori* just as the Oriental King's slave used to do when his master was feasting. But soon after I had descended from the hospital into the crowded street all my phantoms took to their heels and flitted away, leaving my heart and my

mind completely devoid of any thought that was not
of the moment. My friends, too, did their best to chase
away the blues. " Come on," said Corporal Wood—a
beady-eyed little fellow who had draped a flag round
his waist and was prancing up and down like a bucking
broncho. He and his pal Sergeant Turner were good
friends of mine—or rather fellow-vagabonds. They
shared with me an irresistible mania for exploring the
picturesque lower haunts of Italian cities. Whenever
we could escape on any pretext from routine and discipline we would dodge the military police and disappear
in the maze of narrow Genoese streets, ending up as
often as not in one of the sinister little marine taverns
near the Banco San Giorgio.

With my two companions I went first of all to the
Olimpia—one of the big cafés in the central square of
Genoa. Inside the scene recalled pre-War luxury with
its crowds of smartly-dressed men and ladies. At the
end of the hall an American band syncopated and ragged
more and more as the corks popped and the champagne
flowed in golden streams into one glass after another.
The leader, a plump, podgy man, worked himself into an
apopleptic fit as he sweated in his fiddling against the
blaring saxophones and rumbling drums. At one side
of the room a girl, who was sitting with an officer,
suddenly started to sing at the top of her voice and
climbed up on to the table, knocking down all the
glasses as she did so. She was an intoxicated, dishevelled nymph and as she sang her body swayed to
and fro as though she wanted to whip herself into a
triumphant " cancan " but had not the energy. At last
she missed her footing and fell off the table into the arms
of her cavalier. In another corner I saw a fat, sallow-
faced man pull a thousand-lire note from his pocket and
wave it in the air. Then he lit a match and ostentatiously

started to burn the note, but the fair-haired houri by his side took up a bottle of champagne and deluged the note, the tablecloth and the shirt-front of the fat man. After that exhibition of *nouveau riche* mentality they embraced one another affectionately and their neighbours cheered, all except a severe-looking married pair near us who gazed grimly at them, murmuring under their breath, " Pescicani " (sharks), which is the name given by the Italians to war profiteers.

The air in the café was stifling and there was an atmosphere of unreality about it all. " Not many of those blighters ever heard a shot fired in anger," said my friend Sergeant Turner. " Last year they squealed after Caporetto and would have made a separate peace with Austria. To-night they'll binge in honour of ' the glorious victory to which we have contributed.' " Outside in a side-alley we met a trio of wounded Italian soldiers hobbling pitifully along. They were peasants from the Venetian province just released from hospital and they had not a sou in their pockets with which to buy a drink on this night. With them we wended our way to the humbler cafés off the Piazza to drink the health of Italy in Chianti and Barbera. Soon all the miseries of the War were forgotten and those three Italian soldiers became our brothers. There was a fiddler in one of the cafés and Wood made him hand me his violin and I started playing. Rhythm intoxicates people more than drink, and in a trice everyone in the café was as wild as a troop of Indians dancing their war-dance. When we became wearied of the enclosed space I made for the street and continued playing, followed by about a score of excited people singing and capering. My mind was in a maze : the Chianti I had drunk and the frenzy of the people made me play as in a dream. We halted at the Carlo Felice theatre in the shadow of the statue of Garibaldi on horseback. Then a mad idea struck Corporal Wood. " Why not climb up on top of the statue and play your fiddle from there for the crowd ? " No sooner said than done. Intoxicated as I was I managed to hoist myself up the slippery side of the horse aided by my two British friends, but when I got to the top I longed for the powers of a Blondin. Only he could have balanced securely on the perilous saddle. My two companions then climbed up and held me while I played. Meanwhile the crowd below cheered and cried out " Viva L'Inghilterra," and I felt the urge to play " God save the King " followed by the " Marseillaise " and the " Hymn of Garibaldi." Mentally I begged the pardon of the great old hero of Caprera for playing the fiddle standing on his horse. I felt it was blasphemy, for it made me think of Nero fiddling while Rome was burning.

We were now wearied of singing and shouting and the Piazza had no more adventures for us, so we started off to discover the street of the red lanterns, but though we searched we could not find any house that suggested women, wine, and song. We walked up and down many of the narrow streets leading to the Piazza Caricamento, deep in the heart of the port of Genoa, but in vain. At length as we were arguing, a young man approached and said to us in French : " Est-ce que vous désirez trouver des femmes ? " and when we answered in the affirmative he brought us into a narrow street where most of the houses were patronized by sailors.

The night was hot and stuffy : the smell of garlic, rotten fish and latrines wellnigh overpowering. Genoa is an ancient city and the quarter we were traversing lay near the Banco San Giorgio which, history says, lent money to the ancient English kings. The drainage was in keeping with the medieval architecture. It was

so narrow a street that people leaning out of the upper
windows could nearly touch the walls on the opposite
side. Out of every window hung the inevitable ragged
clothing to dry, and in the dim light they gave the
street a fantastic appearance : they were like countless
white flags fluttering to welcome the approach of the
skeleton of death.

These streets to-night seemed strangely silent, but
in the distance I could hear the shouts of the crowd, and
every now and then the long-drawn hiss followed by a
bang of fireworks. Our footsteps echoed as we walked.
There was rottenness in the air and it seemed to permeate
one's bones. All my excitement had evaporated and
depressing thoughts began to crowd upon me like a host
of ill-omened ravens. Every step we took brought up
vague visions which were all the more macabre because
they peered at me from dark corners. In one doorway
I saw wizened, toothless old hags whispering : in another
I saw two deaf mutes with their faces close together
gesticulating with finger and thumb, making ghastly
gurgling sounds in their attempts to convey their meaning. At the corner of one street we ran into a group
of men dressed in black, shuffling along noiselessly,
carrying on their shoulders an empty coffin. At last
our guide knocked at a door, and after a few seconds
a voice cried out from above hoarsely—" Chi è " (who is
it ?) and then we heard the sound of a wire being pulled
and the door suddenly sprang open disclosing a long,
gloomy passage. While we paused at the door a for-
midable-looking woman advanced along the passage
towards us. She was enormous in size, pale, with
masses of black hair, but on her left cheek was a deep
scar that gave a sinister expression to her witch-like face.
After gazing at us from head to toe she beckoned to
us to follow her into the house. My two companions

and the guide entered after her but I stood in the street irresolute. I heard shouts of laughter and drunken singing as a door opened at the end of the passage.

The ravens had now completely surrounded me, flapping their black wings.

I rushed away into the dawn.

CHAPTER IV

WANDERER IN GENOA

GENOA initiated me into Italian life. Now that I have known it for twenty years, it has been associated in my mind with all the different phases of Italian history. Genoa gives me what Goethe called " a sense of the past and present as being one : a conception which infuses a spectral element into the present." Whenever in my mind I try to conjure up in a flash the exquisite loveliness of Italy, I see before me the vision of Genoa from the sea. It is a sunny morning and we are moored outside the harbour. In the clear air the city rises like a gigantic jewel glittering in its rugged Alpine setting. In the distance the bright-hued buildings soaring tier by tier give the impression of having been honeycombed out of the Ligurian mountains. From the boat it looks like a fantastic city of the Genii, created by magic power—a dream city evoked by the caprice of a wizard who might with a sudden Satanic impulse cast it hurtling into the calm waters at its feet. A stronghold of pirates. Even to-day the old boatman wearing his red, worsted cap testifies to a long race of daring devils of the sea. Even in 400 B.C. the Genoese in their rocky fortress traded with Greeks, Etruscans, and Celts. Long before the Genoese republic was established, its sailors were the protectors of the coast towns against the Saracen invasions.

The city ascends from the port in a maze of narrow, evil-smelling streets which dissipate my visions of

26

aristocratic beauty. The proud Genoa of the Republic has been overwhelmed by the populace. From the boat, with distance lending enchantment to the view, I could visualize the city of the Doges, those freebooters who fought and trafficked from the Gulf of Genoa to the Levant and built their glorious palaces with the riches they accumulated in their wars. But before arriving at the Street of the Princes, the wanderer loses himself in the maze of characteristic laneways, amidst an excited rabble, reminding him of the *souks* of an oriental city, for Genoa has been for centuries cosmopolitan, ever since the Brignoles and the Dorias were masters of the Ægean Sea.

The wanderer soon finds that there are three Genoas which he learns to distinguish. First of all, ascending from the port, he penetrates into the crowded district leading from Via Soziglia and Piazza Banchi to the Cathedral of San Lorenzo—a district recalling at times the bazaars in Tunis or Tetuan. It was this ancient Genoa extending from Porta Mare to Porta Soprana that inspired Flemish and French painters of the sixteenth and seventeenth centuries to paint their chaotic genre pictures. Here and there in the midst of these highly-coloured, raucous streets we come across silent *piazzettas* with yellow and pink walls where life has not changed since the days when Christopher Columbus roamed there as an urchin. Alas, those visions of ancient Genoa have begun to disappear beneath the onset of modern civilization and progress. Genoa has become one of the wealthiest cities in Italy, but the descendants of the noble Doges have not always followed the ancient traditions of art and beauty. Vulgar modern hotels with baroque ornamentation have crushed out the austere simplicity of the past. It is indeed a curious experience to pass suddenly from the Genoa of the thirteenth and fourteenth centuries with its Palazzo San Giorgio and the Cathedral of San Lorenzo into the crude twentieth-century decorations of the Via Venti Settembre. But the wanderer who wishes to discover *Genova la superba*—Genoa in all the glory of her Republic—may do so in the two streets, Via Balbi and Via Garibaldi, which lead to the central Piazza de Ferrari. Those two streets are so full of gorgeous palaces that they deserve to be called the Streets of the Princes : they tell us of the fifteenth and sixteenth centuries when Renaissance architecture overspread the medieval city—an age of peace and liberty after the ceaseless internal struggles. In those days art and letters flourished as well as trade, and the city became a meeting-place for brilliant spirits of Italy under the benevolent ægis of the great Andrea Doria. The spirit of Michelangelo survived in his pupil, Galeazzo Alessi, who planned the beautiful street known as the Via Nova until the name was changed to Via Garibaldi.

The Golden Age of Genoese art was a riot of the baroque. The sculptors vied with the architects and after them came the painters of frescoes to cover the walls of those great palaces. Genoa in those days was European, for did she not welcome with open arms the Flemish brothers, Van Deiner, the great Van Dyck, and a host of foreign artists ? When we look at Van Dyck's portraits we can form an idea of the noble lords and ladies who sauntered through those halls. Van Dyck pointed the way to Genoa's greatest painter of that period, Bernardo Strozzi, whose colouring ranges from the sweetness of the earlier Murillo to the magical effects of Velazquez. Strozzi, when he became a monk, ceased to revel in colours and deliberately became an ascetic painter of monks and friars. When he left the monastery he followed the Flemish realistic school.

Nowhere is the charm of ancient Genoa more clearly seen than in the gardens which the nobles laid out behind their palaces. In accordance with the Renaissance notions of harmony and symmetry they laid them out so as to harmonize with the architecture of the period. They are not as grandiose and classical as the famous examples of Le Nôtre with their formal paths, lakes, and little temples. But they are more picturesque because Nature on the Riviera is more bountiful than in France. All the Genoese villas possess gardens, but my favourite is to be found in an ancient villa at Pegli which once was the home of King Victor Emmanuel. To walk through that garden was to evoke many an Arcadian scene from Petrarch, Boccaccio, or Torquato Tasso. First of all we have the spacious lawn edged with a hedge of boxwood and statues of the Seasons. We pass beneath three rustic arches into the garden itself : the broad walk leads in to the artificial ruins of little Roman temples near a lake on the banks of which are weeping willows : by the lake are gondolas made in the shape of swans : a little farther on is a small shrine which we pass by on our way to the Arcadian theatre built in the Greek model and surrounded by rose-bushes. Here the lords and ladies thronged to hear courtiers read, recite, and sing the Arianna and the Didone Abbandonata, and as soon as voices on the stage would die away, the guests would wander here and there through the narrow, intimate walks by the little brook, through a small wood leading to rustic arbours and to the so-called " Trianon "—a circular space surrounded by busts of the Roman Emperors, overhung by scented acacia trees, where the gavottes and minuets were danced to the music of a small orchestra. Such a garden is a continual surprise. Here and there are statues half hidden in shrubs, imitation ruins of ancient buildings, secret paths leading to treacherous bridges over dark chasms. In such a garden a dreamer finds his paradise, for the murmuring fountains bubbling up and flowing through marble channels lull his senses and bewitch him so that centuries disappear and he finds himself among fauns and nymphs of Italy's Arcadia.

But here I am, back again in the Genoa of the nineteenth and twentieth centuries with its broad streets ascending steeply into the mountains. From every corner I can see panoramas of sea and Alps. In the brilliant sunlight the tall modern buildings glisten white, pink, yellow, and orange. The broad roads curve round and round as they mount towards the fort at the summit called Il Castellaccio, but the poorer Genoese do not travel by those circulating roads : they mount by countless steps winding between the houses from the sea-front to the upper part of the city. One of the most exciting spectacles in Genoa occurs at noon when the cannon booms from the fort above. Then a vast migration begins from the lower commercial part of the city to the upper : it is all like an ant-hill in movement : the steps and the laneways resound with the patter of footsteps as the workers hasten up to their homes for the midday meal and siesta. Then between two and three o'clock the descending migration begins and the streets are black with the swiftly moving crowd.

My centre of operations was in a beautiful villa surrounded by a garden in the Piazza Corvetto. Here we had established a big library for soldiers in the ground floor while upstairs in the tower of the villa several rooms were adapted as classrooms for the Army Education scheme. On the sunny days when the fountain in the garden played beneath the palm trees I had the illusion of living as a Genoese aristocrat might have done in the heyday of the city's power. The villa became a meeting-place not only for British troops, but also for Italian friends, for I had a host of helpers. Two boys, Aldo, a Swiss, and Tony, British, assisted me in running the library, and three or four Italian young ladies organized a tea-room for the benefit of British officers. Every moment of my day was occupied. When I was not giving classes in French to soldiers I was helping in Y.M.C.A. huts in the city or working on the trains arriving at Brignole station laden with invalids from North Italy. Another of my duties was to visit the hospitals and play to the patients in the wards. Some of the medical officers in the Italian as well as the British army had a firm belief in the curative powers of music. After all, history has sanctified the custom, for as far back as the Middle Ages the wandering minstrel would play, sing, or recite to the wounded. During those days with the Italian Expeditionary Force the title of minstrel was the only one which I mentally conferred upon myself. A man with a fiddle in his hands and a host of anecdotes on the tip of his tongue could win his way into the hearts of all the soldiers in the world. From my roving minstrelsy I gathered a host of acquaintances among the inhabitants of Genoa. Every day I was besieged by signorinas who were eager to learn the English language. Some there were who had learnt English at school or university and would write long essays on Byron or Shelley which I would discuss with them under the palm trees of the Villa Acquasola : others would come begging me to assist them in the task of writing letters to English admirers. How I wished I had lived in the eighteenth century—the age of gallantry. I was acutely conscious of my deficiencies as a writer of love-letters that would satisfy the passionate aspirations of a signorina of twenty years. For my duty was to play the part of confidant and adviser.

Signorina X would come to me with news of captain or lieutenant so-and-so whom she had known when he was in Genoa. But as the poor girl's English was limited to " good-bye " and " I love you " it was necessary to create in my own mind a letter which would express in English the flutterings of her tiny heart. And when the answering letter in English would arrive she would bring it to me and I used all my imaginative powers in Italian to embroider the blunt, prosaic words so that they might satisfy her eager expectancy. In those months many English soldiers fell madly in love with signorinas without being able to babble more than *buona sera* or *bella bambina*. I often used to wonder what would be the outcome of those war-time love-affairs : what would happen when the warrior departed on his homeward way, leaving the sad-eyed signorina gazing through her tears at her engagement ring ? In the evening when my classes were over I would mount the hill towards the Via Acquarone where I had my billet. Often I would slip away to the Politeama Genovese, where there was a season of Opera. It was a pretty young maidservant, Manina, who made me go to the Opera. One night I noticed that she had rouged herself more than usual, and she rushed us through supper. " Why are you in such a hurry, Manina ? " said I playfully ; " you must have an appointment with your *fidanzato*." " Let me go, signorino," said she, " I shall be late at the Opera : it is due to begin at nine and I've to dress up." She then informed me that she sang in the chorus to make a little extra money. I realized how deeply rooted the tradition of Opera is in the Italian people : singing is the most characteristic gift of the Italian race, and as soon as they sing they begin to make gestures and develop the theme of a drama within them. Opera in Italy springs from a spirit of festival and carnival, and it was natural that our little maidservant should put on her cloak and rush away to swell the chorus of the local theatre. Italian Opera such as I saw in the local opera-houses in those war days was full of spontaneity, without a trace of calculation. Whether the performance was Verdi, Rossini, or Donizetti, the singers sang and acted as if the melodies welled up in their hearts in unconscious improvisation. The joy in song of those people was as natural as the noting of birds. I thought of our theatres at home where Opera is an exotic plant imported at great cost to be a dainty delicacy for the rich. Here Opera belongs to the humble folk and there is complete sympathy between actors and audience. Those who are accustomed to the ceremonial silence of a Nordic theatre audience would be shocked by the behaviour of the Genoese public, who refuse to curb their impulses even during the play. They are noisy and excitable, but they will all of a sudden hush so that you could hear a pin drop when the *primo tenore* sings his aria, only to burst out into full-throated applause if he swells out the high note in the tradition of *bel canto* to which they are accustomed. After a few months of Verdi and Bellini I felt that I had driven all the fog of the North out of my system. Although by nature a fervent Wagnerian I would have subscribed to Nietzsche's plea for Mediterraneanizing music, so bewitched was I by the gaiety of those melodies with their " Southern, tawny, sunburnt sensitiveness."

THE VIOLIN OF PAGANINI

Many of my views on music I confided to my friend, Francesco Simone, an old Genoese gentleman, whose acquaintance I had made on my arrival in the city. I had brought a letter of introduction to him from my

violin teacher in Dublin, Achille Simonetti. Francesco
Simone was a timid, white-haired little man living a
lonely life in one of the narrow streets of old Genoa.
His one passion in life was the violin. In his youth
he had been a violinist and had known most of the
great masters of the instrument. Now in his old age
his one hobby was collecting and making violins.
When I had brought him a letter from Simonetti he
received me with open arms, saying : " There is nobody
in the world I would sooner welcome than Achille
Simonetti, who was a credit to the great traditions of
Italian violin playing. He was the favoured pupil of
Camillo Sivori, the one and only pupil of the king of
all violinists who ever lived, Nicolò Paganini." Straight
away old Simone led me on a ramble through Genoa to
visit the haunts of his idol Paganini. Near the harbour
we went first of all to a pale pink house with green
Venetian shutters, wherein the maestro was born.
Underneath a tiny shrine to the Madonna in the wall
is a marble tablet bearing the inscription :

Il Giorno XXVII di Ottobre dell'
Anno MDCCLXXXII,
nacque
A decoro di Genova a
Delizia del Mondo
Nicolò Paganini,
Nella Divina Arte dei Suoni
Insuperato maestro.

The old man pointed to the inscription, saying : " There
the great virtuoso was born of Genoese parents. He
came into the world with a violin and bow in his hand.
His mother would relate how one night an angel had
appeared to her in a dream and prophesied that her son
would become the greatest violinist in the world. When
other children played ball in the street he was shut up

by his father, a prisoner with his instrument, for he was a hard, avaricious man like most Genoese, and *pien d'ogni magagna* as Dante would say ; he was eager to show off his son to the world and win the boy's weight in gold."

The old man, as he spoke, led me towards the Cathedral of San Lorenzo, where Paganini as a child had sung in the choir. "It was here," said he, "that he received violin lessons from the *maestro di cappella*, Giacomo Costa. In those days it was the custom on Sundays to invite the local violinists to play solos during the Mass. The tradition had been established in the previous century by the father of the violin Arcangelo Corelli, who had felt inspired to compose his church Sonatas for such performances. Many say that the violin is the instrument of the devil, but Papà Corelli certainly devoted it to the glory of God. Young Nicolò Paganini was of a different stamp : look at his tall, gaunt, skeleton figure, his waxen face and long, dark hair, and you would swear he was a vampire, descendant of the Satanic spirit who inspired Tartini to write the 'Devil's Trill.'" From the Cathedral we wended our way to the Municipio where in a glass case the violin of the master is preserved.

"Look well at that instrument," said old Simone, "it is the supreme masterpiece of Joseph Guarnerius, dated 1743, who was a genius only surpassed by the peerless Stradivari himself. He too, like Nicolò Paganini, was tempted by the devil and they say that he passed many a day in gaol—aye, and made fiddles there with wood which the gaoler's daughter brought him."

I gazed at the instrument hanging within the glass case as in a prison and I thought of its romantic wanderings ever since the day when the master received it in guerdon from the French merchant at Livorno. It was in his younger days when he had escaped from the

tyranny of his father and had spread his wings in the
world. Being son of a miser, what could be more natural
than that he should become a spendthrift? He was a
passionate gambler and on that occasion at Livorno
he was forced to pawn his instrument to pay his debts.
He was engaged to perform at a concert but he had no
instrument to play on. It was then that the French
merchant, Livron, came forward and lent him the
beautiful Joseph Guarnerius. After the concert, when
Paganini tried to return the violin, Livron refused to
accept it, saying: " The instrument belongs to you :
my hands will never profane the violin which your
fingers have touched." That golden-varnished instrument followed him all over Europe. Sometimes its
tones soared through the palaces of kings. What
secrets it could tell of the boudoir of Elisa Bacciocchi,
Princess of Lucca, Napoleon's sister, of Antonia Bianchi,
the dancer, of the fierce public contests when Paganini
played against Lafont and Lipinski. No wonder that
the Italian, Viennese, and English journals would publish
rumours of the master's league with the devil. They
would tell stories of his imprisonment in damp cells
where one string after another would snap from the
Guarnerius : but the magic fiddle would inspire him
to play ravishing music upon the one remaining string.
And then, at the end of his life, when he was dying
at Nice in 1840, it is related that on the last night he
stretched forth his hands for the beautiful Guarnerius
which had been his faithful companion. Propping
himself up on pillows, he played and played, awakening
for the last time its golden tones. Those who heard
him say that never in all his life had he improvised as
he did in this swan-song. Better would it have been
for the beautiful Guarnerius to have shivered to pieces
as Tartini's violin is supposed to have done at his death.

Old Simone then brought me back to his lodgings in the heart of Genoa. After climbing a staircase of more than 100 stone steps we came to the apartment which consisted of three rooms crammed with bric-à-brac and *bibelots* of every description. In one of the rooms a fire was blazing merrily and the flames shone upon a multitude of tiny bronze statues. From one side of the room to the other a cord was drawn and on it were dangling from ten to twelve violins. They too glistened in the firelight. One of the rooms was fitted up as a workshop : stray pieces of pine and maple were lying about amidst a chaotic confusion of pots of glue and varnish. On the table beside the callipers lay two pale, unvarnished instruments on which he was working. Everywhere there were reminders of old Simone's heroes. At the end of the room was an old print of Paganini : in the dim light his cadaverous face gazed at us with an expression of sardonic scorn. On each side of him were faded photographs of Sivori and my master, Simonetti.

The picture that fascinated me most of all was one of the ancient Stradivari working in the attic in his house at Cremona. On his head he wore a woollen cap and over his clothes an apron of leather.

Many a day I spent in that dusty old room listening to old Simone's anecdotes, watching him at work in his back room. From time to time I would take down one of the amber or red-varnished fiddles that were dangling on the cord and try it. There was a beautiful amber Landolfi, whose sweet mellow tone still echoes through my memory, though it was not so delicate in tone as a Nicolò Amati which Simone called his princess. He would never keep his instruments in cases : " It was," said he, " the golden sun of Italy that seasoned those wonderful instruments. The particles in the atmosphere

tone the varnish—that is why in the days of Corelli and
Vivaldi it was the custom to hang the new instruments
on pegs in the organ loft, and on Sunday a master
violinist would choose the instrument on which he would
perform the Church Sonata."

ANSELMO

One day when I was preluding on one of old Simone's
violins, I was interrupted by the sound of incessant
coughing. It was an agonized cough such as one would
hear from a consumptive. The old man paused in his
work and shook his head sadly.

" That is Anselmo," said he.

" Who is Anselmo ? "

" You have not met my nephew, Anselmo, because
he is a very sick youth. He fought in the War and was
gassed, and he has come back here completely broken.
They say that he will never recover, for the gas has left
his lungs in the condition of galloping consumption."

The old man then led me in to see Anselmo. He was
seated in an arm-chair by the open window. He was a
very handsome youth with the finely chiselled features
we so often see in the Genoese, but so emaciated that the
delicate bones showed through the waxen skin. His
white hands with long, slender fingers were so fleshless
that they resembled the claws of a bird. All that lived
in his face were his eyes, blazing with excitement as he
struggled with the disease that was consuming him.
When he ceased his terrible spasms of coughing he would
lie back limply like a white flower drooping after the
storm, and with eyes closed he would remain motionless
for a time. Then all of a sudden he would start talking
rapidly in a deep, tragic voice : the words would trip
over one another excitedly as if they were afraid of delay.

Anselmo came to welcome my visits, because during his long, lonely hours, seated at the open window, thoughts would revolve through his mind which he longed to express. Being young and full of youth's arrogance, he did not care to tell his inner thoughts to his uncle who belonged to the past : he welcomed me because I belonged to the present. Anselmo was a characteristic young Italian patriot : if he had lived in 1848 he would have been one of the first to follow the hero of Caprera, but he would have nothing to do with the modern politicians and their crowd, who had reduced, as he said, to commonplace prose the divine poetry of the Risorgimento. The mere thought of the Italian parliamentarians of the day drove him into paroxysms of fury leading to one of his inevitable spasms of coughing.

"What have we fought for?" he gasped. "Have we not fought and died to make a stronger Italy? But now when the generous blood of youth has been shed you will find those black-coated clerks appearing on all sides like vultures and ravens on a battlefield strewn with corpses. They will parley and bargain away the victory won by heroes."

Anselmo, weak and delicate though he was, glorified war. "War," he said, "awakens the energy of men and obliges them to seek an ideal of beauty and duty. In times of peace," he cried, "we do not listen to the seers, but once the drums of war beat we turn to those poets who will lead us into battle as minstrels used to long ago."

Then I discovered that Anselmo's hero was Nietzsche. In a small bookcase by his side he had all the works of that suffering prophet, and the pages were covered with his pencilled annotations. He would tell me anecdotes of Nietzsche's stay in Italy. The philosopher had felt attracted to Genoa because it combined the double

energy of mountain and of sea. He admired a city of
palaces erected by Corsairs who had the courage to follow
their instincts without weak scruples.

" Nietzsche," he said, " lived in a garret in one of
these narrow streets. In the house with him were
many poor people who called him " the little saint."
It was the Genoese with their kindly, ascetic mode of
life who taught him to be independent and full of a
gentle pride that does not try to dominate others but
is able to bear up against the frivolous mockery of the
world." Anselmo would quote again and again the
words of Nietzsche in *Zarathustra* :

" I have been a leader that one day I might have my hand free
to bless : in dying I would offer men the riches of my gifts. It
was from the sun I learnt that message—from the sun who when
he sets is so rich : out of his inexhaustible riches he flings gold into
the sea so that the poorest fishermen row with golden oars."

Anselmo would go on to quote for me passages from
The Dawn of the Day, written by Nietzsche when he
roamed along the shores of the Gulf of Genoa between
Rapallo and Santa Margherita. When he would read
these passages in Italian from Nietzsche, his whole
personality seemed to rise in stature, his eyes would
glitter and his cheeks would flush hectically ; his spirit
for a moment escaped from the dingy, narrow room
into the wide world, and in thought he saw himself at
the head of a band of youthful heroes eager to revitalize
the Italian genius. Or he would quote from *The Origin
of Tragedy* to prove that the primitive Greeks were the
supreme masters because they possessed energy, strength
of thought and of action. " They taught us," he cried,
" to despise the vulgar herd of the market-place and the
democracy of the town. They taught us to forswear a
life of slothful ease and safety and seek danger."

It was a pathetic sight to watch this handsome youth,

broken by war yet gasping out a pæan to war. It was macabre to hear the dying boy say : " Let me sing the pæan of war : the resonance of its silver bow is terrible : it comes to us sombre as night : nevertheless Apollo accompanies it—Apollo the rightful leader of States, the god who purifies them. War is necessary to the State because it exalts the people."

After one of those tirades he would sink back on his pillows coughing his heart out. Then old Simone would softly creep into the room, followed by an old woman dressed in black who tended the invalid. It is strange to note how strong a wish for life consumptives have : even at the point of death their minds possess a vitality which is denied to many healthy people. Anselmo imagined himself as a leader of men in a movement of ex-Servicemen to regenerate the country for which they had fought. But then came the day when they took him away to the sanatorium, and a month later I followed the black and gilt hearse to the Campo Santo.

CHAPTER V

CAPO SANTA CHIARA

THE rocky shore of the Gulf of Genoa which unfurls itself like a gigantic fan edged with the green of its luxuriant vegetation, is studded with many tiny inlets, where from time immemorial the rugged Genoese fishermen have made their settlements. Amongst those little colonies none is so full of tradition as the community of Boccadasse which nestles at the foot of Capo Santa Chiara. Up above on the crest of the Cape are many luxurious villas and castles poised on the edge of precipitous crags, but down by the water's edge, hidden away from the rocks, are many primitive dwellings with which the cliffs are honeycombed. From the summit of the cape a network of stone steps leads down to the rocky beach where the boats are drawn up out of the reach of the waves. A colony of sea wolves. In the evenings the bronzed old fishermen sit on those steps and gaze out to sea as though they were sentries of the coast.

On the day after the Armistice, after rambling through the tiny village I ascended to one of the villas above belonging to the father of the golden-haired signorina of the Italian Red Cross, whose singing had so bewitched me. From the broad terrace of the villa I saw the glorious panorama spread out before me. It was late afternoon and the calm sea shone in the glory of the setting sun. In the distance the graceful head of Portofino, purple-coloured, completed the background of the picture. Below in the wilderness of green emerged here and there gaunt silhouettes of cypress trees and the sunlight catching the window-panes of the neighbouring red houses turned them into dazzling jewels. An atmosphere of peace hardly broken by the gentle tolling of the church bell of the little hamlet of Apparizione in the hills behind. On the terrace there was silence and meditation ; not one of the company said a word, for everyone's thoughts flitted away over the calm sea into dim, distant recollections.

Beside me sat my host, Signor Alberto—Colonel of the Italian Red Cross—a tall, bearded man of fifty-six, and his wife, Donna Delfina—a slender, graceful woman with grey hair, flashing dark eyes, and the brown skin of the Italian from the South. The colonel was the first to break the silence. He began to speak in a rambling voice about the War and Italy's part in it, as though he were arguing aloud with himself : " So the end has come, and we may cry ' Viva l'Italia ' with joy in our hearts. It has been a terrible struggle. Remember those days in 1914 when the most that was asked of us was that we should declare our neutrality. Many there were who advocated the policy of peace at any price. How divided public opinion was in those days ! To-day, for the first time, we may say that Italy is united."

" E proprio così ! " cried the chorus on the terrace. " Now that we have ' Italia irredenta ' we may raise our heads in the world and shout ' Vittoria a noi '—a victory won by Italian arms."

" Victory in the face of superhuman difficulties," said Donna Delfina, turning to me. " You in England seem never to have realized the appalling difficulties that have faced us. We were bound by many ties to Germany and Austria. Many in North Italy were married to Germans and Austrians and looked to those countries as the means of their livelihood."

" And do not forget," said a young man in the uniform of an artillery officer who was sitting beside Delfina, " do not forget that in 1915 when we entered the War many believed that the Central Powers would win. Our fighting was different from that on the other fronts : war for us had to be waged in the Alps amidst snow, ice, and blizzards : we fought on the edge of dizzy precipices or amidst the wilderness of jagged rock on the pitiless Carso."

" Aye," said Signor Alberto, " it was a war of Bersaglieri and Alpini. We had not the money of the British and the French : our regiments in their grigio verde were not so smart as your troops in khaki. It was the first time in our history that we had fought a war on so great a scale, and it was only by bitter experience that we learnt our lesson. The days of Caporetto were bitter, I tell you."

" Caporetto, Caporetto "—the fateful word was murmured dreamily by the rest of the company. " It was Caporetto created modern Italy," said a young naval commander, husband of one of the Colonel's daughters. " The whole nation co-operated with the soldiers after that : rich and poor made sacrifices, and the spiritual link between army and people prepared the ultimate victory." Then Donna Delfina turned graciously to me, saying : " And now, Signor Alleato, we must drink your health : your country and France came to our aid in our darkest hours and your divisions helped us in the days of Piave and Vittorio Veneto."

" Can I, Signora, forget those stirring scenes when we arrived from France ? The stations along the line were crowded by Italian villagers offering us bunches of sweet-smelling flowers as tokens of their gratitude. Let me propose a toast to the friendship of Britain and Italy. To-day the love we bear you is as great as it was in the days of the Risorgimento, when Englishmen fought for Garibaldi, and Mazzini looked upon London as a second home." The Colonel went off to his cellar and returned with a bottle of fragrant Passito di Pantelleria. The golden wine glittered in the slender glasses and reminded me of the tiny volcanic island bosomed in the blue Mediterranean.

As we were chatting gaily there was a loud ring of a bell, and I heard a buzz of voices coming from the narrow lane at the back of the house. "These are the fishermen from Boccadasse," cried Donna Delfina. "'È l'ora della minestra.' Quick! girls! put on your aprons and let us get to work."

Signor Alberto then explained to me that it was Donna Delfina's custom to feed every evening the poorer fishermen of Boccadasse and their families. Ever since the beginning of the War she had carried on this charitable work and her house was always open to the seafaring folk whenever they were in any trouble. "The women often call her 'madre di Boccadasse,'" said he : "she feeds them and nurses them ; she writes their letters to the sons who are at the front, and she reads to them the letters in return. But come and see for yourself."

Downstairs in the kitchen there was great excitement. The three daughters of Donna Delfina were dressed in long aprons and were ladling out a thick reddish-coloured soup full of macaroni, under the vigilant eye of their mother. The fishermen were of all ages : some of them were old sea-wolves, bronzed and gnarled like oak-trees on a windswept plateau ; others were swarthy young fellows with the strength of Hercules in their muscles. There were, however, more women than men, and each woman pulled after her various struggling children. Each had his tin bowl which was promptly filled with soup. Donna Delfina prided herself on her scientific knowledge of cookery. During war-time, meat and indeed grease of all kinds was strictly rationed, but she had made for herself an analysis of the amount of fat contained in each vegetable and so she prepared special vegetable soups that would act as substitutes for the lack of meat. But those women with their struggling children had not come merely for food—each of them wanted a word of advice, consolation, or encouragement. Donna Delfina, while she talks to them, every now and then describes their history to me. She knows all their story and she adapts herself to the varying personality of each one. One woman is hysterical and needs to be treated with good-natured severity ; another is one of those downcast creatures who has no more courage left to face a cruel world—she has lost an only son in the War—and to her Donna Delfina speaks words of gentle consolation. Another woman arrives leading four small children, and she is evidently expecting another one very shortly. " That is Caterina," says she to me, " she's had six children but two of them have died."

" Sì, Signora," answered the woman placidly, " Dio mi aiuta—se l'è presi " (God helps me—He has taken them from me).

" Ah, yes, Caterina," replied Donna Delfina, " but no sooner has He taken one from you than He gives you another."

As she was talking there was a burst of shrill, hysterical laughter and another wizened, little old woman in ragged black pushed forward. The rest of the women looked at her pityingly. Donna Delfina turned to me and touched her forehead, murmuring : " È pazza " (she is mad). The old woman twisted her hands convulsively and made meaningless gestures. Then she would count on her fingers, saying : " Michele, Giovanni, Pasquale, Paolo—four boys, four birds, all flown away, never more return. Where are my children? Give me food, I must feed them or they will die ; they cannot return." Then she would burst again into a shrill laugh and her face would twitch and her eyes start from their orbits.

While Donna Delfina and her daughters were attending to the wants of the women and children, the Colonel told me tales of the fishing-folk.

" They are," said he, " the backbone of Italy. If you travel by any of the big Italian liners you will find that most of the sailors are Genoese. From time immemorial they have been sea-wolves ; even to-day a folklorist would find traces of ancient customs going back to the dawn of history. Some of those old sailors still use magic words to quell the fury of the storm. Their minds are stored with fairy lore mingled with faint echoes of the ancient wars between Rome and Carthage off these coasts. Hannibal appears in the local folklore as a wizard in league with the evil spirits who inhabit deep inaccessible grottoes in the cliffs. Whenever they are buffeted by the elements they call upon their great protector, Saint Antony of Padua."

" Why Saint Antony of Padua : what had he to do with the sea ? "

" The tradition is from the episode in the saint's life when nobody would listen to his austere teaching. So in disgust he preached to the fishes off the shores of Rimini. Isn't that the story, Nicolò ? " said he, turning to an old grey-bearded salt who was hobbling on a crutch.

Nicolò took off his cap and scratched his head before

replying. "It's the honest truth, Signor Colonello : 'After God comes the Saint.' And every woman in Boccadasse brings her mezzetta of oil up to the chapel of the Saint yonder to keep the lamps lighting night and day till they cry out the news : ' Bastimento ed equipaggio salvi ' (ship and crew safe). He who doesn't pay a visit to Sant' Antonio will rue the day. Do you remember, Signor Colonello, the night of the great storm, when the *Silvia* was wrecked out there in sight of us all. Six men there were in her—among them Francesco Ghiglione. If Francesco had visited the Saint he would not have been swallowed up by the waves. But he was a foolhardy fellow full of pride. And the Saint says to himself, ' I'll give him a lesson,' so he took him."

After all the fishermen and their families had gone away Donna Delfina called out to us : " A tavola, Signori." Dinner was served on the balcony—a characteristic Genoese meal beginning with vegetable soup or *minestrone* which in Genoa is called *signor minestrone*. What is the secret of Genoese *minestrone* ? Donna Delfina would not tell me, for every good housewife jealously preserves her magic from prying eyes. It is in any case a symphony of taste and aroma suggesting all the vegetables in the world—a perfect harmony of culinary tones. What shall I say of that meal when superlatives fail me ? Shall I sing the praises of *pasta asciutta* which has been the staple food of Italians since the days of the ancient Etruscans—*trenette col pesto, fainà, burrida, friscieu,* and so on through the gamut of regional varieties ? Shall I rhapsodize on sea-truffles, mussels from the Gulf of Spezia, veal flavoured with leaves of laurel ; or the *scabei* or fritters of Sarzana, or the classical *torta pasqualina* or Easter tart divided into thirty-three pieces in memory of the years of Our Lord?

Night had now fallen and the sea had become transformed from gold to shimmering silver beneath the crescent moon. In a tiny pool in the garden beneath clusters of stars shone like glow-worms. The magic of the moon had bewitched the landscape into the silence of death. The cypress trees with their slanting shadows stood motionless like rigid sentinels at their post.

The moon made us all turn to the mood of reminiscence, for her rays searched out the hidden corners of our minds, drawing out by slender threads a thousand hidden, uncertain thoughts. She awoke thoughts of romance, of wandering over hill, over dale, far from the smoke of cities and buzzing crowds. All the toils and troubles of the sun-world faded away and petty ambitions seemed but false notions created in this Vision-house of life. No wonder the moon was called the only base runagate on earth : she wanders up and down the sky like an antic drawing us all after her by silver threads into the unfettered moon-world.

Signorina Italia began in a low voice to murmur the lines of Leopardi, poet of the Moon :

> " E quando miro in ciel arder le stelle
> Dico fra me pensando :
> A che tante facelle ?
> Che fa l'aria infinita, e quel profondo
> Infinito seren ? che vuol dir questa
> Solitudine immensa ? ed io che sono ? "

ALBERTO AND DELFINA

My host then told the story of his life. He was born at Pinerolo in the heart of Piemonte where his parents carried on a silk industry. " We had," said he, " a fine, square old house in the midst of a vast plantation of mulberry trees. But as the years passed we became

poorer and poorer, for my father gave all he had to the
national cause, and as for the silk industry, it declined
before the competition of the French silk of Lyons."
Alberto then described his life at home, contrasting it
with the life to-day. " In those days," said he, " husband and wife often held the most diverging views.
My father, like so many men of the Risorgimento, looked
upon himself as an *esprit fort* : he read Voltaire and would
have set up a temple to Reason in his back garden had
it not been for my mother, who was deeply religious.
A beautiful woman she was, tall, pale-faced and always
dressed in black. When we were six years of age she
read the works of Saint Augustine to us and she would
make me repeat long passages of the Bible by heart."

At that point Donna Delfina with a roguish smile
interrupted, saying : " Dear me, Alberto ! I never
knew you were so religious."

" My mother's rigid views turned me against religion.
But even if I had been a mystic I should have lost my
faith when I went to the University, for there I came
under the influence of Arturo Graf—a romantic poet of
pessimism who revelled in macabre details of skulls and
tombstones. He did, however, induce me to study
Leopardi deeply, and thereby I lost the last remnant of
religious doctrine I had learnt by my mother's knee.
Soon I neglected Leopardi for Carducci, who was the
civic poet of united Italy. Every student in those
days knew the *Ode to Satan* by heart."

It was my turn to interrupt. " Why, Signor Alberto,"
said I, " did you and your contemporaries heap praise
on the *Ode to Satan*—one of the weakest compositions
of Carducci ? Surely it is nothing more than a pitiful
blasphemy ? "

" In those days," replied Alberto, " Satan became in
our eyes the spirit of progress—a spirit akin to the

Prometheus Unbound of Shelley—the poet whom Carducci later called ' the Titan's spirit in a maiden's form.' Carducci in my youth was for me the personification of rebellion against obscurantism and outworn ideas. Now that I am older and mellower I admire him for his classical measure and balanced mind. But even to-day I am bewitched by his paganism, for I know that it sprang from his intense love of Nature. He had a serene love of Italy springing from his profound consciousness of the ancient classical authors. Italy for him was the farm of Horace in the Sabine hills or the vineyards of Virgil's Mantua and rivers gliding beneath the ancient walls of cities. That is the eternal Italy and Carducci knew it ; hence his indignation against the miserable mongrels yelping at the heels of his hero Garibaldi. His pen indeed was as mighty as the hero's sword which he celebrated in immortal verses :

> " ' Egli vide nel ciel crepuscolare
> co'l cuor di Gracco ed il pensier di Dante
> la terza Italia.' "

Alberto would have continued his quotations from Carducci but Donna Delfina admonished him, saying : " Alberto, Alberto ' revenons à nos moutons ! ' If you start quoting Carducci you will never stop, for you know all the *Odi Barbare* by heart and the dawn will find us here listening to you."

Alberto then continued his story. " Carducci," said he, " distracted me in those days when I ought to have been looking for a regular profession after my University course was over. But I was a rebel and I would not settle down in Piemonte to a humdrum life. I wanted adventure and I was terrified of becoming Monssù Travet. As you are not a Piemontese, I shall explain who Monssù Travet was. He was the hero of a famous

Piemontese dialect play and a symbol of the hard-working, civil-servant of my country : honest, hard-working, disciplined, eager to carry out orders. A model citizen—one to bear all the burdens without the rewards : never a word of complaint, unless occasion-ally a shrug of the shoulders and—' Pasienssa ! ' To-day in my old age I genuflect to Travet who is the backbone of our country but in impetuous youth I foreswore him."

" You were quite right, Papà," said Alberto's three daughters in chorus ; " you were ambitious and you wanted to see the world."

" That is what I said at the time," continued Alberto, " and so one day, to the consternation of my parents, I disappeared from home and went to sea. I engaged myself as an ordinary seaman on board a sailing boat bound for Odessa. For years I wandered from one side of the world to the other : I was like the Flying Dutch-man sailing on the ship with the blood-red sails."

" But," said I timidly, " the Flying Dutchman met Senta and she anchored him safe and sound." I said this with just a trace of a smile at Donna Delfina.

Donna Delfina laughed and said, " Senta was crying her eyes out all the time in Pinerolo waiting for her hero to come up from the sea with his mind stored with fantastic tales and his wallet crammed with fair brocades and ribbons."

Then as I looked at Alberto I could not refrain from quoting from Shakespeare :

> " which he observing,
> Took once a pliant hour, and found good means
> To draw from her a prayer of earnest heart
> That he would all his pilgrimage dilate."

" Yes," replied Alberto, " I told her my story but I was no turbaned Moor. I wanted to make my way in life before I begged Delfina to come with me. But what was I to do? The silk industry had declined : the family business was ruined : my parents were aged and feeble : Italy in those days did not offer prospects to the adventurous. And so, like so many others of my race, I determined to emigrate to South America."

" I imagine you, Signor Alberto," said I, " setting out for that continent filled with the tireless spirit of the conquistador."

" Yes, I had something of the conquistador in me as far as education was concerned, for I remembered that our Mazzini had called education the ' bread of the soul.' In a vigorous new country like the Argentine there was plenty for me to do in those days. After a bitter struggle with adversity I saved enough money to buy land by the River Plate near Buenos Aires and there I founded my own educational Institute based upon the newest European systems of Pestalozzi, Froebel and others. When Delfina came out to join me we made our college a centre of culture linking Italy with the Argentine. Many a politician, writer, or professional man in the Argentine to-day came to us as a student and our house was always a meeting-place of poets, artists and men of letters."

" Did you never regret your mother-country ? " said I.

" Every day that passed made us more conscious of our exile. We for ever dreamed of Italy, and as soon as the Great War began we returned to give our services to our beloved fatherland. I wish you could understand the strength of national spirit among the Italians across the seas. Millions of our countrymen who emigrate to the four quarters of the earth remain faithful to their traditional civilization. Although they work for the benefit of foreign races they never forget the tiny village in Italy whence they sprang. And yet here in Italy the governments in the past have neglected them and consigned them to oblivion. When the Great War broke out, however, the government realized the strength of the emigrants and their descendants when they saw them arrive at Genoa and Naples in their thousands to fight for Italy."

"You, Donna Delfina," said I, "must tell me your memories of the Garibaldian days."

Donna Delfina then began in her soft, musical voice to tell the long story of her father, Count Vincenzo Landi, one of Garibaldi's most faithful followers. "Alberto," said she, "has told you all about Piemonte and North Italy. I want to tell you about the South which played no less noble a part in Italy's Risorgimento. When I think of my father, I feel myself a ' Meridionale ' and I call to mind those Neapolitans and Sicilians who died to emancipate Italy. They too heard the burning words of Mazzini when he said : ' Without country you have neither name, token, voice, nor rights ; no admission as brothers into the fellowship of the peoples. You are the bastards of Humanity, soldiers without a banner.' My father's destiny was decided at birth. He was born in prison in 1810. His father, Domenico Landi, a Neapolitan, had taken part in an insurrection against the Bourbon King and he was confined as a political prisoner in the bleak island of La Favignana off the coast of Sicily. Queen Carolina as a special dispensation allowed his wife to share imprisonment with him since he had been condemned to penal servitude. In that fetid gaol which was built into the rocks beneath sea-level, my father lived the first seven years of his life amidst terrible privations which ended by killing Domenico. When he and his mother left the gaol and returned to Naples they found their home destroyed and the coral industry of the family ruined. My father then entered the military college at Naples and obtained promotion in the Bourbon army. But then came the year 1848 when the wave of revolutionary Nationalism swept over Europe. In Paris there were barricades : in Berlin there were risings : in Italy everyone sang the song :

> " ' Blessed be the hand
> That kills Radetzky.
> Fire, fire, fire !
> We'll have to win or die,
> The banner rose on high
> Green, White and Red.'

" My father deserted from the Bourbon army and entered the ranks of the Northern army of Carlo Alberto. Green for hope, red for joy, and white for brotherhood : those were the colours that henceforth he followed under the leadership of the hero of Caprera. He fought all through the campaigns of 1848, 1849, 1859, 1860–61. There is no need for me to tell you the tale of those long years of struggle, for that has been inscribed in letters of gold in the archives of our nation for all the world to see. But I want to tell you a small anecdote of his life which has a moral to it.

" It was during the campaign of 1859 and Garibaldi had planned a night surprise attack on Fort Laveno which was held by the Austrians. He entrusted the task to a chosen band of *cacciatori delle Alpi* under my father and Captain Bronzetti. They were to attack by land while Major Bixio was to cross the lake in boats and attack the enemy in the rear from the shore. But the night was dark and cloudy, Bronzetti lost his way and my father was left to sustain the whole attack with his small band. Urging on his Alpini, he charged the enemy and drove them back to the wooden gate in the wall surrounding the fort. There a fierce hand-to-hand fight took place : the Austrian defenders fired point-blank at the attackers, who dashed on with their bayonets fixed. My father said that the night was so dark that his soldiers could not see the enemy except occasionally when the flashes of gunfire lit up the scene. All at once a tall Austrian soldier bore down upon him. My father tried to slash at the Austrian with his sword but he slipped on the damp ground, and the Austrian, raising his gun, discharged it into him as he lay. The bullet passed through his side and lodged itself in the spine. Although grievously wounded, he managed to retire with his men. When Garibaldi heard the news of the retirement he thought it was due to fear and he uttered the words— ' Maledetta paura ' (accursed cowardice). Later when he saw my father writhing in convulsions in the ambulance amidst the wounded, he turned to his staff and said with tears in his eyes : ' Questa mattina mi sono sbagliato. Oh Meridionali, Meridionali ! Vittime di ingiusta mala fama ' (this morning I was mistaken. O men from the South ! unjustly victims of bad repute). And straightway he awarded my father the silver medal for valour. The moral of that episode is that Garibaldi's words were a reminder to North Italians not to misjudge their brothers in the South who had come to help them. My father spent his remaining years in Piemonte, but on his death-bed at Pinerolo he said : ' I am sorry to die in exile.' "

As I walked back to my lodgings in Genoa I pondered over Donna Delfina's story. Italy had not been completely united in 1870. There was still a cleavage between the Northern Italians, whose minds were directed against the hereditary enemy Austria, and the Southern Italians with their Spanish Bourbon traditions.

For me that was a fateful evening.

Soon I was to become a member of Alberto and Delfina's family.

CHAPTER VI

THE PROPHET IN THE BLACK COAT

ONE of Alberto's most intimate friends was old Goffredo Palazzi—or Papà Goffredo, as we all used to call him. Papà Goffredo looked upon himself as one of the most authentic Genoese for two reasons—first of all because he had been mayor of Genoa : secondly, because all his life he had been a convinced Mazzinian republican. " The Prophet in the Black Coat," said he, " gave the world one book worthy to be set beside the Bible. If the men of to-day would study the *Duties of Man* they would discover a panacea for all ills ! "

One day the old man took me on a pilgrimage to the grave of the prophet in the Campo Santo. First of all we visited the house in Via Lomellini where he was born. Papà Goffredo took great pains to explain to me the Genoese ancestry of Mazzini. " He was born a republican," said he. " His father, a professor in the University of Genoa, took part in the democratic movements of the time and gave his son the vocation to become the prophet of a united Italy."

" Why was he called the Prophet in the Black Coat ? " said I.

The old man replied : " One day as a youth he was accosted in the street by a tall, bearded man, with a severe, energetic countenance, who held out a white handkerchief, saying, ' for the refugees of Italy.' So

57

deep was the impression made by the incident that the
youthful Mazzini determined to dress always in black,
fancying himself in mourning for his country."

Papà Goffredo brought a small volume of Mazzini with
him and as he walked beside me through the crowded
streets, he would halt suddenly from time to time and
declaim a passage from one of the master's works.
Then he would walk on in silence stroking the little
tuft of white hair on his chin. Soon he began again :
"Mazzini was like Silvio Pellico and many other
Italian patriots : he created his programme in gaol.
After his imprisonment in Savona he wrote the words :
' I see the people pass before my eyes in the livery of
wretchedness and political subjection, ragged and hungry,
painfully gathering the crumbs that wealth tosses insult-
ingly to it.' He was the visionary of the Risorgimento
—he lit the torch and passed it to the others. It was
his immortal example of Faith and Constancy that saved
Italy."

At the Piazza Corvetto we took a *carrozza* out to the
cemetery. Old Papà Goffredo still declaimed in a loud
voice to me passages from Mazzini. The coachman
on his box listened attentively, occasionally adding his
trite comment accompanied by the crack of his whip.

The celebrated Campo Santo is situated in the beautiful
valley of the river Bisagno and it stretches up the slopes
on its north bank. First of all we entered a large
rectangular space full of arcades between which stand
a host of sumptuous single monuments. Beyond lies an
oval space with row after row of monuments in the
recesses. Flights of steps and broad avenues lead to the
upper galleries, which are all built round a huge rotunda
with a dome supported by columns of black marble.
Slowly we mounted the steps, halting every few moments
while Papà Goffredo rested his weary legs. My eyes

had stolen my mind away. I no longer thought of
Mazzini, so fascinated was I by the macabre sculpture
that surrounded us. From the cloister where I stood
I could see beneath me a huge open space covered with
an infinity of white slabs. Those were the graves of the
poor. To-day that space was crowded with black
figures, for the Spanish influenza was still exacting its
toll of victims. But in the cloister where we stood we
were surrounded by a procession of citizens in marble.
So amazing was the technical craftsmanship of those
statues that I had to rub my eyes to see if I was not in
the presence of phantoms from the nineteenth century
dressed up in silks and satins, tall hats, and frock-coats,
parading silently and stiffly in a ghostly church parade.
It was as if the sinister Medusa had gazed upon the vast
concourse of bourgeois and petrified them as they stood.
The garments worn by those phantoms were carved
by the sculptors in all their details. Here and there I
saw folds and creases in the coats and dresses which were
amazing sculptural *tours de force* in photographic realism,
but never did I imagine that art could be so terrifying.
It seemed as if the sculptors had taken the corpses out
of their coffins and dressed them up in their Sunday
clothes which the relatives kept stored in presses as a
pious memory. To make the effects more poignant
the artists had begged the dead man's family to describe
some familiar gesture of his which could be perpetuated
for all time in the marble. So grotesque are the majority
of those funeral statues that one forgets little individual
gems of art by great artists such as Vela, Scanzi and
Bistolfi, who have revolted against this tyranny of the
monstrous commonplace.

Papà Goffredo meanwhile was climbing slowly up the
steps past terrace after terrace towards a high point
on the hillside where stood the tomb of Mazzini. It is

the noblest structure in the Campo Santo : a Mausoleum of marble with massive pillars at the entrance, above which in huge letters is the inscription : GIUSEPPE MAZZINI.   When I reached the old man I noticed that his eyes were full of tears.   Inside the porch he knelt down and said a prayer.   Then he turned to me, saying : " Remember the words he wrote in one of his last messages, ' The Book of God is not closed.   The coming generations are not disinherited ; they who preceded Jesus were not accursed.   Children of God all of them, identical in faculties and tendencies, they transmit from each to each, in brightness growing with the growth of time and their own endeavour, the lamp of life kindled by Him, and fed and nourished by His spirit.   Revelation is the education of the human race ; it descends continuously from God to man ; prophesied by genius, evoked by virtue and sacrifice, and accepted and proclaimed from epoch to epoch, by the great religious evolutions of collective humanity.' "

Now after an interval of twenty years I still remember vividly the passionate faith of old Goffredo in his idol— the Prophet in the Black Coat.   He knew that Mazzini's ideal was unattainable, but none the less he for ever remained faithful to the republican ideals proclaimed by the great Tribune in 1848.   But Papà Goffredo, after his years of struggle as a Mazzinian, became resigned in his old age.   The words of his master might still spur youth on to action and he might be the Ezekiel of the new Italy.   For it is the general message of Mazzini which men must hear : he taught the Italians how to love and acquire a country, and he taught them what were their duties.   His gospel has survived to-day because it is the faith of Italy.   In *The Duties of Man* he says :

That which saps the vitality in Humanity in the present day is the want of a common faith, of a thought shared by all and re-uniting earth and heaven, the Universe, and God. Lacking this common faith man has bowed down before lifeless matter and has consecrated himself to the adoration of the idol Self-Interest. And the priests of that fatal worship were the kings, princes, and evil governments. They invented the horrible formula : *everyone for himself*; they knew that thus they would create egoism, and that between the egoist and the slave there is but one step.

Those words were remembered by the men who fought at Vittorio Veneto.

The first article of Mazzini's gospel was to combat materialism. According to him charity is not the watchword of the future faith—" The watchword of the future faith is *Association*, fraternal co-operation towards a common aim. And this is as much superior to charity as the work of many, uniting to raise with one accord a building for the habitation of all together, would be superior to that which you would accomplish by raising a separate hut, each for himself, and only helping one another by exchanging stones and brick and mortar." Mazzini was profoundly Christian in his teaching. Again and again the word *Communion* occurs throughout his writings. It is a holy word, for it taught men that they were a single family of equals in God. " The Communion was the symbol of the equality and brotherhood of souls ; it remained for Humanity to expand and develop the truth hidden in that symbol. Every step forward in religious thought brings a corresponding progress in civil life."

Mazzini spared no pains to confute the error of those who in the name of liberty wish to found *Anarchy*, and to abolish society so as to leave only the individual and his rights. He used all his invective against the wicked dream which denies progress, duty, human brotherhood, the solidarity of nations. But he showed that those who confined themselves to the economic question demanding the abolishment of individual property and the establishment of Communism, touched the opposite extreme, for they denied the individual, denied liberty, closed the way to progress, and petrified society. " Communism," he said, " would not produce equality among the men of labour ; it would not increase production which is the great necessity of the present day, because as soon as the means of life are secure, human nature, in the average man at least, and the incentive to an increase of production to be diffused among all the members of society, becomes so small that it is not enough to stimulate his faculties. For the evils which afflict the sons of the people the only remedy of Communism is protection from hunger. Now cannot this be done, cannot the working man's right to work and to life be secured without upsetting the whole social order, without rendering production sterile, impeding progress, abolishing the liberty of the individual, and chaining him down in a tyrannic organization ? "

In the days of Mazzini the Liberals looked upon him as the apostle of liberty, but Mazzini said that the true liberty was not that of the individual who refuses to recognize the nation above the individuals. True liberty means sacrifice for the good of all—" Liberty," he said, " is only a means : woe to those who accustom themselves to regard it as an end. Liberty is not the negation of all authority : it is the negation of all authority which does not represent the collective purpose of the Nation." And one immortal phrase of Mazzini was murmured by the idealists who came back from the Front to build up their country : " Una nazione non è un' esistenza naturale, ma una realtà morale " (a nation does not exist by nature : it is a moral reality). Nobody finds a

nation at birth : everyone must work to create it, for a
nation is not geography or history : it is a programme
and a mission.

THE PROPHET IN GREY

A few days later I was standing amidst a crowd of
excited Genoese on the steps of the beautiful sixteenth-
century church of Santissima Annunziata del Vastato.
The streets were thronged, the windows of the houses
were adorned with the coloured brocades of Zoagli
and the flags and bunting were flying. The sky was
overcast and rain fell intermittently, but it did not damp
the ardour of the multitude. One song after another
rang out in full-throated chorus : first, the national
anthems of the allies—" God save the King," " La
Marseillaise," " La Brabançonne," then the Italian hymns.
But there was another song which the crowd wished to
shout to the skies—" The Star-spangled Banner," for
to-day was the triumphal visit of President Woodrow
Wilson to Genoa on his way to Rome. No king enter-
ing the capital of his realm after a victorious war ever
received a more delirious welcome than the " Messiah
from the West," as he was called that day by the Italians
who cheered him. Even now, when I gaze back in
retrospect to that gloomy winter's day, when even
Genoa's blue sky was overcast, I can hear the roar of the
crowd in the distance swelling in volume as the procession of cars drew nearer—" Viva L'America ! Viva
Wilson ! " By my side stood an old man who in his
excitement kept on haranguing me on the virtues of the
President. " This man has brought the olive branch
to Europe : he is the deliverer of mankind." He then
quoted excitedly from the fourteen points, saying that
no prophet had given such hope to humanity since

Mazzini wrote his *Duties of Man*. Meanwhile, the car containing the President and his suite passed slowly in front of me amidst the frenzied cheering and waving of flags. I had the vision of a tall, grey-haired man bowing stiffly from side to side. A vision in grey, for his hair and his clothes were grey and there was a grey tinge about his skin. His face was like a mask, set in a stereotyped smile. It was the face of a University don —a puzzled dreamer with heavy-lidded eyes and a forehead deeply furrowed with wrinkles. Although the upper part of his face was that of a dreamer, the strong jaw and thin pursed lips stamped him as a mulish, obstinate man accustomed to impose his will. But when he passed I felt that the spirit of George Washington had descended on earth and inspired him to lead our world away from the mean, petty animosities of mankind. He was like a visitant from another planet who would judge our strife with calmness and clear vision. " The self-determination of peoples " and " a League of Nations "—those words resounded through my mind as through the minds of all of us like magic refrains. We all had in those early days of 1919 visions of a League of strong, self-respecting nations each taking her place in a new international structure as an independent element—like a single crystal in an ordered group of crystals.[1] The Italians no less than the French and the British believed that a new era had arrived, and Wilson was acclaimed as a Messiah throughout the length and breadth of the country. In Genoa one of the main streets leading from the Piazza de Ferrari was called Via Wilson in honour of the hero of the day.

Then came the fall of the superman. The malignant demon of disillusion who treads in the shadow of

[1] N. Murray Butler, *Is America Worth Saving*, New York, 1920, p. 135.

popular heroes. Of Wilson we might quote Marlowe's mighty lines :

> Base Fortune, now I see, that in thy wheel
> There is a point, to which when men aspire,
> They tumble headlong down : that point I touched,
> And, seeing there was no place to mount up higher,
> Why should I grieve at my declining fall ?

Already in January 1919 the Battles of the Peace began. In Italy we were far from the scenes which marked the beginning of the Great Conference, but right from the start disturbing reports echoed and re-echoed through Italy. If the British plan had been adopted the Conference would have met in a Swiss city far away from the memories of the War. But instead, Paris was chosen— Paris, the capital which had suffered most from tragedies of invasion and bombardment.

Paris of the Conference [wrote Dr. E. J. Dillon] ceased to be the capital of France. It became a vast cosmopolitan caravanserai teeming with unwonted aspects of life and turmoil, filled with curious samples of the races, tribes, and tongues of four continents who came to watch and wait for the mysterious to-morrow. An Arabian Night's touch was imparted to the dissolving panorama by strange visitants from Tartary and Kurdistan, Corea and Azerbeijan, Armenia, Persia, and the Hedjazmen with patriarchal beards and scimitar-shaped noses, and others from desert and oasis, from Samarkand and Bokhara. Turbans and fezes, sugar-loaf hats and headgear resembling episcopal mitres, old military uniforms devised for the embryonic ovaries of new states on the eve of perpetual peace, snowy-white burnouses, flowing mantles, and graceful garments like the Roman toga, contributed to create an atmosphere of dreamy unreality in the city where the grimmest of realities were being faced and coped with. Then came the men of wealth, of intellect, of industrial enterprise, and the seed-bearers of the ethical new ordering, members of economic committees from the United States, Britain, Italy, Poland, Russia, India, and Japan, representatives of naphtha industries and far-off coal mines, pilgrims, fanatics, and charlatans from all climes, priests of all religions, preachers of every doctrine, who mingled with princes, field-marshals, statesmen, anarchists, builders-up, and pullers-down. All of them burned with desire to be near to the crucible in which the political and social systems of the world were to be melted and recast.[1]

Above that chaotic scene sat President Wilson enthroned on high.   He was no voice crying in the wilderness but a prophet sent by the New World to cleanse the impurities of the Old.[2]   The map of Europe lay open in front of him and it was for his pen to draw the boundaries. Men compared the present Conference with the Congress of Vienna when a religious spirit of peace had descended upon Europe and kings representing Orthodoxy, Protestantism, and Catholicism abandoned their differences and declared themselves united in the noble cause of peace.   " All the more reason," said they, " to hope that on the present occasion the treaties settling the terms of the Great War will be written in a spirit of foresight and statesmanship."   Instead, the world to its dismay saw President Wilson and his colleagues forswearing one by one their lofty principles. As General Smuts said later : " It was the spirit of man which failed at Versailles."   The conquerors spoke in the words of the Tiger Clemenceau when he said : " I conceive of life after the War as a continual conflict, whether there be war or peace.   I believe it was Bernhardi who said that politics are war conducted with other weapons.   We can invert this aphorism and say that peace is war conducted with other weapons." The treaty of peace was conceived in a spirit of revenge and fear : it provided the means of continuing the war against the defeated enemy in an even more rigorous form by its arrogant demands.   Instead of being a treaty

[1] E. J. Dillon, *The Peace Conference*, London, 1919.
[2] H. A. L. Fisher, *A History of Europe*, London, 1936, p. 1160.

of peace to create a co-operative world, it laid stress upon vengeance and punishment. Soon there was discontent everywhere and nowhere more than in Italy, whose just claims were neglected or side-tracked by her more voluble allies. The Italian delegates to the Peace Conference instead of being representatives of a Victorious Power appeared to their fellow-countrymen as timid retainers halting at the door of a hall while a great banquet is in progress and waiting hat in hand until some flunkey will cast them a morsel to satisfy their hunger. President Wilson who had said in his Olympian way to the crippled victims of the War in Milan, "I shall give due consideration in Paris at the Conference to the sacrifices made by Italy," revealed himself as a bitter opponent of Italy's aspirations and an advocate for Yugoslavia. He refused to recognize the validity of the pact of London and demanded that all Carniola, all Dalmatia, a part of Gorizia-Gradisca, and the eastern half of Istria should be given to Yugoslavia on account of the racial composition of the inhabitants. Then in manifest contradiction of his fourteen points he insisted that Fiume, whose population was Italian, should be handed over to Yugoslavia, because it would be convenient to that State. Such was the origin of the fierce wrangle which was to last for two years, embittering the relations between the Allies. Luigi Villari, the well-known historian, shows that Italy, in spite of her undoubted rights, did not present her case in the most effective way : she would have done better to insist on the execution of the Pact of London pure and simple in the discussions with the Allies, and then, once having secured that, to negotiate with the Yugoslavs for Fiume in exchange for concessions elsewhere.[1] But Italy herself was not united. Within the Government counsels

[1] L. Villari, *The Expansion of Italy*, London, 1930, pp. 172–3.

were divided and public opinion was bewildered. One thought was uppermost in the minds of the Italian ex-Servicemen : Italian prestige had been shaken by politicians who preferred to barter their country's claims for the sake of party interests. Amidst all this clamour of European nationalities battling for Peace, the grey, statuesque figure of President Wilson was buffeted about like the statue of a patron saint bobbing up and down over the heads of a drunken, gesticulating crowd. In those days I took a pleasure in jotting down in my diary the discordant opinions held concerning the " Messiah from the West." For one brief moment he had been the Prophet of Humanity redeemed from War. But then even his friends began to discover in him the defects of certain well-meaning, religious pastors, who are convinced that they cannot make a mistake. Such men will brook no contradiction, for they have not enough imagination to be generous. Many would repeat the dictum attributed to Clemenceau. The Tiger, shrugging his shoulders, had exclaimed : " Monsieur Wilson m'embête avec ses quatorze points : le Bon Dieu n'en a que dix ! " Then Europe learned with amazement that the Messiah had been rejected even by the West.

Wilson became the butt for attacks at home and abroad. In Paris his standpoint and that of Clemenceau were irreconcilable : in Italy, as day by day scurrilous articles appeared in the press attacking him, he soon became an object of execration. One day when I was walking down a street in Vicenza, I saw a band of men carrying on high a wretched scarecrow of a figure. It was the effigy of the Prophet in Grey, which they proceeded to burn amidst exulting cries of " Down with Wilson ! "

History will look upon Woodrow Wilson as a tragic idealist, whose sentiments were universally applauded but not followed—a vague, unpractical, obstinate personality, who appeared for a brief moment in a flash of sunlight only to disappear suddenly into the limbo of forgotten heroes.   He was a blind and deaf Don Quixote, tilting at windmills which he could not see—a grey figure of disillusion creeping home to die.

CHAPTER VII

THE SACRED MOUNTAIN

" O Monte Grappa tu sei la mia patria."

AFTER the Armistice the main problem was to keep the men amused. " To demob or not to demob, that is the question," was the eternal refrain I heard in every Y.M.C.A. hut and canteen. During those early months of 1919 in Northern Italy, a comic actor, a female impersonator, a juggler, even a fiddler, was worth his weight in gold in the camps up the line. In Genoa I had my own troupe called by the high-sounding title of " The Riviera Concert Party," including three professional entertainers and a pleasant variety of amateur talent. During my peregrinations as fiddler and lecturer I had always kept a watchful eye on the men who offered to take part in our informal sing-songs and recitals in the various huts. It is only by degrees that one can draw out the many hidden talents of the British Tommy. One day, to my delight, a tour of Northern Italy was arranged by the military authorities, and the soldiers selected by me to be members of the troupe were released from their duties. A director of a concert party, however, should never be an optimist, for the gods take a malign pleasure in raising his hopes only to make his dismal fall the greater. I celebrated the star-performance of our party in Genoa with repeated rounds of Capri wine with my companions. In a few days we should set out for the North

70

and be fêted like princes in Thiene, Vicenza, and in all the camp coliseums in Venetia and Lombardy. Next day misfortunes fell upon us like a curse from heaven. One by one my artistes began to disappear : the local majors and colonels refused point-blank to release the men, saying that owing to the stress of demobilization they could not be spared. All my blarney was useless. I had fondly imagined that an order from G.H.Q. was tantamount to a heaven-sent command, but I failed to realize that in peace time, where entertainment is concerned, G.H.Q. may propose, but it is the local choleric colonel who disposes. I spent my days wandering from one side to the other in a desperate attempt to break through the barrage of red tape and army arrogance which was all the greater, seeing that I was but a camp-follower from the Y.M.C.A. I had one staunch friend and adviser in Miss Kit Bowen—a tall, handsome girl who had come out from England to help in concerts and canteen work. Miss Kit had a pleasant voice and a winning personality : I have never seen anybody refuse her anything she wanted. She possessed the most uncanny facility for wangling. Her wangling was artistic because it was imaginative in its indirectness. She had a special technique for the various military ranks and could change from one method to another with astonishing swiftness. I knew from the first that my only chance of working up a concert party would depend upon her co-operation. At last Kit and I set out with the remnants of a concert party. With us travelled my squire, Sniper Kelly, a diminutive Irishman from Cork who boasted of his talents as a conjurer.

When we arrived at Vicenza we were lodged in a gloomy, ramshackle house near the Cathedral belonging to a locksmith.

My first task was to persuade the Y.M.C.A. chief in

Vicenza, a charming Cambridge man called Elmslie, to drive me from one camp to another so that I might collect my full quota of performers. The next task was to bring the artistes together for a rehearsal and fix their places on the programme.

It was a dark day in January when they all arrived at the house in Vicenza. The one room big enough for the rehearsal was the kitchen which the owner of the house and his daughters shared with us. Let no one imagine that it is easy to arrange military concert-party programmes. The jealous temper of the most sensitive prima donna in the world is naught when set beside the susceptibilities of a soldier female impersonator or knockabout comedian. The first clash came when I arranged the order of the programme ; the whispering baritone would not sing after the knock-about comedian because the public would be more in the mood of laughter than tears ; the female impersonator would not sing after Miss Kit ; and the Shakespearean actor wanted double the amount of time of the rest, in order to recite the whole of the Death Scene of *Othello*. The only person of the whole lot with a sense of humour was Sniper Kelly, the Irishman, but at a glance I saw that he would need all his Hibernian wit and charm to put across his very patent conjuring tricks.

One of the most important duties of the director of a military concert party is to discover a means of conveyance, for after all, Thespis needed a chariot to carry his drama round the Greek countryside. To obtain a chariot in modern days needs all the tact in the world and it was necessary to negotiate many a barrier before reaching the source of all authority. Eventually a big lorry was given over to be our Thespian car and we set off in great spirits. For many days our lorry lumbered over the roads of the Venetian province. We arrived at four o'clock, dusty and tired : Miss Bowen and I were shown into the officers' mess and at six-thirty we found the officers at dinner. At half-past seven I strolled over to the theatre to see if all the arrangements were in order. I met the female impersonator and the knockabout comedian at the entrance to the stage-door gloriously drunk. Sniper Kelly was in the middle valiantly holding them up. At the first moment I felt my blood freeze with horror, but there was no time to be lost. I ordered Sniper to bring them into the wash-room and put their heads under the pump. With diffi-culty he dragged them along, for both kept saying in a sing-song : " Where's the bloody concert now ? We've been off on the booze tra la ! " The jazz pianist was not drunk but in a vitriolic humour : " Look here, Mr. Starkie, when we came on this 'ere concert work we thought as 'ow we'd get decent grub. Why, we ain't had anything but bully beef and chunks of bread. That ain't playin' the game, see ? All you folks 'ave been tuckin' in and the men is left to forage for themselves." I devoutly wished I had been a pukka officer of the British Army to rebuke the fellow, but I was a Y.M.C.A. man and so had to humour him ; besides, divine tact is necessary when a concert is about to begin. " Thank God I have Kit Bowen : she ought to back up the audience even if the rest are duds." My sorrows were not yet to end, for I saw my Shakespearean actor approach very much the worse for wear. " I say, Starkie, old fellow, I found a cosy little nook down in this town and they serve you wonderful sherry there—let's see, what did the bard of Avon say about sherry ? ' A good sherris-sack hath a twofold operation in it. It ascends me into the brain ; dries me there all the foolish and dull and crudy vapours which environ it ; makes it apprehensive, quick, forgetive, full of nimble fury and delectable shapes.' " The bombastic fellow then, in an attempt to strike a pose, slipped and subsided to the earth at my feet. " Look here, sniper," I cried, " another candidate for the wash-tap." It was now about five minutes before the performance was scheduled, and I could hear the chorus-singing of the men in the audience. It is astonishing how quickly one's brain works in an emergency, and that night I felt that it was necessary to be ready for any mishap. If the three tipsy fellows could only carry through their performances in a combative way all would be well, for gay drunkenness always wins its way into the hearts of an audience ; but I was afraid that when they got on the stage they would fall into the mournful, flabby state and stare with glassy eye on the audience. I determined to go on first myself so as to measure the public. After a few bars of ' Wieniawski ' and ' Hubay,' I felt that they had settled down, and at the end of a fiery csárdás they roused themselves to a fair degree of enthusiasm. After my turn I put Sniper on and whispered in his ear, " For God's sake put plenty of gag in : remember a lot of them are Scotch and have a hard sense of humour." One of the characteristics of Sniper was that he was an optimist. If you said to him, " Sniper, go off at once and bring me the moon," he would have departed smiling. As I saw him push his little tables into the middle of the stage I felt confident he would blarney the audience. He started all right, but unfortunately conjuring is not all gag : occasionally one must perform a trick. I watched Sniper closely as he took the little coloured balls and put them under the cloth. " Gentlemen, this is a celebrated trick, and I have had the honour of performing it before most of the Crowned heads of Europe. With one touch of my wand I shall transfer one of those balls to the other table." Alas,

Sniper's magic did not work : his hand faltered and at the
precise moment when the ball should have been travelling
invisible through the air, it dropped and rattled along
the floor. Loud laughter from the audience. " Butter
fingers," said one voice. " Don't let your mother send
you for eggs," said another. Sniper smiled and tried
the trick a second time, but this time the ball did not
travel at all. At last at the third effort belated success
came. The next item on the programme was the
Shakespearean actor and my heart sank as I worked the
diminutive switchboard, and turned the spot-light on
him. At the back he was incoherent and he hiccoughed
loudly as he lurched up the steps leading to the stage.
According to the programme, he was to recite the Death
Scene in *Othello*, but he boldly started off the apostrophe
of Macbeth to the dagger. Strange to relate, the moment he found himself before the public all signs of
inebriety disappeared. He braced himself up and rolled
out the great words in a style that brought down the
house. After his turn I knew that the concert was safe
and I left the comic knockabout and the female impersonator to do their worst . . . I was saved.

A few days later we had to give a concert in a camp
at Arcole and we arrived there in our lorry under floods
of rain. At Arcole in 1796 one of Napoleon's most
romantic victories had been won and near the village
in one fierce attack the future ruler of the world was
thrown from his horse into a marsh and saved by his
adjutant Belliard. On this day Arcole was a marsh,
nothing but mud on all sides. The British guns were
lined up, sunk in the morass. In the officers' mess,
before the concert, Miss Bowen captivated the hearts
of everyone by her charming manner. She was able
to draw out the fat old colonel and make him tell all
his chestnuts. As for me, I was deeply engaged in

conversation with an officer who was a keen musician —a highbrow in fact. He insisted on playing the piano for me at the concert, much to the disgust of my jazz player, who looked on himself as the official accompanist. The concert was held in a broken-down old barn which was far from rain-proof. As bad luck would have it, the officer pianist insisted on my playing highbrow music. " We must give these fellows something good, you know soldiers appreciate classical music, so let us play some of the César Franck Sonata." With misgivings I agreed, and we played the first movement. We reached the end amid silence, but when we started the tempestuous second movement I heard murmurs. Suddenly a voice cried out from the back, " For God's sake play something with a bit of tune in it—give us Annie Laurie." My friend at the piano was indignant, as for me I could hardly finish the movement for laughing. During the concert one of the officers of the unit insisted on singing songs. He dressed himself up as a comic bull-fighter, and went on to sing " Montes the Toreador." His voice was cracked and he looked a ridiculous figure on the stage. At first there was a low murmur of conversation, but when he came to the line about the " Spanish Onion " a shower of pennies hit the back of the stage and rattled all around him. This hint did not disturb his sangfroid and he finished amid shouts of derision. Soldiers who are restlessly awaiting demobilization become bitter critics and it is no easy task to win their praise. Kit was popular because, being a woman, she made them think of home. Many of them had not been back to England and Scotland since the first year of the War, and when they heard a girlish voice sing the old songs, they went wild with enthusiasm. After the concert we packed again into our lorry and splashed through the mud towards

Vicenza. Hardly had we gone more than fifteen kilometres through the blinding rain when the lorry broke down. Not a bit would it budge. Here we were, stranded by the side of the road with not a cottage in sight. On this occasion the alcoholic tendencies of the Shakespearean actor saved us from despair, for he apologetically drew out of his pocket a small flask full of issue rum, which he carried with him for emergencies. With the help of that medicine we were able to endure until the lorry was started again, and we reached Vicenza without further mishap.

Soon every small town in the Venetian province became identified in my mind with adventures of our ramshackle concert party. When I read over my diary I find laconic descriptions pencilled as follows :

Montecchio Maggiore.—Country home of Montagues and Capulets —concert a success, marred by blood-thirsty quarrel between Sniper Kelly, female impersonator, and local juggler from the Motor Transport.

Montebello.—Strange meeting with Hungarian prisoners who turned out to be Gypsy fiddlers.

Arzignano.—Lost my heart to black-eyed daughter of tavern-keeper who acted as *vivandière* to us.

Trissino.—Drank too much red wine of the district and put too many gags into my remarks as compère. Very dangerous for a camp-follower to pull the leg of a sergeant's mess.

Schio.—I shall remember it always ; near there one Sunday I listened to the finest sermon in my life. It was a small rustic church, and the congregation was mainly composed of the humble peasantry of the district. The Priest who said Mass was a young man who had fought in all the battles of the Isonzo, and had been wounded several times. He had been awarded the silver medal for gallantry on the field. He preached the sermon standing in front of the altar, and at his feet many tiny children rolled about on the ground ; for it was the custom for the mothers to deposit their infants within the altar rails to keep them out of harm's way. The young Priest took as his text, " Love your enemies." He spoke of War and the hatred it engenders ; he spoke of nights in the trenches ; of bayonet attacks ; of battles in the snows ; and he told tales of heroism and sacrifice. Then he showed us how the same scenes took place a short distance away on the enemy side. What lessons could we learn from this terrible War but the message of love and charity ?

I still can visualize that young priest, speaking like one possessed with a divine flame to that congregation of peasantry, while at his feet the tiny children played, and the sunlight streaming through the windows of the little church illuminated their curly heads.

After an extended tour with " the Riviera Concert Party," I accepted an invitation to visit the Italian armies in the mountains and give concerts. Early one frosty morning I set out on my Alpine journey. The car zigzagged round and round the narrow road, as we sped higher and higher into the towering peaks of Italy's northern boundary. Already the plain of Venetia lay far below us, glittering in the sunshine like a fair ocean of green and gold, studded here and there with the white towers and red roofs of towns. Above us rose rampart after rampart of massive rock, culminating in the long, serrated ranges of snow-peaks. An Italian officer by my side described graphically the salient points of Italy's campaign. His voice merged with the monotonous drone of the motor engine, as we climbed upwards into the vast, solitary spaces of snow and ice.

At the beginning of the Great War there were paths in these mountains, up which the villagers clambered with their packs on their backs, but when the Italians, as my officer friend said, " mounted the stairs to attack the enemy," they built graded and metalled roads rising by spirals into the Alpine valleys, not only for the purpose of carrying up guns, ammunition, and provision trains in time of war, but that they might be a permanent benefit in times of peace. " Whenever we Italians," said

he, " construct a new road, it is to civilize the surrounding
country. That was how the ancient Romans carried the
spirit of the eternal city all over Europe. We are an
economical people, and when we spend great sums of
money we like to draw permanent profit from our work
and expense. That is why you will always see the road-
makers and the soldiers working together." As he
spoke, he pointed to groups of dusty labourers in the
valley beneath us toiling at a stretch of road by a bridge.
The sound of their pickaxes echoed in the morning air,
mingled with the song which they were singing in chorus
as they hammered. I then thought of the ancient Roman
priests, who were called *pontifices*, or bridge-makers.
Their duties were bridge-and road-making—the two most
important functions of a primitive State eager to extend
its power. And what was the *pontifex maximus*, the
head of religion, but the supreme bridge-maker between
earth and heaven ? By these winding roads over which
we were travelling, the Italians were able to supply their
mountain batteries and trenches, hidden in the rocky
cliffs out of sight of the enemy. Here and there we
could still see medium and heavy calibre guns in position
behind rocks camouflaged with trunks of trees and
bushes. The heavy guns were hauled up the snowy
slopes and swung across dizzy precipices by wire hawsers.
There were also telepheric railways, consisting of wire
ropes and sliding baskets which carried wounded men
as well as provisions from one peak to another one lower
down in the valley. Alpine soldiers during the campaign lived like members of a Polar expedition : they
crouched in snow huts and dug-outs to escape the pitiless
blasts of the Alpine storms. The Ice Maiden was, however, most dangerous when she was peaceful and smiling,
for all of a sudden, after the fierce concussion of a
bombardment, she would loosen out of a sunlit sky a

great mass of snow—a *valanga*—sending it thundering down the heights, burying men, cannon, and huts, and sweeping them to their doom below.

From time to time we stopped at villages and towns, which testified by their blackened ruins to the fury of continuous bombardment. Of all the places I visited, none brought before my eyes the destruction caused by War so clearly as the Asiago plateau, or plateau of the Seven Communes. The road passed through a scene of awe-inspiring horror. But not a village in all the plateau escaped : one after another had been reduced to a mass of ruined houses. The Demon of War had descended, leaving scarcely one stone upon a stone. The woods had been raked by shell-fire, so that nothing was left but clumps of naked, tottering stumps, raising their leafless branches like desolate phantoms of the battle-field. Even the War cemetery, with its multitude of crosses, was pitted with deep shell-holes, many of the crosses lay on the ground, and the graves were churned up. The demon of War with ghoulish fury had pursued his victims even as they lay in their everlasting sleep.

As I was looking at the ruined church of Asiago, and wondering how its campanile still stood erect, a bystander told me that once during a bombardment, an Austrian shell burst inside the campanile, and with the force of the explosion set the bells chiming. They chimed so loudly that their notes could be heard tolling all over the neighbouring countryside :

" They were tolling in honour of Italy's victory," said he.

During my journey into the mountains, I became acquainted with many of the regiments of Alpini, who are Italy's *corps d'élite*. To them was allotted the task of defending the Northern frontiers, and most of their fighting was done in advanced posts in the snow, ten thousand feet above sea-level. What tales they told me of the Carnia and the Cadore, of Monte Cavallazza and Monte Cauriol! They know the secrets of the Alps, and are accustomed to thread their way along narrow paths by the edge of precipices. They are immensely proud of their own traditions, and relish dangerous enterprises. Of all the troops I saw in Italy, none impressed me as much as the " Alpini " by their discipline and efficiency. They are eager-eyed, full of animal spirits, and completely fatalistic in their acceptance of the rigours of War. There is a spirit of charming camaraderie between officers and men, which in no way diminishes the excellent discipline of the regiment. The officers play games with the men, and join with them in their sing-songs. After taking part myself in concerts with the "Alpini" in Treviso, Bassano, Schio, and Udine, I came to the conclusion that they were the most musical of all the Italian troops. Their music is not so much an expression of their individuality, as in the case of the Sicilian or Sardinian soldiers, but an expression of collective emotion. They love to sing in full-throated chorus in the mountains, and listen to the sound echoing from crag to crag in the surrounding valley. Singing is for them not only an exercise of the lungs in the clear air, but it is also an antidote against the strange, overmastering feeling of loneliness, which the mountain gives. He sighs for the black-eyed maiden he has left behind in Feltre or Belluno, and the mountains will echo his sighs. Violetta is her name, and as she lays clothes to dry in the meadow at home, she thinks of her Gigín, the " Alpino," fighting up in the mountains. " Come to the War with me, Violetta," says the love-sick swain. " I won't go to the War with you," answers the girl : " the food is too bad, and the earth is too hard to lie upon." But Gigín answers : " 'Tis not upon the ground you'll lie, but upon a bed of flowers, and four fine ' alpini ' will minister to you."

During the War, a wealth of popular songs arose connected with the life of the " Alpini," and many of them became so identified with the troops that they became part of Italy's musical heritage. True to my profession of wandering minstrel, I collected a big repertory of such songs, and kept them in reserve. Some of the Alpine tunes are sentimental and full of nostalgia. Take, for instance, the following, which consists of a dialogue between the girl and her beloved, who is fighting up in the snows :

Dove sei stato mio bell' Alpino   Dove sei stato

mio bell' Alpino   che ti ha cambià colore ?

> " Where have you been
> my fine Alpino ?
> Where have you been
> my fine Alpino :
> you've changed your colour ? "

He answers :

> " On Monte Nero
> there is a storm :
> it changed my colour.
>
> On Monte Grappa
> there is a bombardment :
> it changed my colour.
>
> It was the smoke
> of the machine-gun :
> it changed my colour."

But the girl at the end answers :

> "Your colours will return,
> your colours will return
> to-night when we make love."

Another song which the " Alpini " would sing in chorus
was " The 29th of July," a rousing marching tune :

> "On the 29th of July
> when they cut the corn
>   tralalà :
> a child was born with a rose in her hand ;
> she wasn't a maid from country or town
>   tralalà :
> she was born in a wood by the sea."

Each town has its own song, which serves as a kind of
mascot to its inhabitants, no matter where in the world
they happen to be.   When I was in Bassano, a soldier
taught me " Sul Ponte di Bassano " (On the Bridge of
Bassano), and even to-day I cannot play its tune without
remembering its straggling laneways, the painted façades
of its houses, the castle of the Ezzelini, with its panorama
of the plain of the Brenta :

The song of Bassano is a pledge of faith in North Italy,
and the words " On the bridge of Bassano we'll shake
hands," have become proverbial.   On one occasion in

recent years I heard it sung by Italian workmen in Hartford, U.S.A., while they were building a church. For the Italian, even when he is living at the other side of the earth, never for a moment forgets his small home town. The song is an eternal reminder of the day when he will sail for Italy, with enough money saved to be able to buy a piece of land near the Bridge of Bassano, and build a little house for his family. Among the " Alpini " on the front, I heard one sing a song of the Emigrants, describing the thirty days' journey by ship and train, how they slept on the hard earth like cattle. " But we Italians," he sang, " helped them over there to build cities and make America a great country." Being an Irishman, I felt most drawn towards the songs of the soldiers from Friuli, for there was in them that minor note of sadness and homesickness. Instead of singing their songs in unison, they prefer to sing them in harmony, with little variations which the individual singer adds in at his discretion. I heard the following sung by a bronzed young soldier in a *casa del soldato*:

" Ti ricuardistu, ninine, dis-al
quand ch' 'o jèrin sul rivàl
tra la la
op la le le
magari ch'a 'n foss !

O'ti 'ai dadis plui bassàdis,—dis-al
che no fuèis sul cocolàr
tra la la
op la le le
magari ch'a a 'n foss ! "

("Do you remember, dearest, said he,
when we were on the hill:
would those days were here!

I gave you, said he, more kisses
than the leaves on the walnut tree:
would those days were here!")

Another humorous, rhythmic song describes the men
descending the slopes of the Carnia beating time. They
all have their pipes in their haversack but not a bit of
tobacco:

Vegnin ju i Charniei de Charnie vegnin ju battind il tacc.

The men from Friuli have a song for every hour of the
day. In the dawn, when they hear the cock crow, they
salute the morning with the song, " A'l chiante'l gial "
(The cock crows—the day breaks—good-bye, my dar-
ling—I must depart). When they are in the tavern they
sing the song, " Olin bevi " (We want to drink the
mellow wine from Latisana). When they serenade their
beloved in the village they sing, " Traiti fur, ninine biele,"
(Come to balcony, dearest) in the hope that she will listen
to their song. And up in the lonely frontier outposts
in the moonlight they sing, " Ai preat la biele stele " (I
have prayed to the beautiful star). The myriads of stars
represent to them the saints in Paradise, who will inter-
cede with God to stop the murdering hate of war, so
that the soldiers may return to their homes. " But,"
cries the singer, " you, O star of mine, direct my destiny:
go behind yon mountain where my heart lies."

There was, however, one song which was sung by
all the troops in those days, whether they came from

Friuli, Venice, Sardinia, or Sicily—the song of Monte Grappa. It is not known who composed the song, but it was sung during the darkest days of the War by the inhabitants of the Alpini towns that were occupied by the Austrian enemy. The Italian troops on the neighbouring heights hearing the children of the occupied towns singing the song, wrote it down, and sung and played it during the terrible months of the " watch on the Grappa."

The mass of Monte Grappa rises from the Venetian Alps between the Brenta and the Piave, like a gigantic fortress. In contrast to the neighbouring peaks it is harsh, gloomy, with scant vegetation on its lower slopes. On the day when we mounted to the summit, it was swept by misty clouds, and the wind whistled in our ears. When the mist cleared, I could distinguish the outlines of the principal spurs that surround the central peak— Monte Pallone, Monte Tomba, Monfenera, Monte Tomatico, Monte Asolone—every one of them the scene of fierce battles. It was the heroic defence of Monte Grappa which prepared the way to the final victory. After Caporetto there was danger that the enemy troops would sweep down from the Venetian Alps on to the plain of Lombardy, had they not been stubbornly kept at bay by the defenders of Grappa.

Thus Monte Grappa became the " Sacred Mountain " of the Italians—one of the most hallowed sanctuaries of the fatherland. In those grim days it resembled a solitary ship buffeted by fierce breakers which threatened at any moment to engulf it. When the Austrians had captured the surrounding positions they hurled one regiment after another at the mountain : their aeroplanes swept the skies above it, their artillery raked it with fire, but the defenders held on grimly, suffering appalling privations in their long vigil throughout the

long winter of 1917–18.   The watchers on the Grappa,
when the enemy attack failed, began the task of moulding
their mountain into one of the supreme fortresses of
Italy.   Just below the summit, they hollowed the rock
into a great central chamber capable of giving cover to
more than a battalion.   From this central chamber, many
tunnels branch right and left, leading to posts for
observers, machine-gun nests, positions for batteries,
dug-outs arranged in tiers : the whole place resembles
a vast palace of Troglodytes.   The whole Italian nation
expressed its gratitude towards the defenders of Grappa,
when, after the armistice, the Government decreed that
the mountain should be a national sanctuary, crowned on
its summit by an altar of the fatherland.

From the summit I could see the whole panorama of
the War spread out below me, for the misty clouds had
rolled away and the blue sky appeared.   The peaks
stretched out in a long line like giants : I could follow
them, one by one, from Monte Pasubio to the far-off
Friulian Alps.   I saw below the Asiago plateau, and up
above the mighty peaks of the Dolomites—Fassa, Agor-
dino, Cadore, and Carnia.   In the depths below lay the
plain, stretching from the Adige to the Tagliamento, and
on the horizon the faint blue line of sea.   I felt as if I
were poised on the roof of the world, outside the reach
of humanity.   The crests of the mountains resembled
huge waves of an ocean over which thin wisps of clouds
were scurrying, casting fleeting shadows on the sunlit
spaces.   How peaceful it all seemed !   Not a sound
came from those deep valleys.   And yet a few months
before, the boom and roar of heavy cannon echoed
and re-echoed from those dark crests, and I could have
seen puffs of smoke on the mountain-sides where shells
had struck.   Up in the sky there had been the zooming
of aeroplanes, circling round and round like sinister birds

of prey—living tombs as Æschylus called the vultures. To-day the mountains had returned once more to their eternal silence. At night, however, when the moon shines upon the deathlike scene, there is a slight, rustling sound near the altar of the fatherland. Pale, tenuous figures keep eternal watch on the rocky summit. They are the heroes of the sacred mountain.

CHAPTER VIII

THE WAVELESS PLAIN

" Beneath is spread like a green sea
The waveless plain of Lombardy,
Bounded by the vaporous air,
Islanded by cities fair."—SHELLEY.

AMERICAN military hospital, Vicenza. There I
found myself with two pillows at my back, a
hot-water bottle at my feet, and a symphony
orchestra of wheezes surging within me. I had collapsed
at Venice after my last concert, and my faithful friend, Kit
Bowen, with the aid of a naval surgeon off the British
battleship *Diamond*, had transported me back to Vicenza.
It was an ill wind that blew nobody any good. My faithful hobby-horse of a fiddle was stolen from me while
I lay prone, and I was left like Sancho mourning for
Dapple. Some days later, however, it was discovered
lying in the snow on the slopes of Mount Berici near
Vicenza by a British major who handed it over to Kit
Bowen. With tears in her eyes she brought it to my
bedside, saying : " There is a remnant of the once famous
Riviera Concert Party." It was a sorry object : the
table was cracked and the neck was broken, but I would
not have exchanged it then for a golden-varnished
Cremona. Being by nature a fatalist, I submitted patiently to my second bout of hospital. My first had been
at Genoa during the Spanish influenza epidemic. In
Genoa I had been tended in the British Red Cross hospital

by nurses, most of whom came from that Northern home of wit and beauty, Aberdeen. In Vicenza hospital, most of the nurses came from El Paso, Texas. They had been sent out by the American Government to help in the great scheme of assistance for the wretched refugees from the War-areas in North Italy and Dalmatia. It was a nun, Sister Valeria, who looked after me. She was a bright-eyed, cheery soul, whose presence in the ward was like a ray of sunshine. When I was in one of my most pessimistic and rebellious moods, Sister Valeria would come and smooth out the ruffled surface of my mind by her serene influence. I delighted in arguing perversely against her in order to hear her demolish my objections one by one in her clear voice. She always treated me firmly as an affectionate mother does a wayward child, and when she would leave me I felt as if she had safely tucked my mind in for the night. Our conversation would start as follows :

" I am sorry, Sister Valeria, I have not got a religious nature."

" You are an Irish Catholic, are you not ? "

" Yes, I was born and bred a Catholic, and in my childhood when I came under the influence of saintly women I felt occasionally that radiant ecstasy of religious emotion. It was as if a benign influence had all of a sudden illuminated my soul. But those moments were followed by reaction, when the light was quenched and I was incapable of doing the daily duties of life. Instead of being spurred on, I felt as if my will had collapsed, leaving me in a dim state of futile despondency."

" You are a dreamer," replied Sister Valeria, " and you should have learnt how to discipline your meditations."

" I'm afraid, Sister, I am a Lotos-eater—a mild-eyed, melancholy Lotos-eater, dreaming of rest on beds of asphodel."

"That is only one of your moods—a self-conscious mood," said Sister Valeria severely.

"My disease," said I, "condemns me to inaction, whereas my mind is active and despises my accursed moods of resignation. No, Sister, I have not got a religious nature. My reason is stronger than my sensibility and prevents me from 'emptying my soul of all that is not God,' as Saint John of the Cross used to say. When I knelt in a cathedral and the nave was all in darkness, save for the faint candle-lights twinkling from the altars in the side-chapels, I felt the swift onrush of emotion. The distant chanting of Gregorian music, echoing through the empty spaces, gave wings to my spirit and enabled it to soar, for a moment, above the clouds of incense in the Gothic edifice, which itself was 'music frozen into stone.' But when the chanting stopped, and the incense had floated away, I became again conscious of the malignant demon whispering in my ear : 'You are a sentimentalist, and you mistake your emotional processes for religious feeling.' "

"You should discipline yourself by prayer," said Sister Valeria. "If you told your beads or buried yourself in your prayer-book, you would soon release yourself from vain dreaming."

"Yes, Sister, by repeating litanies I could then release myself from the external world and create my own world. Did not Jacopone da Todi repeat over and over again to infinity the word *amore, amore*? Saint John of the Cross, too, in his passionate lyricism repeated his invocations until he reached eventually the *desnudez de espíritu*, the mystic's nakedness of spirit."

"But," said Sister Valeria excitedly, "you forget that such a spirit of mysticism descended into lives that were full of active, practical sense. Saint John of the Cross was a great master of novices—he trained them for their painful journey through the world. His lessons are full of shrewd commonsense. And what about Saint Teresa, who first recognized the sanctity of the little saint when she saw him through the grating of the *locutorio* at Medina del Campo? She was the greatest woman administrator the world has ever known. Her *Camino de Perfección* was not a book of shadowy dreaming, but a manual of everyday life in those storm-tossed days of the sixteenth century. It tells of the jealousies, the intrigues, the petty tyrannies that members of a community feel. She gives hope to all of us, because she makes us feel that most of the little basenesses and subterfuges sprang from ' conscience and tender heart.' We all need some radiant spirit like hers, or Saint John's, to relieve our faltering footsteps on the journey through life. And she was never weary of explaining her meaning to her nuns, by little images from everyday life. Nature gave her memorials of the Creator. Do you remember how she compares the soul to a little donkey at pasture, cropping its food and eating almost without thinking of it? She was like a sister of Saint Francis in her love for dogs, horses, cows, birds, and even insects. She would say : ' In each tiny creature God has made, be it but a little ant, there is more than we can understand.' She was never weary of comparing our soul to the bird straying from its nest, striving by reason to attain to heights impossible to its strength. But then our Lord comes and takes the little bird, and puts it back in the nest to rest. Remember that simile when you are tempted to rationalize life."

" My education, Sister, led me away, for a time, from the Christian thinkers towards the ancient Pagan world. My father was a great humanist, a Greek scholar, and he made me love the sweet reasonableness of the ancient Athenians—their σωφροσύνη, which we rarely find even in the most religious Christian peoples. Why is it that Christians have combined religion with hardness of heart? Cruelty has done far more harm in the world than irreligion, which is only a negative quality. When I look back on the cruelty of so-called Christian countries in the War which has just ceased, I feel inclined to despair of Christianity, for it has hardly ever attempted to apply Christ's teaching. At times I believe Homer was right when he said that the gods have fashioned war, and have woven the skein of death for men, that there might be a song in the ears of the folk of aftertime. The gods only take an interest in men because Heaven is the abode of 'ennui.' It was necessary to create men that the gods might have playthings. That is what we are—playthings in the nursery of the gods. Most of us lie forgotten in a corner in the jumble of broken toys, while the noble spirits, like Hector and Achilles, fight in the ring before the sweetly-smiling divine audience on Mount Ida. Can you wonder that Hector would not pray? He leaves that to the women. His mother will pour the libation to the gods, and the blind minstrel Homer explains, saying, 'for men must work and women must pray.' I am afraid it has always been so in the world's history."

Sister Valeria drew a long breath, preparing to fulminate me for my heresies, but Sister Phelan, the young V.A.D., appeared with a bottle of medicine and a large spoon, so all arguments ceased. And when Sister Phelan had finished prattling of Houston cattle convention, Galveston cowpunchers, Red Indian festivals at Taos and Acoma, I was handed over to the Irish-American orderly, Joseph Flynn—a fervent Gael from Ballydehob, Co. Cork.

When at last I was alone, I lay for a long time thinking of Sister Valeria, and relating her in my mind to other nuns whom I had known, and whose unworldly spirits had brought to me such spiritual comfort. For no matter how energetically I argued with Sister Valeria, I knew that her spiritual strength would triumph at the end over my restless doubting. I linked her up with memories of convents in Ireland. I remembered the tranquil garden in the Convent of Mercy at Blackrock, near Dublin—the tiny lake with two swans gliding peacefully over its glassy surface—the long corridors with glistening floors and the faint scent of beeswax : the statue of the Madonna with blue cloak and the gentle expression—a mixture of Raphael and Murillo : the incense-scented chapel echoing with the ethereal voices of the young nuns. I remembered what one of those nuns had said to me : " We have many prayers to offer up, for we must say those which you in the world have not time to say."

After I had left hospital I was allowed to go for a few days' convalescence to Sirmio—a health resort on a tiny peninsula jutting into lake Garda. Sirmio to-day is a settlement of fishermen, but in ancient Roman days it was a famous resort of nobles who built villas upon its shores. It was here that Rome's supreme love-poet, Catullus, dwelt, and to-day the traveller to Sirmio never fails to make a pilgrimage to the grottoes of Catullus, as the natives call the huge boulders which are all that remain of the poet's sumptuous villa. The road to the grotto winds in and out of olive trees, whose gnarled, wind-swept trunks seem to be as old as the Roman ruins themselves. Through the branches of the silver-green olives, I can see the deep blue of Lake Garda and the snow-capped mountains, as I rest upon a grassy slope and think of the passionate music of the poems to Lesbia, the notorious sister of Cicero's enemy, Clodius. But even Cicero bore testimony to her proud beauty, when he

wrote of her magnificent burning eyes. They burnt
deeply into the soul of Catullus and drove him to love
her madly, as only such a warm, generous nature could.
His hectic, consumptive passion still rages through those
inspired lines, wherein he describes his obstinate longing :

At tu, Catulle, destinatus obdura.

The words are written with fire. They have rushed
from his soul in such a flood of spontaneous rhythmic
inspiration that even to-day they bewitch us by their
dangerous music. Even the sweetly-smiling gods must
have stopped for a moment their playing when they heard
music like :

> " O di, si vostrum est misereri, aut si quibus umquam
> extrema iam ipsa in morte tulistis opem,
> me miserum aspicite et, si vitam puriter egi,
> eripite hanc pestem perniciemque mihi,
> quae mihi surrepens imos ut torpor in artus
> expulit ex omni pectore laetitias."

To-day, amid the olive-trees of Sirmio, the flame-like
spirit of Catullus sleeps. The bright-eyed children of
the peninsula look upon him as a kind of *folletto*, or goblin,
and as I was climbing over the rocks, they stood in a ring
near by laughing at me and reciting doggerel verses about
him.

Sirmio to-day is as peaceful a retreat as when Catullus
rambled by its shores, seeking to forget in this " eye of
all peninsulas," as he called it, the blazing eyes of Lesbia.
Hither, too, came another Italian poet, Carducci, with his
nymph, Lalage. When he had crowned her with laurel
and myrtle, he made her turn her eyes away from the
grotto of Catullus, to gaze upon the swans floating across
the lake from Peschiera towards Mantua, fatherland of
Virgil. Lalage hears in the distance the soft Mantuan
song. In the West, silhouetted against the red sky, she

sees the rugged castle of the Scaligers. Upon those
battlements stood Dante, and let his frown and furrowed
cheek soften to a smile, as he looked upon the scene of
waters, earth, and sky.

THE OLYMPIAN THEATRE

Life in Vicenza is full of interest for the ·person who
feels the thrill of historical tradition. Many travellers give
it only a casual glance, so eager are they to reach Venice
and the Lido, but few cities can look back with greater pride
on their past than Vicenza, which has always been famed
as the city of struggles. Again and again it was devastated by the barbarian hordes, but the spirit of its citizens
lived on to fight war after war against Barbarossa, against
Frederick II, against the city-States of Padua and Verona.
In the sixteenth century it was full of riches, and palace
after palace arose under the magic wand of the great
Palladio. In the nineteenth century Vicenza played a
patriotic part in the creation of New Italy, and in the
Great War it was again called upon to make sacrifices.
After the defeat of the Italian army at Caporetto, had the
Austrian advance not been stemmed, Vicenza would
have been the next line of defence, and as I motored
through the country outside the city I saw the lines of
barbed-wire entanglement set in position.

Vicenza with its narrow streets and gloomy recesses
awakens the imagination, and when we explore those
corners we suddenly come upon some glorious example
of Palladio's art. It is impossible to walk anywhere in
Vicenza without hearing the name Palladio. He is
looked upon by the Vicentines as the great hero of their
city, and they may well do so, for the term Palladian
was for a long time a synonym of perfection in architecture. I prefer to remember Palladio by his most exquisite

gem, the Teatro Olimpico at Vicenza, with its permanent scenes which inspired the stage architects of France and England, including even Inigo Jones himself, who boasted of the title "English Palladio." Whenever I had a free moment I would hasten to that theatre and sit alone in the empty auditorium gazing at the ornamented proscenium. Through the arches I could gaze along the perspective alleys which seemed to stretch far back and dwindle into the distance. The perspectives represent streets running into a large courtyard in the front of the stage. Through the majestic arches I saw in my imagination the actors of the Renaissance moving across the stage. I saw Œdipus in sixteenth-century costume, followed by Sophonisba and the stilted characters of Trissino. After them came the florid figure of Aretino holding both his sides for laughter as he pummelled the hypocrite. The arena was no longer cold and empty, for it was thronged with the ambassadors from the States of Europe and their suites. In the centre was seated a king, and on each side of him Cardinals in their red robes. In a corner stood Scamozzi, the pupil of Palladio, to whom the master left the task of completing this noble theatre.

Few places give one the sense of actuality as this playhouse which enshrined the drama of the Renaissance. As I gazed at the ornamented architectural façade with its conventional statues of classical antiquity, I thought of the scholars of the Renaissance rummaging about on book-shelves and drawing forth manuscripts of antiquity. *Torniamo all' antico* was the watchword trumpeted forth on all sides then and many a laurel wreath was deposited at the shrines of Greek and Roman deities. Plautus came to life from ancient Rome and was the fashionable dramatist : he was, in fact, the Dumas Fils or the Sardou of those days. Terence, too, was often

played upon such a stage, but as he lacked *gros sel* he
pleased less those devotees of Gargantuan laughter.
Plautus and Terence were the ancestors of many an
Italian literary comedy played upon this stage. That
literary comedy with its rigid, fixed rules was not destined
to bring rich fruit to Italian literature, unless we except
the great Machiavelli, whose *Mandrake*, with its Peck-
sniffian Friar Timoteo, was one of the great comedies of
the world. Nor would that bright-hued audience have
wished to spend all their time gazing at the slow-moving
tragedies of Seneca. Even the red-robed Cardinals
seated in the front row would have yawned at such a
spectacle. They wished to laugh at life caricatured upon
the stage.

Mankind has always welcomed the wandering actor
who is a kind of pedlar of humour, pulling out of his
well-stored wallet many quips and cranks and wanton
wiles. No sooner have the characters of Plautus and
Terence shuffled off the stage than another band of ribald
vagabonds appears in the distance advancing rapidly
down one of the avenues. They are a joyous crew :
they have wandered from town to town playing under
the stars as well as in the palace halls. They remember
a tag here and a tag there from the literary comedies of
old Plautus and Terence, but they rely on their own
mischievous wit to carry them through their performance.
Every one of them has his own *lazzi* or conceits. When
they are not on the stage you will see them carrying under
their arm a well-thumbed parchment volume : it is a
zibaldone, or repertory, in which are written all the witti-
cisms proper to their parts. What a mine of humour
that notebook is ! Yonder actor has written into it all
the fancies that have come into his mind, all the funny
scenes he has witnessed, all the trite poetical aphorisms
he has heard in his wandering through life—nay, that

book is even richer than that, for he had inherited it from
an actor father, who had played the same part upon the
stage and had written down his material. Before we
see them play we know that they have rehearsed with the
stage manager of the play, or *corago*. The author had
written just a synopsis of the play in its broad division
of acts and scenes and he had pinned it up in the wings
of the theatre. After the *corago* had explained the nature
of the plot, the situations, the necessary *lazzi*, the actors
turned to their notebooks for assistance in their improvisation. As I watch them perform I see a similarity
between the plot of their play and one of the ancient
comedies of Plautus. But what a transformation!
Whereas in Plautus morality nearly always triumphed
and vice was represented in its most unattractive colours,
here these masked actors show us scenes of unblushing
grossness as if their joy consisted in deforming the well-
worn themes through their genius for parody. It is,
however, not the network of intrigue that fascinates me,
but the characters themselves with their masks. I see
the two old men of the play crossing the stage—they are
Pantaloon and Doctor Graziano. Pantaloon is dressed
in red doublet, hose, and cloak; on his head he wears
a red cap with a point, and over his face a black mask
with a long hooked nose. He excites a roar of laughter
because of his miserly meanness and his extraordinary
tendency to fall in love with every young girl he meets.
As my imaginary audience is composed of men and
women of Vicenza, the laughter is at his expense, for is
he not a caricature of the rich merchant of neighbouring
Venice? And as for Doctor Graziano—he is even a
greater source of laughter, because he comes from
Bologna University, the home of pedantry. But who
are those two brightly dressed knaves who are perpetually
quarrelling in the centre of the stage? They too are

from this province and they walk together like Tweedle-dum and Tweedledee, always quarrelling, always romping. They are Harlequin and Brighella, the two clown servants. Harlequin wears a doublet of many colours and carries in his belt a wooden sword : he is a doltish fellow. To his lot fall all the buffets and beatings but you will never hear him utter a complaint. As for Brighella, he is a bright-eyed, shifty fellow, for ever side-stepping and boxing his shadow.

Many characters passed before my eyes as I sat in the darkened theatre. The procession of actors disappeared in the distance down the interminable avenues : Pantaloon, Doctor Graziano, Harlequin, and Brighella had departed to enrich the theatres of other countries and contribute to the rise of modern drama.

When I reported for duty, I was sent, first of all, to Arquata, a small Ligurian town on the river Scrivia, which had been the general base for the British Expeditionary Force. There I continued my work of lecturing, fiddling, and organizing concerts among British and Italian troops. A few days later a note arrived from the army authorities appointing me language teacher in an army school which had just been established at Montebello—a small town near Vicenza. This was to be a model institution, organized under the auspices of the War Office and Lord Gorell, to enable the officers and men of the British force in Italy to prepare themselves for their return to civil life. From the school they could matriculate into the universities, or prepare for entrance examinations into the various professions. I was delighted to get the appointment, for I remembered my interview with Sir W. H. Hadow in London, when he had told me that my most valuable work would be to organize in the army classes and lectures, which would encourage the men to turn their thoughts towards reconstruction. " There are," he had said, " two great spheres of activity in which you may exert an influence. You may encourage the British soldier who is full of chauvinistic ideas and prejudice to learn foreign languages and read the history of other countries than his own. And you may also aid in developing the musical side of humanistic education, helping the men to appreciate the masterpieces and to make music themselves."

In those early days after the War, idealists had their way, and there was a generous spirit of co-operation between the army authorities and the educationists in the Y.M.C.A. Not only did we start libraries with books received from London, but we would get letters from active music directors, such as Percy Scholes, offering to send us out musical instruments for orchestras. To-day, in my life of humdrum toil as a University don, I look back with a tinge of regret to those days when we had such youthful enthusiasm and simple faith in our mission of leading the world back to the great humanistic ideals. Our motto was : " Homo sum : humani nil a me alienum puto." Here we were in Italy—in the waveless plain of Lombardy, islanded with cities fair. How could we remain idle and uninspired when we were living in the shadow of Padua, Verona, Vicenza, Venice ? The only difficulty was to possess a broad enough conception of humanism, so that we could unite men and make them conscious of the never-ending adventure of learning. It was not enough to teach the men languages, and talk to them of history and social institutions : they must also hear, play, and sing the music that Marcello, Cimarosa, and Vivaldi created in those cities ; they must train their eyes to see the lights in the mountains or over the canals of Venice, which inspired the flaming Titians ; they must

ramble slowly through the narrow streets of Padua,
Verona, Vicenza, which have been enriched by masterpieces of Palladio and Donatello. We were, in fact,
to look upon the whole plain of Lombardy as our
studio.

The army authorities established the school in a big
country house, a few miles from Montebello. It soon
became, in our eyes, a miniature Urbino. In the morn-
ings we held our classes, and in the afternoon we
organized football matches on the days that were not
devoted to sightseeing in Padua, Verona, or Venice. In
the evenings we rehearsed concert items and plays for
performance on Saturday nights in the little theatre we
had rigged up in one of the stable buildings. Our mess
consisted of six or seven officers, the Church of England
padre (also a Y.M.C.A. worker), and myself. We were
a merry party. The director of the school was Major
Turner—a bluff, hearty soldier who liked to pull the leg
of Moore, the padre. The latter, however, who was a
man of the world, more than held his own. Then there
was Carlo Denza, son of the well-known Italian musician,
Luigi Denza—composer of the immortal Neapolitan
Piedigrotta song, "Funiculì, Funiculà." Carlo, however, though of Italian parentage, was not Italian in
sentiment. He had fought through the War in an
English regiment, and was aggressively British. My
two particular friends were Dowden and Bowman.
Dowden—a Scotsman out of the second Gordon High-
landers—appealed to me because he had a bit of the
devil in him, and was always ready for a spree. In this
he was ably seconded by Bowman—an engineer, who
was in charge of all the transport of the school.

"Let us dash over to Vicenza," said Dowden.

"Done," cried Bowman.

A few minutes later we were speeding along the road

towards Vicenza, and later in the evening, after a Lucullian dinner at the Hotel Roma, we would retire to the Café Garibaldi in the piazza.

On one of the nocturnal visits to Vicenza I had a small adventure on my own. I was seated alone in the Café Garibaldi, waiting for my two friends, when I noticed an attractive lady at the opposite side of the room. She was dressed in a beige-coloured coat with grey fur collar, and she wore a smart little Cossack-style hat at a rakish angle. I am not always the soul of discretion when my eye is ensnared, but the lady returned my stare unabashed. Then she called over Sandro the waiter, and handed him a card which he brought to me. On it was written " Miss Mary Paulon " in large lettering, and underneath in small print the words : " Travaille avec messieurs les officiers anglais." Those words intrigued me. What kind of work docs this lady do, I wondered ? "Miss Mary" sounds innocently English —even girlish ; but, then, why put the rest in French ? And why usc the preposition *avec* instead of *pour*, unless perhaps the work requires the co-operation of *messieurs les officiers anglais*. The waiter said in a low voice : " The signora's address is : busa San Michele, No. 16, and she is always at home if the signore would like to call." When I mentioned Miss Mary Paulon to friends, I found that they knew all about her. One French officer said she was : " Une poule qui a beaucoup de chic " : another said she was a *vivandière*. A British officer said she was a fairy godmother, for her house was the only decent club in Vicenza. " You'll hear all the army gossip anyhow," he added. Some Italians frowned when I mentioned her name, saying that she was a sphinx woman—a perverse, exotic courtesan—a spy. I heard quite enough to enable me to idealize Miss

Mary, and make her into a kind of Mata Hari, and I determined to visit her at the first opportunity. When I did arrive at No. 16 busa San Michele, I found a queue of officers waiting in the passage outside her door. She received her guests in a gaudily furnished drawing-room. A diminutive maid brought in cups of coffee, and Miss Mary herself offered me a glass of strega. She was dressed in a clinging grey *crêpe de chine* frock, which revealed more than it concealed of her sinuous, *fausse maigre* figure. She had three girl friends with her who helped to entertain, but it was she herself who was the life and soul of the party. I have never heard a girl murder English so charmingly : she had a way of blurting out in a childish voice unmentionable English monosyllables, as she twisted the moustaches of a solemn Saxon from Birmingham, twitting him roguishly, mimicking his speech and his walk. She never stopped talking, but rattled on, now in Italian, now in French, occasionally in German, as well as in broken English. Most of the men who visited Mary Paulon did not do so to make love to her. They enjoyed listening to her amusing stories and her smart repartees when anyone started an argument with her. I mentally labelled her Aspasia, for, like the great Athenian courtesan, she had varied accomplishments and even political insight in addition to her beauty. It was amusing to watch her give herself airs when any great person's name was mentioned. If any prince, duke, or general's name came up in conversation, Miss Mary would say : " I know him well. He was here a short time ago. *Mon cher !* you should see him without his uniform—no façade to him at all : *Et quant à l'amour il est absolument moche !* "

" *Monsieur le prince,*" she would say, " is a martinet in war-time. He has a conquering eye : one can't argue with him, but when he visits me he is so humble, you would think he was afraid of losing the battle with me, or at least of going away *bredouille*."

We all welcomed Mary Paulon's wit at the expense of those famous personalities. Her anecdotes gave piquancy to our conversation later on in the mess, when we quoted them to one another as the latest piece of *chronique scandaleuse*. There were many theories about Mary's place of origin. Some said she was Italian with an assumed foreign name : others said she came from Vienna and had been a lady of great wealth and position there before the War. Personally, after hearing her swear in French when she was angry, I came to the conclusion that she sprang from the soil of Montmartre, somewhere in the classic region of Rue des Martyrs. She was a pleasant though exotic addition to society in Vicenza, and she gave many a lesson on continental customs and habits to inquisitive, willing, though stolid pupils from our Northern islands. One of my friends —a grey-haired devotee of Kipling—murmured to me as we descended her stairs : "I learnt about women from her."

One evening, when I went to call on Mary, I found a piece of cardboard hanging from the door-handle with the word *chiuso* scrawled on it in pencil. I knocked and I rang. No answer. What had happened ? As a rule, the staircase and landing at this hour would have been thronged with Mary's visitors. I rang again, and paused, saying to myself : "What does *chiuso* mean ? Does it mean temporary suspension or ' closed for spring-cleaning ' ? " As I stood perplexed, an officer with an eye-glass came springing up the stairs, humming gaily, "La donna è mobile." He hemmed and hawed when he saw me, and adjusted his monocle in order to read the card on the door. A moment later, a choleric, red-faced captain joined us. When he saw the card, he scratched his head and said : " Any of you know what is the meaning of *chiuso* ? "

" Closed," said I.

" What the hell ! " said he.

" Vacation or spring-cleaning," said I.

" I don't think," said the choleric captain. " Mary takes no vacations."

The monocled officer coughed without saying a word.

As we waited, disconsolately, before the closed door, an old charwoman came along the passage, carrying a brush and dustpan. She stopped when she saw us, and pointing with her brush to the door, she said in a wheezy voice : " She won't come back : they've taken her."

" Who ? " said the three of us in chorus.

" The *carabinieri*. I could tell you but I won't," said the old woman.

" Come on, tell me," said I persuasively, feeling for a lira in my pocket.

" Acqua in bocca," said she. " Mum's the word. I'll whisper it in your ear. The police came this morning when she was in bed, and took her away with them. She had hardly time to throw on a dressing-gown. They ransacked every drawer in the house—looking for papers, they were."

While I was listening to the old woman's whispered revelations, the two officers had slipped silently away. " Come with me," said she, " and I'll show you." She pulled out a bunch of keys, opened the door, and led me into the apartment. What chaos and confusion there was ! The cupboards and presses were open ; the drawers were piled one on top of the other : dresses, gowns, petticoats, underclothes were thrown in disorder around the room. It was as if a devastating hurricane had swept down with avenging fury. Amidst all the disorder, perched on the mantelpiece, stood the large

photograph of Mary Paulon, dressed in her clinging evening gown, with a white fur over her shoulders.   She
seemed to gaze serenely over the ruin beneath, and there
was just the suspicion of a contemptuous smile upon her
face.

" Well, well," said the old woman sententiously,
gazing up at the photograph ; " where are you now, my
pretty one ? what's the good of all your finery ?   You'll
be cooling your heels a while, I'm thinking.   And the
two *carabinieri* didn't fall for you ; try as you would
with all your sighs and side-glances, tears and tantrums.
I remember you when you came here first : you weren't
so full of furs and finery then, but you soon had young
and old trailing after you.   You should have stuck to
your trade, my girl, and not gone meddling with politics,
which were not meant for a giddy head like yours.
But there you are ! there's no fathoming the folly of us
women."

The old woman, mumbling to herself, began to tidy
up the room.

Two mentors I had with me in those days of rambling
over the Lombardic plain—Shelley, whose poem written
in the Euganean hills describes in immortal music the
first swift vision of beauty of that sky and earth—and
Ruskin, who from any rock above the waveless plain
can point out in a moment the panorama of history
below. To Shelley, standing on a solitary hill, the
dewy vapours, the clouds fleck'd with fire and azure in
the unfathomable sky, bring love, light, harmony to
people his lone universe. Ruskin, gazing from the
heights above Verona, sees the sum-total of man's work
through the ages.

Now I do not think [he says] that there is any other rock in
all the world, from which the places and monuments of so complex

and deep a fragment of the history of its age can be visible, as from this piece of crag, with its blue and prickly weeds. For you have thus beneath you at once, the birthplaces of Virgil and of Livy; the homes of Dante and Petrarch; and the source of the most sweet and pathetic inspiration of your own Shakespeare; the spot where the civilization of the Gothic kingdoms was founded on the throne of Theodoric, and where whatever was strongest in the Italian race redeemed itself into life by its league against Barbarossa. You have the cradle of natural science and medicine in the schools of Padua; the central light of Italian chivalry in the power of the Scaligers; the chief stain of Italian cruelty in that of Ezzelin; and lastly, the birthplace of the highest art; for among these hills, or by this very Adige bank, were born Mantegna, Titian, Coreggio and Veronese.[1]

The only way to acquire (as the French Renaissance poet said) " *le goust et l'air de l'Italie*," is to become a peripatetic philosopher, for walking in the clear air of Lombardy stimulates the brain, and we soon become as sharp-eyed as the Athenians ἀεὶ βαίνοντες διὰ λαμπροτάτου αἰθέρος (always walking through the clear air). It is useless to sit in a chair and read book after book on Italy: we must walk about the towns and villages with a wallet stored with small, serviceable manuals, to which we may turn to refresh our memories. But our eyes must not become hypnotized by the printed word: we should let them rove restlessly, ever watchful like the eye of a wild bird, otherwise they will miss some sight which is worth all the wisdom in the book we hold in our hand. It took me some time to recover from the books I had read about Padua. I was blind, deaf, and bilious with guide-book learning, and the whole city at first was like a gloomy mausoleum, through which I walked with head down listening to my echoing footsteps. Then I put my books back in my wallet, and I sat in the Café Pedrocchi—the navel of Padua—and kept my ears and eyes open.

[1] J. Ruskin, *Verona and other Lectures*, London, 1894.

Paduans will never allow the stranger to miss any of the beauties of their city. For them Saint Antony, Giotto, Mantegna, Ezzelino, Petrarch, are as living to-day as they were in the Middle Ages, and so vivid in their description that the stranger soon cannot walk down a winding, narrow street without fancying that Cunizza gazes upon him from a balcony, and every serenader with a cloak and a guitar takes on the semblance of the Mantuan Sordello. For a whole day once, I followed mentally in the tracks of the sinister Ezzelino da Romano, because in the morning, when coming out of the Church of Saint Antony, I gave a few centesimi to a cripple who seemed to me to be the living image of the dread tyrant. Symonds described him as a small, pale, wiry man, with terror in his face and enthusiasm for evil in his heart, living a foe to luxury, cold to the pathos of children, dead to their enchantment.

They say that his palace stood in the Piazza Castello, and the tower which contained the terrible dungeons designed by Zilio (who was the first to be confined within them) has now become an astronomical observatory. Ezzelino's reputation in the popular mind has acquired lustre owing to his courage. He is looked upon as one who defended the lower classes against the feudal nobility, and many of his terrible crimes, his mutilations, which won him the fame of monster of iniquity, are forgotten by those who prefer to remember him on the battlefield at Soncino, tearing open his wounds with his own hands rather than submit to the enemy. I can still visualize him as a younger man on the day when, at the entreaty of his aged father, he swore obedience to the commune of Padua. He rode out in armour on a black horse from his castle on the Brenta, and descended to the Paduan camp. He stood with his horse in the river, and swore to the peace treaty, with fierce anger in his countenance, and with a grim look at those who had fought against him, he galloped away to plot his vengeance against the city.[1] His type springs up again and again in the Italian Renaissance, when the spirit of the age was auspicious to the individual who was achieving self-emancipation. But in Italian history, at the very moment when a monster of cruelty like Ezzelino strides across the stage, we behold humanity rallying round the opposite type who preaches peace and love. It was Saint Antony, patron of the oppressed and suffering, who gave men courage to withstand Ezzelino. Saint Antony, like his still greater master, Saint Francis, shunned the pomp of the world, and in spite of the wealth lavished upon his communities, preferred to live in a tiny hut of straw and wattle. Rich and poor alike worshipped a saint, whose life was spent in tending to the sick and weary, and in addition they saw in him a patriot for ever ready to defend Padua. When he died, there was commotion in the city : children ran through the streets, crying out, " E' morto il santo " ; and noblemen, artisans, laymen, and priests hastened to pay homage to his body in Arcella. Less than a year after his death he was canonized.[2] When I wandered through the church of the saint, I could not help thinking all the time of him in his hut of straw, or writing his last sermons, sitting in the branches of a tree, as he is represented in the picture. How ill at ease his unworldly, ascetic spirit must feel in this vast temple amid the countless works of art created in his honour by the supreme artists of Italy. He would smile sadly at the sight of his own chin and tongue preserved for all time in the churchlike reliquary of chiselled gold. Although I fervently touched Saint Antony's tomb for luck, I lost

---

[1] C. Foligno, *The Story of Padua*, London, 1910.
[2] C. Foligno, op. cit., p. 186.

sight of his spirit in the wealth of Renaissance art surrounding his shrine. To rediscover the spirit of Saint Antony or Saint Francis it was necessary to go to Padua's most wonderful monument—the Arena chapel, whose walls are covered with Giotto's greatest paintings. Giotto "whom Cimabue found among the sheep" illustrates the universe of Dante and Saint Francis as well as that of Saint Antony. Even as a child he showed the divine spark of genius and covered the walls of his father's hut with charcoal sketches of the sheep he tended on the slopes of Val d'Arno. He released art from the tyranny of Byzantine tradition and gave it a divine soul and a human interest. At Florence under Cimabue, who was painting in Santa Maria Novella, Giotto made amazing progress. Those were the days when the great Duomo and Sante Croce were being built and Giotto would meet Dante and converse with him about the allegories which were floating through the mind of the great poet. Giotto in painting allegorical scenes was obeying the tendency of the time. In the *Fioretti* Saint Francis tells how one day, when he was walking on the road to Siena, he met three fair maidens, whose names were Obedience, Chastity, and Poverty, the three monastic virtues making up the sum of evangelical perfection. And Giotto's painting of the scene in the Lower Church at Assisi gives the warmth of full and generous life to the pale theological conception. Like Dante, he strove to give eternal forms to human feelings, as when he painted Saint Francis espousing Poverty in the presence of the angels—a scene which might serve as an illustration to the eleventh book of the "Paradiso":

> chè per tal donna giovinetto in guerra
> del padre corse, a cui com'alla morte
> la porta del piacer nessun disserra.

But Giotto, true to his sense of humanity, symbolizes the cynicism of the world in the mocking youth and the group of rich grandees who turn scornfully away from the angels. Of all the works of art I saw in my first journey through Italy none moved me as much as the Giotto frescoes in the Arena chapel. It was in 1303 that Enrico Scrovegno, a noble citizen of Padua, determined to raise on the site of the Roman amphitheatre a chapel dedicated to the Annunciation. Benvenuto da Imola, seventy years after, describes Dante's visit to Giotto when he was painting the frescoes. The poet watched him at work in the chapel surrounded by his children, who were playing on the ground. " They were," said Dante, " as ugly as he was himself, and I wonder that the creations of his brain were so much more beautiful than his own children." Other contemporaries such as Boccaccio and Petrarch refer to the painter's small stature and grotesque appearance, which was always the subject of jests, but they pay tribute to his cheerful good-humour, his kindness, and his power of repartee. Boccaccio gives one instance when he describes how one day he and a lawyer, Messer Forese, and Giotto were riding towards the painter's home at Vespignano, when they were caught in a shower of rain and forced to borrow hats and cloaks from the peasants. As they rode on, dressed in the tattered old garments and mud-stained boots, Messer Forese remarked to Giotto : " If a stranger met you now, Giotto, would he ever imagine that you are the greatest painter in Florence ? "

" Of course he would," answered Giotto, " if on beholding your worship he could think for a moment that you had learnt your A B C." Another anecdote tells how one Sunday, when he was on an expedition with his friends, they met a herd of pigs, one of which ran between Giotto's legs and threw him down. The painter picked himself up, shook the dust from his clothes and said : "The pigs are quite right; when I think how many thousands of crowns I have earned with their bristles, without ever giving them even a bowl of soup."

Giotto was no less outspoken among the great than he was among his boon companions. On one occasion King Robert of Naples was watching him paint on a summer's day and he remarked : "If I were you I should stop painting while the weather is so hot." Giotto replied : "So would I, were I King Robert."

The innumerable anecdotes which have arisen around Giotto, whether they were apocryphal or no, prove how deeply he impressed his personality upon his contemporaries. To-day when we enter the long, low nave of the little chapel with its six narrow windows, we not only live in the mediæval world which culminated in the Divine Comedy, but we become familiar with the ideas and feelings of a great man struggling to express in form and colour his visions. In this small temple there were no other artists to compete with him, and so he had full opportunity to work out his scheme and allow his imagination full play. Although he was a contemporary and friend of Dante, there was in his character, in addition to the serious, mystical spirit of the Florentine, a touch of the gentle roguishness of Boccaccio.

When we consider, one by one, the subjects in the Arena chapel, we see many touches of naïve realism. In the first twelve subjects which are taken from the apocryphal gospels we see scenes which might be illustrations of the painter's own early life : shepherds in rough garments, rams butting at each other, the faithful sheep-dog who rushes to welcome his master Joachim.

Up to the Annunciation, the culminating point in Our Lady's life, Giotto had followed the legendary texts of pseudo-Matthew and of the Golden Legend, but from now onwards he abides strictly by the Gospels. One of the most moving scenes of all is where Mary is welcomed by her mother, Saint Anna. The contrast between the calm, radiant grace of the Virgin and the tender sympathy of the aged mother, as she gazes at her divine daughter, has hardly ever been surpassed by any later painter. According to Ruskin, it is practically independent of the whole system of decoration of the chapel, and beneath it there is an allegorical panel by Giotto representing a lamp hanging from the ceiling of a room with a Gothic window. Giotto, whenever he attempted to paint strictly according to the scriptural tradition, is disappointing, but in the fresco of the Entombment, where he drew from his own imagination, he created a scene of the most poignant beauty. A faint light seems to shine from the face of the dead Saviour upon his Mother and upon the other grief-stricken watchers. But the artist, not satisfied with this scene of sorrow on earth, has added an ethereal beauty to his picture by showing the angels in the clouds in all the attitudes of uncontrollable sorrow. We see them in the gloomy sky above the trees : their white wings gleam as they fly hither and thither like frightened birds before the storm, and their bodies twist in agony. Few pictures I have ever seen moved me as deeply as Giotto's beautiful expression of naïve sorrow. It has remained ever since hidden away in a shady nook of my mind. At certain moments of solitude it returns like a gentle memory—a divinely sad melody heard " in the silence of the infinite spaces."

"Let us go in search of Romeo and Juliet," said one of my soldier pupils. We were standing in the ruined courtyard of the so-called Romeo and Juliet castles at Montecchio Maggiore. As the traveller comes along the road from Montebello, in the distance over the plain he sees the massive walls of those two castles. They belonged to the Scaligers, but the folklore of the people associates with them the names of the star-crossed lovers. It was said that the Montagues and the Capulets retired to these retreats in the summer from Verona, and there is not a peasant girl who will not tell you the story.

"I don't believe they ever were here," said my pupil firmly.

"Why?" said I.

"Because two households who 'from ancient grudge break to new mutiny' would never spend their holidays in two castles that are cheek by jowl with one another."

"Let us then go to Verona and search for Capulet's orchard."

As we drove through the fields spring was in the air. The countless phantom mulberry trees had suddenly sprouted and all the earth was throbbing with life. Under the trees were lumbering wagons drawn by white oxen with swinging gait. Here and there were women in red skirts trailing the vines on the trees. It was near the time,

When well-appointed April on the heel of limping winter treads.

The Piazza delle Erbe, a market-place of Verona, with its large white umbrellas like the tents of a Gypsy tribe, was ablaze with colour and animation. Threading our way through the excited throng of vendors, we entered the narrow Via Cappello, where tradition insists that Juliet lived. Over the door of an ancient house there is a tablet commemorating Verona's heroine:

These were the houses
Of the Capulets
Whence sprang Juliet
For whom
So many noble hearts have wept
And poets have sung.

What a disillusion descends upon the sentimental
traveller who enters the courtyard of that house and
gazes up, repeating softly : " What light through yonder
window breaks ? It is the east and Juliet is the sun."
There was no orchard, nothing but a stable-yard with a
cart or two drawn up in a corner. There was no balcony
at Juliet's window to tempt the lover " bestriding the
gossamer that idles in the wanton summer air." The
ground beneath was pitted with puddles of dung and in
the corner of the yard a garbage heap tempted the
covetousness of neighbouring mongrels. And our disillusion grew still greater when we visited the so-called
" Tomb of Juliet " surrounded by its modern romanesque
cloister. The Tomb, which is made of Red Verona
marble, had been a washing-trough before false senti-
mentality (or was it grotesque Italian humour ?) converted it from its prosaic functions into the resting-place
of legend's fairest lovers. The genius of each country
creates its own immortal victims of star-crossed love.
Shakespeare gave England Romeo and Juliet, on whom
" Death lies like an untimely frost upon the sweetest
flowers of all the field." Italy pays scant heed to the hero
and heroine of Luigi Da Porta's romance, because Dante
had given her Paolo and Francesca, those wearied souls
fleeing hand-in-hand through space for all eternity,
crying out in anguish, " Amor, che a nullo amato amar
perdona."

So while we are in Verona let us forget Romeo and

Juliet and seek rather for Dante's host, Cangrande della Scala, " the Great Lombard," whom Petrarch called " the consoler of the houseless and the afflicted." As I stood before his majestic tomb outside the romanesque church of Santa Maria Antica I thought of the words which the historian Cipolla wrote of this the greatest of the Scaligers :

More fortunate than Uguccione della Fagguiola, who lost in a moment all that he had gained, less fortunate than Matteo Visconti, who left to his valiant sons a state firmly established, Cangrande by daily and continual wars acquired an extensive lordship, but one without stability ; based only on the valour of him who formed its head. The Scaliger power disappeared rapidly in a few years after it had been founded.[1]

Significant words when we reflect on this man who welcomed with princely liberality not only Dante but Giotto, Albertino Mussato, and a host of poets, musicians, and scholars. In battle no one was more reckless, for he would allow no other man to captain his forces. To the conquered foe he was humane and even generous, as in the case of the Paduans, whom he treated with a father's tenderness once he had vanquished them. Mere personal ambition did not satisfy one who saw visions of a united Italian state free from foreign suzerain. But Destiny struck him down with cruel suddenness. As Ruskin says : " He died, at thirty-seven, of eating apples when he was too hot," [2] and all the schemes for Italy's greatness evaporated into thin air.

Day by day as I wandered through those cities of the waveless plain the panorama of Italian history passed before my eyes in a succession of powerful individuals advancing, one by one, out of the huge anonymous

---

[1] C. Cipolla, *Storia delle Signorie Italiane del 1313 al 1350*, Milano, 1881, Bk. I, 4.

[2] J. Ruskin, *Verona and Other Lectures*, London, 1894.

mass of Italian humanity. At one moment the mass casts out into the arena a wolf-hearted conspirator like Ezzelino, at another a noble visionary like Cangrande. No sooner does the individual fly out of the humming mass than, like the queen bee, he leads a swarm after him to form a new community. Woe to Italy when she does not produce the great individual *condottiere* who will rule the mass, for then the power falls into the hands of anarchical secret societies and Italian life becomes unhistorical like the life of peasants. As Count Keyserling said in his essay on Italy :

Democracy in the French or English sense has never existed in Italy. If there was no outstanding figure the power fell into the hands of the secret societies, who after their fashion, again, represented the principle of minority rule. In Italy the democratic façade was never anything more than a façade ; if it ever became anything more, anarchy inevitably followed. The great Italian individual's qualities issue forth in a marvellous earth-bound realism of the spirit. He finds the necessities of political life just as natural as the mother finds the needs of her little children.[1]

Historical reflections are inevitable in these Lombard cities where an eager wanderer is unable to wander up fifty yards of street without some monument or other halting him and prompting him to philosophize. But in Verona, which has been called " the hostelry of the peoples," there are just as many old-world taverns to waylay the traveller as monuments. In England we call such frequent haltings for refreshment by the disagreeable and vulgar words " pub-crawling." It is a contemptuous term invented by Puritans, who cannot look at a snug, peaceful hostelry without seeing visions of purple-faced inebriates crawling from its secret back door in the direction of a further rest-house on Sin's road. In the North of Italy they use a more delicate

[1] H. Keyserling, *Europe*, London, 1928, p. 157.

phrase to describe the wanderer with a palate for varied wines. *Andar per ombre* (to go shadow-chasing) means to go from tavern to tavern tasting (not guzzling quantity mind you!) the mellow produce of those vine-clad hills of Lombardy. When I taste my glass of golden Soave, its delicate aroma recalls the memory of vines clustered round a mediæval castle, and as for Valpolicella, its sparkling fragrance tells of red Veronese marble from Saint Ambrose. The hardened " shadow-chasers " of the waveless plain will tell you that there's a wine for every hour of the day, and they are as particular about their ritual of drinking as any Indian with his magic " rag." " Give me Soave," says one of those hawk-eyed fellows, " when it is noon and I am lying in the shade of an olive tree picking my teeth after a plentiful meal of *tagliatelle al sugo*. Give me Bardolino, Raboso, or Vino Santo in the afternoon when I'm parched and uncritical, but keep, I pray, some Recioto or some special red Valpolicella for me to drink in honour of the setting sun." Val-policella is the wine for such Epicureans who sit in shirt-sleeves under the pergola of a small inn with their companions and gaze dreamily at the River Adige flow-ing beneath the Bridge of the Boats. The hum of the city has died down and all we hear is the shock of the *bocce* or bowls played in the lane beyond.

I was enjoying this melting sunset mood with my companions in the tavern when I was rudely awakened out of my reverie by the noisy entry of an excited young man. The fat, sleepy old padrone murmured : " Ecco Luigi : catastroffico come al solito ! " Luigi was the nephew of the house and he had just come from Milan. " The 23rd of March," he cried, " will live for ever in the annals of Italian history."

" What has happened ? " cried the chorus.

" The first Fascio has been formed," cried Luigi.

" Fascio ? " said I, puzzled.

" The word," said one of the bystanders by way of explanation, " springs from *fascia*, a band holding a bundle of faggots together. It signifies the axe and rods of the Roman lictors."

The young man continued without paying heed to my interruption.

" There were a hundred and fifty at the meeting of Benito Mussolini in Milan. Every word he said was received with ovation." He then pulled a crumpled paper out of his pocket and began to read excitedly. " Here are the three declarations he made :

" I. We turn our thoughts to the sons of Italy who fell for the greatness of the Fatherland and the freedom of the world.

" II. We insist on the annexation of Fiume.

" III. We pledge ourselves to sabotage the candidature of those neutrality-mongers of 1915 who seek re-election.

" The news of the meeting spread like wildfire in Milan. All my companions are joining the new movement. Mussolini's speech is the best answer to those in the factories who are calling out ' Viva Lenin ! ' Everyone of us is ready to go back to the trenches if necessary." The youth, after his harangue, paused for breath, rushed over to my table, seized my bottle of Valpolicella, poured out a glassful, and cried out : " Viva il Fascismo ! Viva Mussolini ! "

Such was my first introduction to Italy's new *condottiere*.

CHAPTER IX

D'ANNUNZIO SPEAKS TO THE PEOPLE

VENICE in the early days of 1919 was a city of
the dead : the palaces on the banks of the Grand
Canal were closed and shuttered : in front of
the Basilica there were piles of sandbags : the black
gondolas were funereal. Where was the Venice of
gaiety and feasting when men and women wearing masks
would throng the square singing and the narrow streets
would resound with the twang of guitars and mandolines ? Venice in its sadness reminded me of that day
in the year 1509 when the League of Cambrai threatened
to overthrow the Republic. As the chronicler said :
" No one was seen in the Piazza, the Fathers of the
College were broken with anxiety and the Doge Lorenzo
Loredan who never spoke looked like a dead man."
One feeling was uppermost in the mind of every visitor
to Venice after the War : gratitude to the city's destiny
for preserving it from the Austrian aeroplanes. So eager
were the gondoliers to tell me their experiences in the
city when the enemy roared overhead that they forgot to
fill my mind with the usual fantastic stories of Desde-
mona's house, the glass works, the Bucintoro and the
Bridge of Sighs.

In the courtyard of the Doge's Palace we came upon
a pathetic sight : the four gilded horses that should
crown the pediment of the Basilica were lying on the
ground, for they had only just been taken from their

121

place of safety. What stories could you tell, O gilded
steeds, of the days of Alexander the Great, of the conquest
of Greece and the triumphal cars of Rome? Did you
not look down from the triumphal arch, upon Nero,
Trajan and Constantine, before you wandered East again?
And later, were you not the symbol of Venetian conquest
when the ships of the republic returned laden from
Constantinople?

Venice to-day was the city of feasting : it was the
24th of April, the day of Saint Mark the patron of La
Serenissima.

The sun shone brightly, the water sparkled, as we
sailed up the Grand Canal. To-day all traces of war-
time have disappeared. Many of the palaces we pass
have open windows, through which I can see stately halls
with Venetian chandeliers glittering as a roving sunbeam
catches them. The fish market and the *erberia* or fruit
and vegetable market are a riot of colour. Even the
Rialto Bridge in the glory of the morning sun cast off
its modern squalor and recalled the days when it was the
" Heart of Venice." As we got nearer to the traghetto
of Saint Mark the crowd of boats and gondolas began
to increase in volume. Right in front of the Piazzetta
Italian and American battleships were moored. As soon
as we disembarked, we found ourselves in the midst of
a motley crowd of merrymakers. No people in Europe
know the art of spontaneous enjoyment so well as the
Venetians when one of their festivals comes around.
At the slightest excuse their pleasure-loving nature takes
a naïve delight in sumptuous displays. As we gaze at
the gay crowds chattering volubly we imagine what
Venice must have been in the days of its power, when
Venetian festivals were encouraged by the Doge and his
advisers. To-day, however, Venice was excited—not
because it was the day of her patron saint, but because

the poet-hero, Gabriele D'Annunzio, was going to speak to the people from the *loggetta* of Sansovino in the Piazza San Marco.

With difficulty I elbowed my way through the crowd until I reached a vantage-point, whence I could hear the words of the orator. I was flushed with excitement as if some strange experience was about to befall me. For many years D'Annunzio had appeared before my eyes as a legendary figure surrounded by a halo. It was not the personality of the poet himself which fascinated me so much as the consciousness that he had soared above modern Italy upon the wings of Wagner and Nietzsche. As I waited in the humming crowd I called to mind, one after another, the heroes and heroines of the D'Annunzian world—every one of them with the temperament of the Nietzschean superman, strutting slowly across the crowded stage. Andrea Sperelli, exhausted through self-indulgence ; Giorgio Aurispa, sadistic intellectual ; Tullio Hermil, victim of his insane jealousy ; Claudio Cantelmo, incestuous Don Juan and inconsequent Nero of a decadent Rome.—Every one of them contributed to create a portrait of the author—a jaded, aristocratic artist, a dilettante of sensations, as the philosopher Croce had labelled him. Here in Venice, during its carnival, I imagined him in the gilded gondola beside La Foscarina, gliding past the palaces of the Grand Canal amidst the plaudits of the crowd. And Venice, in the over-ripeness of its autumn beauty, was the setting to La Foscarina, the famous actress eager to be loved, the lonely wanderer who seemed to carry in the folds of her robes the frenzy of the multitude.

But then I thought of the War and the famous speech which he had delivered on the 5th May 1915, the anniversary of Garibaldi's departure with the thousand for Sicily. I thought of those words of burning patriotism delivered from the rock of Quarto, which had heralded the entry of Italy into the Great War. Even then he had wielded the magic of a wizard over the crowd, but he had thrown off his bardic robes to become a warrior filled with the impetuous passion of a *condottiere*. No enterprise throughout the War was too foolhardy for this modern Giovanni delle Bande Nere. His aeroplane, on which was painted the motto " Iterum leo rugit " surrounded with seven stars and a tongue of blue flame, descended like a bird of prey upon the Austrians at Pola and Cattaro : his name was linked with Luigi Rizzo's in the famous enterprise of Buccari, when, in a few swift motor-boats, he had attacked the Austrian fleet.

Suddenly I was roused from my meditations by a roar from the crowd. Looking up, I saw a tiny, bald-headed man upon the balcony. He stood motionless for a moment before beckoning the crowd to be silent. He then began : " Volete dunque che io parli ? Avevo rifiutato quando mi fu chiesto. Perchè mi forzate ? " (Do you then want me to speak ? I had refused when they asked me. Why do you force me to do so ?) As I gazed at the little man, all my illusions fell in a heap like a house of cards. I had created my image of the poet from a world of towering supermen : instead I see before me a dwarf of a man, goggle-eyed and thick-lipped—truly sinister in his grotesqueness like a tragic gargoyle.

Is this the man that Duse loved ?

Little by little, however, I began to sink under the fascination of the voice, which penetrated into my consciousness, syllable by syllable, like water from a clear fountain. It was a slow, precise voice accompanying the words right to the last vowel, as if he wished to savour to the utmost their echoing music. The tones rose and fell in an unending stream like the song of a minstrel, and they spread over the vast audience like olive oil on the surface of the sea. Never a hurried, jerky gesture : occasionally one arm raised slowly as though wielding an imaginary wand. He went on to tell how he had come among the Venetians as a Venetian, wishing to pay tribute to this sacred city. But it is no longer the time for words—" We have," he cried, " been too prodigal of words ever since we stood with arms at the ready. If words belong to women and deeds to men, then to-day every fighter silently takes his place in the ranks. Yesterday on the field of ' La Serenissima ' I spent two quiet hours adjusting my machine-gun and packing bombs in my aeroplane."

The crowd in answer shout the words " La Serenissima," for they remember that this was the name of the poet's squadron of planes, so called in honour of Venice.

The poet continues : " The machine-gun is silent until the practised hand presses the trigger ; the banners are silent until the storm of battle descends upon them. This banner of Fiume does not speak—it commands. Out of the distant centuries it commands the future like the gesture of the returned *condottiero*, like the bronze of Alexander of the Horse."

Again the multitude burst in chorus with the shouts of " Viva Fiume ! "

The voice of the poet rose sharper in tone in continual crescendo. He played upon the emotions of the crowd as a supreme violinist does upon a Stradivarius. The eyes of the thousands were fixed upon him as though hypnotized by his power, and his voice like that of a *shanachie* bewitched their ears.

" The standard of the Dalmatians to-day waving in the sunlight takes on again its original colour of red. To-day red overshines all our banners. What do we care about green in future? What do we care about hope?"

"Noi non più speriamo, ma vogliamo, Intendete? Vogliamo."

The orator paused for a moment after the word *vogliamo* and then cried to the people : "Repeat that word."

All the people with one roar answered : "Vogliamo!"

It was no longer a speech by D'Annunzio, it had become one of his dramas. My visions of the master's theatre again crowded upon me. I saw Basiliola, the fierce heroine of *La Nave*, when the prisoners invoke death at her hands, and cry out : "We die for thee—we die by thee—we die before thy eyes, Basiliola " : and Sebastian martyrized before the crowd, where the chorus of youths answers the chorus of maidens in an ever-increasing orgy of excitement. There is always the scene when the superman invokes the crowd, calling up their answering refrain. As in a dream, I heard again the poet's voice :

"Saint Mark, our gallant, wise Saint Mark, when he thought the time had arrived to curb the eloquence of his ambassadors, would close the book. Our leaders, too, seated at the table of swindlers and card-sharpers, have followed the example of our lion-hearted patron saint and closed the book. They closed it at the page of falsity and lying. All praise to them!"

At these words the whole *piazza* broke out into a tempest of applause, for these words were the announcement that on this day, the 24th of March, the Italian delegation, under Orlando, had withdrawn from the Peace Conference in consequence of President Wilson's anti-Italian manifesto concerning Fiume. The wild applause was a clear confirmation that the will of the Italian people would support their leaders who had resigned when the honour of the country was involved.

And Gabriele D'Annunzio, the *condottiere*, knew that Fiume would be the next name to be added to the archives of the Risorgimento.

Then after the thunderous applause the poet began in a low voice the peroration to his speech. The crowd was so hushed that I could hear the whirr of wings of Saint Mark's pigeons, as they fluttered in droves above our heads. "One question and one only I shall ask to Italy which has grown in one night to giant stature like those vast blooms which burst out in a night into violent splendour. To defend your right and to preserve the pact of the dead, are you ready to fight again?"

The whole crowd with one accord thunders : "Yes."

"One question I'll ask this patient, heroic people of Venice. To defend your sea and the peace of your dead who lie in its depths, are you ready to suffer again?"

The whole crowd answers with a still louder "Yes."

"Then I say that we have won. Let the Dalmatian cry ring out from Venice to Rome : 'Ti con nu, nu con ti !' Let it ring out from Venice to Fiume, Zara, Sebenico, Traù, Spalato, Ragusa, Cattaro. Let it stir up the waters of the Adriatic. Long live Saint Mark !"

The poet disappeared, and the whole *piazza* became a seething mass of cheering humanity and fluttering banners. That evening American sailors were not allowed on shore, for the Venetians were in a boisterous mood.

Such was the beginning of the famous Fiume expedition which was to culminate, later in the year, in the occupation of Fiume and the Statute of Carnaro. D'Annunzio, in those months, lived the life of one of his own supermen. He was the hero of the moment, and he could afford to snap his fingers at the weak-kneed Government and shout out his "Me ne frego." In an

Italy torn asunder by bitter controversy and haunted by disillusion, he represented the ever-youthful spirit of tradition. It was his legionaries marching from Ronchi to Fiume that were the first to sing Italy's new war-song, "Giovinezza, giovinezza." It is said that Lenin, at a Congress of the Third International in Moscow, remarked that there was only one revolutionary in Italy : D'Annunzio. But D'Annunzio, in spite of being a modern Italian, belongs to the generation that welcomed the pale, æsthetic pre-Raphaelites with their haunting harmonies. His speech, his gestures, even his literature with its slow heart-beat, belonged to the so-called naughty nineties. In answer to his melodious phrases, there arose menacingly the strident, harsh tones of Marinetti, urging the youth of Venice to burn the gondolas, those swings for fools, and erect up to the sky the rigid geometry of large metallic bridges. It was D'Annunzio's destiny to be the first to destroy his own image which he had created particle by particle, with all the loving care of a Renaissance craftsman. There are few greater paradoxes than this poet of enervated impressionistic art who became the hero of action and prophet of a re-invigorated Italy.

Soon he would retire to the villa on Lake Garda which had once belonged to the widow of Wagner, and write his spiritual autobiography of the War that had opened the graves wherein lay buried all things accursed long ago, and he would transform that hill-top with its tresses of pine into an artificial labyrinth expressing his own tortuous mind. Like an oriental mystic he would erect a host of symbols, recalling the dreams of his active life : a medley of columns, each recalling a battle ; a host of statues, guns, and shells ; an armoured prow of a cruiser, from which he could watch over the lake. And as a contrast to those memories he would set in his house

a host of symbolical rooms ; a macabre " burial room " ;
a Franciscan refectory ; hidden passages and grotesque
corners that would make you swear the Vittoriale was
Vathek's magic castle.   In that dream-castle the poet
would play his part to the end before a select audience
of pilgrims.   Occasionally, the visiting pilgrim might
be the victim of the master's sardonic sense of humour.
There is one anecdote which they are very fond of telling
in Italy about the Soviet Minister Chicherin's visit to
D'Annunzio in his palace.   Dinner was served in the
Franciscan refectory.   At the end, two legionaries came
in bringing a beautifully damascened scimitar and withdrew, locking the door after them.   D'Annunzio took the
sword in his hand and fondled the blade, gazing fixedly
at his amazed guest.   Then he said : " My dear friend,
for certain reasons which I did not wish to tell you
beforehand, I have resolved to cut your head off."   And
then he stopped and waited for the effect his words
would have upon his guest.   Chicherin grew pale, saying
to himself : " Who knows what may happen ?   With
this mad poet, anything would be possible ; and if he
does cut my head off probably Europe would not care."
After a few moments' silence and after fondling the blade
lovingly, D'Annunzio frowned and said in a peevish
voice : " What a bore !   I am not in form to-night :
I am afraid I'll have to postpone the matter till another
day."

CHAPTER X

THE SWAN OF THE LAGOON

NEXT day I visited my favourite retreat in Venice
—the island of Saint Lazarus bosomed in its
cypress trees. In the midst of Venice's Pagan
splendour we are surprised to discover this tiny paradise
of peaceful meditation. Saint Lazarus of the Armenians
in the twelfth century was an asylum for those afflicted
with leprosy or Saint Lazarus' evil. At the end of the
Middle Ages it was abandoned and remained uninhabited
until in 1717 it was given by the Venetians to the famous
Armenian monk Peter of Manug, surnamed " Mechitar "
or " the Comforter." He had founded the Armenian
Mechitarist order and established a monastery at Modone
in the Morea from which he was expelled by the Turks
in that year. The little island in the Venetian lagoon has
become ever since the centre of Armenian civilization
and its printing-presses have turned out books in all the
languages of the world. Here it was that Byron used
to come in 1816. He would swim out from Venice and
spend the day in the gardens beneath the cypress trees
conversing with the superior, " a fine old fellow, with
the beard of a meteor, " and learning Armenian from
Father Paschal. The monks to-day show with pride
the room in which the poet worked and the pen with
which he wrote the fourth canto of *Childe Harold*. They
also printed some of Byron's letters to John Murray in
which he tells of his progress in Armenian and his delight

in the society of the Convent of Saint Lazarus. " It appears," he said, " to unite all the advantages of the monastic institution without any of its vices. The neatness, the comfort, the gentleness, the unaffected devotion, the accomplishments and the virtues of the brethren of the order, are well fitted to strike the man of the world with the conviction that there is another and a better even in this life." He then goes on to make an impassioned plea for the oppressed and noble nation which has partaken of the proscription and bondage of the Jews and of the Greeks, without the sullenness of the former or the servility of the latter. " It would be difficult," he said, " to find the annals of a nation less stained with crime than those of the Armenians, whose virtues have been those of peace, and their vices those of compulsion."

The chief reason for my repeated visits to Saint Lazarus was the desire to converse with my friend Father Simòn Eremian, poet, scholar—and Armenian patriot. Up and down the island's flowering garden we would walk, gazing all the while at the panorama of La Serenissima in the distance—the faint pink and white lacework of the Doge's palace, the dome of Saint Mark's, the slender campanile, the ever-changing colours of " La Salute." Father Simòn in his gentle voice would talk to me of Armenia where, according to the Scriptures, Paradise was placed.

" Armenia," he would say, " was the cradle of the world. It was there that the flood first abated and the dove alighted. But the unhappiness of that country might be said to date from the disappearance of Paradise."

I would leave the island in my gondola just before sunset so as to reach Saint Mark's *traghetto* at the magic hour when every Venetian thinks of listening to the military band in the *piazza* or of launching himself upon the great

S of the Grand Canal. At the hour of sunset as we float gently over the golden water towards the animated city, I feel that my gondola has been truly called the " Swan of the Lagoon." It is yet another symbol of that cultured primitiveness which we discover in every manifestation of the Italian genius. When I gaze at the gondola I see in a flash the whole panorama of Venetian history. In the sixth century Cassiodorus, the secretary of Theodoric, found the earliest ancestor of the gondola—a light skiff or *barchetta* tethered to the huts on the island shores. Art and literature show its gradual evolution from a rough boat into an object of beauty expressing that harmonious balance between the useful and the beautiful. The gondola, like the violin, reached its perfect shape in the Renaissance. In the pictures by Bellini and Carpaccio we see the gondola as it is to-day, all but the " Swan's beak " or *Ferro* which was added in the seventeenth century.[1] The making of a gondola is a complicated business, for three metals—iron, steel, and brass—must be used and four kinds of wood—walnut, cherry, pine, and oak.

It is fascinating to watch how the old white-haired gondolier can make his craft respond to his rhythmic movements as he propels it with his single oar and spins it round the sharp corners of the narrow canals. As we glide through their maze, under bridges, passing from shadow into sunlight, my eyes become intoxicated by the sudden visions of coloured perspective which change with the rapidity of a kaleidoscope. At one moment it is the dim grey-green of shady walls covered with lichen ; then all of a sudden the sun shines on a red door in a tottering mildewed tenement transforming it into an entrance worthy of a *palazzo*. The sun's rays have an elfin capriciousness : they may alight one

[1] H. Brown, *Life in the Lagoons*, London.

moment on a beautifully carved marble balcony and flit
the next on to a broken window from which hangs
a torn orange petticoat. When the sun has set the
narrow canals subside into dim tranquillity. The silence
is broken from time to time by the voices of children
which echo and re-echo from wall to wall. As we pass
the doors of taverns I hear songs and the querulous
plucking of mandoline strings. Heavy odours rise from
the green waters and the mustiness enters into my bones
as I loll back on the black cushions in my *felze*. The
thrill of vigorous life in a sunlit world is quenched and
a languid mood of sadness descends upon me as though
I were passing through a city of Death peopled with
phantoms. The sight of these dilapidated palaces inhabited by an emaciated, poverty-stricken people who
camp in them like Gypsies during their wintering makes
my mind dash off in search of the triumphant Venice of
Giorgione and Titian. Giorgione the " fire-carrier " as
D'Annunzio called him—the Prometheus who handed
the flaming torch to Titian the mountaineer from the
snowy peaks of Cadore, to enable him to drive his
chariot of fire through the clouds. Give me music which
Leonardo da Vinci called the sister of painting, for what
are those flame-spirits of triumphant Venice but divine
musicians pursuing infinite harmonies in a world symbolized by Giorgione's " concerto," where the monk seated
at his clavichord creates his dream-city of magic
sound ? . . .

I awoke hearing a distant sound of violins played
together in harmony. The music prolonged itself in
echoes over the water. It was pitch-dark and the
gondola stopped near steps against which the water was
lapping gently. The distant music fascinated me : it
was an ancient melody in a minor key and it floated into

my mind like a faint memory from long ago. At the top of the steps before me I saw a dark passage with a faint light at the end. I rose from my seat in the gondola and mounted the steps, groping my way along the dark passage towards the light. I followed the tune as if it was a golden butterfly flitting in front of me. When I reached the light I found that it shone from an old lantern of beaten iron which must have hung at the gates of a *palazzo* in the time of the Renaissance. Near the lantern was a half-open door and I could see twinkling lights within. Yielding to my curiosity, I pushed open the door gently and entered. No sooner was I in the courtyard than the door slammed behind me and I was unable to open it. " I am caught," said I to myself. " What shall I do if they accuse me of trespassing ? " The music grew in volume, and in addition to the concerted violins I heard voices of women singing madrigals. The air was fragrant with the scent of orange blossom. At the far side of the courtyard the twinkling lights came from men and women who were carrying torches and moving to and fro through a leafy pergola like glow-worms. They were dressed up in ancient Venetian costume : the ladies in voluminous dresses of velvet, the men in slashed doublets and hose, and their long hair fell over their shoulders.

" This must be a fancy-dress ball," thought I. " What shall I do ? I cannot escape from the courtyard, for the wall is too high to climb, and I cannot hide myself in the crowd of guests, for I am conspicuously the only person not in fancy dress." I did not go unperceived for long. A lean, pallid man carrying an ivory stick strutted up to me and after gazing at me for a moment said : " You are from some distant country, I am sure. Welcome, sir stranger ! This house is a seaport open to all. Here is a hostelry for afflicted pilgrims, a refuge for knights-errant." He spoke in a mellifluous, affected tone of voice and to stress his words he twirled his stick in the air.

" What a wonderful party this is," thought I, " they are even able to talk in the style of their period costumes. This man's speech is pure Renaissance." Without more ado I followed him towards the palace. A few servants carrying torches preceded us up a noble staircase of white marble and bowed us into a spacious hall. For a moment my ears and eyes were dazzled by the blaze of lights and the charivari of voices and instruments. Occasionally the murmur of conversation would die down and I could hear the performers on the stage singing their madrigals. •It was a long, narrow hall with spiral columns at the end. The ceiling was of carved wood and the walls were covered with rich tapestries and hangings. of gilded leather. Some of the windows were thrown wide open and I could see the tiny lights of gondolas passing along the Grand Canal beneath : others were closed and their little, circular panes of glass glittered in the lights of lamps and torches. Never have I seen so many varied lamps : there were lamps of bronze, lamps of silver, lamps of brass, lamps of every kind of workmanship, and the countless quivering flames gave a restless vivacity to the scene. It was the hall of an art-collector, full of inlaid tables on which stood a multitude of amphoræ of porcelain, vases of chased silver and gold, exquisitely carved figurines. Here and there I noticed books bound in gilt leather decorated with arabesques. A fragrant scent came from reed baskets full of flowers and herbs. I have never felt so self-conscious as I did in the midst of that throng of revellers. My khaki uniform was such a drab anti-thesis to the gorgeous satins and brocades around me that I was tempted to dash out of the hall and down the stairs, but my natural inquisitiveness and thirst for adventure retained me.

" What a wonderful masquerade ! " said I to myself. " Fancy seeing this in a city that has suffered so much in the Great War. None of the people here look as if they had ever had a sad moment in their lives. Such ogling, hand-pressing, whispered words, flirting technique with feathered fans I have never seen ! " I longed to take part in the revels with one of those damsels, for they looked more light-hearted and vivacious than any Italian girls I had met so far and they roared with laughter at the Rabelaisian jests which were bandied about by their cavaliers.

My friend with the ivory stick led me through the throng to salute my host. We passed between the spiral columns into an inner room where upon a dais enthroned in a gilded chair sat he whom they called " master of those who know " (*maestro di color che sanno*). He was a massively built man—so massive that he dwarfed the throne he was sitting on. He had a noble, spacious forehead and bright, humorous eyes, but his mouth was coarse with red, sensual lips, half hidden in his fleecy, luxuriant beard. He was dressed in a sumptuous cloak of velvet with satin facings and around his shoulders he wore a heavy gold chain of exquisite workmanship. With one hand he clutched the edge of his cloak and with the other he leant upon an ebony stick at the end of which was a knot of turquoise. " An arrogant fellow," thought I, " he thinks himself master of the universe, but there is a humorous glint in his eye and that mouth of his is full of covetousness."

After gazing gravely at me for a moment he said : " I am told that you are English. My name is celebrated in your country. Your King once sent me a present of three hundred crowns, but his rascally ambassador kept them for himself, and when I claimed them he hired assassins to kill me in the English way—that is to say, with cudgels. But I beat them back : I am proof against the tricks of such trash. I do not need to seek the great, they come to me in their thousands, for they know that I possess a weapon more fatal in its effect than all their knives and cudgels—the pen which is mightier than the sword. That is why the world calls me the ' Scourge of Princes.' A stinging pamphlet from my pen can stir up the passions of the people. And so France sends its legates to me and Spain offers presents to beguile me. But I contrive to play with France, Spain, Germany as I would with pawns on a chessboard, and I play on until the game wearies me. For in the end those gentlemen bore me by their visits. My stairs are worn by their feet like the pavement of the Capitol with the triumphal chariots. I do not believe Rome ever witnessed a greater collection of nationalities than this palace of mine. When Turks, Jews, Indians, French, Germans and Spaniards besiege me with petitions, you can imagine how many Italians come ! I say nothing about the common folk. I am never without a flock of priests and friars. I have come to be the oracle of truth, the secretary of the universe."

After his long speech the great man stroked his silky beard and glared fiercely at the company. His face when he was speaking fascinated me. Arrogance, Snobbery, Meanness, Servility, Megalomania passed one by one like shadows over his mobile features. After a long yawn he stood up, calling out in a stentorian voice : " Where are my sisters, my daughters, my *mammole* ? " There was a rustling and whispering among the satellites and in a moment I saw six girls appear. " Come here, my doves," cried the host. " Come here, my *cortigiane da candela*, my Ministresses.' Then turning to me he continued : "Let me, sir stranger, present these beautiful goddesses of Italy to you. I have no steward, no major-domo—only these six fair maidens who minister to my wants and distract my boredom."

The six girls varied in age as well as in figure. Adriana, the eldest : black-haired with opulent curves, breasts of Juno and the proud profile of a Roman matron. Marieta was a Venetian girl of the people : seventeen, mischievous, witty and full of sparkling repartees in her Venetian dialect. She was dressed in red to show off her flaming hair. Agnola : deliciously snub-nosed with freckled face full of mockery. She was dressed in dark green velvet and her brown hair was bound up in a gold net. Ersilia : deep blue eyes, flaxen hair and a far-off *sainte ni touche* expression as the French would say. Between her white breasts hung a little gold cross. As for the last two, Martinella and Fulvia, they were a contrast to each other. Martinella had eyes like sloes and skin as dark as a Gypsy, while Fulvia resembled a chubby little fish-wife from Chioggia full of frisky impudence. In accordance with the fashions of the period all the girls had their breasts entirely uncovered with the tips rouged. Opening his arms wide as though he wanted to gather the six girls into one embrace, our host exclaimed : "I am, gentleman, an idealist : I go through life in quest of the peerless Aphrodite. The ideal courtesan must have beautiful eyes, a face of honey but a heart of gall. She must be sweet-lipped, sugar-tongued but miserly in mind. Her breasts must be of alabaster, her hands soft as the plumage of doves but greedy as a vulture's talons. Where shall I find among mortal frailty such a goddess ? Must I not like the great painter Zeuxis create my sum-total of beauty from the individual excellencies of many women ? My heroine must have the Roman profile of Adriana, the sweet lips of Marieta, the sinuous figure of Agnola, the nerve of Fulvia, the alluring innocence of Ersilia, the diabolical perversity of Martinella."

As he was speaking a weird figure dressed as Harlequin appeared in the doorway and blew three blasts on a trumpet. It was the signal for the banquet to begin. I followed the host and the throng of guests into a smaller hall where a long table was laden with a Lucullian profusion of dishes. Gold and silver candelabra shed a soft light over the fantastic scene and made me wonder whether I had not been spirited into the world of Trimalchio. There were delicacies from every part of Italy ; there were thrushes from Perugia, geese from the Romagna, quails from Lombardy, tripe from Treviso, cakes from Genoa and cheese from Piacenza. Every dish was seasoned with pepper, cinnamon, ginger, nutmeg and perfumed essences which reduced me soon to a condition of sickly bewilderment, coming as I did from a country where, according to Voltaire, there are " a hundred religions and only one sauce." Little boys filled our cups with wine from gold and silver beakers. We drank Hungarian Tokay, Canary Malvasia, Malaga from Spain, Monte Moro and Old Moscato from Cyprus. Between the courses, which amounted to about fifteen, there were musical, dramatic and even acrobatic interludes performed upon a small stage at one end of the hall. At one moment at the behest of our host a flock of white pigeons and doves was loosed from the roof and fluttered down over our heads and perched upon the chandeliers.

My neighbour at table was Marieta, and a vivacious little companion she was—always twitting me in an ironical tone. Sometimes she would recite in verse for my benefit, gazing at me and sighing with mock-seriousness :

" Oimè! che'l' sento un fuoco dentro al petto
che ogni mio senso per amor si duole,
d'amarti son fortemente costretto :
abbi pietà di me, poi ch'amor vuole !
Io ardo, Signor mio, io tremo, io moro ;
socorri, tu sei pure il mio tesoro."

Her conversation was full of conceits and Petrarcan
hyperbole which I tried to interrupt in order to make her
flirt with me in more *terre à terre* fashion.

" What lovely red hair you have, Marieta," said I
sentimentally.

" All Venetian girls have red hair," said she. " We
dye it and then we lie on the roof under the sun to dry
it." Marieta then coquettishly arranged her long pearl
necklace so that it fell in a white cascade between her
breasts.

" The girls here in Venice," said I, " put on a lot of
rouge and powder—far more than the girls in my
country."

" And why not ? " answered the girl quickly. " Our
duty in life is to please, is it not ? When my mother
taught me the seven liberal arts she would say to me :
' Beautify your body as the painter does his picture."
That is why I paint in red my cheeks, my breasts, my
finger-nails and even toe-nails, and every day I bathe
my body in water perfumed with myrrh, cedar, and
lavender. You men do not know what apprenticeship
a girl must serve if she would become an artist in her
beauty. No painter—not even our master's boon companions, Titian and Sansovino—ever laboured at their
art as we do when we set out to become *maestre di segreti*
(mistresses of the secrets of men). We must be princesses
in our speech and action. That is why you will always
find us with a volume of Petrarch or Boccaccio in our
hand."

I was rapidly becoming sentimental about Marieta and I was like wax in her hands. Then, to my surprise, I heard the booming voice of our host declaiming against courtesans in general. "What a fine world it would be," said he sententiously, " if mean mankind were not subject to the baneful influence of courtesans. Boys would go to school and youths would work at their arts without disturbance. Wives would have their husbands home at dinner-time and bedtime. Fathers and mothers would not only be revered by their sons but even cherished by them and they would die in happiness as well as sanctity."

There was an outcry at this tirade and the six girls cried out in chorus : " What would your life, master, be without us to inspire it ? We are the stars in your firmament."

On the other side of me was a pale, bilious man with a bitter expression, called Niccolò, the secretary of our host. He resented his master's remarks and said to me in a low voice : " A pretty preacher forsooth. Soon he will call for the habit of Saint Francis and the discipline. It is more than I can endure. Were I not his secretary I would spit in his face."

This was all said in a low tone, but Marieta heard it and interrupted sharply, saying : " Turn a deaf ear to him, he is jealous of our master's genius. He should mind his own duty, which is to ferret in dusty libraries for Greek and Latin quotations to put into our master's pamphlets."

Niccolò made a grimace and held his tongue, but later when he saw that Marieta's attention was occupied elsewhere he continued his attack upon our host.

" I am not jealous," said he, " of his genius, for it is I who wrote a great part of those famous letters and pamphlets addressed to Kings and governments of

Europe. Let me tell you more about him. No bird of prey is more rapacious than that boastful man. He says he was born in a hospital with the spirit of a King, but I say he was a whore's bastard, born and bred in the stinking atmosphere of the servants' hall. Even as a youth he was notorious. At Perugia he saw one day in the *piazza* a picture of Mary Magdalen at the feet of Christ with arms outstretched in grief for her Saviour. Our scapegrace, when no one was looking, painted a lute between her hands. He became a nomad adventurer and he arrived in Rome with nought else but the clothes he stood in. But soon by shameless flattery and evil tongue he won even the favour of the Pope, and from being a lacquey he rose to be the confidant of noble spirits such as Giovanni delle Bande Nere. No one knew better the secret of alternately caressing with one hand and stabbing with the other.

" Hence the flood of panegyrics and satires that flowed from his pen, most of which in latter years have been polished and sharpened by my wit. Do you see the big gold chain he is wearing ? That was given to him by Francis I, King of France, as a mark of his esteem, for the great are always ready to be tricked by cynical flatterers. Soon people began to fear his pen as they would the plague. His satires were repeated in the *piazza* by the people as well as in the ducal palaces. And so he waxed great in power and influence. Occasionally men of courage would face him boldly and threaten his life. He has been called the ' loadstone of clubs and daggers,' and if you were to see him without his doublet and hose, you would find his flesh streaked all over like a chart of navigation."

" He must," said I, " have a thick skin to stand such punishment."

" His conscience is tougher than his crocodile hide.

But I have seen him cringe in fear of the assassin's dagger. Did you never hear of the famous meeting he once had with Tintoretto, the painter, whom he had often abused ? Tintoretto invited him to his house on the pretext of painting his portrait. But instead of taking up his brushes the painter drew out a large pistol and levelled it at his guest. The terrified libeller cried out for mercy, but Tintoretto said solemnly : ' Compose yourself whilst I take measure of you.' He then moved the direction of the pistol slowly from head to foot, adding : ' I find you are just the length of two pistols and a half.' My master understood the lesson and henceforth he was always one of Tintoretto's warmest friends."

Niccolò would have told me many more anecdotes had our host not addressed the whole table as follows : " Friends ! The night is still young and there is still time for us to drink and be merry. This is the house of pleasure in the city of pleasure, where it is better to be a gondolier than a chamberlain in any other capital. I want everyone to be happy and so I have always opened my doors to rich and poor. I take no delight in seeing my neighbours go naked and I would share with them the shirt off my back and the crust of bread upon my plate. My servant-girls are my daughters, my lacqueys are my brothers. Peace is the pomp of my halls and Liberty the major-domo of my palace. From my windows you may gaze upon the eternal beauty of Venice, the queen whom our Doge marries to the Adriatic on the day of the Ascension. My palace is a watch-tower whence I cast my eye over the universe. I am acquainted with all the foibles of men and women. I can unearth the impostors, hypocrites, and rascals, even though they burrow in the earth like moles. I am the only free man and I can speak my mind, hence my sincerity has found favour in the eyes of all the princes

in the world. That is why they all come to me. I
swear by Pegasus that none of you has heard one-half
the hymn of my celebrity. It is I who teach men to
laugh without restraint, for my life is as full of sap as
trees in the spring. Come, my six children ! Let the
merrymaking continue."

So saying he rose from the table and walked slowly
and majestically, preceded by torch-bearers and musicians
playing. We passed through several anterooms, the
walls of which were covered with pictures by famous
artists such as Titian and Sansovino, who were friends
of our host. When we reached the big hall he ordered
the six ladies to perform short dramatic sketches for the
company. No sooner did they start improvising than
our host would spring to his feet and add his witty
comments to their scenario and soon the fun became
fast and furious. As the jokes became broader the
excitement of the audience became more demonstrative
and a wave of mad sensuality surged over us all. One
of the little sketches was taken from a story by Boccaccio
and was entitled *The Girl and the Nightingale*. Adriana
recited the words of Boccaccio describing how a maiden
called Caterina, who was in love with a young swain
Ricciardo, played a trick upon her parents. The parts
of the lovers were played by Martinella and a young
man of the company. It was at the end of May and the
nights were sultry. Caterina said to her mother :
" Mother, I cannot sleep in the house. Let me make
my bed on the terrace outside my room overlooking the
garden. There I could fall asleep listening to the song
of the nightingale." The mother then asked Messer
Liziò, the father, but as he was old and crotchety ; he said :
" What nightingale is this she wants to hear as she falls
asleep ? I'll make her sleep to the song of the grass-
hopper." To this the mother made reply : " Can you

wonder that she should wish to hear the nightingale
sing? Is she not a young girl? Young people long
for things that are like themselves." The father at
length gave his consent on condition that Caterina put a
serge curtain round her bed. And so night came and
the parents went off to bed, leaving Caterina on the
terrace behind her serge curtain.

At this point our host interrupted Adriana, saying:
"Let me embellish the words of Messer Giovanni
Boccaccio to give a touch of art to the scene that is
coming. Instead of saying 'Night had come' you
should say: 'Night came with eyes bandaged, without
saying a word, grave, melancholy, full of dreaming, like
a widow cloaked in black. The stars, gilded by the
hand of Apollo the goldsmith, put their noses at the
windows of the sky one by one, by two, by three, by
four, by fifty, by the hundred, by the thousand.'"

After this interruption the play continued. We saw
Ricciardo creeping tiptoe into the garden with a ladder
which he laid against the balcony and climbed up like
a cat.

"Now the song of the nightingale must begin," cried
our host.

Ricciardo with a sudden gesture pulled aside the
curtain and there upon a wide couch of damask lay
Caterina naked as Eve before the fall. The whole
audience burst into loud applause as Ricciardo threw
himself on the couch and embraced his beloved before
pulling the curtain across. Then we saw old Messer
Liziò shuffle on to the stage dressed in grotesque bonnet
and nightshirt with a candle in his hand. On tiptoe
he approached the serge curtain, saying to himself:
"Let me see if the nightingale has made Caterina sleep
this night." When he pulled aside the curtain he
saw the two lovers lying asleep in one another's arms.

"Come here, wife," cried he excitedly, "and look at your daughter. She loves the nightingale so much that she has caught it in her hand."

The audience rocked with laughter, and as for our host, he stood up waving his hands and shouting: "Now for another story from the Decameron. Adriana will dramatize the tale of the girl who put the devil back in hell." He paused and I suddenly saw him totter and fall with a thud upon the marble floor. Then a scene of chaotic confusion took place. There arose a sound of wailing and shouting and people were running in all directions. The six girls carried their master from the hall and I saw him no more. I followed the distracted crowd down the stairs and into the courtyard. They flitted away like phantoms and I was left alone with the sardonic Niccolò.

"The scourge of princes is dead," said he malevolently. "He died with a blasphemous joke on his lips. When they anointed him he said: 'Guardatemi da topi, or che' son unto' (Protect me from rats now that I am greas'd)."

Niccolò held the door of the courtyard open, making signs to me to go. But there was one question I wished to ask. "Tell me," said I, "what was his name?"

"Peter Aretine, surnamed the Divine," said he as he slammed the door in my face.

How I got to the gondola I know not, but after stumbling in the dark I found myself gazing up at the face of my old gondolier.

"How long have I been away?" said I anxiously.

"You haven't left this gondola," said he, eyeing me with surprise. "When I saw you dozing I stopped for a moment's rest before turning back in the direction of San Marco."

CHAPTER XI

OFF TO THE SOUTH

WE are off. The long troop train begins to move away from the little station of Tavernelle. A loud roar of cheering breaks out and the strains of " Tipperary " float faintly through the barrage of discordant voices. We were like wild beasts in a cage : our railway carriage before demobilization had been a cattle-truck, and the smell of hay and stale cow-dung brought back thoughts of the farms of Britain. There was hardly any room to move about and the heat was stifling. Some of the men were convinced that they were going home and began to sing " Home, Sweet Home." They were already in fancy seated by their firesides smoking the pipe of peace. Then suddenly another voice broke in on the idyll : " Not bloody likely, you fellows : we're not goin' home, worse luck : we're off to Egypt." A loud snarl greeted the speaker and a few voices said : " Chuck him out, chuck him out, the bastard." There was an air of restlessness over all of them. Gradually the certainty dawned upon the troops that they were not going home to England. For days past in the various camps around Vicenza there had been rumours of the Egyptian expedition and many of the men were in a troublesome mood. Many had not been on leave for three or four years : from the trenches in France they had been transferred to Italy, and after the Armistice they had dawdled on the plains of Lom-

bardy awaiting the demobilization that never came.
Now after packing up, as a last straw came the news
that they were to travel still farther away from home.
Hence the loud imprecations, the threats of mutiny.
A few evenings before I had witnessed a nasty scene
at Montebello where some tipsy " Jocks " broke into a
quarrel with Italian sentries and casualties were reported.
The men were restless and it only needed a tiny spark
to cause conflagration. The military authorities left
nothing to chance : the station of Tavernelle was
mounted with barbed wire entanglements to prevent
escape and the military police were vigilant.

On the morning of our departure a tragic event took
place which brought back to mind the horrors of war.
After the Armistice most soldiers stationed in the little
Lombard villages owned dogs. When orders to quit
came they had to leave the dogs behind, and as it was
impossible to discover new masters for them, there was
nothing for it but to kill them. At Tavernelle scores
were awaiting execution : terriers, bull-dogs, collies,
poodles, a pathetic yapping and tail-wagging multitude.
A pitiful sight it was to see those struggling creatures
dragged to their doom and one that might be entitled
the slaughter of the Innocents. Where were you, O
sweet and merciful Society for the Prevention of Cruelty
to Animals ? The spirits of those murdered dogs still
cry out to you to wreak vengeance for the bloody deeds
of that dark day in April 1919.

The journey down through Italy was long and tedious.
Some days we would remain stationary, shunted away
in some side-line : at other days we would plod on
steadily towards the South. In addition to the dis-
comforts of congested quarters in our cattle-trucks,
there were those due to dirt and heat. The complica-
tions of washing and shaving at wayside stations, the

ineffable monotony of days and days journeying onwards lulled by the inevitable rhythm of the wheels. A tantalizing vision for a moment of the dome of Saint Peter's in the distance, followed by weary waiting in a Roman siding.

At last we reached the parched countryside of the South, after passing by the port of Bari into Apulia with its dusty roads and white towns glaring under the piercing noonday sun. Taranto was the end of our journey, for from its harbour the transports were to sail with the men for the East.

Taranto, the famous city of Magna Græcia, is to-day one of the big ports of Italy, and its bay during the War harboured many a battleship. It was humming with activity. Ships were arriving daily laden with troops from Salonica, and others were setting sail for the East. Taranto stands on a long peninsula which divides the small inland sea from the great sea outside. In the *mare piccolo*, or inland sea, with its twelve miles' circumference, we found the transports moored, and along the coast were the big camps, thronged not only with European soldiers but also with the West Indian negroes of the Labour Corps.

Taranto was to be the last stage in my military life. More than five months had elapsed since the Armistice and I was now demobilized. In the North Camp on the shores of the *mare piccolo* I spent my last weeks under the Colours, and on my farewell evening I gave a musical recital in the Camp Coliseum, a huge marquee fitted up as a soldiers' music-hall. There were over fifteen hundred soldiers in the audience and for two hours and a half I had to play music for them, ranging from Spanish Gypsy dances to Scotch, Irish and Italian melodies. Nobody in the world is more responsive than the soldier when once you have won his sympathy. If he thinks you are a " highbrow " he shuts himself up in his shell and refuses to let your spell creep into his ears. But if you tell him some stories about the music and describe the life of the wandering fiddlers who play those tunes in the villages, he will hearken to you and allow himself to be touched.

On that last night as I played in the Camp Coliseum I felt like the boy leaving school who plays football in the dormitory with his tall hat and romps madly with his companions. It was the end of a chapter.

ROVING LIFE

The thought of getting out of uniform gave me the uneasy feeling of being thrust into an outer world of darkness to fend for myself. There is in T. E. Lawrence's great work one passage which I have read over and over again in recent days, when so many of the youths of Europe clamour for uniforms, or rather shirts, whose colour will symbolize their party.

The secret of uniform [said Lawrence] was to make a crowd solid, dignified, and personal : to give it the singleness and tautness of an upstanding man. This death's livery which walled its bearers from ordinary life was sign that they had sold their wills and bodies to the State ; and contracted themselves into a service not the less abject for that its beginning was voluntary. Some of them had obeyed the instinct of lawlessness : some were hungry : others thirsted for glamour, for the supposed colour of a military life : but, of them all, those only received satisfaction who had sought to degrade themselves, for to the peace-eye they were below humanity. Only women with a lech were allured by those witnessing clothes : the soldier's pay, not sustenance like a labourer's, but pocket-money, seemed most profitably spent when it let them drink sometimes and forget. Convicts had violence put upon them. Slaves might be free, if they could, in intention. But the soldier assigned his owner the twenty-four hours' use of his body; and sole conduct of his mind and passions. A convict had license to hate the rule which confined him, and all humanity outside, if he were greedy in hate : but the sulking soldier was a bad soldier; indeed, no soldier. His affections must be hired pieces on the chessboard of the King.[1]

Such were the thoughts of a man who had crowded into his short life a Homeric record of achievement ; who, in the midst of the conflict, had kept his vision unclouded, so that he could distinguish the thin-tempered, hollow, instinctive fighters from those who " held together in the war-time yearning to keep within four ears such thoughts as were deep enough to hurt." Not one of all those soldiers of many nationalities whom I saw awaiting demobilization at Taranto but would feel a sense of dazed timidity at being pitchforked into a world which had grown unfamiliar—a world of freedom after years of restriction and discipline. Even I, the camp follower, longed to postpone the return to a life of duty day by day. Already the vision of a new world fit for heroes, full of peace and good-will to all men, had faded into thin air. The outlook in Europe seemed plunged in gloom : nothing but the spirit of hatred, vendetta, and the threat of further wars. At one moment I read of Bela Kun's orgies of Bolshevism in Budapest and the invasion of the Roumanians : at another I buried myself in the report issued by the Crimes' Commission of the Allies, in which Germany and Austria, Turkey and Bulgaria, were declared solely responsible for the outbreak of war. The Commission produced thirty-two categories of crimes to be imputed to those countries, and it went on to speak of

the most cruel practices which primitive barbarism aided by all the resources of modern science could devise, for the execution of a system of crimes carefully planned and carried out to the end.

---

[1] T. E. Lawrence, *Seven Pillars of Wisdom*, London, 1935, p. 641.

After announcing that the conscience of mankind would be outraged if the Kaiser escaped and underlings were punished, the Commission stated that it was not prepared to recommend that the Kaiser or the rest should be tried for acts leading to the outbreak of the War or for breaches of neutrality, but they should receive " formal condemnation " by the Peace Conference.

And the letters I received from my own country did not fill me with optimistic thoughts on the future of the Emerald Isle. They gave a dismal catalogue of calamities in true Irish fashion.

The more I thought of Ireland the less I relished the prospect of returning to Dublin and swelling the ranks of lean job-hunters. My father, in one of his letters, urged me to return and fit myself to take a part in the reconstruction of the State which would follow the War.

If England is to remain England, her heart must be changed, and she will need men of character and intellect to do the necessary work. Return as soon as you can and make preparations for having a profession, as you must have something to live on. The men who have served at the Front will have a claim for all the jobs in the Government Offices, and besides, those jobs are not likely to suit you, for you are not temperamentally suited to routine work. In Dublin you might do a bit of coaching and stray journalism to pay your expenses while reading law. When you are called to the Bar you will have a career open to you.

My imagination conjured up visions of my future life in Dublin. I should find myself out of touch with the young generation that had grown up, filled with thoughts of liberating Ireland. I was born with the old régime in my bones, and I should assist as a passive spectator at the barricades just as I had done in the tragic Easter week in 1916, when a handful of young poets and desperate revolutionaries had roused a slumbering nation. I saw myself wandering through the stately streets of Georgian Dublin with mind torn this way and that by conflicting thoughts and emotions. A sad destiny, that of us Anglo-Irish, with the tensions in our nature drawing us alternately towards Britain, whose Empire we helped to create, and Ireland, the land that bore us. I could not think of Ireland's civil conflicts without remembering that Easter Monday, when I saw that fine sportsman F. H. (Chicken) Browning lying in his blood, slain by a young fellow-countryman who from a window had sniped at the old man when he was marching with his company of G.R. volunteers. But that vision immediately gave way to another, wherein I saw Sackville Street thronged with men, women, and children waiting for the news of the executions after the Bloody Week. Every half-hour we would hear the cry of " Stop Press," and the crowd with a gasp of horror would murmur the name of yet another youthful leader who had been shot by the Court Martial. I saw myself back in Dublin, losing, day by day, the illusions of humanism which had lifted my life out of the weary Limbo in which I had vegetated. I should take refuge among the scoffers of Dublin who " monologue " in the pubs to admiring audiences knowing the jargon. Ireland, England, Europe would be fruitful themes for mocking laughter among those who hide their disillusion behind the mask of jeering. I envied my colleagues in the Y.M.C.A. who would continue to wear their uniforms and perform their regular daily task unmoved by the storms that were shaking the world. Such a uniform is the same as the habit of a monk : it enables him to live in Paradise, which, according to Orientals, is a place surrounded by a high wall. If I had lived in the Middle Ages I should have knocked at the first monastery I came across in Italy and entered the contemplative life, vocation or no vocation, for then I should be at peace with myself.

"No, you would not," said Dobson, my friend and chief under the Y.M.C.A. education scheme. "There is a nomadic streak in you which would never let you settle down behind the high wall of any Paradise."

Dobson encouraged me to play my part as minstrel among the troops. On the day of my demobilization I received a letter from him which made me blush with pride, even though my pitiless self-analysis told me that a man's friends tell him what he wishes to hear. Dobson's letter ran as follows :

I wish I could recompense you adequately. I shall never forget you, your wonderful music, and the many pleasant hours I have spent in your company. It is only natural, I suppose, to envy you your gifts. The gods have been kind to you. But I am sure that they must look down and smile with pleasure when they see how selflessly you use their gifts, and how much men are made happier by you. Let me say once again how much I count it a privilege to have known you, and to have had as much as I have of your company. I only wish these months had not been as unsatisfactory in many ways; the constant upsetting and re-making of plans : the fair hopes and bitter disappointments. You have had a full share of these—and so have I. But there have been many compensations—and of the choicest to me I hold the delights of your company. I hope that when you get back, and look, in detachment of time and place, upon these months in Italy, you will find only good things in memory. Time does mercifully tend to blot out the memory of things that were trying and painful at the time. And we have had a great boon in being in Italy.

Such a letter, instead of lulling me into a mood of serene complacency, stirred up a hornet's nest of conflicting thoughts and fancies in my mind. My prudent Sancho Panza personality tugged at my coat-tails, saying : "Music has been your bane ever since childhood : it has made you into a Lotos-eater—a Richard Yea and Nay—always dreaming your way through life without a profitable thought for the morrow. Put away that fiddle of yours : it is always leading you off on a goosechase." But immediately my slender, ramshackle Quixotic personality would retort indignantly : " Prudence has played hell with your life. You have always been too ready to follow the advice of your elders. That is why your life has been so unadventurous. Follow your fiddle as Don Quixote did Rozinante and you will save your soul." After a short struggle I determined to postpone my return home and have a further spell of wandering in Italy. At Taranto I had made the acquaintance of a charming family who were accustomed to give entertainments in their palatial house. One evening I was invited to give a violin recital to an audience of cultivated amateurs. Among them was a musical critic who wrote for the Roman newspaper *Il Messaggero*. A few days later I was surprised to see the following notice in that paper :

SERATA MUSICALE

Tra uno stuolo di elegantissime e colte signore, ieri sera abbiamo avuto l'occasione di gustare della musica meravigliosa che ci fece passare delle ore di vero godimento spirituale.

Il signor Walter Starkie, che ebbe a maestri due illustrazioni italiane, eseguì magistralmente " Concerto Vivaldi," " Ciacconna Vitali," " Leggende Wieniawski," " Notturno Chopin," " Danse Hongroise Hubay," ecc., destando ammirazione ed entusiasmo nei numerosi ascoltatori. Egli suonò con arte veramente squisita, con delicato sentimento, imprimendo nelle note tutto l'ardore del suo animo giovanile. Le corde del suo violino avevano gemiti e fremiti sotto il tocco del magico archetto che faceva venir fuori delle note or carezzevoli e passionali, or turbinose ed incalzanti come il ruggire della tempesta.

Il signor Walter Starkie non é il manierato esecutore, ma l'artista che sente tutti i fascini dell'arte sua, quasi inspirato e rapito al murmure di un'armonia lontana che e come l'eco soave di un'elegia elevantesi dalle sue balze natie.

That florid tribute to my powers was a veritable god-send. It gave a certain *cachet* to my performances in barn or tavern. When I had played the village Paganini and dazzled my audience, I could always give the final touches to my supremacy by pulling out the crumpled newspaper and pointing to the notice, saying : " Look what *Il Messaggero* says about me. Next time I come to this town you must let me give my concert in the town hall." With such a notice in my pocket I was ready to face the roughest audience in any local music-hall. They would not throw carrots, cucumbers, or orange skins at me when they knew that I was quite a personage in the eyes of the Roman critics. During my stay in Taranto before demobilization I had made the acquaint-ance of many members of the wandering confraternity of variety artistes—not those who perform in the big theatres, but those who roam from village to village and town to town, sometimes with pockets bulging with lire notes, other times lurking hungrily in the neighbourhood of inn or tavern.

One of my good friends was a juggler called Delco with whom I had, before demobilization, performed on many an occasion in the Camp Coliseum. Delco intro-duced me to many singers, acrobats, and clowns of every variety, who earn their living roaming from Taranto to Reggio. Most of the time, however, I led the life of a lonely minstrel, trudging for miles along the dusty roads, and halting in the cool of olive trees during the heat of the day. At cottages by the way I would buy some bread and *ricotta* (a cream cheese of Calabria), which satisfied the appetite. As for wine, there was always plenty—a delicious, fragrant Calabrian wine full of sun-shine and memories. In the evenings I would go to this or that café in the villages and pull out my fiddle. The host would be glad to see me, for in the South of

Italy all life is full of song. The men smoking their cigars and sipping their wine would ask me to play some canzone, mostly from operas by Verdi and Mascagni, or else war-songs such as the " Canzone del Piave," or the " Bells of San Giusto." All the little towns around Taranto—Massafra, Palagiano, or Mottola —heard the strains of my violin in the cool evenings when the sun sank and the moon rose in the sky, illuminating the ghostly white walls of the houses clustering round the central square. Now there followed days of real freedom. As soon as I got out in the open country I changed my personality, for my thoughts travelled back to those days in Ireland when I used to go about from fair to fair with old blind fiddlers in Dowras Bay and Cushendun. I remembered the day when one of the Coffeys of Killorglin put a tinker's curse on me, saying in his wrath : " May you tramp the roads till the feet wear off you, and may they find you dead in a ditch."

On our way from village to village I played truant more often than not. I made the acquaintance of a heap of disreputable friends—street arabs, beggars, hobos —and I accepted with gusto the brotherhood of the road. Occasionally, these vagabond friends were an embarrassment, for they would try and attach themselves to me as permanent confederates, whereas they belonged to my personality of " over the hills and far away " and were meant to be discarded lightly. During those early days of roving I developed a most subtle talent for escaping from humdrum life without anybody being the wiser. I have never believed in being an out-and-out revolutionary, because as soon as you stick out your jaw and contradict the will of the majority you become a victim, and you spend your life battling unsuccessfully for principles that others will not accept. I learnt the secret of wearing lightly the mask of society and following outwardly its rules, so that I might not awaken the suspicions of the interfering busybodies. But when everyone thinks you are obeying the rules, it is possible to mount the hobby-horse and off like hey-go-mad—just as if you had rubbed your armpits with the magic ointment which gives a man the power to ride through the air on a broomstick. At times I am ashamed of this evasive personality of mine, and I curse myself for my insincerity and lack of sound principles; but I hear a sardonic voice murmuring: " What odds, if one can escape from the crowds and rejoice in one's own freedom."

CHAPTER XII

TARANTELLA

LIFE had not changed in the old part of Taranto since the Middle Ages. The streets were so narrow that the sun was unable to pierce the gloom and they were crowded at all times with a picturesque rabble, for the Tarentine lives in the street and very often sleeps there. Down near the water were open booths where old men made objects of terra-cotta. One of their specialities was pipe-making for the Tarentine smokers—pipes made of red clay, the bowl of which was fashioned in the form of the head of a bearded man, and into this a reed was inserted. Near the harbour along the Via Garibaldi I met the fishermen who have inspired poets without number. In the cool of the evening I saw them mending their nets. They were tall figures of bronze, most of them as classic in their features as the Greek athletes we see on the red-figured vases. As they worked patiently in the setting sun they made me think of the Disciples by the Lake of Galilee, and if ever I see Saint Peter I am sure he will be in the semblance of one of those bronzed sons of the sea drawing up his nets on the rocks. They have not changed their customs since Plato visited the schools of the city and saw them gathering their sea-harvest. Motor-cars, motor-boats, and aeroplanes may come and go but there will be no change in those men who live as a race apart. Their face is like copper, and their wild black hair and arrogant mien recall the Gypsies of South Spain. Their dialect resembles Greek closely and they use words that we hear among the Greek peasants of Bova and Terra D'Otranto. As I stood on the sea-wall talking to one of them he sang a beautiful song about the tunny-fishing expeditions in Sicily and told me tales of storms and shipwrecks.

Around Taranto the country was parched and desolate save for the countless grey olive-groves which gave a pleasant shade to the traveller. It was a country that appealed to my spirit by its elemental nature. The ancient world of Magna Græcia with its brilliant cities had disappeared without leaving a rack behind, but the peasants whom I saw working in the fields still bore traces of the past. Here and there were piles of Murex shells from which the ancient Greeks extracted purple dyes. In the evening as I gazed at the city beneath the glory of the setting sun, a feeling of melancholy crept over me. I could not help comparing the city of purple and gold of the Greeks five hundred years before Christ with the sleepy city of to-day. Greek literature tells us of its laughter and joy, its beautiful women and proud athletes. Alas, in company with Sybaris and Croton, it crumbled away in dust centuries before the Christian era. Yonder peasant resignedly labouring his piece of land with the plough of Hesiod was a symbol of all that Magna Græcia has left to the world—a slight fragrance, a pillar or two, a few lines of poetry to remember its past greatness. Who knew whether the peasant with his rude plough might not that evening turn up a vase whose figures traced out in the clay might remind the world of what once was? Taranto to-day gallantly proclaims to the world its greatness as a seaport, but its blocks of modern apartments, its big harbour full of ships, seemed pathetically unreal to the lonely traveller

dreaming of Greater Greece.   The proud fishermen and
patient husbandmen looked on those modern buildings
with as much stupefaction as though they had been set
there in the night by the genie of Aladdin's lamp.

Before I left Taranto on my wanderings I did not
forget to walk along the shores of the *mare piccolo* until
I came to the tiny brook meandering through the swamp
seawards which tradition says was the *dulce flumen Galæsi*
of Horace :

> " Ille terrarum mihi praeter omnes
>   angulus ridet, ubi non Hymetto
>   mella decedunt viridique certat
>   baca Venafro :
>   Ver ubi longum tepidasque praebet
>   Juppiter brumas, et amicus Aulon
>   fertili Baccho minimum Falernis
>   invidet uvis."

(" Of all the earth's corners that allures me most,
   which with Hymettian-flavoured honey flows,
   where fine as green Venafrum e'er can boast the olive grows.")

Gissing went in search of the Galæsus—the river beloved
by Horace with its banks pasturing a famous herd of
sheep, with fleece so precious that it was protected by
a garment of skins.   I walked the three miles under
the broiling heat of the June sun to discover the spirit
of Gissing.   Gissing, disappointed and brooding at the
insignificance of the Galæsus, followed its current sea-
ward and upon the shore, amid scents of mint and rose-
mary, sat down to rest.   Across the water he saw
Taranto ; the old town on its little island, compact of
white houses, contrasting with the yellowish tints of
the great new buildings.   With half-closed eyes he could
imagine the true Tarentum.

Wavelets lapped upon the sand before me, their music the same
as two thousand years ago. A goatherd came along, his flock

straggling behind him; man and goats were as much of the old
world as of the new. Far away, the boats of fishermen floated
silently. I heard a rustle as an old fig tree hard by dropped its
leaves. On the sea-bank of yellow crumbling earth, lizards flashed
about me in the sunshine. After a dull morning, the day had
passed into golden serenity; a stillness as of eternal peace held
earth and sky.[1]

Gissing was but one of the innumerable Englishmen
whose souls were haunted by the beauty of Italy and
whose words echo through our minds as we linger amid
the same scenes. Gissing, the sad poet of suffering
humanity, released himself from the disillusion of
" Demos " and the starving world of " New Grub
Street " when he visited the shores of the Ionian Sea,
for his mind when illuminated by his enthusiasms soared
in quest of the ancient world of classical humanism. " It
is strange how these old times have taken hold of me,"
he cried. " The mere names in Roman history make
my blood warm." He was one of the silent band of
Romantics who escaped joyfully out of the monotonous
machine-made ugliness of the modern world into memories of the ancient world.

As I walked back across the barren field I met a
woman carrying an infant in her arms. I noticed that
she was crawling along with difficulty and every few steps
she rested by the side of the road. She was a young
woman, but her yellow, emaciated face, seared with
wrinkles, and her stooped shoulders, gave her the appearance of an old hag. Only her eyes glittering with
fever lit up her weary face. The tiny child, too, was
sickly-looking as though the Angel of Death had already
touched it lightly with its wing. I stopped to question
her and she told me that she, like the rest of her family
at home, were victims of malaria. " We are no worse

---

[1] G. Gissing, *By the Ionian Sea*, London, 1905, p. 57.

off, signore, than most of the people in the country. When the summer comes we all begin to shiver with the ague. Not one of us is spared." She made a gesture of resignation, saying : " Pazienza ! If we hadn't the malaria we'd have something worse—God help us ! " When I thought of that haggard woman with her feverish eyes, I saw in a flash the destiny of Magna Græcia, once the richest land of classical antiquity. When it was not torn asunder by earthquakes it suffered the devastation of continuous wars, and its fertile fields became derelict swamps—breeding-grounds for the mosquito. Never in its later history had this land the population to pursue the peaceful Arcadian arts which Horace and Virgil had celebrated.

Those of us who dwell in the North of Europe do not realize how all-embracing are the activities of the café in the South. The café might be called the parliament and theatre of those Calabrian villages, for in it men discuss politics, hear music, tell stories as well as drink and eat. And in those humble cafés the wandering musician wields the powers of a wizard. He is the stranger from far-off countries and an object of curiosity to those men, for he may tell them stories of queer customs and a life that they have never tasted. When he tunes his fiddle they listen intently, for he will play them songs that bring pictures into their minds. In the café at Massafra the host was a musician, and when I played he produced his mandoline and improvised an accompaniment. Soon the figures around the walls of the café would join in our song and the street would resound with music. Night after night I went to that café and the host would feed me in return for my music. When I had played for an hour or more he would come up to me and say : " Maestro, you have played like an

angel : you need wine. Let us drink to Italian Victory
and our brothers in Fiume."

Then a storm of conversation would break out, for
every Italian had his thoughts set on Fiume ever since
the day when D'Annunzio had made his great speech
in Venice and expressed the will of the whole nation that
Fiume should belong to Italy. Whenever the crowd
in the café would start arguing, one man immediately
assumed the leadership and imposed his reasons on the
company. This was the village schoolmaster, to whom
the others always gave the title " don." He was a
grotesque little man with grey whiskers, dressed in a
tight-fitting frock-coat, very threadbare and green with
age, and very baggy trousers. Only on rare occasions
did anyone raise his voice to contradict him, and when
that happened the little man would puff out his chest,
roll his eyes and fulminate his adversary. Don Riccardo,
as he was called, had one inveterate enemy, the Government, and he gloried in attacking it on every occasion.
He used to tell his awe-struck friends in the café that
he had written to this or that Ministry at Rome to get
redress for wrongs real or imaginary. Music he affected
to despise, but when I started to play the host would
serve him some marsala to keep him in a good humour.

When I had finished Don Riccardo would announce
to the company that he was going to recite verses in
my honour. He had the most astounding memory, for
not only did he recite poems of Carducci, Manzoni and
Pascoli, but one night he recited the whole of Dante's
" Inferno " by heart after his glass had been well filled
by the host. In the South of Italy it was no uncommon
thing to meet in the villages old men and women who
could recite by heart most of the *Divina Commedia*.
They recited it in the same way as the old rhapsodists
used to do, halting for breath at certain introductory

lines which aided their memory.   In this way the Divine
Comedy became an immense source of inspiration to the
country people and the figure of the austere poet loomed
in their lives as the first great Italian of history.

From Don Riccardo I heard about Gypsies in Calabria,
and he would speak of them by the hour, for they were
his pet abomination.

"They are an accursed race," he would say, "and all
my teaching in school is useless.   I tell the boys and
girls of those cursed vagabonds and their ways, but as
soon as they go home, if a ' vecchia Zingara ' comes
round to their cottage they will be after her.   Their
parents are no better : why, they would sooner go to
' vecchia Religione ' for a cure than to the doctor."

The old man hated Gypsies with ferocity, chiefly
because they wandered from one place to another.
According to his theory of life, a man should find his
little corner and stay there all his life.   He should buy
a little piece of land and till it himself.   " If every man
tilled his own little piece of earth and put away all
thoughts of ambition and roaming, the world would
be a different place," he would say sadly.   Gypsies,
according to him, were a race accursed by God far back
in history, and like the Wandering Jew they would have
to rove for ever over the earth, never doing any useful
work for humanity but always living as parasites on
the State.

" Look at them," he would say, " none of them have
ever tilled the ground and so they are useless drones and
should be exterminated."

He could not understand my position at all and he
would admonish me severely in the following terms :
" You are a young fellow : why do you wander about
like a vagabond ?   Take my advice and settle down to
a trade here which will bring you in honest money."

"I know what is wrong with the signore," said one of the company. "He has an attack of 'Tarantismo.'"

"What on earth is that?" said I, alarmed.

"Have you been eating too many oysters or periwinkles?"

"Not a single oyster: this isn't a month with an 'R' in it."

"Oysters give hysteria, which they used to call here 'Tarantismo.' When you have an attack of that fever you can't stop dancing: you become a Tarantist and you go gadding around like a lost soul."

"He can stop his dance," interrupted Don Riccardo, "if he plays the Tarantella. That will cure him. They used to say in these parts that the bite of the Apulian spider, the Tarantula, gave its victims terrible fits of depression which could only be relieved by dancing continuously for three or four hours without rest like one possessed by a demon. In those days when a girl had been bitten by the spider they used to make her perform a whole ritual. When she would dance the Tarantella they would make her carry branches of trees and coloured ribbons. Woe to anyone dressed in black! The sight of black clothes was enough to send the patient into violent hysterics. All had to be done to cheer the girl up by flowers, silks, satins, and mirrors."

"Well, Don Riccardo," said I as I departed, "I'm afraid I really have an attack of 'Tarantismo' and I have the itch to keep on the move. The only cure for me will be to play Tarantellas all the way through Calabria."

I was so interested in the subject of the Tarantella that I searched in the libraries for information on the subject. In Niccolò Perotto's rare book, *Cornucopia linguae Latinae*, published in 1489, there is the earliest notice of the strange disease of tarantism, which increased to an alarming extent in the sixteenth century and lasted

until the end of the seventeenth century in South Italy.
It resembled the St. Vitus's dance mania in mediæval
Germany, or the Tigritija dance in Abyssinia, in that it
was endemic. People who suffered from it were sometimes seized with an unconquerable thirst and tried to
cast themselves into the sea : others worked themselves
into fierce frenzy at the sight of certain colours. In
order to combat the disease, musicians were made to play
certain dances for the Tarantists, or victims, until the
latter fell to the ground in exhaustion. In the Jesuit
Father Kircher's book, *Magnes*, which was published at
Rome in 1641, there is an actual air called *antidotum
tarantulæ* which was used as a cure :

It is strange that the above tune is written in common
time and not in the tripping rhythm of 6-8 or 12-8 as
the following, which is called the traditional Tarantula
tune :

That tune was quoted by Storace, a well-known
eighteenth-century contra-bassist (father of the opera-
composer, Stefano Storace, the friend of Mozart), in a
letter describing how he had cured a person near Naples
who had been bitten by the Tarantula spider. Storace
said that he was asked to play the special tune connected

with the cure, but, as he did not know it, he tried various jigs without success. Finally an old woman hummed the correct tune for him and he played it for the patient with perfect result. Kircher, in his account of the Tarantella, tells a quaint anecdote of an experiment carried out in the ducal palace at Andria in Apulia by order of the Duchess. Tarantula spiders were caught and placed on little sticks laid horizontally in bowls of water. As soon as the musicians began to play quick rhythms, the spiders began to move their feet and jump in time to the music. When the music stopped they ceased their dancing.

The Tarantella has fascinated more than one great writer who has visited Southern Italy. Goethe, in fragments of his Travel Diary, described how the young girls in Naples spent long hours jumping rhythmically to the rhythm of the Tarantella, unmindful of spectators, and he added humorously that the movements of the dance might be an admirable cure for ladies who were downcast, or who had been bitten by the famous spiders (they probably cured themselves by perspiring freely).

It is not to Goethe we must go for the most picturesque description of the dance, but to Madame de Staël, who in her romantic novel of Italian travel, *Corinne*, makes her heroine dance the Tarantella for Lord Nevil.

Corinne wore a light and elegant costume for the dance, her hair gathered into a silk net—Italian style—her eyes bright with pleasure. Before she began, she saluted the company gracefully, and turning round, took the tambourine which her partner, Prince Amalfi, presented to her. She then began the dance, beating the air with her tambourine and showing in all her movements a grace, a lissomeness, a blending of modesty and " abandon " which gave the spectator some idea of the power exercised over the imagination by Indian dancing-girls when they are, so to speak, poets in the dance, expressing varied feelings by characteristic steps and picturesque attitudes. Corinne was so well acquainted with the different attitudes which painters and sculptors have depicted, that by a slight movement of her arms, holding the tambourine sometimes above her head, sometimes in front of her, while the other hand ran over the bells with incredible swiftness, she would recall the dancing-girls of Herculaneum, and present before the eye of painter or artist one idea after another in swift succession. Corinne, dancing, made the onlookers sharers in her feelings, just as if she were improvising, playing the lyre, or designing figures; every motion was to her as expressive as spoken language. The musicians looking at her were inspired to make the genius of their art more felt; and it would be impossible to tell what passionate joy, what ardour of imagination thrilled at once all who were witnesses of this magic dancing, which carried them away into an ideal life where one dreams of happiness not to be found in this world.

Madame de Staël saw the Tarantella in all the aristocratic elegance it acquired in the *salons* of the late eighteenth and early nineteenth centuries. I never saw the Tarantella in such august surroundings. To me it personifies the crude, barbaric rhythms of the folk of South Italy. Such a dance is the artistic attempt to express by movements of the body the emotions of Joy or Grief. My first vision of the Tarantella as a dance of the folk was on the feast-day of the Irish saint Cataldo, the patron of Taranto. The silver statue of the saint was carried on the shoulders of the populace through the streets from the cathedral : in every restaurant there were special cream cakes in honour of the *festa*. Down in the fishing quarter I saw a Kermesse at sunset. The Via Garibaldi was thronged with a chattering crowd. I heard the rat-tat-tat of drums and the sound of fiddles, harmonicas, and mandolines amid the full-throated babel of voices.

In an open space I saw two girls and a young man dancing the Tarantella before a crowd of stamping and gesticulating revellers. One of the girls held her tambourine above her head as she beat it while she circled

gracefully around her companions, exciting them by the
ever-increasing speed of rhythm. The other girl, with
both arms raised and gesticulating fingers, alternately
advanced within the orbit of her cavalier and retreated.
She was the personification of Circe, the witch whose
fatal grace hypnotizes the youth as the serpent mesmerizes
the humming-bird. On and on surged the music, faster
and faster. The tambourine banged and jingled, the
bystanders clapped and stamped. The barbaric element
of rhythm lifted those people out of their environment,
far away from the miseries of their daily life, and made
them one with Nature. The Tarantella, like the *fandango*
in Andalusia, the *jota* in Aragon, the *csárdás* in Hungary,
the *Hora* in Roumania, acted as the *Katharsis* in the lives
of the folk. It gave expression to racial emotions that
would otherwise remain starved in modern mechanical
civilization. As Havelock Ellis said : " Pantomimic
dances with their effort to heighten natural expression
and to imitate natural process, bring the dancers into
the divine sphere of creation and enable them to assist
vicariously in the energy of the gods." [1] Woe to the
South, the day when it loses its dances of race memory !
In the Tarantella as danced by the Ionian Sea may we
not hear a faint echo of ancient Hellas which Pindar
described as " the land of lovely dancing " ?

[1] H. Ellis, *The Dance of Life*, New York, 1923, p. 41.

CHAPTER XIII

DIARY OF A TARANTIST

ONE of the results of being a Tarantist was that it made me place too great a trust in my feet. I was determined to walk across the heel of Italy from Taranto to Brindisi. Memories of Horace who had journeyed to Brundisium with his patron, Mæcenas, in 37 B.C., and of Virgil, who had died there in 19 B.C. on his return from Greece, echoed through my mind as I plodded along the dusty Via Appia in the scorching sun. Fortunately, Apulia is full of olive groves which tempt a weary pedestrian to throw himself down on a bank and sleep in their shade. The landscape of vast pastureland undulating gently towards the horizon did not stir my imagination. It brought to my mind Laurence Sterne's reflection on plains in *Tristram Shandy*.

There is nothing [said he] more pleasing to a traveller—or more terrible to travel-writers—than a large, rich plain, especially if it is without rich rivers or bridges, for after they have once told you that 'tis delicious, or delightful—that the soil was grateful, and that Nature pours out all her abundance—they have then a large plain upon their hands, which they know not what to do with.

Following Sterne's example, I do not wish to expatiate on the Apulian plain, but return to my feet. The tutelary genius of the Via Appia is unkind to pedestrians, and he blighted my feet the day after I left the town of Franca-

villa.   While I was resting by the road, gazing dejectedly
at my sore foot which I had relieved of its sock and shoe,
an old peasant passed by in a cart.

" Have you been wounded ? " said he, stopping the
mule and peering at me with curiosity.

" My feet have given out," said I piteously.

" I'll cure them for you," said he quickly.   " Jump
up."

He took me to his cottage a little farther along the
road.   He put me sitting under a tree in the yard and
went to fetch his wife, saying : " We'll get the saint
to cure you."   He returned, followed by a grey-haired
woman carrying a bottle.

" Show me your foot," said she ; " Saint Nicholas will
soon cure it."

" Who is Saint Nicholas ? " said I, puzzled.

" Have you never heard of Saint Nicholas of Bari ?
You ought to be ashamed of risking yourself on the
roads without his protection.   He can even raise a man
from the dead, and as for sickness—there isn't one disease
sent to us from Satan that the manna of Saint Nicholas
won't cure."

With these words she opened the bottle and poured
some oil on my foot.   " This oil," said she as she rubbed
my sore limb tenderly, " is indeed a miraculous manna
and I got several bottles of it on the eighth of May last,
when I made pilgrimage to the crypt of San Nicola in
Bari."

As a result of the woman's kind ministrations I was
enabled to continue my journey towards Brindisi.   Later,
when I visited the twelfth-century basilica of San Nicola,
which rises from the sea like a tutelary shrine of Bari,
I laid in a stock of bottles of his manna.   I recommend
the oil, not only for sore feet, but for any other ailment.
And if we believe the following hymn sung by the

pilgrims to his grave, Saint Nicholas's manna cures soul
as well as body :

> Sospitati dedit aegros
> Olei perfusio,
> Nicolaus naufragantum
> Adfuit praesidio.
>
> Relevavit a defunctis
> Defunctum in bivio.
> Baptizatur auri viso
> Judaeus indicio.
>
> Vas in mari mersum, patri
> Redditur cum filio.
> O quam probat Sanctum Dei
> Farris augmentatio.
>
> Ergo laudes Niccolao
> Concinat haec concio.
> Nam qui corde poscit illum
> Propulsato vitio,
> Sospes regreditur.—Amen.

(The sick are given health by the miraculous oil, and Saint Nicholas
saved those in danger of shipwreck. He raised to life a man who
had died by the roadside. A Jew was baptized who had miracu-
lously recovered his money. A jar lost in the sea and a lost child
the saint recovered. O how great a saint he showed himself
when he increased the harvest's yield. Wherefore sing hymns
in praise of Saint Nicholas, for he who drives away his vices and
prays to him, will return safe and sound.—Amen.)

I discovered later that Saint Nicholas of Bari was no
other than our homely Santa Claus, who descends our
chimneys at Christmas-time to fill our stockings with
toys. Saint Nicholas is the hero of many picturesque
stories told in the *Golden Legend* of Jacobus de Voragine.
But none is quainter than the following, which the
waggish citizens of Bari love to tell the inquisitive
traveller. Nicholas came of a wealthy *Greek* family.

When his parents died, he determined to give away the wealth which he had inherited for the glory of God. Now one, his neighbour, had then three daughters, virgins, and he was a nobleman; but for the poverty of them together they were constrained, and in very purpose, to abandon them to the sin of lechery, so that by the gain and winning of their infamy they might be sustained. And when the holy man Nicholas knew thereof, he had great horror of this villainy, and threw by night, secretly, into the house of the man a mass of gold wrapped in a cloth. And when the man rose in the morning, he found this mass of gold, and rendered to God, therefore, great thankings, and therewith he married his oldest daughter. And a little while after, this holy servant of God threw in another mass of gold, which the man found and for which he thanked God, and purposed to wake for to know him that so had aided him in his poverty. And after a few days Nicholas doubled the mass of gold and cast it into the house of this man. He awoke by the sound of the gold, and followed Nicholas, which fled from him, and he said to him: " Sir, flee not away so but that I may see and know thee." Then he ran after him more hastily and knew that it was Nicholas ; and anon he kneeled down, and would have kissed his feet, but the holy man would not, but required him not to tell nor discover this thing as long as he lived.

When Saint Nicholas, who had become bishop of Myra, died, his death was the occasion of many miracles. No sooner was he laid in his sepulchre than a fountain of oil issued therefrom, which, as Voragine said, " is much available to the health or sickness of many men." After the Turks had destroyed the city of Myra, forty-seven knights of Bari went there and opened the sepulchre. To their amazement they found the bones swimming in the oil, and they bore them away honourably into the city of Bari in the year 1087.

Saint Nicholas, who has always been regarded as the patron of boys, had also the power of protecting honest humanity against robbers, footpads, Gypsies, who were called " Saint Nicholas's clerks " in Shakespeare's day. No sooner did I utter the word " Saint Nicholas's clerks "

than they appeared. In the distance, over the plain I
saw a Gypsy encampment. Saint Nicholas's oil must
have brought me within the ken of those wanderers.
Would it be powerful enough to protect me against
the magic spells of Romany?

It was sunset and the parched land was the colour
of burnished copper. The hush of evening had come
upon the earth, and the sky was harsh, metallic. In
the shade of an olive-grove the caravan had halted.
Already the brown tents were pitched and the fires lit.
Who were they? Brown were their faces and their
speech was strange. Around the fires they were gathered
and the women were stirring the cauldrons, while brown,
naked children darted here and there amidst the mules
and donkeys of the tribe. Night advanced silently.
Then suddenly a voice lost itself in the void. The song
of the wanderer. " Here to-day, there to-morrow, for
ever wandering on our way through the desert of the
world. Who knows whence we come? Who knows
the secret of our origin? The Destiny that drove us
inexorably since the beginning of history will not dis-
close." After the music had died away, all was hushed
again, save for the tinkle of the mule-bells. Then rose
the moon, as a ghost, and cast the paleness of death upon
the scene. Voices arose again in songs : " We are thy
minions, O Diana, goddess of the Moon : let thy kingdom come, for thou art the Mother of our witchcraft :

> " Amariden shao tshin
> ardel shune sfintoshin,
> tendji nao t'avel kraïa
> t'avel, t'avel tiri voia
> a da, Mene, pe Krishnata."

In the silver night, men, women, and children fell and
worshipped the full moon, for her daughter, Aradia,

was the greatest witch in the world and the peerless teacher of the lonely wanderer. In accordance with the teachings of Aradia it was their duty once a month, when the moon was full, to assemble in some desert place, or in a forest, and there to join in adoration of the potent spirit of the great Mother Diana. For this was the gospel of witches preserved by the wandering folk since the beginning of Time in every country.

Such were my thoughts as I stood on a tiny knoll, eyeing the Gypsy camp below. I had not met Gypsies since I had said farewell to my blood-brother Joska, a Hungarian Gypsy prisoner, in Lombardy. Joska had said that I was possessed of a *Romano nak*, or Romany nose—" Wherever you go," said he, " your nose is sure to lead you to a Gypsy camp "; so here I was, standing timidly at the entrance, waiting to be invited in. I did not go long unperceived. Two mangy dogs, followed by a cluster of boisterous brown children, dashed up to where I was standing. Soon I was surrounded by most of the tribe.

" Where are you going ? " said I to the tall, swarthy leader, who was wearing a black sombrero and a torn orange-coloured muffler round his neck.

" We're off to Taranto," said he curtly, eyeing me from head to toe.

" Now that the war's over," said I, " you can wander from North to South and East to West without fear or hindrance."

" War's no hindrance to us," said he. " Austriaci Tedeschi o Italiani è lo stesso ! We've come all the way from Zara, always keeping to ourselves and minding our own business."

As he spoke, the rest of the tribe gathered still more closely around, staring at me as if I was some strange animal. Then a waspish-looking young girl in a ragged smock, but with a red kerchief and enormous earrings, came up behind me and gave a tug at my fiddle.

"All right," said I, "I'll play for you, but *per carità* stand back and give me some air."

We retired beneath the olive trees, and I took out the fiddle and played a few dances. Ragged children gambolled at my feet, dogs barked, lean donkeys brayed dolefully, and as for the men and women—they sniffed, grunted, and expectorated as I played. They would have aroused nothing but contempt from my friend Joska, for they did not react to the rhythm as the Hungarian or Spanish Gypsies would have done. As I played, various remarks about my clothes, my face, my hair, my eyes, came to my ears.

"What a fair man—yes, look at his blue eyes : he's no Italian.

"Of course not, you idiot : *è Tedesco.*"

"Look at the red handkerchief in his pocket—I'd like it." An urchin darted forward, and before I could say a word had snatched the handkerchief from my pocket. Several others also made a dash for me, and I should soon have found myself as ragged as the Gypsies themselves had not the elder woman drawn me aside to tell my fortune.

Fortune-telling is the fundamental ritual of the Gypsies : it enters into every one of their actions in life. What is fortune-telling but primitive magic, enabling them to dominate or wheedle their victims ? Even their exciting dances and their strange passionate music is nought else but fortune-telling. I had no silver on me, which was a mistake, for a Gypsy fortune-teller, according to ritual, will cross the hand with no other metal. She did not, however, refuse the five-lire note I offered, and she drew an old coin out of her pocket and crossed my palm. She then started her long invocation, calling

upon spirits to help her in drawing out the secrets of my
destiny.   As she prayed, she scrutinized my face eagerly,
and I was conscious that the prayer was a ritual which
enabled her to read my thoughts.   According to the
Gypsy belief, every particle of our destiny is written in
the palms of our hands.   In them the witch can read not
only the physical traits, but also the intellectual.   She
can tell what passions agitate us, what ideas are in our
minds.   She spoke to me of the " Auguriellu," or little
monk, who appears as a goblin in one's infancy ; of the
beautiful lady who must be propitiated.   She asked me
whether I had lucky charms with me, such as a horse-
shoe or two-tailed lizard.   " Let me sell you," said she,
" a piece of coral or horn to protect you against a *jettatore*,
who would wither you with his evil eye.   That hand of
yours is a fair one : there's gold and silver—aye, and
beautiful women in it ; but there's a power of trouble in it
also.   In a short while you'll meet a bitter sorrow, after
you've crossed the sea ; someone will give you a *colpo
d'occhio* when you haven't Santa Lucia to help you : you'll
find trouble over there, but you'll be pining to come back
here : mind the dark lady with the cast in her eye—
she'll be unfaithful to you : turn a deaf ear to her, and
go down to the sea ; take the boat back here, for there's
one waiting for you night and day—fair-haired she is—
una bionda bella come il sole.   You'll come back, but you'll
find trouble here too, and you'll have to fight knife in
hand with your rival."

" Come, come, signora," said I, " I've no knife, and
besides, what woman is worth fighting for to the blood ? "

" No knife, son ? " said the woman.   " That's not
possible.   Nobody in Italy courts without a knife ; it
makes the girl respect you, and it's prettier to serenade
with than a mandoline."

" Come here, Adamo," said she to the surly man,

" show the gentleman your knife—tell him how they throw it in Naples."

The man whipped out from inside his coat a villainous stiletto, and lunged with it towards my belly with such a realistic gesture that I winced in terror.

" Never mind, son," said the old woman calmly, " you'll soon learn how to use the knife ; besides, I see no death in your hand. After the storm comes the calm weather. You'll find hidden wealth here, and you'll marry the fair-haired lass—aye, and twice she'll be calling on Saint Joseph, and there'll be plenty of butterflies flitting round the cradles."

When it came to meal-time I was hospitably received, mainly because my own haversack was well stocked with provisions, which I shared with the rest. The pot over the fire contained a varied assortment of meats, for Gypsies cook whatever comes to their hand. Any young birds they find in the nests, any hens they manage to decoy into their voluminous skirts, find their way eventually into the simmering pot. I was interested to hear that those Gypsies of Southern Italy considered the hedgehog as great a delicacy as any Romanichal in England. The boys of the tribe were as skilful at stalking those elusive animals as my old friend, Ithal Lee, whose idea of heaven, I am sure, is " a large garden full of fine fat hedgehogs." Anybody who has eaten a hedgehog roasted on a camp-fire will never eat another rabbit as long as he lives.

How could I find words to describe my feelings of ease and freedom as I rested by the smouldering fires, surrounded by those dark-eyed vagabonds ? At night even the familiar sounds of the camp—the shrill shouts of the children and the harsh voices of the men—were stilled. Occasionally, the chief with the surly face broke the silence to tell me anecdotes of his wandering. He would speak of the War and its horrors. He had wandered as far as Serbia and Montenegro, and he would tell tales of the metal-working Gypsies from Albania. Sometimes the waspish young Gypsy girl, who was sitting by his side, would interrupt his tales with exclamations of surprise. Her ferret eyes spied something moving in the undergrowth just beyond the tents. Then three or four boys would spring to their feet and dash off to investigate. A few minutes later they would return with a rabbit they had managed to capture. When I questioned the chief about the customs and habits of Italian Gypsies, he became strangely secretive, but his wife, who had read my hand, would draw me aside and tell me about charms and spells against the Evil Eye.

" Would you like to meet a pure race Italian Gypsy ? " said she.

" Certainly."

" If you go to Brindisi I will give you a message to my sister, Carlotta, and she will introduce you to Cesare, the finest mandolinist and harmonica-player in the Kingdom. Cesare will take you along with him, and who knows but we may all meet in Taranto, Cotrone, or Reggio. But you must go and see Carlotta first : she is a Settimana."

" What is a Settimana ? " said I.

" A Settimana is a seven-months' child and full to the eyes with *vecchia religione*. Carlotta has been called a witch : she was not born any more witch than I was, but she inherited the gift from one."

After the rest of the tribe had retired to their tents, I sat alone by the fire which was still smouldering. In the sweltering climate of the South, night comes as a grateful release. During the day every living thing on earth seems to be scorched into a coma, but at night-time the sleepers rouse themselves, and, hour by hour, a certain wakeful influence seems to increase in intensity. Gradually one's senses become attuned to these stray voices of Nature. There is the far-distant, ringing sound of myriads of frogs in a marsh ; the faint buzzing of flies ; the gossamer note of the mosquito orchestra. A cock crows in the void, followed by a few birds, noting softly. Even the stars in the sky seem to increase this wakefulness and ruffle the calm of resting humanity. Then, just before the grey light of dawn, there is a momentary pause—a hushed preparation for the new day.

And so passed the first night I ever spent in a Gypsy camp. Those Gypsies in Apulia must have cast a spell upon me that night, for, ever since, I have felt at certain moments a longing to be away on the plain, near the tents of the wandering folk. Many a night have I spent in the last eighteen years among the copper-working nomads of Transylvania, or the horse-dealing *chalanes* of Andalusia, but I have never captured so deep a thrill of Nature's freedom as I did on that first night of initiation into the mystery of the Gypsy camp-fires.

As soon as I reached Brindisi, I made my way to the address given me by the Gypsy. In a small room of a back-street tenement I found Carlotta. She was a fat, sallow-faced woman, dressed in a tattered red gown. On her head she had tied a yellow handkerchief in Romany fashion. She wore long ear-rings of gold, and her bodice was studded with various little amulets. Hardly giving me the time to deliver my message, she started to speak breathlessly :

" So you've come from my sister. Why has she sent you ? I suppose you are unlucky in love—isn't that so ? Well, you have come to the right person—I am known all through Apulia and Calabria for my *scongiuri* and charms. They fear me more than they do the devil himself. Come over here and I'll show you."

Still chattering volubly, she led me over to the far side of the room and pulled aside a curtain, behind which was a table covered with a green cloth and laden with flowers and various objects.

"That table," said she, "is an altar : it's all of wood —not a nail in it, for iron is unlucky. On the table you will find flowers, candles, incense, verbena, sandalwood, and the little sack of green silk to correspond with the tablecloth. Come now, tell me your trouble and I'll soon cure it. But you must first of all put on the white cloak."

Carlotta paused and seized a white cloak which was hanging in the corner. She was just about to throw it over my shoulders when there was a knock on the outer door.

"Who can that be ? " said Carlotta, as she rushed out of the room. After a few moments she came back, and said in a low voice : "There is an unhappy girl outside who needs my help in her trouble, but she must not see you here : I told her that I was all alone. Go in there quick—I shan't be long."

She pushed me into an inner room and closed the door upon me. I found that by opening the door a little I could see what was happening without anyone being the wiser. The young girl who came to consult Carlotta was evidently in deep distress. She was lean and haggard, and her eyes were red with weeping. She kept wringing her hands, and her voice was choked with sobs. Carlotta put her arms round the girl, and said to her :

"Do not weep, child ; he will come back to you. All you have to do is to follow my directions."

"All is useless," cried the girl tearfully—"it's my

destiny. That other woman has bewitched him : I have lost him."

" Tell me, child," said Carlotta sharply, " have you brought what I told you ? "

" Yes, here they are," said the girl, pulling out a small packet—" here are what you asked me to bring—the hairs off his head, pieces of finger-nail parings, a piece of cloth off a suit he wore, and the photograph."

Carlotta took the packet and said : " Did you bring me the money I asked for ? Remember that this charm cannot be worked unless you pay the full value of your wish."

" Here it is," said the girl eagerly, " all my savings for the past few weeks."

Carlotta took the money and counted it carefully before she put it into a small box on the mantelpiece. Then rubbing her hands and smacking her lips, she said to the girl :

" Now let us begin. You must calm yourself, my dear, and dry those tears. The moment I put this white cloak over your shoulders, you should forget everything in the world except your love for him. For seven minutes you must stand in silence, thinking of him."

The girl, with the white cloak over her shoulders, stood motionless as a phantom. Meanwhile, the old woman went behind the curtain and lit the two wax candles on the little altar. When all was ready she pulled aside the curtain, and I could see that she had arranged the objects according to a certain ritual. In the middle, between the two candles, was the photograph of the youth. On the left was a little copper vessel, from which issued a tiny cloud of incense. There were also rose-leaves strewn upon the table, and on the right was the little bag of green silk containing the hair, nail parings and cloth. Carlotta then awoke the girl from her meditation, and led her over to the magic altar.

"Here," said she, "is the place where you will find relief from your distress, provided you do all I tell you. On the table you see the photograph of your beloved between the candles of pure wax. Your wish will be all the more powerful because it is accompanied by incense, verbena, and rose petals. In that little green silk bag are the personal relics. Stretch out your arms towards your beloved, and pronounce three times, after me, the invocation."

The old woman then invoked the occult power in a low, sing-song voice.

She started off by calling the name of the man, saying : "Come to me guided by Aradia now that I invoke you. Already by my will you have become absorbed by my desire. May your Spirit be touched, and your soul join my soul, and your body consent. May the propitious powers stirred up by my words help me and link you to me. May my will be accomplished—Amen." It was a fantastic sight to see the witch bending over the girl, who was standing like a statue with arms outstretched. There were no other lights in the room save the two wax candles, and as the witch stood there, the quivering flames cast her monstrous shadow upon the wall.

After that ritualistic performance was ended, Carlotta blew out the candles, pulled across the curtain, divested the girl of the white cloak, and dismissed her gruffly. She then called me out of my hiding-place.

"You may come in now," said she. "I have cured the patient : it is now your turn. Come, put on the white cloak."

"Look here, Signora Carlotta," said I, interrupting her with determination, "I have not come here to work magic on any mistress. I am safe and sound, hard-hearted and hard-bitten—a man of the roads and not of the town. I have come to see your brother—your brother, the Romanichal—and see here I carry a fiddle : I'm not a moper, I'm a minstrel."

"Why didn't you say that before ? " said Carlotta excitedly. " If it's Cesare you want to see, come with me."

She put on a black cloak, and led the way down the stone steps of the house into the street.

" Cesare," said she, as we walked through the narrow, dark streets, " is always known as *il gobbo* around here."

" Ah, so he's a hunchback—that's lucky in Southern Italy."

" Yes, he's hunchbacked, bow-legged, and as ugly as sin, but he has a heart of gold."

At length we reached Cesare's lodgings, which consisted of a tiny, dark room just off the street. It was more of a den than an apartment—a riot of junk of every description—broken chairs, books, stringed instruments, a table, a dilapidated cottage piano, a wooden bed covered with a faded patchwork quilt. The only bright object in the room was a pink and blue statue of the Madonna in a corner, with a red lamp burning in front of it. Out of the gloom, Cesare advanced to meet us. Carlotta had not exaggerated his ugliness. He was small in stature, but thick-set. His hump was so aggressive that it gave him the appearance of being as broad and deep as he was tall. He had a great skull covered with thick, black, tousled hair, but his neck, which was long and slender, drooped, as though unable to bear the weight resting on it. His face was square-cut with prominent cheek-bones, and his eyes had a crazy expression, due to a malignant squint. As for his skin, it was brown, but wrinkled and furrowed like a piece of old

leather. He was dressed in a baggy pair of blue serge
trousers and a faded green shirt open at the neck and
revealing a chest covered with black stubble. Cesare
received me with cordiality. No sooner did he see my
fiddle than he rushed over to a corner and brought
out his mandoline. Then a battle-royal of music took
place. I played and he interrupted me with his metallic,
pecking music. Then he abandoned the mandoline for
a harmonica, and the harmonica for a guitar, and the
guitar for a one-stringed fiddle on which he scraped with
gusto. Finally, when neither of us had any more breath
or energy, he suddenly stopped and said:

" Molto bene, molto bene, adesso combiniamo ! You
play by the grace of God and so do I. Every man for
himself and the devil with us all ! We must combine ;
four eyes see better than two, and four hands working
together are as good as a regiment."

Cesare spoke in a raucous voice, and he had a disturbing habit of punctuating often a fragment of sentence
with a grunt or a scarifying clear-throat. Carlotta
gazed at Cesare admiringly while he played :

" Isn't he a wonder ? " said she to me : " he'll play
any instrument ; and with his music he is cuter at coax-
ing money out of the people than I am, with all my cards,
scongiuri and love-philtres."

We retired to a tavern to celebrate our meeting and
make arrangements for the future. When we were
seated before a bottle of Moscato, my two companions
bombarded me with questions. Where was I from ?
German ? Austrian ? Hungarian ? Americano ? " Sud-
Americano, perhaps," interjected Carlotta. " I know
Brazil and Rio, the best place in the world for fortune-
telling."

" That's true," said the hunchback.

" You must have learnt much of your witchcraft from

the *zingari* over there," said I, wishing to draw out some of her experiences.

"Of course I did," said she, "but I learnt more in Barcelona and Marseilles. But nobody can learn the *vecchia religione* by word of mouth : a *zingara* in Italy inherits it as she would an heirloom."

"That's true," interjected the hunchback. "A *zingara* would never carry her art beyond the grave. She must hand it on to another before she gives up the ghost."

"I got the gift," continued Carlotta dreamily, "from an old aunt who lived at Basilicata. Just before the rattle came, she whispered to me : 'It's not gold nor silver I'm leaving you, Carlotta, but the religion of the blood : mind you use it and hand it on ! '"

Carlotta's account of the transmission of witchcraft from one to another fitted in with the general theories of deathless vampires, which were current in some primitive parts of Italy, if we believe authorities such as Leland. He quotes a story at Florence of an old witch who lay dying in a hospital ward next a young girl.[1] "The witch kept on moaning that she had no one to whom she could leave her possessions. The girl, thinking she meant money, asked the dying woman to leave all to her. But, alas, it was the gift of sorcery not money that the girl received, and she had to become a witch. Her brother, the story relates, determined to save her, and so, one night, when she went out to the Sabbat, he followed her. He caught her by the hair and twisted it, and a great number of cats came up and miaoued. He held on like grim death until the cats vanished. The girl then ceased to be a witch and became a *buona donna come era prima* (a good girl as she was originally).

[1] C. G. Leland, *Gypsy Sorcery and Fortune-telling*, London, 1891, p. 150.

Carlotta continued her reminiscences, whilst every now and then the hunchback interrupted, to add his comments.

"Fortune-telling is not what it was," said she, "for the world has changed. In the old days, when nobody left his village, it was easier for the story-teller. Down in the South, where there was greater hunger and suffering than in the North, it was easier for a *zingara* to find clients among the poor. There were fewer doctors and fewer curates. Many were the cures I used to do in the old days. Many's the night that I led girls out to a deserted ruin under the moon, and recited the gospel of the witches. For you know, young man, though you may not believe it, I have a remedy for everything."

"Tell me some charms," said I, "to help me in love."

"Listen," said she, "the next time you need a charm, pull three hairs out of your left arm-pit, burn them on a hot shovel, and reduce them to powder. Put the powder in a crumb of bread, and when the girl is not looking, slip it into her soup or coffee. As soon as she's eaten the bread, she'll never leave you."

"I'll tell you a better one," interrupted the hunchback. "Go into a meadow before dawn, and catch a little frog in a white napkin. Put it into a box in which you have made nine holes. Then go to the foot of a tree where there is an ant-hill. Make a hole in the earth, and put your box there. Then cover the box with your left foot, saying : 'May you be confounded as I wish.' At the end of nine days, go at the same hour to fetch your box. You will find two bones in it—one in the shape of a fork, and the other like a little leg. If you touch the girl with the little leg, she'll love you, and if you touch her with the fork, she'll take to her heels. That's a better charm, my friend, for with women it's always best to have two choices open ; a man never knows where his whim will lead him."

Carlotta and the hunchback were characteristic scions of the Gypsy race, which is very difficult to run to earth in modern Italy. Unlike the Romanies of Southern Spain or Hungary, the Italian Gypsy is not pre-eminently musical, and he has not preserved, as a living language, the ancient dances of the country. The Italian Gypsies have become more absorbed by the population than their Spanish or Hungarian kinsmen. In Spain and Hungary the Gypsy has played the part of a minstrel for centuries, for he calls forth that Dionysian element which is so strong in those two races. In South Italy the Gypsy has adapted himself to the humble tasks of the countryside ; but occasionally, in out-of-the-way places we do come across Gypsies who keep alive the ancient traditions of witchcraft, which are part and parcel of the Italian race. In ancient Roman times there existed the religion of Diana, the goddess, and her daughter, Aradia (or Herodias), the female Messiah. And Diana, the goddess of the moon, who was worshipped with a crescent horn, is connected with Bacchus, the god of wine. Leland, in his *Legends of Florence*,[1] tells one of the *Via del Corno* (street of the horn), in which the hero, falling into a vast tun of wine, is saved from drowning by sounding a horn with tremendous power. The sound of the horn penetrates even into the depths of heaven, and Diana, when she hears it, leaps through doors and windows to save the vintage of the one who blows. Even to-day, the wanderer through the villages of the South may hear echoes of the ancient religion of the red goblin, of Laverna, the goddess of thieves, pickpockets, and hypocrites, mentioned in Horace, who was worshipped in perfect silence. Even

[1] C. G. Leland, *Legends of Florence*, London, 1896.

to-day, in South Italy as in other Mediterranean countries, in spite of modern civilization, there exist, deep beneath the veneer of Society, brotherhoods founded on superstition and fragments of old tradition.

The origin of this secret anarchy was during the Dark Ages, that is to say, from the downfall of the Roman Empire until the thirteenth century. Men discovered that the world was full of wickedness and injustice, due to the crushing tyranny of Church and State. Those who rebelled against injustice, and those whose weakness left them unprotected, turned to the ancient superstition of Diana the protectress. Christianity did not, until the end of the Middle Ages and the emancipation of the serfs, diminish the sufferings of the vast majority of mankind. The reason, as Leland shows, was that in the old " heathen " time the humble did not know or even dream that all were equal before God, or that they had many *rights* even here on earth as slaves ; for in fact the whole moral tendency of the New Testament is utterly opposed to slavery or even severe servitude. Every word uttered teaching Christ's mercy and love, humility and charity, was in fact a bitter reproof not only to every lord in the land but to the Church itself and its arrogant prelates.[1] Hence the vast development of sorcery as a religion for the rebels and outcasts, with wizards as their priests. Even to-day, there are secret places near old ruins, where the tradition of the witches' sabbath still lingers. And in the chaotic, disillusioned Italy after the War, among the poverty-stricken population of the South, fortune-tellers like Carlotta reaped a rich harvest.

Cesare, the hunchback, and I became confederates, and we were rarely out of one another's company. I

[1] C. G. Leland, *Aradia or the Gospel of Witches*, London, 1899, pp. 105–6.

soon began to learn the tricks of the itinerant musician's trade, and what was more important, the philosophy of " nichyevo," as the Russians would call it. I learnt how to endure with equanimity the sordidness of poverty, for there were many lean days when we needed the frenzy of a Tarantist to make us dance in search of centesimi. The heat, bugs, and smells, we had with us always. But there were compensations, such as the prolonged siesta in shady courtyards, or in dingy taverns, lulled by buzzing flies. I was not an exacting partner, for I left the hunchback to hold the money bags. I had a little money of my own for emergencies, but, I must say, Cesare, though tending to avariciousness, did not cheat me out of my share. Mine was an easy life, for all I had to do was to play and obey my companion. He organized our performances ; he passed the hat round ; he arranged where we were to sleep ; and he even looked after the welfare of my immortal soul, on Sundays, for Cesare, in spite of his Gypsy traditions, was religious. Whenever he came back to his den, he would first of all say a prayer to the Madonna, and he left strict injunctions to the women living in the neighbouring rooms that the red lamp was always to be kept lighted. After hearing him talk with Carlotta about Diana, Aradia, and the Gospel of Witches, I wondered whether his attitude of mind towards the statue of the Madonna was not the same as that of the Gypsies in South Spain, who threaten to throw the statue of their favourite saint, Antony, on to a dung-hill if he does not bring them luck in their undertakings.

I shall always remember the day we set out on an extended ramble from Brindisi to Taranto, and from Taranto, down through Calabria, to Reggio. We were given a triumphal send-off by the dishevelled inhabitants of the tenement, after a parting stirrup-cup in which all joined. We were a grotesque sight. Bow-legged Cesare stumped along the road carrying his hump with majesty. Although the heat was stifling, he had two coats on him, one of which, he said, was for change. He carried a mandoline and a guitar strung round him, as well as his bulgy sack. In his right hand he brandished a bamboo cane, with a horn handle against the evil eye. As for me, I was dressed in grey flannel trousers, a dark blue shirt open at the neck, and a woman's red scarf tied around my waist like a sash—this gave me a slight buccaneering air and attracted attention.

The pleasures of wandering lie mostly in retrospect. I cannot say that I enjoyed at the time the following weeks of roaming from Brindisi to Reggio. But now, I look back upon that period of sweated labour with compassionate envy. Nowadays the South of Italy has changed : there is less poverty, less malaria, and the people live under a strong, stable government which is alive to their problems. But in the year after the War, there was more chaos and wretchedness in South Italy and Sicily than in the rest of the country ; and living, as I was doing, among vagrants, whose activities would have awakened the suspicions of the police, if there had been an efficient force at that time, I was able to plumb the depths of human poverty. The Sicilian proverb says that " the sun is the father of the ragged," and that is true. The warm sun enables the vagabond to thrive on a starvation diet. In Northern countries, where there are grey skies, snows, and stormy seas, men are forced to discipline and organize their existence. In the South, men can live instinctively and passionately. If I had remained much longer with my hunchback minstrel, I should have become completely a nomad. I should very soon have conquered my repugnance to squalor and even hunger in that land of Lotos-eaters ;

for it takes but little energy there to earn enough to support life. What were my needs? A crust of bread, some sardines, olives, and a few glasses of Calabrian wine, were enough to set me at peace with the universe. And as soon as I had begun to despise the idea of work for work's sake which I had learnt from my parents and at school, my mind was free to dream.

> Let us alone. What pleasure can we have
> To war with evil? Is there any peace
> In ever climbing up the climbing wave?
> All things have rest, and ripen towards the grave
> In silence: ripen, fall, and cease:
> Give us long rest or death, dark death, or dreamful ease.

Soon the yellow, pinched faces of the coast populations, wasted by malaria, no longer haunted me. If I had been stricken down with the disease I should have accepted it as they did, for was it not their destiny? Even one's moral nature changes in that land. What is the good of boiling up in indignation at the wrongs of the world, when around me there lie so many memorials of the folly of past struggles? Take, for instance, Metaponto, with its Palatine Tables, where tradition says that Pythagoras, the Greek philosopher, held his school. I insisted on tramping all the way from the station to see those venerable columns, much to the disgust of the hunchback, who had no taste for historical antiquities. " Who but a fool," said he, " would cry out with admiration at the sight of those ruins? Any Gypsy feels contempt at such a sight. We never built temples of marble in our wanderings: instead we folded our tents and passed on, leaving no track behind us. There is more wonder, my dear friend, in that wood of eucalyptus trees and tamarisk bushes over there." It was useless for me to tell Cesare stories of the days when the Golden Sheaf at Delphi symbolized the fertility of the land of Metapontum.

Cesare had an uncanny faculty for discovering hospitable resting-places. Probably much of his success was due to his hump, for humps in the South, in spite of the laughter they arouse, always bring luck; and when you are a minstrel and story-teller as well as hunchback, life becomes one long series of invitations.

Along the coast, we spent much of our time among the fishing population, which has suffered none of the changes of civilization. From father to son they have inherited with their love of the sea many of the ancient traditions. The arrival of the little fishing-boats is quite a ritual in these parts. The boys lie in wait on the cliffs to catch the first glimpse of the returning fleet, and when it heaves in sight they rush down to awaken the village with their shout, " Barca ! " and they are given a reward by the grateful inhabitants, who look upon their fleet of fishing-smacks as the provider of God's bounty. The customs which are still prevalent in Calabria reveal that man is helpless in the face of Nature, and the gods must be propitiated in every way. And so the youth who returns from work in the evening, casts down a faggot at his mother's door before he dares to cross it. Just as we see occasional ancient columns lying in the deserted fields—a memory of Greater Greece—so do we hear echoes of past rituals from the peasant folk. I was also struck by the firm belief that those people have in the talisman as a means of averting disaster. Not one of those brawny old fishermen could swim, but all of them wore little amulets suspended from a string round their neck. Those charms, they told me, protected them against the power of the sea.

Each town had its own little characteristic, but I can only

remember them to-day by some personality, or adventure which is of no interest to the reader, though it had consequences for me at the time. Policoro I remember because two brutal mongrels took a sudden dislike to my red sash, and sprang at my throat. Cesare paused to utter a *scongiuro* against dogs before he beat them off. I then discovered that the best dog technique for a tramp is to pick up a few large stones, and fling them at the dogs before they come too near. Those mongrels are cowardly, and they slink behind the unwary traveller, waiting for their chance to jump at him. Amendolara I remember only because it was there that we were turned out of a house in disgrace, because I smiled and paid compliments to the pretty wife of my host. A wanderer should always act cautiously where women are concerned, when he is in Calabria or Sicily. In Northern climes, a husband expects other men to pay tribute to his wife's good looks, hence the elaborate art of flirtation. But in the South, where happiness is " short, sudden and without reprieve," a husband draws his knife when Don Giovanni's shadow falls across the courtyard. She was a Calabrian beauty, with eyes like two live coals in her wax-like face, and black hair drawn back from her brow, moulded to her little head—a statuette of Tanagra in her gracefulness. I was no Don Giovanni, but merely a humble retainer paying my court.

One of my wishes was to visit the site of Sybaris, although I should have been warned by Gissing's melancholy description. The land of Sybaris when it flowed with milk and honey must have looked like the garden of vines and olives where we had slept; but now it is a fever-infested fen, and the traveller who stands on the banks of the River Crathis must gaze deep into those muddy pools to imagine what the city might have been.   Perhaps beneath those heaps of mud there may be streets that await the excavator, like those of Pompeii and Herculaneum.   To-day nought is left of Sybaris but the name, which has been given to the ugly railway station by a government trying to encourage in the people a knowledge of Greek history.   The Crathis, in spite of its melancholy desolation, evokes many memories.   In 600 B.C. Sybaris was the proudest city of the Mediterranean, and this river was crowded with boats laden with merchandise.   Near here were mines of silver, from which were minted those beautiful coins bearing on them the figure of the bull—symbol of the fertility of those plains once overflowing with wine and honey.   It was in those days that the word " Sybarite " became the equivalent of our word " millionaire." Historians said that the city was not enclosed within its circuit of nine kilometres, and its population reached three hundred thousand.   In those days it welcomed the wealthy merchants of Greece and Asia Minor : the women in their palaces wore robes of priceless Ionian silk ; the men were no longer the hardy pioneers of the Achæi with muscles hardened by the chase.   Instead of preserving the humble virtues of the peasant, they acquired the indolent refinements of the oriental in their houses, with their plates of gold and their candelabra from Etruria.   And, strange to relate, that period of effeminate luxury, which had given their name to be a warning to the world, tallies with democratic government.   Destruction came from the aristocratic Croton which looked with envy on the flourishing democracy of its neighbour.   As in the case of Athens, democracy was unprepared for war and the city which rendered cult to the athlete Milon won a smashing victory in 510 B.C.   For seventy days the siege lasted, and at last Milon and his band of warriors entered.   What destruction must have been seen that day! Milon's men hesitated before they sacked such beauty : their eyes had never seen such numbers of golden vases, such brocade of silver strewn about in hopeless confusion, or such hosts of fair slaves cowering in terror behind the overturned statues. For the Sybarites had not the noble frenzy of the Saguntines, who cast themselves and their wives and daughters into the flaming pyres on which their wealth had been piled. The destruction of Sybaris came to remind mankind of the fate of Sodom and Gomorrah : its people had grown in pride and insolence, forgetting the revengeful " Atē," and they had outraged the gods by their impiety. On that day of reckoning Milon became the instrument of the gods as he drove his bands to plunder, and rough soldiers raped the women on their couches of purple. Towards evening the flaming piles bore witness to the city's fate, but still Milon's men did not stop : down fell the temples and the buildings, and the soldiers knocked asunder the walls. Then that the name of the city might be effaced for ever, the course of the River Crathis was turned so as to submerge the mass of smoking ruins. The destruction of Sybaris made a deep impression upon the ancient world, and moralists were never weary of quoting it as an example of the downfall of sinful pride.

While I was sentimentalizing over Sybaris, my practical hunchback had gone off to order food in the station buffet. My historical rhapsodizing always irritated him, and he would interrupt me with a grunt and an expectoration, saying : " You are the strangest fellow I have ever come across. You can't visit a town without imagining what it was like thousands of years ago. A plague on the past, say I ! I'm thinking of the present. Look around you. Do you see that wood of eucalyptus trees ? Why were they planted ? Because the land is full of malaria. Look at that fellow over there with a face as yellow as if he had jaundice. Why have they malaria ? Because down here the people live like serfs in the past and cling to their feudal history. They become mildewed by their past. The only ones who escape are those who throw their bundle over their shoulder and tramp off to Naples and board the steamer for America. They would need a man down here who would prod them out of their sleep and say to them : ' To hell with the feudal past ! We're living in the present. The world begins to-day, and you've got to colonize your own land. I'll break up the large estates and divide the land among you, and I'll give you money to drain it free from malaria.' "

" Those are true words," chimed in the shabby porter of Sybaris station, who was listening attentively. " A strong man should come along and take the land from those rich noble families. They spend their time in Rome or Milan living like Sybarites on the money wrung from the poor slaves down here. It's no wonder that there are more Calabresi in the Argentine than there are in Calabria itself."

I felt in my pocket for my bottle of quinine and I swallowed two tablets extra in honour of Sybaris.

One of the charms of a journey through Calabria is that it sets in continual antithesis the coast and the mountain. After travelling along the sea-shore and mixing with the fishing population, we would turn inland and ascend into the mountains. In Corigliano, which rises out of a forest of olive trees, we saw the convent of Santa Maria del Patire, whence the wise men used to descend to preach in the towns of the plain. From Corigliano we followed a mountain path towards the Byzantine town of Rossano perched upon a neighbouring peak of the Sila range. Up in these towns there was no trace of malaria, and the children were vigorous and apple-cheeked. The mountaineers have their own customs and folk-poems. At one moment, while we were resting in the mountains by a clump of prickly pears, we heard the distant sound of a bagpipe. I thought for a moment I had been spirited away to the glens of Donegal or Antrim. At the end of the path I saw a swarthy shepherd playing as if he was the Pied Piper followed by a flock of sheep. He was a tall, gaunt fellow with olive skin and straggling black beard, dressed in a dark cloak and top-boots. After saluting us gravely he sat down upon a neighbouring rock and made the mountains echo to his wild music, while his sheep clustered around munching with rustling sound the fragrant herbs. After playing for a while, the shepherd would put down his pipes, rub his mouth with the back of his hand, and gaze round restlessly like a startled animal, then he would continue his music. He played till the sun sank behind the ridge, and then with a muttered farewell he strode away followed by his bleating sheep. I am sure he was not a Græco-Calabrian nor an Albano-Calabrian, but a descendant of the primeval Bruttians who dwelt in the forest of the Sila mountains. The Greeks despised these primitive Italians as savages and the Romans later branded them as the descendants of escaped criminals. Few parts of Italy offer greater problems to the ethnologists than Calabria with its many racial types.

With Cesare I had great opportunities for observing the variety of human types in the quaint little coast train whose locomotive was driven by wood instead of coal. Behind the passenger coaches were many trucks full of logs which served to fuel the hard-working little engine. Travelling by train in Calabria was an hilarious

amusement : the compartments were crowded with
peasants carrying baskets full of hens and ducks, and
sacks of vegetables. It was remarkable to see how
much luggage those chattering women were able to carry.
In our compartment, in addition to fishermen and
mountaineers, there were three girls going for an outing
to Cotrone. They were full of fun and laughter : the
eldest was immensely amused by Cesare's face and
hump. After touching his hump for luck, she pointed
to his guitar and asked him for a tune. Cesare gravely
complied with her request, and soon three of the girls
were singing lustily to his playing. It was my turn
next, and I stood up and played to the eyes of the first
girl who had spoken to us—they were deep blue eyes
set in a fair, sensitive face. " She is a Græco-Calabrian
maiden," said I to myself as I played, " one of the
five peerless beauties of Croton, after whom Zeuxis
painted his Helen." They were going to Cotrone and
so were we, but when we descended from the train
they tripped away from us with a merry farewell greeting.

Gissing's account of his visit to Cotrone in 1897 gives
it very little credit for anything, so I expected to find a
miserable little malaria-infested town, where the life
of the inhabitants is one dreary protest against the inept
government of the country. Even in the other Calabrian towns people had warned me against the dirt of
Cotrone. I was surprised, therefore, to discover as
sunny and smiling a town as I had seen in South Italy.
I then came to the conclusion that Gissing's mind was
prejudiced against the place because he had been stricken
down there by malaria.

Cesare led the way to lodgings belonging to a friend
of his—a villainous-looking old woman called Leda.
She looked about ninety years of age, but her agility
was so surprising that I expected to see her ride in

through the door on a broomstick. Her face was a
mass of wrinkles, and her grey, matted hair hung half
down her back. Her gums were toothless, and she had
a queer habit of smacking her lips with a noise that
made me jump. She had eyes as sharp as gimlets, and
when she looked at me they bored deep into me. Leda
hemmed and hawed when she saw me : she sniffed at me
and held a candle up to my face. Finally she shuffled
along a dark passage and gave us a room—a den as black
as the Hole of Calcutta, without a window in it. The
whole house seemed to be tottering on its foundations.
It must have been a relic from the Middle Ages, when
Cotrone was attacked by the Saracens, and freebooters
and desperadoes hid away in those humid passages.
The scene in the living-room reminded me of Ali Baba's
cave during a meeting of the robbers. There were
various men with the appearance of cut-throats, and
among them I recognized my Gypsy acquaintance,
Adamo, the chief of the nomads I had met near Brindisi.
Adamo, seeing I was in the company of the hunchback,
welcomed me cordially and made room for me on the
bench beside him. Near us was a tall, athletic fellow
with black curly hair and side-whiskers—a Southern Don
Juan—who was cracking jokes with a plump, red-
haired, heavily rouged girl.

" Who are they ? " said I in a low voice to the hunchback as we sat in the corner.

" That is Aldo," replied Cesare : " we always call
him *argento vivo* because he can do anything with his
fingers or his body : he can do card tricks, conjuring
tricks, juggling, somersaults, cartwheels, and there isn't
in all Southern Italy his equal at imitating the twittering
of birds, the lowing of oxen, or the braying of an ass.
He has only two failings——"

" What are they ? "

"He's a little too fond of playing the finger-wizard off the stage, and then he has to cut and run for it. His second failing is more serious : he's too fond of crying out ' cuckoo ' in other men's houses."

"What do you mean ? "

"Do you see this stick of mine with the horn on the end ? When Aldo is around every man scratches his forehead to see if any horns have sprouted in the night, and if he is wise he keeps his wife under lock and key."

"Who is the plump girl—is she his wife ? "

"Not on your life. That is Susanna—a whore on holiday. She has her ticket in Naples."

"Who are the two fellows who look as if they would cut my throat for a lira ? "

"Those are Riccardo and Edoardo. We always call them the twins, but they are not even related. They are never separate. They do odd jobs in the port—just enough to keep body and soul together, but most of the day you'll see them lying asleep near the pier. As a matter of fact, Riccardo is the more helpless of the two. He never makes up his mind but leaves every decision to his younger companion, Edoardo. Edoardo plans everything while he lies on the stones with his hat over his eyes, and Riccardo then goes into ecstasy over his friend's genius for *la combinazione*. They never do much more than plan, for the days are too hot and the nights are too cold, and a hungry belly saps a man's ambition. So with a shrug of the shoulders they lie down again and snore to their hearts' content."

The hunchback would have continued to enlighten me still further concerning the personal characteristics of the company, when old Leda shuffled up to me and said with a wheezy cackle :

"You haven't paid your share of the *cena*."

" What does she mean ? " said I to Cesare. " I thought you were doing all the paying."

" Yes, my friend," replied the hunchback, " but here there is something to pay extra for the establishment. It's worth paying a handful of money to keep that old hag's mouth shut. She has the *malocchio* and she'd wither you while you were sleeping."

I paid under protest some of my hidden reserves, with the feeling that I was standing the meal for the whole company. From the way everybody wolfed his food, I inferred that there had been lean days. Nobody spoke, and the room resounded with the clicking of jaws and the crunching of teeth. When the first pangs of hunger had disappeared, the swash-buckling Aldo stretched out his legs, picked his teeth with a match, and called for wine.

" There's no wine," said Leda crustily.

" No wine ? " replied Aldo, casting up his eyes in amazement. " Is this a Christian house ? Surely we must toast the stranger," said he, leering at me.

The old woman hobbled over to me, saying : " Hand us a few lire : we want to drink your health."

I paid, and the old woman brought out a bottle of very watered wine, from which she filled the glasses.

The wine loosened the tongues. Conversation became a series of anecdotes from each in turn. Susanna described her life in the purlieus of Naples, making the rest roar with laughter at her grotesque mimicry of the clients who visited her house. Adamo told blood-curdling tales of his life in the underworld of Rio de Janeiro, Pernambuco, and Santos. Edoardo argued with Aldo about the Social Revolution which was coming in Italy, and called him a " Mafiuso."

" Of course I'm a Mafiuso," retorted Aldo with a grin.

" What would happen to us down here if we hadn't the Mafia ? "

" The Mafia is the curse of the country," said Cesare.

" Rubbish," replied Aldo. " What would any of you do without the organization of the Mafia ? Every one of us is powerless as an individual : we don't count the snap of a finger while we walk alone, but when we combine together and create our own secret organization, we can shake the world. The Mafia is the friend of the poor : it protects us against the landowners and the capitalists who would grind us to powder. A Mafiuso with a knife up my sleeve—that's what I am, and I'm proud of it."

As he said these words he puffed out his chest and glared round at the rest of the company.

" That's the sort of man I like to meet of an evening," said Susanna with a giggle. She then put her arms round Aldo's neck and rested her head on his shoulder. Aldo pushed her away roughly, saying : " And I know how to keep women in their place too : they can't get round me with any soft talk."

The rest of the evening we spent in making arrangements. Cesare said that we should take Aldo and Susanna with us as partners.

" I don't like it," said I. " As far as I can see, I am the poor fool in this business. That fellow Aldo is too tough-looking a customer for me, and as for Susanna —what womanly accomplishments has she except the oldest one in the world ? "

" You haven't seen her dance with Aldo," said he coaxingly. " The two of them can dance tarantellas, habaneras, fandangos, till Kingdom come. Aldo is a decent fellow except when he gets in a temper—then I admit he treats women rough."

It was settled that we should all set out together the following morning on our trek towards Reggio.

Now I had not forgotten my romantic-travel personality. When I arrived in Cotrone I was determined to reach, by hook or by crook, the Lacinian promontory, for there stands in lonely majesty the single column of the temple of Hera, which once had been one of Greece's most hallowed shrines. The difficulty was to persuade the hunchback, who looked with scorn upon my pilgrimages in search of history. However, while the company were engaged in fierce argument, I managed to slip silently out of the room and down into the street like a flash. I tramped the eight miles along the low cliffs following the rough track. After passing a graveyard, I reached the little harbour of Porto Berlinghiere, and then mounted steep cliffs over the sea. Luckily the moon was shining brightly, and I could see where I was walking ; but once or twice, as I negotiated the rocky path, I was so dizzy that I nearly slipped and fell over the precipice into the sea below. After passing the deep valley which is called " La Fossa del Lupo " (the wolf's lair), and ploughing through some undergrowth, I reached the head of the promontory, and there before me in the moonlight rose the lonely column of Hera's temple.

Nothing else that I had seen in my travels gave me such a vivid impression of the sad majesty of that Greek world which has faded away. That lonely column brings the whole of ancient Greece before one's memory. On this promontory, the legends tell us, Hercules landed and founded the temple. Other legends describe its foundation to Thetis, who gave it to Hera, and every year the women of Crotona used to come here as suppliants to mourn the death of her son, Achilles. Virgil, in the Æneid, describes the temple as standing when

Æneas sailed past. In the ancient world the whole headland was a sanctuary and sacred flocks rambled in the valley, which was called in later times the wolf's lair. In the heyday of Crotonian supremacy, the temple was the holiest sanctuary of Magna Græcia—so full of splendour that it tempted the sore-pressed Hannibal to loot its treasures after the Second Punic War. Before I took leave of it, I thought of the mystic philosopher, Pythagoras, who tried to establish a Utopia here at Croton. Pythagoras, like so many of the great men who led the Italian race, was an idealist. He believed in founding an aristocracy of individuals who would educate the populace, and so he became at Croton a great moral reformer, preaching the joys of hard work and the simple life. His fate was the same as that of many leaders who have tried to better humanity. His followers were butchered by the populace, and he was driven out to die in exile at Metapontum.

While I was resting on a rock, gazing out at the silver sea, a fisherman paused to talk with me of the *capo nau*, as he called it. " Over there," said he, " is the shrine of the Madonna."

" What Madonna ? "

" The Madonna of the Cape : she protects the ships that pass. If you were here on a Saturday, you would see the *le verginelle* like white fairies coming over the cliffs."

" Who are the *verginelle* ? "

" They are young maidens of Cotrone. My own daughter was one of them. They dress in white and come barefooted in procession, from the town to yonder shrine of Our Lady."

I thought of those girls in white, singing as they come over the rocks, following the same path as those ancient Greek maidens, suppliants of Hera.

CHAPTER XIV

MUMMERS

WHEN I returned to my lodgings I found the hunchback fuming. " Where have you been ? " said he : " we thought you had been spirited away by the *folletto rosso*."

" I tramped out to the Column," said I.

" What in heaven's name for ? "

" To pray to the Madonna of the Cape for guidance. I'm thinking I'll need it badly with the lot of you."

" Aldo and Susanna have gone off with Adamo. We have to meet them near Cutro, where the tribe is resting."

Just outside the village of Cutro, we came across the familiar tents. Adamo entertained us royally, and as for his wife, she greeted me as a long-lost friend. Nevertheless I had to draw still further upon my meagre reserves of money, in order to give a festive air, as Cesare said, to our alfresco banquet. It was a gay scene. I can still visualize us lolling beneath olive-trees near the three brown tents. The two donkeys were browsing peacefully beside the carts, and various ragged children darted here and there, rolling and turning somersaults. It was a joy to pull out fiddles, guitars, and mandolines, and play tunes in friendly rivalry. Aldo sang in a high falsetto voice street songs he had picked up in his rambles, and every few moments he would stop singing suddenly, spring up like a Jack-in-the-box, and twist his lithe body into incredible shapes. Then he would take Susanna aside and teach her new steps in dancing, abusing her roundly when her portly frame did not respond to the rhythm which he kept beating with a stick upon a stone. Next day, on leaving Adamo and the tribe, we set to work in earnest. Our intention was to make for the mountain town of Catanzaro, capital of the province, where, according to the hunchback, there was plenty of money. At Catanzaro Marina, a modern seaside resort, Cesare and I gave a performance on our own, for Aldo and Susanna had gone above to Catanzaro city to prospect and arrange our future shows. In two hours of playing in the sweltering heat we made six lire. The funicular train led us into one of Nature's paradises. Every kind of fruit flourishes in such profusion that Gissing called the land around Catanzaro, the Gardens of the Hesperides. After so many days of heat and squalor, it was a relief to inhale mountain breezes, and see men and women resembling North Italians in vigour and hardiness. The city was built upon a mountain spur, from which we could gaze down upon a rich valley undulating towards the sea. It was Robert Guiscard, the great Norman, who made Catanzaro into the strongest fortress in Calabria, and the ruins of his castle lie to-day within a vast garden.

One of the citizens in describing the past, said to me : " In those days it was *la città dei tre V—Venti, Velluti, e nostro santo protettore, San Vitaliano* " (the city of the three V's—wind, velvet, and our patron-saint, Vitaliano). As late as the seventeenth century the warehouses of Catanzaro were filled to overflowing, and its merchants were known throughout Europe. But in 1668 a terrible plague struck it and reduced it to ruin. " It was not the plague, however," said the citizen, " that laid Catanzaro low, with a succession of devastating earthquakes, which shook it to its foundations." As a result, Catanzaro to-day is a modern-built town, perched perilously on the edge of the precipice as if it wished to defy the next earthquake to do its worst. When I looked out of the window of our lodgings, I seemed to be poised in mid-air over the valley thousands of feet below.

By the time we arrived in Catanzaro, Aldo had made all the preparations for our performance. He had settled with the police authorities, fixed the open space where we were to play, bribed loungers to do publicity work for us, so that when we started our show there was a good sprinkling of people present. He had fixed four sticks with small lanterns at the top to mark out the stage, and the people stood round, forming a big ring. After introducing us, Aldo did various acrobatic tricks : he got Cesare to tie him up with chains, from which, with cat-like skill, he managed to extricate himself. Then he did juggling tricks, and imitated skilfully the clucking of a hen, the quacking of a duck, the grunting of a pig, and the braying of an ass. This last part of his turn was enthusiastically applauded by the younger members of the audience. Cesare and I then did our duet performance—all I had to do was to play what I was told, for the hunchback kept the audience amused by his ceaseless patter and his gags. Cesare's hump excited vociferous laughter, and many were the exclamations : " Let me touch your hump for luck.—I've got a lottery ticket here, let me rub it on.—Come here, hunchback, tell me the numbers you dreamt last night and I'll sell my shirt to buy them."

A couple of women made remarks about Cesare's squint : " Don't come near me, old squint-eye.—You've got the evil eye.—You should be packed out of the town before we all fall sick."

After we had finished our combative performance,

Aldo took the floor again, this time with Susanna. Both
of them did a tarantella, followed by a fandango, and a
jota. Then he said to the audience : " Now I'm going
to work a magic spell upon you all."

" Lord bless us ! " said an old woman near me : " I'm
afraid with this old squint-eyed hunchback present.
This is witchcraft and the devil must be in it."

She blessed herself, and gazed with still more interest
at the stage. Aldo made Susanna sit down on a chair
and throw back her head. After making various passes
with his hands over her eyes, saying that he was hypnotizing her, he blindfolded her. He then took up a piece of
paper and asked her what was written on it, and she
straightway recited it in a sing-song voice. The audience
were amazed, and I heard the old woman near me mutter :
" It's wicked magic : the devil is in it, I'm sure." But
she did not slacken her attention. Aldo made great
play with his hypnotizing stunt : he asked for letters
and papers from people in the audience, whose contents
Susanna might declare. Then when excitement was at
its height, he interrupted the performance, saying :
" To-morrow at the same hour we shall continue our
magic performance." He then pretended to raise
Susanna from her hypnotic trance, and while I was
playing to the hunchback's mandoline accompaniment,
he passed round the ring with a little wooden tray for
money.

Such was our first collective performance. Day after
day we gave such shows, not only in Catanzaro, but in
most of the towns and villages on the way to Reggio.
It was a wearisome and monotonous life, for I felt
that we were all slaves of the imperious Aldo. He was
impresario, manager, first tenor, prima donna, money-
collector—all in one. I have never met anybody more
tyrannical. We were mere pawns in his game, and we

had to sink all our individuality in order to contribute to his glory. " What we want," he cried, " is co-operation : we must sink our individuality for the good of all." My feelings of rebellion grew apace when I discovered Aldo's method of sharing the money. When we retired to our lodgings, full of eager expectancy, Aldo would come in a little later and hand each of us his supposed share. Then a fierce quarrel would break out between Aldo, Susanna, and the hunchback. The quarrel would mount in a gradual crescendo to a climax, when Aldo would suddenly adopt a fighting pose, saying that his honour had been touched. When he was in that mood, he would beat Susanna and reduce her to floods of tears. Then he would go for the hunchback, threatening to cut his throat, and Cesare would slink into a corner without a word. As for me, I adopted a passive attitude, and remained timidly on the outskirts of those violent scenes. It did not matter to me how much I got, for I knew that before the day was out I should have to supplement the common treasury out of my own reserve funds. The first to break the partnership was Susanna. When we reached Reggio she disappeared suddenly before a show, and though Aldo searched high and low, he could not find her. Later on in the evening I saw her laughing and joking with a man of the commercial traveller type in a café. She had forsworn the Bohemian life and returned to her old profession.

As for me, I was determined to escape from bondage too, for I wished to visit Sicily, but not in company of Aldo. I was sorry to say farewell to the hunchback, for we had wandered through the whole length of Calabria—sleeping, working, and breaking bread as brothers—without a quarrel. And that is saying a great deal when Romany and Gorgio travel together.

And so, leaving a note for the hunchback, to say that I was going back by train to Taranto, I slipped out of the house early in the morning when everyone was sleeping, and made for the pier at Reggio, where I took the little steamer for Messina.

CHAPTER XV

RITUAL OF THE TRAMP

THE last part of my journey through Calabria had been a preparation for Sicily, for from the moment I rounded Cape Spartivento I saw before me, across the blue Ionian Sea, the unbroken outline of " snowy Ætna, nurse of endless frost, the prop of heaven," as Pindar called her. That distant outline with smoke issuing from its white crest became an obsession. No matter where I happened to be, my thoughts would fly away to that mountain, which artists have compared to Fujiyama. I got into the habit of looking out for it at particular hours of the day. At sunrise, when the red beams touched the snowy crest with pink ; at midday, when the sea rippled with gold and a slight haze hid the distant presence ; at eventide, when its dark blue mass began to recede into the dusk. Calabria became my initiation into the Greek world of Sicily. Even the language of the tall, handsome peasants of the settlements that cling to the crags of Aspromonte —" the Bitter Mountain of the Storms "—seemed to my ears to be the language of ancient Greece. It is, as scholars tell us, modern Greek, affected by the dialects of Italy, but with scarcely a trace of Turkish or Slavonic words. In Squillace, Bova, and Ammendolea, one still could meet peasants who prided themselves on their Greek ancestry, and called themselves " Greci," even though they ignored the significance of Greater Greece.

In Bova, I bought, from a little peasant girl, some of the most fragrant honey I have ever tasted. It had the aroma of all the wild flowers I had seen growing on the mountains ; and as I savoured it I gazed, from the rocky ledge where I was sitting, at Ætna, thinking of the beehives of Sicilian Hybla. The Greek Calabrians love bees as they were loved by the idyllic poets, and they say of a kindly and helpful man that he has the heart of a bee.

As we sped over the blue sea, my thoughts turned to Scylla, the castellated rock on the mainland, and Charybdis, the whirlpool, but I was rudely awakened from my meditations by a seedy-looking individual who insisted on attaching himself to me with the air of a proprietor.

" Tedesco ? " said he.

" No," said I.

" Austriaco ? "

" No."

" Français ? "

I shook my head.

" Engleesh-Americano," said he with a cry of triumph.

Seeing that I did not contradict him, he continued rapidly : " Sure ! I know you American—I go to America—I work on ze roads—I save money in ze God-damned country—I tired working for ze God-damned sons of bitches—I come home to Sicily. In Sicily many Americans—much money."

As he said these words he made an expressive gesture with finger and thumb, signifying the tip, before he continued his lingo.

" You American—I understand people. I show you Messina—earthquake, churches—I be your guide."

I already saw myself bound, gagged, and delivered over to my tormentor for the rest of the day, so I answered him in Italian, saying that I was not Inglese or Americano, but an honest to God Genoese from Zena

(I took care to add in a few telling phrases in the dialect), and that I was absolutely broke, hadn't a *palanca* nor a clean shirt, nor the prospects of finding a roof to shelter me. The fellow gave a whistle of surprise and lost further interest in me.

I stayed one day in Messina, more for the sake of adding to my financial resources than for sight-seeing. There was precious little to see in Messina, anyhow, for the city had never recovered from the terrible earthquake of the 28th December 1908.

On that day at 5.20 a.m. [Baedeker informs us], the destructive shock took place and lasted for thirty-two seconds. The disturbance of the ocean bed was followed by a tidal wave, which added to the disaster in the lower-lying portions of the coast ; it reached the height of 6–10 feet at Messina, and 11½ feet at Reggio. The damage to life and property caused by the earthquake was greatest at Messina and Reggio, both of which were simply wiped out. At Messina the coast has sunk twenty-six inches, at Reggio twenty-one inches. About ninety-six thousand lives were lost, an appalling total never exceeded in any disaster of the kind since the Syrian earthquake of A.D. 526, in which one hundred and twenty thousand persons are said to have perished. The Sicilian earthquake in 1693 had about fifty-seven thousand victims, that in Calabria in 1783 about thirty thousand. The damage to property is estimated at one hundred and sixty-five million francs.[1]

Baedeker announced in 1912 that it had been resolved to rebuild the town on its former site, but very little had been done when I visited it in 1919. When the traveller leaves the harbour, which is one of the best in Europe, and still carries on extensive shipping traffic, he passes huge camps of wooden barracks in which the present inhabitants squat. The countless shacks made me think of a mushroom town which had sprung up in the night during a gold-rush. The sight of Messina was an index to the mentality of the people. When I compare the

[1] K. Baedeker, *Southern Italy and Sicily*, London, 1912.

Sicilian with the South Italian, I find that the latter expressed the thoughts and impulses that bubble up within him in a wealth of gestures and gesticulations. The Sicilian, on the other hand, is more of a fatalist, and there is in him a certain gravity of demeanour which we associate with the Arabs. How can the Sicilian help being a fatalist when he sees around him the debris of such a disaster as the earthquake of 1908 ? Nature, the Steward of God, gave him a paradise to dwell in, but in compensation, to convince him of the vanity of all that beauty, God, with one fell blow, laid it in ruins about him.

I have rarely seen greater hosts of hobos than those which welcome the lonely traveller in Messina. I arrived in the city on a Saturday, hence the number of arrogant beggars, for Saturday in Sicily is the day of charity. I was told that it was the custom for shop-keepers to distribute centesimi to the habitual mendicants—the *divuteddi*, as they call them in the island. A *divuteddu*, as far as I could make out, is a professional beggar who goes at the stated times to demand his salary, mind you, not charity by the grace of God. A few days in Messina convinced me that most of the other days of the week are considered sacred by the ragged confraternity. On Sunday, after Mass, it is very unlucky to refuse charity, or, as the beggar puts it, " to help the dear dead by a charitable action on earth." Tuesday is sacred to the souls of those who have been condemned, and so is Friday. Wednesday would be a very unhappy day to let slip without giving charity in honour of its patron, Saint Joseph, for he is called the Father of Providence, and provides for all material and moral wants. On Thursday, charity must be given in honour of the Blessed Sacrament, and finally, on Saturday, who would refuse the woman in a shawl with a scrofulous baby in her arms, who begs a coin in honour of Mary, the mother of all grace. That leaves only Monday when a man may stick his chin out and rap out, with a viperish expression, the words : " Via ! niente ! "

The Sicilians enrich their everyday speech in dialect by picturesque epithets and metaphors. A beggar will say to you, as he holds his hand out for alms : " I'm hungry : my belly's like a lantern." A woman will point to her eyes red with weeping, saying : " My eyes are like prunes "—that is to say, red with crying. A man of poor spirit is accused of having a neck like a stork, but if he is a daredevil his admiring companions say that he has seven spirits like cats. In Messina, according to Pitré, when the wags see a scraggy, skinny girl pass by, they say : " She has no bottom and no breasts like the saints of Reggio." Ask a peasant how he is getting on, and he will reply, shrugging his shoulders : " Slow and hugging the coast like the ships from Cefalù," meaning so-so or poorly. The proverbial phrase originated in the little coal-boats plying between the ports on the Northern coast. When a quarrel breaks out among Sicilians it becomes a contest as to which of the rivals possesses the most imaginative vocabulary. First a few spirited rounds of the following :

" May you have an earthquake."

" May you have an attack of diarrhœa ! "

" By and by, say the English ; you'll soon see ! "

" I'll make you see green flies ! "

The world has never yet seen green flies, nor has it ever seen such vengeance as the irate speaker will wreak upon his rival. Then we come to the more breathless, scarifying threats which work up to the climax of the tongue-fight :

" I'll make you bite the devil's paps."

" I'll leather you until the devil cries : Hail Mary."

A footsore traveller jogging through the Sicilian countryside in 1919 did well to learn off the *scongiuri* collected by Pitré, the celebrated folklorist, and others from the mouth of tramps, witches, and quacks.

Every illness has its own special exorcism which must be pronounced according to ritual. Generally it is Saint Joseph who is the great curer of all ills. But the women must be careful not to laugh at him, as is shown by the following *scongiuro* which is recited by women when they are breast-feeding their infants :

> Saint Joseph stood on the balcony ;
> Three maidens passed on their way to the well.
> " Why do you laugh at my beard," says he,
> " Is it making a joke of me you are ?
> A hair off my beard on your breasts I'll throw,
> and not a wink of sleep you'll get,
> nor a drop of milk from your breasts will flow."
> " Mother, help us," cry the girls, " we're laughing no more,
> we'll make no joke of your flowing beard."
> " If that is the case you'll be able to rest,
> and milk for your children in plenty you'll press."

The woman who follows the ritual must, after repeating the spell, pretend to comb her breast. Occasionally Saint Joseph the wizard finds a rival in some strange, deformed character who wanders round the villages working magic spells. Dwarfs, especially, are credited with supernatural powers, because it is an old belief that in their infancy they were fairy changelings. The following exorcism is an invocation to an old dwarf called Citranu—a word that is a corruption of the word *gitano*, or Gypsy. It is one of the best Gypsy spells I have heard, and it should be recited in a submissive tone :

> The old Gypsy tramps the world :
> three hands long he was
> three hands long his beard.
> Two women pass by to the washing-trough.

They laughed and they laughed
and they mocked the Gypsy dwarf.
Says he : " Is it laughin' ye are
mockin' and makin' a jeer o' me ?
May ye die stone dead yerselves and the child
for a hair off this beard o' mine."
And the women cried :
" We're laughin' no more
nor mockin' nor jeerin'."
Cried the dwarf :
" Since ye're laughin' no more
nor mockin' nor jeerin'
here's a hair off me beard,
'twill comfort yerselves and the child.

There is no need to fear malaria in Sicily, if one carries
about a *scongiuro* against the disease, for in the opinion
of many country people, such a charm is worth all the
quinine tablets in the hospital.   But there is quite a complicated ritual in exorcising malaria : first of all, we must
call a woman who is known to be an experienced curer,
for malaria, in popular belief, is caused by witchcraft.
As soon as she approaches the sick person, she takes a
cup of water, dissolves salt in it, and asperges the house
with its contents.   Then she makes a little cross of palm
leaves and puts it on his chest, reciting, as she does so,
a credo.   She also drops on the sick man's feet some
leaves, saying :

" I salute you bread and boxwood !
Here I leave both hot and cold ;
I lighten his head,
I burden his feet,
So health returns to him again."

She then recites the first part of an Ave Maria, while
the women of the house reply with the second part in
chorus.   The next part of the ritual consists in burning
dry herbs and incense in the middle of the room,

and when the smoke rises, the witch uncovers her breasts, throws herself face downwards on the floor, and recites in chorus with the others the following magic exorcism :

" Ti toccu e nun ti toccu !
Ti viju e nun ti viju !
Furcu, befurcu, lurcu, cataturcu !
Ti curcu, ti sturcu, ti 'nfurcu
Cu acqua e sali
E 'ncenzu chi la virtù havi.
Pri li chiaghi di Gesù, non cci accusentu !
E 'ncenzu e sali e acqua ogni mumentu !
Dintra la fossa
Li luti e li scrizzati vilinenti :
Sutta li denti
Ti strudinu l'ossa ! "

(" I touch you and I don't touch you !
I see you and I don't see you !
Gibbet, tibbet, flibberty-gibbet !
I lay you, flay you, betray you
with water and salt
and incense which injures.
By the wounds of Jesus, I don't approve !
Incense and salt and water at every moment !
Down in the grave
are worms and poisonous lice ;
between their teeth
they gnaw your bones ! ")

Every village in Sicily possesses a wealth of this folk-magic, which has been transmitted down the centuries from generation to generation. On my journeys by foot, I learnt how to say Saint Julian's Paternoster, which is the surest protection a traveller can have against misfortunes on the road. But I also learnt, off by heart, the most useful *scongiuro* against being bitten by wild dogs. More than once on the way from Messina to Taormina I recited it, holding in one hand a flat stone :

> " St. Vito, St. Vito,
> I call you three times,
> I call you for those dogs
> who want to bite me.
> Tie their muzzles
> with a red rag,
> tie their flanks
> with a white rag."

With the help of Saint Vito I arrived at my destination without mishap. It is a fortunate country that has such a rich calendar of Saints, eager to help us mortals.

CHAPTER XVI

THE VEIL OF SAINT AGATHA

AFTER Messina, my next halting-place was Taormina. It was not desire for gain that made me stop there, but sentiment ; for from the heights of Taormina one may see the most beautiful panorama in Sicily. Taormina is a peerless watch-tower ; it is poised upon a mountain-ridge, from which one may gaze at majestic, snow-crowned Ætna. The finest view of the volcano is obtained from the celebrated ruins of the Greek theatre, which cling to a ledge above the town. Many travellers climb up with the intention of visiting this theatre in detail, for has it not preserved almost complete its proscenium and back wall of the stage ? But no sooner have their eyes caught a glimpse of the incomparable vista of mountain, sea, and Riviera than all thoughts of Greek or Roman antiquities disappear, and the blear-eyed guide is left to mumble his message to deaf ears.

I have seen many different kinds of traveller arrive in Taormina—idle travellers, lying travellers, proud, vain, and splenetic travellers—but no sooner do they mount to the Greek theatre in face of Ætna than all their eccentricities disappear, and they become nothing but Lotos-eating travellers. Taormina should be let out by the Italian Government as an open-air asylum for Anglo-Saxons who live their lives according to the adage " Time is money." It would soon cure their restless

efficiency. Nobody ever looks at a clock in Taormina ;
and as for money—who needs it in summer-time in
Sicily ? Sardines, olives, juicy *nespole* or medlar fruits,
are enough sustenance for one who has tasted Lotos.
It is curious to note how even the moral character of
North Europeans seems to change in this fantastic scene.
People who in England are proud of their puritanical
conduct, find their frosty virtue thawing away under the
influence of Vulcan, or is it his wife, Venus ? That at
least was the opinion of two Danish spinster friends of
mine at Taormina—living in a villa just below the main
street of the town. The elder one I called Miss Hetty,
the younger, Miss Julia. Both of them had originally
come to Taormina in search of sunlight, for they were
delicate. They intended to stay a few weeks and recuperate, but the months had followed the weeks, and now
they had been established in the town twenty-five years.
" That is what happens to so many people who visit
Taormina," said Miss Hetty ; " they go up to the Greek
theatre in the early morning and gaze at the panorama
of Ætna, the lemon groves, and the blue sea, saying to
themselves : ' I wonder what it all looks like at midday.'
Then at midday they murmur : ' Very beautiful ; but
I am sure it is even more wonderful at sunset.' When
sunset comes they linger in ecstasy, waiting for the
sudden dusk and the gradual rise of the moon which
will transform the golden panorama into a nocturne of
silver. Once Ætna has hypnotized their soul, there is
no escape : they become so intoxicated by this scene of
Paradise that they have no thoughts for the world of
daily tasks."

" Scores of artists," interrupted Miss Julia, " have
come here intending to paint great pictures, but the eye
of Ætna burns up their canvases. Go up at any hour
of the day to the Greek theatre and you will find artists

sketching. They start full of energy, but little by little
the landscape bewitches them and saps their will-
power."

The villa of the two Danish sisters was a watch-tower,
from which they were able to spy the land : nothing
escaped their notice : nobody passed unperceived. At
the back of the villa they had a big sloping old-fashioned
garden—a wilderness of wild shrubs and plants with
shady walks beneath medlar trees, and there the two little
old ladies would walk up and down, talking broken
Italian in high-pitched voices. They looked upon me
as an incorrigible nomad. On one occasion I stayed a
few days in their villa with a friend I had known in the
Y.M.C.A. On another occasion I arrived late at night
and played a tune outside their door, as a beggarly
minstrel. But Miss Hetty's hawk eye recognized me
at once, and instead of tossing me a coin or two, she
insisted on feeding and lodging me for the night. " You
should be ashamed of yourself," said she to me, " a
young man like you has no right to be gadding around
scooping up pennies : you'll become a waster like most
of those foreigners who come here."

" Yes, Miss Hetty," said I, " if I stay any longer here
I'll become a Lotos-eater, so I'm moving off to-morrow
to Catania."

And while Miss Hetty adopted the severely maternal
tone with me, Miss Julia would look up at me with her
large romantic eyes, and question me in detail on my
ramblings. I can never think of Taormina, perched on
a spur of Ætna, without thinking of those two quaint
little Nordic women in their watch-tower villa with its
old-fashioned garden. Although they are patriotic
Danes, and for ever in their conversation laying stress
on the superiority of Nordic to Latin civilization, yet
I do not believe that they would leave the slopes of

Ætna, even if the King of Denmark were to offer them the palace in Copenhagen.

After leaving Taormina I passed the Castello di Schisò, which stands above the ruins of Naxos, the first Greek city in Sicily. A lemon grove rises to-day above the site of the sanctuary of Apollo Archagetes, where the Greek envoys used to offer sacrifice on their return from Hellas. On the journey to Catania I passed various ancient lava streams, which were a reminder of Ætna's sinister power. In one place I came to a huge chestnut tree called the " Chestnut of the Hundred Horses," which, the peasants told me, was the oldest tree in the world. It was so called because once a Queen of Aragon took refuge beneath its branches with a hundred of her knights. As I rested near the chestnut of the Hundred Horses I thought of Dionysius, tyrant of Syracuse, who built his fleet from the brothers and sisters of this ancient tree. So large was its trunk that it appears to me like the Yggdrasil or World Ash of the Edda, in whose shades the gods held their court and whose sap conferred immortality. At Aci Castello the Middle Ages and Greek antiquity join hands, for at one moment one gazes upon the flowering land devoted to the myth of the nymph Galatea, beloved by the Cyclops Polyphemus; at another, the romance of Sicily becomes embodied in the Castle of the Norman Roger de Loria, where he resisted the power of Frederick II in 1297. Off the coast are the rocks which the infuriated Cyclops hurled at the escaping Ulysses.

After such picturesque scenes, Catania comes as a disappointment. No more guide-books for the present, said I to myself—earthquakes and eruptions have seen to that. Catania is a populous modern city without any temptations for the inquisitive historical traveller. " But you have forgotten Saint Agatha," said an Italian friend of mine. " No matter how modern and go-ahead Catania becomes, its citizens still have Saint Agatha to give a touch of old-world romance to their prosaic lives." No less a person than King Richard the Lion-hearted gave a crown to that Saint, whose name is glorified in the most ancient Martyrologies. Every day her name is mentioned in the Canon of the Mass. Fortunatus put her amongst the most illustrious of virgins : St. Ambrose spoke of her with highest eulogy : Methodius, Patriarch of Constantinople, celebrated her in a panegyric in the ninth century. So glorious was she that both Palermo and Catania disputed the honour of having cradled her, and, in 1534, a great law case was held at Rome to decide which of the two cities gave her birth. In the end Rome decided that the victory should be given to neither, and in the Breviary it was stated that the two cities laid claim to the Saint. In any case, Catanians were able to claim more miracles of the Saint in their favour. They could claim that Frederick II, when he wished to destroy Catania which had revolted against him, took up a prayer-book to aid his delibera-tions. But when he opened it he found nothing written but the following : " Do not do injury to the country of Agatha ; she would avenge it." Frederick, being convinced that Agatha was protecting her own city, contented himself with building a citadel there.

The story of Agatha deserves to be remembered. She was as beautiful as she was wealthy ; and Quintian, the Prefect of Sicily under the Emperor Decius, resolved to corrupt her. So he arrested her and gave her into the hands of a debauched woman called Aphrodisia, who trafficked in women's dishonour. Agatha refused to imitate her evil example, and when the Governor threat-ened her with torture she cried out that she feared nothing. " If you expose me to the wild beasts," said she, " the name of Jesus Christ will tame them ; if you throw me into the fire the angels will quench the flames with dew, for I have in me the Holy Ghost which enables me to despise all torment."

Then the Governor ordered one of her breasts to be torn off ; but at night in her cell St. Peter appeared, and with a single word restored it to her. The Governor, seeing that she was still obstinate, rolled her naked over burning coals, but all of a sudden a terrible earthquake took place, killing two friends of Quintian and rocking the town of Catania to its foundations. Agatha, at last, in response to her prayers, died, and was buried by the people with great honour. Both Jews and Gentiles respected her tomb, but Quintian's rage against the saint grew, and he determined to confiscate her wealth. When he was escaping in a boat, two horses jumped at him, bit him and kicked him into the River Simæthus. Then Ætna erupted and the lava began to descend upon the doomed city. The people rushed to the tomb of the saint to implore her protection, and taking the veil which covered it, they held it out as a protection against the flaming streams of lava, which thereupon suddenly ceased. This took place on the 5th of February, the day of St. Agatha, and ever since, the veil of St. Agatha is recognized by the Catanians as the supreme protection against the devastations of Vulcan.

As far as I was concerned, the veil of St. Agatha, instead of protecting me, led me into the only quarrel I had in Catania. We were in a bar and one of my companions, a saddler from the neighbourhood, was replying to my queries concerning St. Agatha's powers when he was interrupted by an arrogant youth who was dressed in a greasy navy blue suit of clothes and a crimson muffler tied tightly round his neck.

" Cut out St. Agatha," said he in a rasping voice.

" She's as dead as a door-nail. It is time such stuff and nonsense was driven out of men's heads. There's too much superstition in this bloody island of ours."

My companion, the saddler, drew himself up proudly, saying :

" You're not a good Sicilian or you wouldn't talk that way. St. Agatha has always been a good patroness to this city, and anyhow, who are you to talk ? "

" I know what I'm saying," replied the other hotly. " St. Agatha is good enough for priest-ridden fellows like you, but I tell you the War has changed things. You can't deceive the poor devils all the time. The curse of this country has been religion and the black plague of priests. They find it easier to keep their hold over the men and women of Sicily with their St. Joseph, St. Agatha, and the whole crew of wizards and charmers. ' Have you got the Evil Eye ? ' says one. ' St. Lucy will cure you if you say a prayer to her. Look at her. She has her eyes on a plate. Have you got a belly-ache ? St. Joseph will touch you with his white lily provided you say ten Hail Marys. Do you want a good harvest ? St. Cosmo and Damian will give you plenty, provided you say your prayers and pay a fat fee to the priest.' To Hell with the whole lot of them," say I. " All they do is to trick us and throw up a smoke-screen to prevent us seeing the truth."

" Look here, sir," said he, turning to me eagerly, " the fact of the matter is that we're all starving down here. And yet it will be the devil to get the people to rise up and demand their rights. They've no more spunk in them. If they would only realize what their life would be if they put away worn-out superstitions and fairy-tales that are good enough for a nurse to sing as she nurses a child to sleep."

The saddler then interrupted the revolutionary outburst, calling the youth Bolshevist, international agent, with the addition of a host of epithets. The arrogant youth continued to pour out a flood of oratory in a still louder tone. The saddler drew himself up proudly, saying :

" I have done my share in the War, anyhow. I was no imboscato."

" You were cannon fodder, like the rest of us," said the youth. " Cannon fodder of the capitalists, who made the War. What had any of the Italian workers to do with the War, anyhow? What business was it of ours to fight and kill the workers of other countries ? What we want is Communism, Russian Communism which would put an end to all wars and give us and the proletariat a right share in the products of our own work. 'Viva Russia,' say I, and I am not ashamed of it."

The quarrel had now grown to bigger proportions. Suddenly, the saddler, without saying a word, lunged across at the hot-headed youth and struck him, saying :

" Take that, you Communist cur. We didn't fight for three years to hear such talk on our return from the Piave."

Then pandemonium broke out. The youth sprang at the saddler and various champions sprang to their feet on both sides. I hovered gingerly on the outskirts of the crowd to see what would happen. All of a sudden the owner of the tavern bore down on the quarrellers, accompanied by three pale-faced young men of serious, efficient appearance. One of them called the saddler by name, saying something to him in a low voice. He and his supporters immediately stopped fighting and stood by sheepishly, as though waiting for further orders from the imperious young men. They then turned to the youth in the red muffler, took him by the shoulders

and literally pushed him out into the street, saying :
" We heard what you said and we have your name
checked off. Mind your step, for we know where to
get you."

The youth with a muffled curse slunk off into the night.

It was no uncommon occurrence in those days of 1919
to find oneself pitch-forked into the midst of violent
political quarrels. There was suspicion everywhere.
All through the towns of South Italy there was talk of
revolution, and those who felt most disillusioned were
the ex-service men who had returned to their homes.
They felt under the immediate necessity of banding
themselves together to resist the influx of foreign revolutionary ideas which had transformed the Italy they had
known before they went to fight.

CHAPTER XVII

SICILIAN TRIPTYCH

As one that for a weary space has lain
Lulled by the song of Circe and her wine
In gardens near the pale of Proserpine.

L OOKING back upon my wanderings in Sicily after
the War, I try to capture again that sense of
wonder which I felt as I visited, one after another,
the cities sanctified by ancient Greece. In recent years
Sicily has received the benefits of modern civilization,
and she extends a generous welcome to every kind of
traveller. But in 1919 there was an atmosphere of unrest
in the island : in every town I came to I heard the same
piteous tale of national disillusionment. " Italy has won
the War, but we Italians are no better off down here than
if we had lost it," was a phrase I heard repeatedly. At
the same time I noticed in the Sicilians, high and low, an
Italian national spirit. In every village, for example,
the subject of Fiume was discussed daily in the cafés,
and D'Annunzio was no less a hero in the town of Noto
in Southern Sicily than he was in Venice. How shall
I describe the national Sicilian type ? It is difficult,
because in an island which has been a meeting-place of
races we find a great variety of human traits. There is
in the Sicilian, as in the Andalusian, a great deal of Arab
solemnity as a background to Italian vivacity. We have
only to listen to the villagers singing their national songs
to note that vein of oriental seriousness which is part of

their character. Very often, as in Calabria, I met the
Greek type—small, bright-eyed, fair-skinned—but there
were fewer of them in comparison to the bronzed Berber
type with thin, wrinkled faces and lithe bodies. It is
a mistake to exaggerate the melancholy and gravity of
the Sicilians, for no Italian on the mainland is more
easily moved to frenzy ; no audience, not even the critical
Florentines, express such collective excitement as the
Syracusans or Palermitans.

With the exception of the South of Spain, no country
is more generous to fiddler, guitarist, or singer, than
Sicily. It is a country of music and poetry and the
open air, for the people do most of their domestic work
out in the sunshine. Go through a village in the early
morning and you will see the women sitting outside their
cottages, combing out their long hair, and the historical
traveller will recall to mind that Carthaginian siege when
the Sicilian bow-strings gave out, and the women cut
their hair to make them rather than surrender to the
enemy. As those girls do up their hair they sing, and
when they are not singing they are listening to some
distant *ciuri d'aranci* (or orange-blossom songs), which
may be the first serenade of love. Every hour of the
day in Sicily has its song—there are aubades in the
early morning ; there are serenades at night ; there are
ciuri and *canzuni* for the afternoon ; and when a young
man wants to give his *innamorata* a special gift he sings
her an aria, which is more pretentious than a mere folk-
poem.

The first eternal figure I met in Sicily was that
of the eighteenth-century Abbé Meli. Although Meli
died as far back as 1815, yet he tramps to-day through
every village in Sicily. He was a pedlar of arias—an
Arcadian born in an age of convention, whose muse would
every now and then revolt against the pretty shepherds

and shepherdesses of Arcady and flit off in search of the
ancient Greek tradition of folk lyrics which has never
died out in the "island of fire," as Dante called it.
When you hear the village barber, schoolmaster, or
saddler recite an aria, you can be sure that he will attribute
it to the Abbé Meli. For Meli is a magic minstrel as
Stesichorus was in primitive Greek Sicily. Meli has
become a mythical character : according to the historians,
he was not an abbé at all, and it is said that he adopted the
clerical habit when a young man in order to practise
medicine, to gain access to convents, and to make himself acceptable to the nuns.[1] Meli was more than a folk
minstrel—he was a follower of the Lonely Knight of La
Mancha, as he showed in his poem " Don Chisciotti e
Sanciu "—an allegory on the theme of Resignation.
The moral of the Sicilian Quixote is that only a fool
would believe that society can be freed from the evils
of the world. The best plan is to resign ourselves to
live on the little that Destiny gives us. A satire on
enthusiasm—that is what Meli's poem amounts to. I
can still imagine the gentle-mannered singer wending his
way through the fields of Sicily followed by a company
of youths and maidens chanting the choruses of his
poems.

If I were asked to paint a Sicilian triptych which would
represent three eternal personalities of Sicily, I should
place the portrait of the benevolent Abbé Meli as the
central piece against a background of Indian fig and olive
trees. On one side of him I should paint a picture of the
Swan of Catania, as the Sicilians called their ill-fated
composer, Vincenzo Bellini. If Meli personifies Sicily's
gift of lyricism, Bellini, with what D'Annunzio called
his *meravigliosa verginità dell' anima primiere*, personifies
the divine gift of melody which Italy gave to the

[1] Countess Martinengo Cesaresco, *op. cit.*, p. 122.

world. When I reached Catania I visited the house where the creator of *La Sonnambula* and *Norma* was born. Seated before the piano of the master, I evoked his personality. He was fair-haired and blue-eyed—"fair as corn, sweet as an angel, young as the dawn," as his black-eyed mistress, Giudetta Turina, said of him. I thought of this restless, consumptive genius wearing itself out before its time. What triumphs he crowded into his thirty-three years of life, surrounded by friends and admirers who saw in him only the laurel-crowned hero! Heine alone saw the dark shadow descending upon the brilliant youth. I imagine the scene between the two friends. Bellini flushed with success, Heine full of melancholy forebodings, with phrases on his lips about the asphodels of the underworld. Bellini filled with the Sicilian's horror of death would call Heine his *jettatore*.

"I believe," said Heine, "that the most dangerous period in the life of a genius lies between thirty and thirty-five years of age. You're a genius, Bellini, and you'll die quickly, for you are just at the critical age."

Bellini would then raise his two fingers and make the ritualistic sign to drive off the evil eye. The idea of death tortured him, for he had such a longing for life, and he feared death as a child does the dark. Hence his ceaseless industry : feeling that his end would come soon, he gave to music all that remained of his strength. Near Paris, in a villa, he died on the 23rd of September 1835. It had been a race with death, for in the last months of his life he had managed to complete the score of *I Puritani*. A week after his death the opera was played before an enormous audience, all of whom were dressed in mourning. Early the next day the whole of Paris followed the funeral, and by the graveside stood Cherubini Chopin and Rossini, weeping. The *Bel Canto* and the sinuous recitative of Bellini transport us to an ethereal universe made up of the beauties of Greece and Italy. His pure song is emotion recollected in tranquillity ; his music springs from drama and is full of human emotion. But when Norma sings her supreme aria, she has conquered passion and sublimated it : the sufferings of humanity have merged into religious feeling.

And so I imagine the blue-eyed, fair-haired Bellini against the background of a Greek temple in Sicily, through whose slender columns I see the blue waters of the Mediterranean sparkling in the sunlight.

To complete my Sicilian triptych I must come to modern days. I need as a third figure someone who will tell of the sorrows, the struggles, and the ambitions of the humble folk in the inland regions and by the sea. I want to know what goes on in the minds of those who are too wretched to recite or sing. It is not enough for a traveller to get his ear full of tunes, for, as Goethe said, it is by the eye one understands the world ; and it was the eye of Giovanni Verga that revealed the lives of the Sicilians to modern Italy. After I had visited Bellini's house I went in search of Verga. It was not difficult to find the old master, for he was the chief glory of his native place, Catania. " We Catanesi call him Giovannino," said a chatty barber as he lathered my face. " Go and see his nephew who has just come back from the War."

The old maestro was like a lonely survivor of a world that had passed away. A dark-skinned, aristocratic figure with drooping moustache and snow-white hair. I longed to question him about his early days in Milan, about the famous *cénacle* of the Caffè Gova with Boito, Rovetta, Giacosa, and other stalwarts. I wanted to know about Capuana : was it true that he had turned Verga's thoughts back to the Sicilian peasants and fishermen just

as Yeats led Synge to the Arran islanders ? But Verga
would make a deprecatory gesture, saying, " It was the
journal of a sea captain that taught me to write." No
more would he tell me. " I have written in the past,"
said he with a sigh, " but it is all over now." Then he
would question me about *la verde Erinne*, and sit listening
silently and gravely to my timid explanations and gazing
at me all the while with his large, sad eyes. Such was
my impression of Sicily's great poet of the humble—" I
Vinti," as he called them in his cycle of stories. In the
era when men worshipped the D'Annunzian superman
I could imagine him shaking his head sadly, saying :
" My poor sons of the soil would never dare to draw
near to that temple of the arts. They know that their
life is the story of every day, and men must know how
to suffer in silence."

I imagine Giovanni Verga in my Sicilian triptych
surrounded by the heroes and heroines of his *novelle*.
On a hill behind them stands a chapel, from which
streams a procession of girls with faces half hidden in
their cloaks. The chapel bell tolls, and Verga seems to
say in his soft voice : " The only remedy in life is to make
oneself as small and as humble as possible : the only
reward will be for those who have faith in the next world.
This world is a vale of tears : the good are victims, the
bad sometimes triumph. The nobler a man is, the surer
he is to tread his *via crucis*." But the old master then adds
in a louder tone : " Why should you despair when I
show you a picture of life as it is, without trappings and
baroque ornaments ? I see anarchy and chaos around
me, and I refuse to buoy myself or my people on false
hopes. We must be stoics : we must face life bravely,
and plumb the depths of the human soul, as the hunchback author of *La Ginestra* did."

And so my Sicilian triptych is complete. The Arca-

dian Abbé Meli, with his soutane billowing in the breeze,
looks perplexed as he gazes to the right at the melancholy,
youthful Bellini, and to the left at the taciturn, white-
haired Verga.   I think I hear him mutter to himself :
" By Santa Lucia, a shadow has fallen across my path
since I joined these two kill-joys.   I am the friend of
haunts where peace and quiet meet.   When I lay my
head upon my pillow I sleep safe and sound as a top, and
my mind flits from one fair dream to another.   But this
old curmudgeon on my left, with his talk of poverty and
humility, lays a weight of lead upon my soul, when I
want to fly away and sing like the *cicaledda* for the joy
of it.   I am not humble, I am not poor : I can in the
twinkling of an eye vault over the moon, and travel
wherever my fancy leads me, and possess the world and
all its wealth :

> " Ora volu com' un cignu,
> ora sulcu undusi vii,
> e, durmennu, disimpignu
> li capricci e li disii."

And then our minstrel begins to sing to himself ; the
cicala chirrups, the waters murmur in distant harmony,
but the song is no longer jovial, it is mingled sadness and
joy, as though the bard was gazing down upon the
panorama of the world :

> " While I sing
> I see beneath my feet
> the earth the sea and all
> that man desires but ne'er achieves."

And while the minstrel sang his simple song, Bellini, the
fair youth, and Verga, the old man, listened entranced,
for both of them had heard it in their childhood from
mother or sister in the village, when the women combed
their long tresses in the morning sun.   And when the

minstrel stopped Bellini exclaimed : " The minstrel of Sicily taught me more than I ever learnt in school or conservatory. He taught me that serenity only comes to those who have had sad experiences in life. He taught me the Greek quality of measure and balance, and enabled me to forswear the Romantic Manfreds of 1830, trailing their long cloaks and posing as noble spirits damned by a cruel destiny. But the most priceless gift he gave me was love for every inflexion of recited poetry. Following the spoken voice, I traced the slender musical line of my recitative leading up to my own lyrical moment of melody, wherein I express the sum-total of the drama that has gone before. And the divine Maria Malibran receives my song from my lips."

As Bellini spoke, the aged maestro, Verga, swayed his body as if responding to the rhythm of the young composer, and when the harmonious voice ceased, he said : " How I struggled throughout my eighty years of life to reach in my art that serenity which you, Vincenzo, found before you were thirty years of age ! We Sicilians cannot help our heritage—our eyes still long to gaze upon the immortal beauty that was Greece : our ears still echo with those harmonies, which, as that Greek-loving solitary Leopardi said :

> " alto mistero d'ignorati Elisi
> paion sovente rivelar."

CHAPTER XVIII

THE GREEK THEATRE AT SYRACUSE

SYRACUSE on a stifling summer's day. Do not ask me to fiddle for pennies in the via Maestranza : I have no wish for anything in the world but my patch of shade by the shores of the Great Harbour. So hot was the weather when I arrived in the city I did not trouble to search for lodgings, but spent the first two nights under the stars. Syracuse, with its gardens, temples and its Greek Theatre, is a paradise for the Lotos-eater and Hellenic traveller but a lean place for a picaresque minstrel. With a Thucydides and a Theocritus in my hand I had more thoughts for the ancient Greeks than the modern Syracusans. Syracuse is the city in Sicily where the contemplative traveller may get his eye full of dreaming. If he lingers near the columns of Olympian Zeus he sees below him the great harbour full of Athenian ships drawn up for the fatal fray : if he lies beneath an olive-tree on the Epipolæ watching a goat-herd leading his flock across the drowsy, sun-drenched, landscape he will dream of Daphnis and Thyrsis. Ortygia is sacred to the memory of the goddess Artemis, for when she played in the meadows of Enna with Athena and Persephone had she not chosen this island to be her home ? And to remind us still more forcibly of the bond with Greece, have we not the fountain of Arethusa invoked by Theocritus in his idylls ? The celebrated fountain with its gold-fish, papyrus plants and "railed round like a bear pit" as J. A. Symonds said, disappointed me and drove all thoughts of ancient Hellas out of my head. If only the modern world would leave the ruins of the past in peace instead of tidying and beautifying them so that they lose all their charm of suggestion. Poor Arethusa! Your ghost mourns disconsolately over the wild flowers you gathered with Persephone. With Milton you may well cry out:

> Return Sicilian Muse
> and call the vales and bid them hither cast
> their bels and flourets of a thousand hues!

For the first few days I devoted myself to the task of creating my vision of the ancient Greek city. I forswore the maze of narrow, mediæval streets, the catacombs, even the Roman amphitheatre. First I went to the famous statue of Aphrodite Anadyomene—the Venus of Syracuse as she is called by the inhabitants. I was eager to see her because I had read Guy de Maupassant's passionate description. No sooner had the great French writer seen in a traveller's album her photograph than he decided straightway to make the journey from Paris to Syracuse to see her. "Je devins amoureux d'elle," he cried, "comme on est amoureux d'une femme. Je parlais d'elle et je rêvais d'elle à tout instant, avant de l'avoir vue." She has no head and one arm is missing, but still her beauty of form seduces, nay, even troubles her countless devotees. She has not the pure outline of the Venus of Milo or the majestic dignity of the Venus of Medici: 'C'est la femme telle qu'elle est, telle qu'on l'aime, telle qu'on la désire, telle qu'on la veut étreindre." In the eyes of the ingenuous, sense-indulging poet the Venus of Syracuse appeared as the embodiment of all his heroines. She is the symbol of flesh and Woman. He compares her with Leonardo da Vinci's Gioconda, saying that the latter leads her devotees in quest of mysticism and dreams that can never be realized. Poets, whom he calls *impuissants décrocheurs d'étoiles*, pursue such a dream-Woman as if she was the fire bird, but the Venus of Syracuse belongs to the category of Women who excite in men the impetuous love whence springs our race.

From the museum I used to wend my way to the celebrated Latomie—the deep quarries from which the city was built. Originally those vast quarries—over 100 feet deep and open to the sky—were grim abodes of death. According to Thucydides, seven thousand prisoners, captured by the Syracusans after the Athenian defeat and the destruction of their fleet, were confined in those stone quarries. They were herded together in those deep, narrow places and the sun beat down inexorably upon them by day, while the cold autumn nights of exposure made them victims of fever. They were oppressed by hunger and thirst, for the Syracusans only gave them half the rations of slaves, that is to say, half a pint of water and a pint of food a day. They were huddled together in the enclosed space, surrounded by the pile of corpses of those who had died of wounds, fever, or starvation. Above, on the edge of the rocks the populace of Syracuse would stand jeering at their wretched victims below. It is said that some of the captives would recite by heart the choruses of Euripides and the theatre-loving Syracusans, spellbound by the beauty of the verses, would release the Greek who recited best and take him into their own service as a slave. The verses of Euripides stirred the Syracusan hearts to more pity than the sight of the intolerable agony of the Athenians. To-day it is difficult to believe that these Latomie witnessed such tragic scenes, for they have been converted into paradises of shrubs and trees.

As I lie in the shade of a cypress tree in the " Latomie dei Capuccini " listening to the insistent song of birds near by I feel as though I had strayed into the gardens of Epicurus. In the summer the wanderer who comes here may rest upon mossy banks listening to the drowsy murmur of cascades. In the winter, when all the rest of Syracuse shivers in the wind, down in this retreat scarcely a breeze shakes the olive trees and the flowers blossom out in tropical profusion. " It is haunted by the ghosts of those Athenian lads," said an old guide to me. " Of an evening you could hear their sorrowful lamentations. They recite their choruses in the light of the moon." In another of the quarries which, by the way, is called " Latomia del Paradiso," there is the famous " Ear " of Dionysius. The " Ear " is a cave resembling the human ear in shape and at the top it has an opening leading into a small cell where Dionysius is said to have sat and overheard the slightest whisper of the prisoners. I brought my fiddle with me and played softly a slow melody. The tones of the violin, echoing and re-echoing through the cave, swelled in volume like an organ and the overtones of thirds and fifths orchestrated my melody as if a band of fifty players were playing it in five or six parts. The guide was impressed by my performance and he went on to tell me of the famous singers who had roused the echoes of the cave. His most cherished memory of all was the visit of Caruso, whose voice, as he said, ' awoke the sleeping soul of Dionysius."

No matter where my wanderings led me in Syracuse I always returned before sunset to the city's supreme monument—the Greek theatre. Looking back over my impressions of Grecian Italy, I cannot remember any place that awoke in my mind such a wealth of images and emotions. To sit in one of the seats of the upper tier and gaze at the city on the island of Ortygia and the blue sea beyond was to call up before one's mind the whole panorama of Greek history.   I always arrived at the theatre before sundown when the golden light mellowed the modern city.   At that hour, gazing down from the Nymphæum, I imagined the ancient city on the island with its painted temples.   There before me was the Lesser Harbour and the Great Harbour stretching as far as the Cape of Plemmyrium.   I could see the whole valley of the River Anapus and the solitary columns of Olympian Zeus.   From my point of vantage I could reconstruct in my mind not only the vast tragedy of the Athenian expedition, with its final battle fought out in the Great Harbour in full view of the opposing armies and populace, but I could also evoke the scenes in the theatre ever since that day in the fifth century when Gelon's workmen cut it out of the hillside sloping to the shore.

First of all I thought of the day when that peerless minstrel, Pindar—"First Violin of King Hiero," as Voltaire called him—recited his odes to the multitude seated tier above tier.   He slowly advanced in trailing robe across the stage carrying the lyre of Apollo.   His gift of song had made him the peer of any king, for "his soul possessed the sun and the stars" and men would gather his words and inscribe them in letters of gold in the temples of the gods.   I can imagine him declaiming to the hushed audience the words : "Golden pillars will we set up in the porch of the house of our song, as in a stately palace hall ; for it beseemeth that in the forefront of the work the entablature should fire its splendour."   Pindar was indeed the poet-builder of song, and he was proud of his liberty as a minstrel. "I would not," cried he, "live at a tyrant's court because I would rather live at my own behest than

another's." He was as proud a guest in the court of
Hiero as Dante was in the court of Can Grande della
Scala at Verona.

Hardly had the stately notes of Apollo's lyre faded
away than I heard the lively, bustling rhythm of the flute
and I saw the procession of Dionysus enter the orchestra
of the theatre. I saw in the distance the figure of the
god, half male and half female, holding a sword in one
hand and a mirror in the other. At the head of the
procession came a maiden adorned in gold, bearing on
her head the sacred basket, and she was followed by
others carrying grapes, figs, jars of wine, and the phallus,
and when they had reached the thymelē or altar of the
god in the centre of the orchestra a hymn was chanted
by the chorus accompanied by the gestures of mummers
as they told the episodes of the life of Dionysus. And
then I saw a stately, bearded figure approach and a
murmur rose from the crowded auditorium. "It is
Æschylus, the creator of Greek tragedy." According to
old tradition, when he was a boy the god Dionysus
appeared to him in his father's vineyards at Eleusis and
ordered him to write a tragedy, and Æschylus had steeped
himself in the Dionysian choral poetry. He had followed the processions in the Spring when the earth
sprouted in blossom and the wine of last year was ready
for drinking, and again in winter after the labours of
the year he had watched the choral dancers celebrating
the completion of the vintage and the gathering of fruits.
His whole life was moulded according to the ritual of the
gods, for was he not sprung of the Eupatridæ at Eleusis,
sacred to Demeter and Persephone ? Year after year in
childhood he had seen the torchlight procession advance
along the sacred road from Athens and the solemn
initiation by night. Such was the man whom the
Syracusans welcomed in 472, when his play *The Persians*

was performed in this theatre. It is a solemn play describing how " the wrath of God tramples with heavy foot upon the nations of Persia." Atossa, the queen whose soul is shrouded in gloom, awaits news of her son, Xerxes, and chants ritual verses as the libations to the dead are poured and she calls up the ghost of Darius. News is brought that Xerxes has been defeated by the Greeks and Darius gives scant comfort to the queen when he says : " Right soon has come fulfilment of oracles and upon my son Zeus has inflicted the doom decreed by Heaven. I felt assured that only after many days the gods would bring it to accomplishment. But when Man is hurrying to his own doom the gods, too, lend a helping hand." The audience in this theatre, as they looked enthralled upon a play so full of the war-god, must ever anon have raised their eyes to gaze out at the blue sea beyond, as though half expecting to see some hostile fleet loom up ready for battle. But not a sail was to be seen on the blue expanse.

Do not think that this theatre witnessed only the masterpieces of tragedy. We are told that the famous Greek comedies were played here in the days of the art-loving Sicilian princes. I can imagine the rustic masqueraders, mummers, and flute-players approaching with their faces stained with wine lees, dancing in the wild transports of Bacchic intoxication, improvising satirical sallies against the well-known figures among the bystanders. Think what a performance in that theatre of an Aristophanes play must have been with its mixture of irony, seriousness, grotesqueness, obscenity, and lyrical beauty which made Heine, a modern Aristophanes, say that " a deep sense of world-destruction lies at the root of every Aristophanic comedy, and like a fantastically, ironically magic tree springs up in it with blooming

ornaments of thought with singing nightingales and
climbing, chattering apes." In the *Persæ* of Æschylus
we saw a drama full of the war-god, but in Aristophanes
we see a peace-lover. " War," he said, " was anti-
hellenic. Peace is the feast of Greek brotherhood.
War debases the frugal temperance of rural Attica, for
the peasants leave the fields for the city and sell their
souls. No sooner do they enter the city than they
become victims of the orators who blow their rhetoric
and drive away peace, knowing that the poor are without
strength." " Deliver us," cried Aristophanes in 421 B.C.,
" from Cleon the leather-seller who corrupted the soul of
Athens."

Many an hour I spent in the Greek theatre gazing
out to sea and dreaming of the Athenian Expedition, till
in the end I thought of it as an Æschylean tragedy full
of dark and mysterious presentiments and foreboding.

Thucydides in his calm Olympian way unfolds the
story like a tragedy with its background of Atē. First
of all he recalls the terrible treatment meted out by
Athens to the Melians. According to the Greek doctrine of Nemesis, the Athenians for that crime were fated
to commit acts of greater folly until the day when the
whole fabric of their world would come crashing down.
Arrogant ambition tempted the Athenians in the middle
of the Peloponnesian War to make a wild grab at Mediterranean empire. Syracuse they hoped to seize without
difficulty, then Sicily, then Carthage, and finally the
whole Peloponnesus. It was the handsome, brilliant,
capricious Alcibiades who conjured up before his
countrymen the vistas of empire and urged them to
follow the motto " live dangerously." Right from the
beginning of the Thucydidean tragedy we see clearly
before us the contrasting personalities of Alcibiades, the
fickle child of fortune and the slow-witted, vacillating

Nicias who begged his countrymen not to engage in yet another war when they still had a host of enemies to fight in the Peloponnese. Needless to say, Alcibiades won his way and the finest fleet that had ever been fitted out by a Greek city set forth from Athens.

At the end, after describing the pitiful plight of the Athenian remnant trudging wearily after their leader Nicias, who in the hour of defeat becomes heroic, Thucydides takes on the functions of the ancient chorus of tragedy and closes his drama with the words :

> Thus ended the greatest of all Hellenic actions—the most glorious to the victors, the most ruinous to the vanquished ; for they were utterly and at all points defeated, and their sufferings were prodigious. Fleet and army perished from the face of the earth ; nothing was saved, and of the many who went forth, few returned home.

Such was the downfall of Athens, and the Syracusans might well boast that their city was the best of all Greek cities. For now a towering personality occupies the stage—the tyrant Dionysius, who filled the four cities of Syracuse with the populations conquered in his various wars and enclosed the quadruple city within the strongest fortifications of antiquity. Dionysius was the product of the age which had witnessed the downfall of Athens—an ancestor of Machiavelli—ambitious, cynical, persevering. He had no scruples when carrying out his policies : he had no respect for either gods or men. Even an Oath to him was of no account. " One must amuse men with oaths just as we amuse children with dice and little bones." His cynical humour at times prompted him to play practical jokes, as when he invited the staid matrons and maidens of Syracuse to a great feast in the temple of Demeter where they wore their finest silks, brocades and precious jewels. Dionysius, when the festivities were at their height, ordered every one of them to take off her beautiful clothes and jewels, which he sold to make money, telling the frightened and embarrassed damsels that it was the will of Demeter. Such was the man who launched Syracuse upon her career of conquest, filled the citizens with overweening pride in their state and blinded them against the approaching Nemesis. But the final day of reckoning eventually came for Syracuse when in 212 B.C. Marcellus sacked her after the famous siege. Livy, in a beautiful passage, described how the Roman general, gazing down from the heights upon the city, shed tears, partly from joy at having accomplished such a success, partly from the remembrance of the ancient glories of the place. But it was the works of art carried by Marcellus to Rome which gave the Romans their first vision of Greek beauty and culture.

The old custodian of the theatre, who became my friend and counsellor during my stay at Syracuse, would not admit that Greece had anything to do with it. " It was," said he, " the Syracusans who civilized Rome. Ah, yes ! Signore ! remember what the divine Petrarch said : ' I Siciliani che fur già primi '—the Sicilians were always the first in everything. When the Greeks came here they found music, poetry, and drama all over the island. It was a Sicilian shepherd invented the flute, and, as for the great man from Agrigento, Empedocles, he taught the Greeks the art of music. Wrestling, too, was invented by a Sicilian, and dancing, and when it came to war the Syracusans taught not only the Greeks but even the Romans a mighty lesson, I tell you. So it has always been in history, signor. In modern days when they created *il regno d'Italia* they couldn't have done it— no, not by half, if they hadn't found Sicily ready to obey the trumpet call. Garibaldi knew it ; that's why he sailed straight for Marsala with ' The Thousand.'

And to-day we are neglected and left out in the cold by the Government of *mascalzoni* in Rome who would sell Sicily just as they tried to sell Fiume. But we Sicilians keep our peace and wait for the day when a man comes along ; we'll show him that we've kept our powder dry."

After his long tirade the old custodian stroked his white beard thoughtfully, saying in a resigned voice : " The people down here are forgotten by the Government, which thinks of the North Italians because they shout louder, and tells us to keep quiet and pay our taxes. No wonder the Mafia is worse in Sicily to-day than it has been since I was a lad in the eighties."

" Surely," said I, " it would be easy to put down the Mafia here if the Government placed power in the hands of one efficient man."

" If you lived in Sicily," replied the custodian, " you would not say that. Only a Sicilian knows the ramifications, the never-ending subtleties of the Mafia which follows every Sicilian as closely as the shadow does the body."

We finished our conversation in a tavern close to the theatre which gloried in the name—" Bar Dionisio." I toasted the custodian in a bottle of Syracusan Moscato —a brown, sulphurous, sweet and heady wine which remained as an uncomfortable memory for the rest of the evening. Afterwards, before returning to the city I mounted to " Street of Tombs," which leads from the theatre. On each side of the street which is cut in the rock are huge tombs of gaping darkness dating from late Roman times—a ghostly street with chariot ruts deeply furrowed in the stone. Up here I cannot hear a sound save the insistent murmur of water from a neighbouring grotto called the Nymphæum. From the Nymphæum I could see deep into the " Latomia del Paradiso," where so many of the Athenian prisoners languished. I

thought of them reciting verses from the dramas of
Euripides in that pitiless dungeon practically within
earshot of the theatre which had witnessed so many of
the master's plays.

CHAPTER XIX

THE MAFIA

IN Syracuse I made many varied friends. There is no profession like that of a wandering minstrel for bringing you into contact with humanity without its trappings. It enables a man to shun the great monotonous and anonymous mass of the people and devote himself to certain individuals who are in sympathy with him. In Syracuse there were waiters in the cafés who welcomed my daily tunes, not so much for their musical magic as for the fact that they led to frenzied discussions on politics. There was a fat old lay-brother, custodian of the famous catacombs to whom I once gave a concert standing on an empty tomb in one of the dark subterranean chambers. The music sounded weird and fantastic in the bowels of the earth. If the fat monk had allowed me I would have played in the crypt of St. Martian, which, according to legend, marked the place where St. Paul preached when he landed in Syracuse. In the morning my beat was in the neighbourhood of the cathedral and I came to know the vagabond fraternity that gather there to practise their various picaresque arts.

As compared with the rest of the Sicilians, the Syracusans struck me as more akin to the Greeks. I could find very little trace of Arab or Spaniard about them. The urchins are bright-eyed, agile and full of roguishness and are a contrast to the peasants from the interior. The peasant, even in summer, wears his dark blue-hooded cloak called *scapularu*, and probably has in

addition a scarf wound round his neck as if he was
terrified of falling a victim to the sudden attack of malaria.

The most lively of all the Syracusans were the
hawkers, who astonished me by the ingenuity which they
displayed in earning a livelihood. They reminded me
of South Spanish picaroons by their pride in their own
wares. They did not seem to care whether people
bought anything from them or not. Their salesmanship,
in fact, was merely an excuse for idling in the sunlight
and commenting upon life as it passed before them.

I made the acquaintance of some of the fishermen off
the coast. Fine, bronzed men they were, reminding me
of my friends at Taranto. On one occasion I had the
fortune to see the famous *mattanza*, or killing of the tunny
fish. Few sights are more profoundly dramatic than this
ritual which goes back even to Phœnician times. The
huge fish, running to hundreds of pounds in weight, is
caught by being driven into a canvas enclosure off the
coast called *isula*. The *isula* is divided into seven compartments, each one separated from the other by vertical
nets and communicating with one another by a door.
The tunny fish cruising off the shore are unwary enough
to enter the enclosure and are driven from one compartment to another till they reach the last one, which is
called "La camera della morte" (death-chamber).
Then all of a sudden begins the *mattanza*. No sooner
does the head of the band of fishermen shout the signal
than all the rest dash along in their little boats to the side
of the death-chamber and the ritual begins accompanied
by the traditional song *La Cialoma*. The men sing in
rhythm with the movements of their arms as they pull up
the nets heavy with the tunny fish, driving them into the
death-chamber. As soon as the glittering fish sparkle
in their prison in the water beneath, the song becomes
strident and savage. The singer declaims in song, calling

on the queen of the sea, the queen of the world, the queen
of increase, white-bearded St. Peter who carries the keys
of hope in his girdle, and in answer to the singers
the crews shout rhythmically the words : " Guanzò,
guanzò." Meanwhile the fishermen bend over, armed
with harpoons, and strive to hook the victims and pull
them up into two big open boats, but the huge fish leaps,
wriggles, and jumps in its attempt to escape the cruel
barb. Soon its radiant silver flesh is stained with blood,
but it still leaps up and down so that it takes the strength
of three men finally to heave its trembling mass into the
boat. One after another the fish are caught on the cruel
hooks and soon the foaming water is deeply tinged with
blood. Never in all my life had I seen a more savage and
yet exciting scene. For an hour there was nothing but
the sound of foaming waters, the dull thud of blows, the
hoarse shouts, and above all the strange rhythmic song
which seemed like a dirge sung over the sinister sea of
blood.

As a contrast to the passionate *cialoma* we can discover
to-day many idyllic landscapes and individual types who
suggest the world of Theocritus. It is impossible to
wander up the papyrus avenues on the banks of the
Anapus towards the fountain of Cyane without recalling
scenes from the idylls which the great poet sketched
suggestively. At one moment we lie on a heap of
feathered ferns which make a " couch more soft than
sleep " ; at another the sight of a fair hillside beyond
an olive grove, full of rocks and thorns and aromatic
plants, suggests the haunts of Thyrsis. It is impossible to
ramble through the countryside without hearing Daphnis
and Menalcas sing in rivalry some such song as the
following while their brown goats browse beside them :

To read Theocritus is to find oneself for ever lulled by the music of water that falls from the high face of the rock or the murmurs of the sea.

I had left my friends the tunny fishers. I climbed a cliff above the shore and there I came across a young goatherd playing a flageolet as he gazed from his rock down upon the fishermen below. He was a roguish, sloe-eyed little boy with big ears and tiny, wizened face like one of the satyrs sent by Pan to haunt this idyllic landscape. When he stopped his fluting I could still hear in the distance far below the weird, rhythmic song of the tunny fishers. Occasionally, too, I would meet a young peasant maiden—a shy, fleeting creature, black-haired, with pale face and large, melting eyes, but not a word would she say to the stranger unless I happened to meet her with her companions at a well or at a washing-trough. Then she would pluck up courage and lead a chorus of mocking, bird-like laughter at the vagabond with the fiddle passing by. Women in Sicily keep in the background, for no other country is so dangerous for Don Juan the playboy, against whom the proverbially jealous Sicilian wages ceaseless war. I was even told that the law had to be administered differently in Sicily than on the mainland on account of this mad, un-reasoning jealousy which rises like a hurricane in the minds of the Sicilian Othellos.

When I was in Sicily there was one idyll of Theocritus which I read over and over again because it seemed like a slice of life, true for all time. It describes how the passionate maiden, Simætha, who is madly in love with the shepherd Delphis, tries to subdue him by magic after he has forsaken her. The scene is laid in some garden beneath the moonlit sky near Syracuse and within sound of the sea. Simætha, assisted by her handmaid Thestylis, invokes Hecate the witch-goddess of the moon. She

tells the tale of her unlucky passion and vows vengeance
if the magic ritual she performs is unsuccessful. One by
one Thestylis brings the fetish charms, the laurel leaves,
the bright red wool, which must be knitted into witch-
knots. Against her lover the distraught maiden revolv-
ing her magic wheel invokes the goddess of Hell, the
vampire goddess who fares through black blood across
the barrows of the dead. Thestylis tosses the barley
on to the fire and the laurel crackles in the flame : even
thus, so Simætha prays, may the flesh of Delphis waste
in the burning. Then Simætha melts wax and casts a
fringe reft from her lover's cloak into the flame, and
thrice she pours libations to Lady Moon, and all the time
the brazen wheel whirls restless under Aphrodite's spell
as she intones again and again the magic refrain :

"My magic wheel, draw home to me the man I love."

And so Simætha, nursing her passion in the telling of
it, describes how she had wooed her lover, how they
twain had come to their desire, but now that he has
forgotten her she will bind him with magic rites and he
will beat, she swears by the Fates, at the gates of Hell.[1]

To-day, in this Greece-haunted land we may in some
of the primitive villages come across Simætha. We need
not follow the avenue of cypress trees towards the moonlit graveyard to discover the vampire spells in the small
villages. There are witch-wives who specialize in charms
and rituals for enabling a girl to win a man's love.

Marriage becomes somewhat of a tyranny in Sicily
if we believe the proverb, "With a girl of 18 years,
marry her off or slaughter her." When we remember
how strictly the girl is kept by her parents it is no easy
matter to become engaged at an early age, for there are
very few opportunities of meeting the eligible youths.

---

[1] *Idylls of Theocritus*, translated by A. Lang, London, 1889.

Perhaps a glance from two dark eyes when she is filling
her pitcher at the well, perhaps a moment's conversation
with the goatherd while she is standing at the door of her
cottage—otherwise what can she do but pray ceaselessly
in the traditional Sicilian manner to the three saints—to
St. Antony, that he may start her fiancé on his way to
her ; to St. John, that he may soon afterwards write up
the banns ; to glorious St. Onofrio, that he may bless
her union with the gift of a fair man-child.

From personal experience I found that the Sicilian
matron was more charitable to the foreign vagabond
than the master of the house. A tramp soon learns the
subtlest method of winning good cheer. The whole
problem is to become known to the village as soon as
possible, for hatred, intolerance, and lack of charity are
only due to ignorance. When a stranger first enters a
village he is immediately a suspect and consequently an
object of hatred to every man, woman, child, and dog.
First of all, the lean and hungry dogs dash at him with
a fury of a hundred devils. The children gambolling
in the streets transfer their attentions to his lonely figure
and he becomes the butt of all like an Aunt Sally at a
fair. The men look daggers at him and the police forth-
with regard him as a potential spy. Besides, who knows,
he may have the evil eye and the *malocchio* or *jettatura*
may be of two kinds. If we believe the authorities, the
stranger may have an eye which produces evil because
it envies the good of others or else he may have come
into the world with an eye that withers up its victims.

Beware, O stranger, if you have a squint in your
eye, for you'll not find a bed in the village. On one
occasion in Sicily I had to take to my heels and away,
not because I had the Evil Eye but because an old
woman who was washing clothes in a ditch did not like
my face and shouted to her companions that I had a

sinister eye (*occhio sinistro*).   Ever afterwards I laid in a
store of amulets, that is to say, coral charms, key charms,
and bits of ox- and sheep-horn, but as I said before, it is
only ignorance which prevents people from being kind
and charitable to the stranger.   The first day I entered
the village I was an object of suspicion.   Two days later
I was the white-headed boy of the place with a herd of
children at my heels eager to hear tunes and stories.   In
the villages it is always the women of the house who
thaw first of all.   When you arrive at a farmhouse and
you ask for a corner of the barn to sleep in or a hunk of
bread and cheese and some wine, the man will scratch his
head and look at you sullenly from head to foot, but the
old matron in the back of the kitchen will immediately
become practical and instead of arguing she will shuffle
off to fetch the wine-jar and the slab of goat's-milk cheese.
The Sicilian peasant, like the Spaniard and the Greek,
feels that it is unlucky to turn away the genuine vagabond from the door.   Besides, he has his own dignity
and point of honour which is celebrated in the proverb,
" Proud as a Sicilian."   No matter how poor a Sicilian
is, he always behaves in his hut or hovel as a perfect
aristocrat.

I shall always have a soft spot in my heart for the
towns of inland Sicily, for there I received hospitality
on all sides, and, indeed, the lonely vagabond tramping
through those parched, barren lands in summer needs
to meet a Philemon and Baucis in every cottage.   As he
approaches the grim fortress of Castrogiovanni the
traveller becomes a victim of a mirage created by the
authors of antiquity, for is not Castrogiovanni the
Enna of Persephone ?   In the famous fields, at the foot
of the mountain, Pluto, the god of the underworld, is
supposed to have appeared to the goddess as she played
in the fields gathering the blooms of narcissus.   In this

mountain fortress, too, was the holiest shrine of Demeter or Ceres, the corn-goddess. And the fields of Enna gave Sicily the fame of being the granary of Europe. But to-day the land is desolate and instead of corn and flowers I see nothing but heaps of sulphur which impress upon me that this must be indeed the entrance to the lower world. Sulphur is the principal industry of these inland towns, brilliant yellow sulphur which gives a dash of colour to the brown parched fields. From the railway station and the malaria-stricken plain I mounted the winding road to the fortress of Enna, which is over 3,000 feet above the sea-level. I was not alone, for on the way from Syracuse I had made friends with two blind musicians, a guitarist and a mandolinist, and their *carusu* (guide), a shock-headed youth who led his two charges as if they were two muzzled bears at the end of a rope. The two blind men kept up a continual chatter. One of them was tall and lanky with joints that crackled as he played, a melancholy, dyspeptic individual with toothless gums and shaggy mat of grey hair. The other was small and wiry, with a face malevolent in expression owing to his sightless eyeballs. I was glad to meet the three of them because I wondered what their method would be when we entered the town. We took a long time to mount the hill towards the town because the blind men insisted on halting by the side of the road and playing.

"Let us rehearse," said they in chorus; "play with us and you'll get your share."

The *carusu* then began to explain to me the secrets of street musicianship. It was necessary to get permission to play, and in addition it was necessary to grease a few palms, for as the youth said, making a gesture with his fingers :

"Every man his share, then there'll be no quarrels."

It was in Castrogiovanni, as a result of my experience
with my blind minstrel friends, that I discovered the
intricate ramifications of the Mafia. As far as I could
make out, life was easy for the wanderer who did not
forget to pay his little tribute in every village to the
representatives of that far-reaching organization. Our
audiences consisted mostly of mountaineer peasants, tall,
fair-haired, enveloped in big hooded cloaks of dark blue
material. But Castrogiovanni in 1919 was not a happy
hunting ground for the minstrel because it was so infested
with beggars. Truculent they were, too, and for ever
ready to quarrel with their fellow-picaroons. Most of
them in addition to their cloaks wore top-boots which
gave them a swashbuckling air. I was glad to make
but a short stay in Castrogiovanni because I went in
terror of those truculent beggars after the experience
which befell me up on the Rock of Ceres near Manfred's
castle. Up there I had forgotten all about the miseries
of hand-to-mouth existence and was gazing at the marvellous panorama, the great snow-white mass of Ætna in
the distance, the peak of Calascibetta near at hand and
down below the fields of Enna and the sacred lake of
Pergusa where Persephone disappeared. Even when
Cicero visited the island, from the Rock of Ceres he
could have seen below a vast ocean of cornfields stretching across the plain, broken here and there by the groves
of Lake Pergusa and the countless masses of fragrant
flowers, whose perfume was so sweet that dogs when
hunting lost the scent. To-day the ground is sterile save
for groves of olive and the almond trees which bloom
into a few days' paradise, in the Spring.

I was gazing entranced upon the panorama when
I felt myself suddenly jostled and thrown on my back.
With a curse I struggled to my feet, but my assailant
had already darted away. As he sped along I saw

to my horror that he had managed to seize hold of my fiddle-case while I was lying on the ground. I dashed after him as fast as I could, but I soon lost sight of him and my cries of " Stop thief " did not awaken much excitement in the few beggars that were hanging about. The loss of my fiddle was about the worst misfortune that could befall me, for it was not only my companion but my support. What could I do to earn my living without my faithful instrument which had shared my wanderings ? I had no money to buy another, and, besides, what other fiddle would console me for the loss of my own ? I descended disconsolately into the town. I told the police, but I got scant consolation from them, for they looked upon me as a down-at-heels vagabond outside the pale of the law. The only words of comfort I heard were from my blind companions :

" Why didn't you fight him ? " said the *carusu*. " Those fellows would never stand up to you if you showed a bit of fight and pulled out a knife."

" He was too quick for me," said I. " He was off like lightning, and besides, I have no knife."

" No knife ? " said the three of them in surprised chorus. " Fancy travelling alone without a knife ! Why, even a blind man never travels without a dagger of some sort."

" Did you tell anybody how you had been robbed ? " said one of the blind men.

"Yes, I told the police, but they didn't take much notice."

" You idiot," cried the three in chorus. " You must be fresh as a new-born babe as far as Sicily is concerned. Police, indeed ! If you don't clear out you'll find them after you, tracking you down, and you'll find yourself behind the bars instead of the fellow who robbed you. We'll tell you what to do."

" Come on, tell me. I'll do anything to get back my
fiddle."

" All right, then," said the *carusu*, " come with me and
we'll see somebody who may help."

To cut a long story short, the youth brought me to
a certain individual who kept a small tavern. He, after
listening to my description of the instrument, scratched
his head and hemmed and hawed, saying he would find
out whether any such fiddle had been found.

" I can't give you much hope for the present," said he,
" but would you be prepared to give a reward ? "

" Of course," said I, " within reason."

I paid a small sum on deposit and to my surprise next
evening when I visited the tavern the owner called me
into the back of the shop and, lo and behold, there was
my fiddle, case and all. On payment of another small
sum it was handed over to me.

" It's a miracle," said I.

" Not so much of a miracle," answered the *carusu*.
" You can thank the organization of the Mafia. Remember that it always keeps its eyes open and it's the only
friend the poor man has in this rotten world."

From Castrogiovanni to Caltanisetta I enjoyed the
company of the blind men, and the *carusu* so enlightened
me concerning the functions of the Mafia that I saw its
hidden arm in everything. In Caltanisetta I sought the
help of Mafia agents, for the blind men warned me
that if I was continuing my journey on foot from one
village to another it was always better to pay a small
sum in order to avoid trouble. " A lonely man," they
said, " has every man's hand against him. Sometimes
in the evening when he is far from the village he may
meet tough customers—*malandrini*. You can never tell
with *malandrini* whether they will let you go free or not.
They may pick a quarrel with you, say they don't like

your face, or they may ask you for some money with threats, or they may blackmail you, whereas, if you hand over a small sum and put yourself under the protection of the village Mafioso you will be as safe as in your own home."

And so, during my trip from Castrogiovanni to Caltanisetta and from Caltanisetta to Girgenti and from Girgenti to Palermo I came to believe implicitly in the Mafia. Walking through the country I frequently came across men on mules with a gun slung from their shoulders. Taciturn fellows they were, those muleteers, and I never heard them sing the lilting songs that one often hears from the muleteers of Syracuse or Catania. However, as soon as a traveller got in touch with an agent of the Mafia in any village he found plenty of introductions to help him on his way.

Looking back over Sicily as I remember it in those days after the War, I often try to sum up in my mind the origin and meaning of the Mafia. There is no doubt that the word is connected with the admiration felt by the Sicilian for *omertà*, or full-blooded manliness. The word Mafia means a certain swaggering insolence which the bully uses towards other men. The word Mafioso is used in the sense of one who has confidence in his own good fortune and it is often applied to girls who are proud of their own beauty. The Mafia, according to Sicilian authorities, arose from centuries of corrupt Government, and it signifies the silence which true manliness, called *omertà*, prescribes when questions are asked by the authorities. It was the result of the long, disastrous period from 1200 to 1860 when Sicily was the victim of a series of foreign conquerors who ruined the island to satisfy their war-lust. The Sicilians had no say in their island's affairs. They were divided with the land and handed over from one master to another. Every government that dominated the country found fresh victims and crushed them with taxation. There was no attempt made to link up the people in feelings of nationality and brotherhood.

The result of centuries of evil government was to prevent friendly communication between the town and country people. Hence the disdain with which the poorest hawkers and picaroons of Syracuse or Catania looked down upon the peasants of the interior. Sicily, even in 1919, suffered from the worst results of feudalism. It was Pliny who said of Italy : " Latifundia Italiam perdidere " (great estates were the ruin of Italy). Pliny's remark might be aptly applied to Sicily in modern times, where a man may tramp all day in the interior of the island without seeing any attempt at cultivation or even of civilization. There are many districts where one rarely sees a farmhouse, and the traveller has to content himself with bivouacking like a Gypsy in the open or else squatting in some convenient cave. The labourers in those districts live up in the hills to avoid malaria and they descend in groups to work, and more than once I came across gangs camping in decrepit huts which reminded me of those wherein dwelt Don Quixote's goatherds in the Sierra Morena. When Sicily was so full of large and productive estates, was it any wonder that it became the home of brigands ? The wretched peasant never meets the owner of the property, for he has to deal solely with the *gabelotto* in whose hands lies the task of dividing the farms into fields and organizing the work on them. When tyranny and enslavement reaches such a pitch as it did in Sicily, the only relief lies in a lawless organization such as the Mafia, which makes some endeavour to punish the oppressors. The Government was never able to cope with the Mafia because it could not collect enough evidence to convict the guilty, for according to the

Sicilian code of true manliness, the highest virtue lay in refusing to denounce the guilty or betray him to civil justice. And so the Mafia continued to extort blackmail from all classes in the island. The rich soon came to terms with the gangsters and paid up rather than risk the depredations of the *Malandrini*. In some cases the Mafioso used to plunder the large estates and steal the crops or drive off the cattle. The proprietor at first would resist, refusing to pay tribute or to accept the employees nominated by the organization. Then anonymous letters with black hands and coffins on them would begin to pour in on him. If he did not come to terms with the Mafia he was denounced by them to the police and it was said that brigands were encamped in his property. The police would then break in and destroy his crops and garden in their search. In every village I visited I heard amazing stories of the Mafia, generally told with a naïve pride by the people of the district. Sometimes they gave me grisly details of executions in lonely places by the Mafia. " When," said they, " a man is condemned the Mafiosi cast lots among themselves for the executioner. The members of the shooting party are made to stand in a ring. The executioner takes the gun from a companion, fires it at the victim, and passes it back to his companion, and from him it goes to the next, and so on. The murderer, meanwhile, walks on and arrives at the place where his victim lies. He is now a simple bystander who has seen the occurrence."

Whenever one of the Mafia murderers fell into the hands of the police every possible ingenuity was adopted in order to secure his release. First of all, there was a campaign of anonymous letters, articles appeared in the papers and dozens of false witnesses turned up as if by magic. Then attempts would be made to tamper with the jury, the members of which were told that the man was innocent. Information, too, would be given of the poverty of the prisoner's family and the jurors would be bombarded by letters telling them how the accused and children of the accused would die of starvation if he were imprisoned. But the most powerful argument of all was the veiled threat that if he were condemned various powerful friends would see to it that he was avenged.

As a result of the Mafia there were various forms of duel common in Sicily.

After hearing from morning till evening bloodthirsty stories of the Mafia and its sinister ramifications, I never believed that Sicily could ever shake off the Mafia, but the miracle has happened, as anybody who has visited the wilder parts of Sicily since the advent of Fascism can testify. When I returned to Sicily in later years I hardly recognized the country without the Mafia. Nowadays the traveller can roam right through the wildest parts of the island without hearing the word Mafia mentioned. Occasionally in the village casinos and taverns the inhabitants will tell anecdotes of the romantic days when gangs of outlaws used to waylay law-abiding citizens. Where is the famous Carlino band who used to frequent the wild places near Caltanisetta and whose exploits caused me to shudder when I walked the lonely roads near that town in 1919? Where is the famous Grisafi band who used to raid the villages near Girgenti? The lurid stories of the bandits who lived in robbers' dens in the Madonian mountains now are told to children. My friend the guide in the Greek theatre at Syracuse was a prophet when he said that the Mafia would only be stamped out when a great ruler of the Italians would give *carte blanche* to one of his lieutenants to put down the Mafia. Mussolini's speech on the 26th May 1927 started the final campaign which smashed the Mafia.

" Gentlemen," said the Duce on that occasion, " it is time for me to unmask the Mafia. First of all, I wish to deprive that association of brigands of all that fascination and poetry which it does not in the slightest deserve. Let nobody speak of the nobility and chivalry of the Mafia unless he wants really to insult the people of Sicily."

One of the Duce's edicts was to call up Cesare Mori, whose whole life had been devoted to the task of fighting the gangsters of Sicily, and give him full powers to destroy the organization root and branch. The adventures of Mori the Prefect would fill volumes. He himself has described many of them in his book *Con la Mafia ai Ferri Corti*. Instead of making a tentative, secret campaign he brought the war out into the open and appealed to the civic pride of the Sicilians. By building up the people's courage and belief in themselves he soon weaned them of their fear of the Mafia. With a strong police force under him, backed up and supported by the Government in Rome, he soon introduced an entirely new spirit into the countryside of Sicily. Mori, in his campaigns to awaken civic spirit in the villages, even adopted music as a civilizing force. He would organize at sunset in the villages concerts for the whole population, in which everyone was encouraged to swell the chorus and sing as an expression of solidarity.

As early as 1919-20 the name of Mori was one to conjure with in Sicily, for even then he was busy fighting the Mafia, but it was the coming of Fascism that gave the great impetus to his work. It is true to say that as a result of his campaign the mind of the Sicilian was changed. I remember on one occasion seeing an old woman in a village chapel near Palermo light a candle in front of a statue of the Madonna to the honour of Prefetto Mori, who not only had saved her son from the

Mafia but also had delivered the whole island from bondage.

It was a relief after days of monotonous tramping to arrive at Girgenti and enter once again the world of ancient Greece, for to stand upon the hills of Girgenti and gaze down over the trees at the long line of temples silhouetted against the sea is to see in a flash a complete vision of Greek antiquity. Whereas in Syracuse the view of the Great Harbour and the city from the Greek theatre is one which stirs the soul of the traveller owing to its historical suggestiveness, the view of Girgenti's row of temples rising out of the landscape like a magic city becomes the epitome of all that one has ever dreamt about the Greek world. Those temples poised on its hills in their ethereal beauty against the background of the blue sea fill the wanderer with a tragic sense of the futility of all that the world has created ever since. To gaze at those slender columns in the clear morning air meant to banish from one's mind the world of Carthage, Rome, the Middle Ages, and the Modern World. My journey through Southern Italy and Sicily had shown me here and there lonely columns and statues which were an ever-present reminder of the glory that once was Greece. But here at Girgenti for the first time I saw a complete vision occupying the whole mind. Girgenti is a dangerous place for a wanderer to halt at, for who would want to leave this spot once the spell of its temples has bewitched him? It is as dangerous as harkening to the sweet song of the Sirens which fills one's mind with overmastering longing. Even the mediæval city with its cathedral built upon the towering Acropolis seems to have kept away respectfully from the lonely line of temples standing on the ridge above the sea. That harmonious world of ancient Greece is unapproachable. It flowered for an instant and disappeared, never to return. Let us rather consider it a fragile memory which we may carry hidden within ourselves. Occasionally the swift vision of Girgenti, which Pindar called "the fairest of mortal cities," will steal into our mind to console us as we plod through a barbarous world. On a moonlit night, as I gazed at the temples silhouetted in ghostly outline against the silver sea, the stillness of the countryside became oppressive as though the weight of history overhung the land. But then the buzz of insects, the metallic note of the grasshoppers, the occasional sad cry of an owl seemed to awaken myriads of tiny particles from the throbbing earth. Even the olive-trees seemed strangely watchful as if they, too, were in sympathy with insect and bird. Before these temples I felt as if I was an interloper, a wanderer lingering on his way, who suddenly comes across a fairy ring and watches scenes that were not meant for him. At night the Temple of " Concord " in the light of the moon becomes the most beautiful Greek monument in the world standing between the stately ruins of the temples of Lacinian Hera and Heracles. I longed to prolong this moonlit hour, but already it has passed and I must hasten away.

I must descend from the heights and follow the road through the Golden Gate down to the plain and on to Porto Empedocle, the modern harbour of Girgenti. What better illustration of the abyss separating modern from ancient world than that mean, miserable, industrial town built by the sea ? The ancient Greeks, with the help of the slaves they had captured in war, raised their beautiful city of palaces and temples along the heights following a harmony. The modern barbarians, following their instincts of greed, closed their eyes to the beauty above them and erected at random a straggling settlement by the sea from which they might export in huge quantities the sulphur which their slave-labour has extracted from the bowels of the earth. And so the traveller's wistful vision of Greece fades away, and he is conscious again of the hideous sulphur inferno of Sicily —the sterile land fissured with artificial volcanoes, with its furnaces to purify the mineral, its blackish, yellowish, whitish heaps dotted about the squalid countryside, with here and there a broken-down shack dwelling. And there is the great band of workers creeping out of the dark holes in the earth, bearing their loads towards the furnaces. Never had I seen a more wretched, hang-dog crew. Not one of them looked as if he had ever eaten a square meal. The older miners, gnarled and twisted like stunted olive trees, were not as pathetic as the young porters shuffling along like ghosts of the damned. Their pinched, yellow faces, already doomed by the sulphur fumes, malaria and malnutrition, haunted me for many a day. Pirandello the Sicilian writer, who was a native of Girgenti, in his greatest novel *The Old and the Young*, has described the scene that took place every day at Porto Empedocle.

A few days' stay in the sulphur districts of Caltanisetta and Porto Empedocle was enough to convince me that the depression of the sulphur trade and the slave conditions of labour were the main reasons why the worst criminals of Sicily and the most sinister agents of the Mafia came from the districts around these two cities. The inhabitants of Porto Empedocle, for one thing, are a contrast to the peasants of the inland. It is said that they spring from African stock, for Girgenti, after it was taken by the Saracens in the ninth century, was colonized by the Berbers. To-day one may search in vain for the bright-eyed, vivacious Greek street-arab who was so characteristic of Syracuse. Even the beggars and hawkers here are surly and quarrelsome. They have none of the placid resignation of the Moslem beggars of Tetuan or Tangier : none of the jauntiness of the picaroons of Cadiz and Puerto de Santa María. They are, instead, the starved, gloomy victims of industrialism which has failed—as hideous as the sulphurous earth itself with its puddles of hot mud and its countless, tiny, suppurating volcanoes. Before I said farewell I gazed once again at the slender line of temples poised on the edge of the precipice and I thought of Renan's melancholy philosophizing over the lonely temples at Paestum. Farewell, O Empedocles, philosopher, musician, engineer as well as democratic leader, who could say of the Agrigentines that they built as if they were to live for ever and feasted as if they were to die on the morrow ! Farewell, O Gellias, the King of hosts, who kept your slaves standing all day in the street to invite every passing stranger to banquet in your house ! Farewell, O Akragas of Pindar, where men erected monuments to horses who won a great race and maidens built marble tombs for their dead songbirds ! Such were my thoughts as I played for the crowd in Porto Empedocle and drew after me the herd of hungry beggars as if I had been the Pied Piper himself.

CHAPTER XX

THE GOLDEN SHELL

AFTER the squalid misery of Porto Empedocle
came the paradise of Palermo's Golden Shell
—the fertile valley stretching like a vast garden
behind the city into the mountains. Nature by its
barrier of mountains has created an amphitheatre to show
off the beauties of Sicily's city of the Arabian Nights.
No longer do I think of Syracuse with its Greek theatre
or Girgenti with its Greek temples, for here the scene
is not European but Oriental. The " Conca d'Oro,"
with its orange and lemon trees, its figs, almonds and
palms, reminds me of North Africa : the countless
gardens full of murmuring cascades planted here and
there like tiny oases recall Granada's " Generalife " or
Xauen bosomed high in the mountains of the Riff.
The contrast, too, between the white, blazing piazza
and the narrow, shady streets full of tiny booths beneath
the awnings is characteristic of the eastern world.
Palermo is most brilliant in the spring when the Golden
Shell is a mass of flowers. So heavy is the scent of
orange, lemon, and almond blossom that people close the
windows of their villas to avoid swooning through
excess of sweetness. Here in Palermo amidst these
flowering gardens a special art grew up, made up of
conflicting influences of Egyptian, Phœnician, Greek,
Roman, Arab, Norman, and Spanish. All the time we
are conscious of mediæval Sicily, when the Byzantine

changed to the Arab domination and the latter was succeeded by the Norman supremacy. But the Normans did not follow the example of the Carthaginian barbarians who sacked and burned the temples of Girgenti. The conquered Saracen absorbed his Norman conqueror. The Norman government of Sicily succeeded because they adopted the tolerant administration of the Moslems and their higher culture. Instead of persecuting the Mohammedan religion they allowed it freedom and set themselves to enjoy the benefits of Moslem civilization which they had inherited. Roger became one of the richest kings in Europe and Palermo became the greatest cultural centre in Europe, where the Eastern met the Western world, where scholars, poets, musicians, and scientists chosen from Christian, Moslem and Jew created the ideal of a courtly society.

To-day we can catch glimpses of that fantastic world when we enter the little churches of that period which are sprinkled about Palermo. These little churches sprang from Byzantine originals : with their rectangular hall and square spaces in the centre enclosed by four pillars, they resemble the little oratories, which the Arabs built everywhere and handed on to their Norman successors. My first impulse whenever I reach Palermo is to go to the Cappella Palatina in the Royal Palace. This was the parish church of King Roger I, dating from 1132, and it is generally considered the most beautiful chapel in the world. The glittering gold mosaics illuminate the tiny chapel, casting strange lights over the mosaic pictures of sacred subjects. The golden background to those pictures leads us into a vague, luminous dream-world, where we see a gigantic figure of Christ surrounded by winged angels and the desert, with bluish mountains in the distance, where St. John is preaching to a few of the faithful.

But of the tiny oratories in Palermo my favourite was San Giovanni degli Eremiti, the most Arabian of all. It was built for the Normans as a church in 1132, but its five domes and its minaret crowned with a dome suggests Islam to me more than any Mosque I have ever seen. Not all the thousands of masses said here for centuries, not all the tombs of Norman nobles buried here, can change the poetical imagery of the East which it suggests. Off it opens a delightful little cloister, full of fragrant flowers with a fountain playing in the centre. This was my favourite rest-place in Palermo, and I know of no fairer one in the world. It is a reminder of the spirit of those Moslem rulers who possessed the secret of true earthly happiness. No matter where they settled, whether it was Palermo, Granada, Cordova or Xauen, they knew that water was the blood of the earth and they created the veins through which it might flow and fertilize their Moorish gardens. The tiny cloisters of San Giovanni reminded me of the garden of Lindaraja as well as the " Generalife," and I remembered the sad song of longing chanted by the Moorish minstrels in Africa lamenting the gardens they had lost in the Andalus. The longer I stay in Palermo the more I am amazed that the Norman dynasty was strong enough to preserve the nationality of Sicily without diminishing the Arabic and Byzantine influences. How was it that the Norman conquerors of Sicily were able to subdue their stubborn national characteristics which left such permanent impress upon North France and England ? In the North they gloried in their rugged and heroic qualities and expressed them in their churches and castles. Beneath the golden sun of the Mediterranean they allowed their souls to become absorbed by the magic of the Orient. The murmuring cascades and gardens of the Arabian Nights made them forget their Northern ancestors. Even in

death their monumental sarcophagi of porphyry surmounted by canopies resemble the tombs of Oriental
potentates.

One afternoon in Palermo I turned aside to visit the
convent of the Capuchins, which contains the famous
cemetery. In the subterranean passages of the convent,
which dates from 1621, have been preserved the mummified bodies of citizens of Palermo. This method of
interment sprang into being owing to the singular
properties of the soil on which the convent is built.
As soon as a dead body is put into the earth it becomes
dried up within a year and mummified, and so after
the deceased have been buried in the ground for a year
they are taken out, dressed up in habits, and suspended
in long rows in the corridors. The sight is one that
should only be recommended to the inquisitive traveller.
My first impression was one of horror, but I gradually
became fascinated by a display which is eminently
characteristic of the Mediterranean love of the macabre.

What terrified me about those pathetic, mummified
corpses strung up in rows was their varied agony of
expression. Every one of them seemed to be racked
with suffering. Some still had hair on their skulls ;
others had even the remains of a beard bristling from the
dry, parchment skin. Some cast their eye-sockets towards the ceiling ; others bent their heads over, as though
twisted in pain. Not a single one amongst the hundreds
had the appearance of having died peacefully. I was
surrounded on all sides by the hideous mask of death
agony. Many were dressed simply in the monk's
habit ; others were dandified with a touch of elegance
which gave a pathetic and yet comic effect to the
grimacing corpse. From this point of view the women,
with their laces, ribbons and silks, were more ridiculous
than the men. What can be more horrifying than to

see skeleton hands covered with a wisp of wrinkled skin sticking out of velvet and satin sleeves? The young maidens of seventeen and eighteen wearing around their skull the crown of metal, symbol of virginity, were the most hideous of all. Their youthful skeletons aged quicker than the adult and began to crumble more easily in these dusty corridors. Many of them had to be put lying, for their spine was not strong enough to prop upright. As for the children, they were often unrecognizable, for their bones had melted away, but when they were laid here in their little glass coffins their parents dressed them up in the little suits they wore when they were running about. All the stations of society were represented here, from the rich man dressed in grotesque elegance, down to the poor beggar wrapped in black sacking; great lady and peasant child, doctors, men of learning, even the priests, who were strung up together in a specially privileged corridor. They were even more macabre than the rest because their vestments and robes had more pomp and colour and thus accentuated the grotesque contrast with the pitiful grimacing mask of death. Every one of them had a different expression. Some twisted their faces in an unearthly grin; others opened their mouth, gaping. Even their gestures varied: one skull bent one way, another bent the other way; one skeleton arm was raised, another one lowered. If I gazed long at those interminable rows of dead I should end by considering this the Carnival of Death full of dancing, rattling skeletons. The lay-monk whom I took as my guide had a red face of beatific contentment. He pointed out to me the various categories of bodies, speaking in a placid voice. Not one macabre detail did he let me miss. At one moment I heard a strange rustling sound and the bang of something falling.

" The worst of this place," said he gently, " is that it is infested with mice. There are thousands of them. They gnaw the sinews of the necks of the corpses. Often you'll hear the sound of a skull rolling off the skeleton on to the ground."

" It's a terrible place," said I. " How can you stand it ? "

" It's practice that counts," answered the monk. " After a few weeks one hardly notices them. One ends by feeling an affection for these poor remains of humanity. I shouldn't like to be shut in here, though, at night. It has happened before now, and they say it's a ghostly experience, what with the rustling of mice and the crackling of skeletons and the occasional fall of a skull. It's enough to drive a man crazy. There was a case once where a man fell asleep here one day and awoke alone at night. He shouted and banged at the doors, but nobody heard him. In the morning when the custodian found him he was stark, staring mad."

Just then the bell rang and I was glad to escape into the open air and the sunlight once again.

By the time I got back to the sea-front it was sunset, and at this hour the Marina is crowded, for every Sicilian, poor and rich, would not think of retiring to his home for dinner without that hour or two of loitering on Palermo's fairest promenade by the sea. I often used to ask myself when Palermitans ever withdrew to their own houses, because, as far as I could see, they spent day and night in the open air. The Marina at sunset becomes a vast carnival of colour, sound and movement. The voices of men, women and children swell the chorus. Most of them parade up and down in serried ranks. Children dart in and out pursuing one another. There are countless little taverns full of men drinking penny-worths of Marsala or good, honest Sicilian red, and

booths crowded with women and children gorging themselves on the varieties of Sicilian ice-cream. In front of
us the blue sea is dotted with tiny craft and an occasional
red sail adds vigour to the kermesse of colour.

Occasionally I met people who could not sympathize
with my enthusiasm for the beauties of Palermo. In a
tavern I came across a soldier, a native of Milan, who
was sent to do his service in Sicily. Over several glasses
of wine he confided in me that a Milanese would sooner
go to Hell than be sent for his sins to Sicily.

" The folk down here," said he, " are as different to us
as chalk is from cheese. I can't get on with them.
They are not of the same race as we are—' È la bassa
Italia.' Every day I spend down here I feel that I am
sinking into barbarism. What a backwater this is for
anyone who was born and bred in Milan, the most
modern and go-ahead city in the world."

The soldier's words interested me because they tallied
with many remarks I had noted on my journey through
South Italy and Sicily.

" There's no doubt," said I to myself, " that Italy has
not yet become one united country in spite of the
struggles of Garibaldi and the Great War. Even conscription has not accomplished the task. What is
needed is a moral revolution which will finally achieve
the full significance of Italian nationality."

One evening, as I was walking along the Via
Maqueda, tired and weary after giving a series of performances and making exactly the sum of three lire,
thirty centesimi in four hours, I heard some music in a
side-street. A man was singing in a hoarse voice to the
accompaniment of a guitar. So familiar was the hoarse
voice that I stopped and listened. I couldn't mistake
that voice, and besides, the song was one which I had
played *ad nauseam* during my peregrinations through

Calabria. " Nobody else in the world could own that hoarse voice except my old friend Cesare the hunchback," said I to myself as I turned down the street whence the music came. Sure enough, it was Cesare seated on a stool near a small tavern, singing, and accompanying himself on the guitar for the benefit of a small audience of messenger-boys, women with babies in their arms, and a few workmen in shirt-sleeves.

As soon as Cesare saw me he stopped singing, gave a long whistle and beckoned me with his first finger. Instead of continuing his song he received me in the most theatrical way possible by calling out that I was a long-lost friend and confederate. The audience began to grow in numbers, and in spite of my protests I was drawn into the circle and made to play. Not a word did Cesare say to me except :

" Out with your fiddle, man. *Combiniamo.* Do you remember so and so ? Play up as loud as you can and I'll follow you." When we had finished playing, Cesare turned to a lanky, squint-eyed individual who was standing beside him and called out : " It's your turn now, Michele. Go on, tell them a story. Listen, Signore, to my companion : he is one of the best storytellers in Sicily—he's a Catanese, born and bred."

The lanky Michele then started to tell his story, a traditional one, like the subjects I had seen painted on the carts, for it was all about Rinaldo, Orlando, Clarice, and Bradamante, but it was not the story-telling to which I was accustomed. Rather was it a species of monodrama in which Michele spoke and made all the gestures of a whole company of actors. He told the complicated story of the Paladin's enterprises, their battles against the Saracens, and as he became launched into the throes of the drama he intoned his voice like a priest. He moved his body up and down. He stepped forward and backwards as if he was dancing in honour of some ritual. He stamped upon the ground and at times raised his voice into a hoarse shriek. When the battle scenes reached their height he overwhelmed his audience with a torrent of adjectives, describing the flashing of the swords and the resounding blows on the armour, the horses rolling on the plain, the heap of bleeding corpses and the cries of triumph of the Christians. The behaviour of the rustic audience was at times as surprising as that of the rhapsodist. At moments they hung upon his words, at other moments they gave shouts of approval when the favourite Christian Paladin destroyed his enemy. Occasionally they would burst into harsh roars of laughter when the story-teller gave some humorous twist to the events. Occasionally, also, they would curse under their breath and roar their disapproval when a traitor escaped punishment for his misdeeds. After it was all over, the lanky Michele subsided on a seat and flicked the sweat from his brow with a weary gesture, while Cesare, with that swift movement of his which I knew so well, darted round the assembly with his cap ready for contributions. A little later, the three of us sat down to a meal of salame, bread, and a rough, red wine. Only then did Cesare question me about my disappearance.

" I mourned over you as a lost soul," said he with his mouth full. " You might have been my brother. Why did you leave us ? "

" I was afraid of Aldo," said I. " He was too much of a Mafioso for me. Besides, I wanted to move on more quickly and see the world. I have been right through Sicily since I saw you last."

" Oh, well," answered Cesare ; " we were bound to meet some day. Everyone turns up in Palermo."

" What about Susanna ? " said I.

" She's fixed here now for the present."

" Not with Aldo, I hope ? "

" Not on your life. She's in a house here in a street off the Via Roma. That's all she's fit for. She's a decent girl, though, and we'll go and see her."

With Cesare and Michele I set up partnership, and instead of loitering about the streets I found myself working again according to a system. Cesare was the usual hard task-master. But there were compensations, and one of them was that it gave me introductions to some of the picturesque little marionette theatres which are so characteristic of Sicily. Cesare knew most of the puppet men and boys in the *teatrini* in Palermo, and in the evenings we spent our centesimi in return for seats as near to the stage as possible. This was no easy matter, for puppet shows draw a full house in Palermo, and when there is no room on the rough benches, the *facchini* and street-arabs squat on the floor or else hang in clusters over the edges of the narrow gallery which runs round the theatre. In order to whet the dramatic appetite of the audience the promoters of the show display outside the theatre a florid poster on which are painted exciting scenes from the plays to be represented. It took me some time to accustom myself to the cramped space, the suffocating atmosphere, and the deafening din of excited hoarse voices. At last there was a hush and the curtain rose, disclosing a scene from one of the romantic stories of Charlemagne and his paladins. The cloth-painted scene changed from baronial hall to battlemented wall and then to the forest of the dragon. The puppets were of varying types—those who played secondary parts in the drama were simply made, but those who acted the heroic parts were carved with all the loving care of Sicilian artisans, who have inherited the traditional craft. Orlando, for example, was one of the gorgeous puppets : he was decked out in brilliant costume and he could move his body with as much agility as if he had been an acrobat. This he had to do because he was the favourite hero of the audience and his great scene was the duel with his rival. The sword-duel, I was told by connoisseurs, is always most elaborately done in the marionette theatres because the Sicilian populace understand all the finer subtleties of fencing and would howl derision at an Orlando who was not master of the art. Then there were other puppets, so cleverly contrived that they would split into two parts or lose their heads when Orlando or Rinaldo's sword delivered the fatal blow. It is important to remember that the marionette drama is patronized by connoisseurs, who insist on the traditional costumes, gestures, and actions being preserved. Every detail of Orlando's duel, his fight with the dragon, the bloody battles with Saracens, are regulated with the utmost precision, and any attempt to deviate from the tradition would arouse a storm of booing from the excited audience. Cesare and Michele, the *cantastoria*, tried to explain to me the symbolic gestures of the puppets, but it was no easy matter for the uninitiated to understand whether Ruggero was expressing sorrow or anger by his motions with his hands or what the princess meant when she waved her arms. It was, however, easy to know who was the villain of the piece, for the crowd of sweating *facchini* and street-arabs hurled curses at him and demanded his instant execution. When Orlando appeared he was saluted by a torrent of applause which reminded me of the way in which audiences used to greet the blameless hero in the old red Adelphi melodramas.

When the show was over and we had pushed our way through the throng, Cesare said: "Let us go to see Susanna. We'll give her a serenade." After a short walk we came

to a house in the courtyard of which there was a tiny
lamp burning in front of a picture of the Madonna.
" It's on the first floor," said Cesare as he climbed
the dark staircase.   When he knocked, a tiny spy-hole
opened in the door and an old woman looked out at us.
After some parleying we were admitted into a small,
gaudily furnished *salon*, the floor of which was covered
with a grey carpet burned in many places by the cigarette
butts of visitors.   In the hall outside three old women
were seated round a stove sewing.   In a moment I
heard a woman humming in a loud voice and Susanna
burst in upon us.   She greeted me with as much
affection as if I had been her long-lost brother.

" We've come here to serenade you," said Cesare,
pointing first to his guitar and then to my fiddle.   " Here
is Michele, too, who will tell stories."

Susanna clapped her hands, saying : " To-night will
be a festa.   There are only a few here at this hour.
Come on, I'll introduce you to the *padrona*—Signora
Valido."

With those words she led us into a large brilliantly
lit room where we met the rest of the company.   Signora Valido was a plump, masterful woman with hair
sprouting from her upper lip which gave her more of a
swashbuckling air than the usual Celestina.   When she
spoke she pursed up her lips and wrinkled her nose as if
she was trying to avoid some unpleasant odour.   One
by one she introduced the various girls.   They were a
nondescript collection with the exception of the sprightly
Susanna and a rollicking Rubens wench with black hair
and merry eyes called Adriana la Mantovana.   In the
background were two solemn-faced, furtive-eyed citizens
of the type that lounge against the walls of such places
watching sleepily what goes on.   When the fun becomes
fast and furious they rouse themselves slightly, take

their hands out of their pockets and cast a swift glance in the direction of the temporary host as much as to say— "What about us ? We are guests in this spree, too, aren't we ?" Beside Adriana la Mantovana there was a tubby little Frenchman with a sweaty red face and bull neck—a petty officer—who breathed potent garlic fumes over all of us and rattled off in a wheezing voice French of the Marseilles quality. Adriana did not understand one word of his lingo, but his fumblings and slippery gestures expressed his meaning more clearly than words. Signora Valido, the *padrona*, mobilized us all. The French petty officer stood the first bottle of red wine in return for some music. When Cesare and I had finished our pot-pourri of tunes, Susanna insisted on singing " Funiculì, Funiculà," the famous old Piedigrotta song, because it reminded her of Naples, which she wished she had never left to come to Sicily. No sooner did she finish amid a chorus of bravos than the plump Adriana puffed out her ample bosom and sang at the top of her voice a Venetian pastoral song on the theme of " When April comes and a young maid's fancy "—

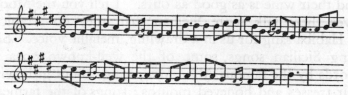

" Quando che Avril torna fora, e ch'el sémena
    margaritine e pavegie sul prà,
    e sora i muri ch'el sol novo ilumina
    le usertoline se sconde qua e là."

After Adriana it was the turn of Michele, the *cantastoria*. He started off on a rigmarole account of Sicilian clown-like types, interspersing it with ejaculatory comments. We laughed at the ugly fellow's grimaces, gestures, and twisting motions, which made him look more like a monkey than a man, but the Frenchman yawned ponderously, expectorated, breathed more garlic over us, and finally stamped his feet, calling out for more music. Then Adriana and Susanna called out : " Habiba ! Habiba ! " Habiba then sheepishly came forward out of her corner. I had not paid much attention to her before now. When I saw her close at hand her face interested me. " She's half Arab," whispered Adriana to me. " Her mother was Moorish and her father Tunisian." She was a complete contrast to the other women, a dark-skinned Moslem with black hair, big lustrous eyes, a bony woman with skin like tanned leather. I expected her to spout French to us seeing that she came from Tunis, but to my amazement she conversed in Sicilian dialect.

" Why does she not talk French if she is a Tunisian ? " said I to Cesare in a low voice.

" Why should she ? " answered he. " There are more Sicilians in Tunis than French. Why, all the cultivation of vines over there is done by *contadini* from this island and their wine is as good as ours. I tell you the Moors over there talk more Sicilian than they do Arabic."

Habiba sang for us in a drawling, metallic voice. She sang Sicilian songs, some of the well-known ones to words by the famous Abbé Meli, songs about girls with fair tresses and honeyed mouths ; songs of the farmer's daughter, whose skin was as white as snow and whose bodice was rich with arabesques and lace :

Her voice, with its nasal harshness, called up visions of Moorish singers in the Soukhs and bazaars of Tetuan, Tangier, Tunis or Marrakesh, but the tunes were Sicilian in lilting 6-8 rhythm and the words incongruously described fair hair and fair skin, which is uncommon in Sicily. I then realized that Sicilian folk-singers devote their songs to the uncommon rather than to the common. It was that queen of Italian folklorists, the Countess Martinengo Cesaresco, who remarked that the " Beautiful ideal " of the Sicilians seemed to be the white rose rather than the red. Golden heads suggested angelical associations and led the Sicilian folk-poet to scorn the national black eyes and olive-carnation colouring. Habiba, however, with her droning voice, transformed the songs into Oriental incantations. She had a whole repertory, prison songs, songs of love delirium (" Pri tia deliru e spasimu "), and songs of muleteers which sounded Spanish in type with their significant turns and grace notes. In the end Cesare roused the whole room to rhythmic fury by rapping out on his guitar the stirring rhythm of the Beating Song.

After that rousing song it was time to break up the festa. The grey dawn was stealing in through the windows. We were all tired, tousled, and thirsty, for there were no more funds left to buy wine, and so I departed with my two companions and wended my way to our temporary lodgings near the Piazza Caracciolo.

The three of us camped in a dark, rat-infested room in a little street called by the picturesque name " Discesa delle Capre " (the descent of the goats). Even in this early hour of the morning the fish-hawkers were beginning to busy themselves. There was fish everywhere and the smell penetrated to my bones. Near the fish-market were the sellers of oranges, lemons, onions, hard-boiled eggs. Gradually the humble life of the city

began to awaken into activity. Soon with the full
blaze of sunlight those little piazzas and narrow streets
echo and re-echo in noisy dissonance. Even the smell
of those streets in Sicily is different to the smell of
Naples, Genoa, or Venice. There is more of the burnt
smell of an Eastern port than we find in the mainland
of Italy, and the crowd are more noisy, for the sun
makes these Southern people more vocal than it does the
Italian. They sing in the streets here in Palermo just
as they do in Seville, and if you walk through the narrow
Via degli Aragonesi or the Piazza Sant' Onofrio, you will
hear the tuneful cries of the hawkers, for in Palermo the
lemon-sellers, onion-sellers and hard-boiled-egg-sellers
have their own traditional musical cry.

I spent some days more roaming with my two friends
as musical picaroons. It was a rough-and-tumble life,
for we lived from hand to mouth and I thought only of
the day and never of the morrow. Then came a sleep-
less night when I suddenly remembered with a pang my
real life which I had escaped from in order to become a
gad-about and a vagabond. Full of remorse, I rushed
off the next morning to the poste restante and found
several letters from home, chiding me for my silence
and wondering what had become of me, and begging me
to hurry back because my father was ill. When I had
finished the letters I sat for a long time in a secluded
garden looking out to sea. I could not bear even to go
back and say farewell to Cesare and his companion. It
was best to break off at once ; and so that same night
I set out on the boat for Naples. In the dark, the
flaming volcano of Stromboli lit up the sea and sky
and gave me the last reminder of Dante's Island of Fire.

CHAPTER XXI

THE END OF MY GRAND TOUR

I HASTENED on my way.

No more for me the delights of leisurely travel which consist in the possession of unlimited time. I actually bought a cheap second-hand watch in a small shop in the Via Toledo, Naples, in order to impress upon myself a régime of punctuality. I resisted the blandishments of guides and commissionaires who offered to show me Pompeii in a morning, Vesuvius in an afternoon and Pozzuoli in an evening. " I have seen them all," cried I. All I saw of Rome on my hurried journey was a series of swift visions : the Claudian aqueduct in the setting sun seen from a third-class railway carriage ; the Forum by moonlight, the Castello San Angelo, the dome of St. Peter's, and the yellow winding flood of the Tiber. At the station I was handed over by the ticket clerk to the police and severely questioned by them for having in my possession a forged 100-lire note—it had been palmed off on me by a dealer in bric-à-brac in the Via del Panteon.

" I suppose you are waiting for the Rome-Paris express," said a talkative fellow-traveller.

" Certainly, sir," said I.

" I'm afraid," said he, " you won't get a through carriage to Paris. The railway service is very bad at present. I don't know what the country is coming to. Yesterday the train was four hours late reaching Livorno."

" Fa lo stesso," said I.   " Provided the train takes me as far as Genoa I'm satisfied."

I was determined to visit once more Capo Santa Chiara and say farewell to my kind and hospitable friends of my Genoa days—Don Alberto, Donna Delfina, and their daughters. I have never forgotten fair-haired Signorina Italia, whose singing had bewitched me that day in the Red Cross Hospital. As long as I had been stationed in Genoa I had gone out every Sunday to Capo Santa Chiara to call upon her. We had made music together : she had sung arias from the operas for me and ancient songs of Vivaldi, Cimarosa, and Marcello. She had read to me Italian poets and initiated me into the harmony of the world's most musical language. In her home I had found that culture of the mind and serenity of outlook for which my restless personality craved incessantly. When I left Genoa on my wandering tour I continued to write to my fair-haired friend and she wrote to me—letters full of serious comments on cathedrals, statues, poems, symphonies such as two young people of different nationality would write to one another while they are still radiant friends, *sans arrière pensée*.   We corresponded in French because my Italian in those days was too clumsy and her English was non-existent.   And now, after all my adventures and all my sight-seeing, I longed to recite for her my rhapsody from the first canto to the last.   And yet, in a sense, I dreaded to return to Capo Santa Chiara, for as soon as I should find myself within the orbit of my friends, I should only increase my deep pangs at having to say a final farewell. I had fallen in love with Signorina Italia at first sight, but in the early stages I rationalized my feelings into friendship and companionship. Day by day I used to say to myself : " Do not fall deeply in love : you will only suffer agonies of unhappiness and you will make her miserable. You are only a passing figure—a phantom who is here to-day and gone to-morrow. As soon as the War is over you will return to your far-off land and you will never see her again." Whenever I talked to myself in that strain I used to determine never to visit Capo Santa Chiara again. But an hour later my will would weaken : I imagined her standing on the terrace of the villa in the sunlight waiting for me to arrive. All my resolves would blow away like leaves in a storm and I would rush out to see her, carrying a big bunch of red carnations, and I would spend the afternoon and evening listening to her singing songs. When I had to leave Genoa and start off on my Grand Tour I felt that Destiny would decide the matter and I should gradually forget her in the stress of new adventures and the vagabond life, but such was not the case. I discovered that absence creates stronger bonds : all the ups and downs of the picaresque life, all the sordid chaos of a truant minstrel, with its days and nights of loneliness, only increased my hopeless longing. I was for ever imagining myself as a modern Ulysses—an ex-serviceman lingering on his return from the wars in order to collect a crop of adventurous stories which he will tell Penelope when eventually he reaches home. How profound the blind minstrel Homer was when he called his story of Ulysses a νόστος, or return home. Every wanderer's story is a return home. From the moment he sallies forth on his adventures his thoughts lead him on ahead, forecasting his arrival at the last mile-stone on the road home. He imagines the familiar scene : the village in the distance, the barking dogs, his own hound who will be the first to recognize him, the old nurse who tended him when a child, and finally his fair lady waiting for him in the shadowy halls. And so all through my long circular journey I thought of the

moment when I would descend the steep little laneway
near the villa on Capo Santa Chiara. I should ring the
bell, the white house-dog would bark and at last she
would appear. I had rehearsed that arrival so frequently
in my mind that I actually dreaded it. If we have not
seen a beloved person for a long time we feel afraid
when the moment for the meeting arrives. Intense joy
always creates an antidote against itself in the mind,
for, as the Greeks knew, the gods are jealous and send
disaster swooping down upon mortals at the climax of
their happiness. With those thoughts dominant in my
mind I did not tell her the day or hour of my arrival,
for she would have met me at the station. I reached the
Capo Santa Chiara on a sunlit afternoon : the air was
clear and my eye took in the full panorama of graceful
coast outline ; the Ligurian mountains and hills studded
with cypress trees and dotted with white villas ; the
distant purple headland of Portofino rounding off the
landscape. In the laneway above the villa I paused,
for in the distance I heard the ethereal notes of a woman's
voice. For me there was all Italy in that voice. Floating through the clear air it awoke in me the thrill of
magic casements opening on fairylands forlorn. The
tune was the following :

O cessate di piagarmi O lasciatemi morir   O   lasciatemi   morir

Whose voice could it have been but hers ? What a
magic coincidence ! A reminder of the past, a prophecy
of future destiny. What could a minstrel do but pull
out his fiddle ? I played the ballade of Dvořak, a piece
which I knew she loved. A moment later she had
rushed downstairs to meet me, and we both felt as if
we had never been separated. Then she led me into

the villa. Alberto poured me out a glass of wine and I had to begin my story from the beginning. After I had exhausted my theme it was my turn to ask questions.

"What has happened to the country?" said I to Alberto. "There's nothing anywhere except talk of strikes, revolution and civil war. In Rome there has been an ugly strike as a protest against the dearness of food. Here in Genoa you seem to be in as bad a state."

Alberto sighed and raised his hands with a gesture of despair. "Things are going from bad to worse," said he. "We are in the hands of Bolshevists. Soon they will seize all the factories and plunder the country in the name of Socialism. There has been, indeed, an epidemic of strikes, and can we wonder after all that the nation has suffered in the War? When you saw us last we were riding on the full tide of victorious enthusiasm. We sang the national anthems until we had no more voice left. We thought that a new era of prosperity would arise. Instead, what do we find but weariness and disillusion? I don't blame the workers. They must feed their wives and children. No wonder they wreck the food shops when they see the prices soaring to the skies."

Delfina interrupted, saying : "It isn't the workers who cause the strikes but the Socialist committees of action who try to foment political disturbances in the name of the Russian Millennium. Our country at present is the victim of international Bolshevik agents."

"I should not mind," said Alberto at length, "if we could even hold our heads up and say that our foreign policy was worthy of our country, but, speaking of Government, we have fallen out of the frying-pan into the fire. If we had to choose between Orlando and Nitti as Prime Ministers, I would choose Orlando every time. Orlando was weak and vacillating, but he would never have let the mob take the bit between its teeth as L'onorevole Nitti did when he took office. It was Nitti who let the mob impose its *calmieri*, or maximum prices, regardless of value. Why, there are people here in Genoa who say that Nitti crows with delight at these riots, for he hopes to terrify all of us into supporting his Government as the only hope against red revolution."

Italian politics was a depressing theme, so I tried to change the subject. I asked Alberto how he spent his time now that his war service was over.

"My dear boy," said he, "I am spending my time in the most profitable way possible, by going back to school. I am 57 years of age, *bien sonnés*, and yet I have signed on at the University of Genoa as a first-year medical student. Every day I go off to do my dissecting, and if you met me you would find me surrounded by young students of 19 or 20 years of age."

"Bravo, professor," said I. "I know of very few men of your age who would go back to the class-room, for was it not Socrates in the *Gorgias* who advised him who had reached man's estate to put away the things of childhood?"

"You are wrong there," exclaimed Alberto. "It is from the young that we older men must learn and draw our strength. Much of what I have seen in my life has made me pessimistic and cynical. Pessimism and cynicism are not what we need in modern Italy. The young have taught me to sweep those dark and gloomy thoughts out of my mind as if they were chaff. They have given me hope in the future. I wish you could see those youths who are beginning their university courses. When you hear the sad tale of political chaos, strikes, war-weariness, and social injustice, you would imagine that the future was black for Italy, but I tell you there is a new spirit in the air."

" I know," said I, " you mean the Fascist Movement of Benito Mussolini. I should think I have heard of it. Here and there, up and down the country, I have met members of the Associazione dei Combattenti (Association of Ex-Servicemen). They are determined to oppose the Bolsheviks and all those who insult the men who defended their country in the War, but are they strong enough ? "

" Wait till you see," answered Alberto ; " the Ex-Service men will follow Mussolini to a man because their best members already belong to the Fasci di Combattimento, but to them you must add the great mass of generous youth who have allied themselves with their elder brothers of the Fasci. They are gradually uniting their forces and preparing for the big struggle in the near future. Let Nitti govern with the help of your mass parties. He will not be able to lead the country back to normal by his semi-socialist tendencies. What is the good of his decrees ordering the splitting up of the large estates into small holdings if he does not provide the new peasant proprietors with housing, cattle and agricultural implements ? "

Our conversation was interrupted by the arrival of a group of friends from Buenos Aires, and then the room became a babel of many tongues. I marvelled at Alberto, Delfina, and their daughters : they passed with incredible swiftness from one language to another. With Signorina Italia I soon learnt the technique, but I reserved French for our *tête-à-tête* because I could express my meaning better. As we saw the rest of the company deep in discussion we slipped out on to the terrace. The moon was shining, the sea glittered beneath us. I persuaded her to follow me and we crept noiselessly down into the garden and out on to the steep, stony path leading to the edge of the cliff. For a long time we sat on the fisherman's seat gazing out to sea, listening to the gentle ebb and flow of the tide. From time to time tiny lights floated over the calm surface of the sea and we could hear the distant voices of the fishermen.

How I longed to prolong this moment when both of us felt the harmony of the whole universe. As I gazed down at the dark sea with its patches of molten silver, the gentle lapping waves awakened in me eddies of sound which prolonged themselves into the immense music of the night with its myriads of stars. Time was abolished and our two lives became eternal. We had always loved each other and we had always heard this boundless music. Italia, too, was bewitched by the night, for she was silent, but her silence told me more than any words.

On the following day I spoke to Alberto and was accepted formally as the *fidanzato* of Signorina Italia. There was a touch of ritual about the betrothal. We dashed off to a goldsmith in Genoa to buy the rings which Delfina presented to us with due ceremony. On the inside of the rim was engraved the name and the date of the engagement. At last the day came when I had to say a final farewell. "You will come back soon," said she bravely. "Remember we are both young : we can live on nothing. I'll give you plenty of courage."

"I shall return in a very short time," said I as I waved to her from the train. No sooner had she disappeared from my sight than I felt myself rapidly sinking back into my old condition of despairing uncertainty.

CHAPTER XXII

IRISH-ITALIAN INTERLUDE

DUBLIN, 1919–20. I found myself back again in my students' rooms in the university. Trinity College is set in the heart of Ireland's capital —it is a paradise in the oriental sense of the word, that is to say, a place surrounded by a high wall. The tide of traffic swirls around it like angry waves around a rock, but as soon as I pass through its venerable portals out of the crowded College Green I find myself in an abode of peace. The roar of modern life becomes a distant murmur and my eye is charmed by pleasant vistas of green lawns and gardens surrounded by the massive granite buildings of the Georgian epoch. When I returned to Trinity College I found it transformed. The lecture halls were thronged with a bewildering variety of individual types : there were students in cap and gown, who some months previously had been colonels, majors, captains : men limping on crutches, others minus an arm ; a weird assortment of costumes could be observed, for many still wore khaki breeches, leggings and British " warms " which gave them the appearance of gunmen on holiday. There were warriors from the dominions—Canadians cheek by jowl with Anzacs and South Africans—Americans from the Middle West, Indians and Egyptians. In contrast to that varied multitude of returned soldiers there were the students from Ireland—north, south, east and west—who had not been to the wars, but had lived through the stormy years of Irish affairs from Easter Week 1916.

Those first two years after the War were the most colourful in all the chequered history of the college of the undivided Trinity—mother of a university. They marked the beginning of a new epoch. I was more conscious of the changes than many others because my college memories reached beyond my own short span of student life. My father had been a Fellow of the College and his recollections became mine. He had transmitted to me many of the anecdotes which cling to the university figures of the past as moss and lichen do to monuments, making them venerable. One by one the great personalities of Trinity's Golden Age of scholarship had died off, leaving as a valuable heritage a few quips and cranks and anecdotes to add to the repertory of college rhapsodic minstrels, in this way bearing out the truth of Homer's adage that the gods weave the destruction of men that mortals of future ages may hear a theme for song. As for the anecdotes of university dons, they have always a Greek sense of balance—μηδὲν ἄγαν—not too much sadness, but just a slight, fragrant melancholy like the bouquet of a venerable wine that has lost its strength. Tyrrell, the most elegant of Hellenists, had died early in the War; Provost Mahaffy, the greatest personality of them all, whose manifold talents and deep knowledge of life were more worthy of a Medicean court than of a soulless, modern age, had passed away in the spring of 1919.

The survivors of the great band were objects of curiosity to the bronzed young ex-servicemen. " They are wraiths of a world that is about to disappear," said one full of the insolent arrogance of youth, but he deserved a rebuke from his elders for misunderstanding the meaning and function of a university. The great provost

Mahaffy, had he been alive, would have chided him in his icy, lisping tones, using the words he once said of an Irish poet : " Poor fellow ! He is an αὐτοδίδακτός— he never worked under a master." In the modern world the university is the last home of true intellectual freedom where old age possesses its special virtues. Inside the fortress walls every kind of learning, even that which is scorned by the omniscient materialists of the outer world, should bloom freely and shed its radiance : every variety of human personality should be welcomed, every lost cause, every vagary of human fantasy should find its tiny plot of ground whereon to prosper. And so every individual eccentricity of those old men had its value, though the young, ignorant Freshmen regarded them as ancient, bearded senators of Rome sitting in silent conclave, awaiting their doom at the hands of the invading Gauls. One must work under a master and one must learn to look with affection on those old men's foibles, for they will in after-life be the freshest memories that keep echoing through the mind. Thus we junior lecturers cultivated the patriarchs : we listened in raptures in the evenings when T. T. Gray, senior Fellow, ninety years of age, described Irish life in the days of Charles Lever, or analysed for us in detail the tactics of the Duke at the battle of Salamanca, using a salt-cellar and a mustard-pot to illustrate the Arapiles. Inside the university, with its calm squares and lawns, there was complete harmony in those days—an equilibrium caused by innumerable tensions. Just as every intellectual and athletic activity was represented, so was every nuance in political opinion. Trinity was a melting-pot of dissonant views : there were ex-servicemen full of belief in the ideals of the British Empire waiting their turn for administrative jobs in India or Africa ; passionate Gaels eager to work for an Ireland completely

independent of England ; dour Ulstermen equally determined not to yield an inch of their Northern Kingdom
to Sinn Fein threats. Strange as it may seem, there was
unity in all this diversity. Within the walls differences
of opinion never went further than arguments conducted
according to the rules of the debating halls. Some of
the closest friends in post-war days were those who
belonged to diametrically opposite political camps.

No sooner did those students pass through the portals
of the Front Gate and enter the humming life of the
city than they were caught up into the vortex, for outside was College Green, the scene of many an Irish battle.
And in Ireland troubles were growing in intensity.
Hardly a day passed without some political crime. From
within the gate I could hear the high-pitched voices of
the newsboys announcing yet another ambush, assassination or burning. From my windows I could see
the ceaseless dashing to and fro of lorries full of soldiers
with guns and tin hats. Those few years were one
long-drawn-out agony for those of us who were unable
to wall ourselves up in a paradise of learning and forget
the world. How I had envied my father's serenity
during the rebellion of 1916, when the streets echoed to
the rattle of machine-guns and bursting bombs ! He
had sat calmly in his study working away at a transla-
tion of *The Knights* of Aristophanes ! How I cursed
my return to my native land ! Out in Italy there was
the same chaos ; there were bombs and shooting, but
there was hope. I knew that the university students
out there had joined with the ex-servicemen to create
a new movement of national solidarity, and I had profound faith in their ideals. In my own country I was
torn by agonizing doubts. If I had only been a hardened die-hard I could, perhaps, have sympathized with
the sinister brutality of the Black and Tans, whereas I

felt nothing but indignation against England's politicians for using such a dastardly weapon against Ireland. Had I only been drawn into the Gaelic orbit, I should have felt the passion of Pearse and Plunkett and even accepted the cruel, cowardly assassinations which besmirched the fair name of Ireland. And so, in common with many of my companions, my mind was divided this way and that. Could anyone blame us for seeking to forget the present in a round of fruitless orgies ?

In those days Dublin was a sinister city ! Everyone lived on the edge of a volcano. City life went on as usual : shops and theatres were open, football matches played before crowds, but then all of a sudden in some street crowded with shoppers shots would ring out— horrified silence—high-pitched shrieks of women— " Who has been hit ?—there he is lyin' on the ground —merciful God protect us ! look at the blood flowin' from his head."

In those days, even in the dead of night, the feeling of tension did not cease. I remember on one moonlit night gazing out of my windows in Trinity on the beautiful vision of a deserted College Green. Not a sound. Two outside cars were parked near Grattan's statue and their jarveys were sound asleep. The Bank of Ireland—Ireland's Parliament in the eighteenth century—with its columns shining white in the moon, reminded me of Italy. Suddenly I heard the crackle of revolver shots in the dark street below and a man moaning for help. A few seconds later I saw two ghost-like figures run across towards the Bank and disappear. The moaning soon ceased. By the time the ambulance arrived he was dead. In some cases the tension was too much for men's nerves and they went crazy.

Life in Dublin in those days was hectic as well as

cruel. In addition to the tragic feelings which were
uppermost in our minds there was the tremendous urge
to unbridled enjoyment characteristic of the post-war
years. When I compare the behaviour of British with
Continental youth in those days I find that the stolid
Britishers showed less restraint than the temperamental
Latins. In Italy there had been a great deal of shouting
after the Armistice and singing of patriotic songs but
comparatively little of that spirit of unbridled licence.
Instead, after the first glorious triumph of victory there
was a spirit of mournful disillusion and drab poverty
in Italy. Among the youth and the ex-Servicemen so
much plotting and counter-plotting was going on that
there was very little time for dancing or drinking.
Political excitement, due to the fierce struggle between
the two ideologies of Communism and Fascism, grew
apace and absorbed all men's energies. In England and
in Ireland, among those who had suffered in the War,
a hectic, tragic spirit swept men and women off their
feet. " Who says the British are a calm, solid, sensible
people ? " said a Frenchman to me as he stood watching a crazy party of drunken revellers. " Why, they
drink themselves into oblivion as the Russians used to
do *quand ils avaient le vin triste.*" The fitting symbol
of that mad period when one tried to forget the tragedy
of the Great War and one's own tragedy at home was
the bouncing, negroid Charleston which made the
veteran composer Saint-Saëns say as he watched the
frenzied couples dancing it : " Ils ont la figure triste
et le derrière gai." But all the time we in Ireland were
dancing and spreeing there were other young men
working out steadily and pitilessly their plans to put an
end to British power in Ireland. Those eager, sharp-
eyed young men lived as ascetics : they did not drink
or dance the Charleston. Like the revolutionaries in

Italy, they laboured underground, gradually creating a secret service with ramifications through all the land, which became a model for foreign countries to copy.

When I look back on those days of national struggle, I smile as I recall to mind those who fondly believed that their nationalistic schemes would be achieved by normal Parliamentary procedure. What great movement has ever taken place without fanatical extremists to lead it? The imaginations of men are always stirred by the fierce extremists—who cry out " all or nothing." Compromise is fatal to those movements whose intensity postulates violence from the first. For national movements, if they are to triumph, must sweep irresistibly forward in a surging tide, overwhelming all those who waver, and their motto is " the doubter damned."

As day by day we watched the ever-vacillating British policy in Ireland, weak at one moment, too drastic at another, for ever snatching at compromise as a man slipping into a precipice clutches at a clump of grass, few of us doubted that the grim, tight-lipped Sinn Feiners would win the day. Every week I received letters from Italia giving me the story of chaos and misgovernment in her country. She was now at Milan, taking singing lessons at the Conservatorium, and as that city was particularly affected by Communist propaganda there were ceaseless clashes between the Reds and the Fascists. On one occasion a house a few doors from where she was living was wrecked by bombs. It had been my wish that she should go to Milan to take up the singing lessons she had interrupted during her period of War service. I wanted her to specialize in old Italian music of the seventeenth and eighteenth centuries to which her light soprano voice was suited. Alone in my gloomy college rooms looking out on

College Green I dreamed of an ideal life with her—a
life spent under sunny Italian skies—not a domestic,
bourgeois life burdened with children and a bank over-
draft, but one spent in the manner of a "dilettante"
(using the word in its true Italian sense of one who
savours refinements of life). I imagined myself owner
of a tiny villa in Posilipo or Portofino with a terrace
looking out to sea. Our days would be spent listening
to music or playing violin sonatas or reading together
Italian and Spanish authors or visiting picture galleries.
In order to prop up my courage and prolong my Italian
dream I used then to go off to my violin master, Achille
Simonetti. With him I would talk of his friend Simone,
the old violin-maker I had known in Genoa, of Giuseppe
Oddone, the luthier of Turin, of Sivori, the only pupil of
the Genoese king of violinists, Paganini. But Simonetti
felt the blight of revolutionary Ireland no less than I
did. He lived in terror of his life ever since the night
when the Black and Tans raided his house for arms.
The poor old man was not in the least warlike, but he
had the misfortune to rent a house from a lady who
was one of the leaders in the Sinn Fein movement, with
the consequence that it was repeatedly raided. But
Simonetti and I consoled ourselves in music. We
gathered a 'cellist and a viola player and we played
Brahms and Beethoven quartets—the best antidote to
world chaos. Poor Simonetti! He never recovered
from those troubled years in Ireland. Not long afterwards he left the country and went back to France, the
country of his wife. He sank into deep poverty and
at the time of his death was in actual physical want.
But although starvation stared him in the face, he refused
to the end to part with his beautiful Bergonzi violin on
which he had played when he was in his prime. It was
sold after his death by friends to provide money for his

children. It is strange to note how some Italians lose the vigorous and combative qualities of their race when they live too long abroad. Simonetti was a Piemontese and should have possessed the hard-bitten characteristics of his region, but when he came to Ireland he lost heart and let himself dwindle into the position of a *buon violino*, which in Italy is the expression of mediocrity : he became, in fact, resigned to his fate. Not so Esposito, the Italian pianist, composer and conductor, who for more than forty years directed musical life in Dublin. Esposito, though he came from Naples, the so-called home of *dolce far niente*, had all the hard-bitten qualities Simonetti lacked. Right to the end he refused to resign himself to the Celtic Twilight. He cursed us as a nation for our lack of logic, our faulty sense of rhythm, and he ruled us as a dictator. Then when he had by superhuman exertions given two generations of our people a musical tradition, the little man got down off his rostrum, packed up his traps and went back to Florence to die, and Ireland still awaits his successor.

My father died on the 20th of July, 1920. He had been unwell for over a year, but his illness, instead of diminishing his energies, seemed actually to increase them. He died at Cushendun, a tiny village in the glens of Antrim where he had gone to visit schools. Looking back to those days, I sometimes think that it was fitting that my father should have died when he did. With him passed away many of the schemes for which he had struggled stoically for many years. At the end of his career as Resident Commissioner of National Education he saw the old régime tottering to its close, but he was spared the sorrow of witnessing the division of his country into two irreconcilable governments which would fan the flames of national hatred for all eternity. My father believed that he could hold the balance, as far as education was concerned, between the warring factions north and south, because he was completely devoid of prejudice or bigotry.   He was a Catholic and a devout one, but he never let religious considerations bias his judgment.   He believed passionately that religious bigotry had always been the curse of the country.   His early training in classical scholarship had clarified his mind and given him a stern critical sense of values. " If we Christians could only learn from the sweet reasonableness of the Greek thinkers " was his constant refrain.   In him, as in so many courageous men, there were two personalities tugging viciously at one another. He was born to be a scholar and he had the scholar's power of being able to immerse himself in his subject of research to the exclusion of all mundane doings.   His greatest happiness was to shut himself up with his books.   In one of my last conversations with him he said in a mood of melancholy retrospection that his life would have been a happier one if he had only stayed on as a Fellow of Trinity College and become Regius Professor of Greek.   But he had a second impatient personality driving him to be a man of action.   He was a reformer, and he longed to impose his ideas on men and lead them.   This second ambitious personality gave the scholar in him no rest, for it made him fret and fume at the cramped life of a don within the university paradise.   And so he vaulted over the high walls and followed his ambitions and became the most attacked public man in Ireland, for whoever tried to be a reformer in Irish education received buffetings from all sides impartially.   My father enjoyed the excitement of those struggles.   When they threatened, his nostrils would dilate like those of a war-horse scenting the coming battle. After they were over he would return home weary in mind and sit down to work at his text of Aristophanes.

One great reform he managed to carry out in Ireland : the encouragement of Shakespeare in the schools. Year after year he fought for the plays, saying that they were the greatest educative force in the world. Some years later, when I became acquainted with the philosopher Gentile, whose great reform revolutionized education in Fascist Italy, I was interested to find that he too laid stress on the importance of Shakespeare's universal spirit in the school curriculum. My father did not believe in ruling education like a bureaucrat from the capital : he wanted to follow the work of the schools all over the country. He was devoted to the cause of the national teachers and he genuinely enjoyed meeting and discussing with them their individual problems. " The good ones need encouragement," said he, " and the slack ones need continually prodding." And so he would spend a great part of the year roaming round Ireland in a car, visiting the tiny village schools in the remote parts of the country as well as the big city institutions. As children, my sisters and I used to be taken on some of those tours, and there were always a few friends who accompanied us.

" We should call this the chariot of Thespis," said I to him one day as we drove off.

" Call it rather a roaming symposium," replied my father, laughing. " Have we not Dr. Mahaffy, the arbiter of all polite conversation, and Mr. Waldron, the most authentic descendant of the eighteenth century ? "

In the earlier part of the day during those journeys my father would enter the schools, look at the reports given by the inspector, talk to the teacher and then make the children recite or read scenes from *Julius Cæsar* or *The Merchant of Venice*. L. A. Waldron, bearded, carrying his ponderous Falstaffian paunch, would survey the class with the solemnity of some oriental Potentate. Meanwhile, Dr. Mahaffy would lead us children into the meadow outside and talk to us by the hour of wild flowers and birds. When our chariot moved on we would choose some tranquil spot by a stream for the picnic lunch, and when the shades of evening began to fall, the question would arise where we were to lodge for the night. " I think we had better go to the Four Counties Hotel," said the sybarite Waldron, " the food is less execrable than at the other hotel and there is some good Larose claret if I am not mistaken." But Dr. Mahaffy would interrupt : " I was just thinking that Lord X lives near here. He is a dear friend of mine. I always stay there when I am up in these parts."

After many an argument our car would lumber up the avenue to the noble lord's manor house, where, on the strength of the learned doctor's introduction, we would generally find a hospitable welcome. My father's personal tours through the country schools were certainly responsible for increasing Ireland's love for Shakespeare. Even to-day, when his name is forgotten in Irish education and many of his reforms have been superseded, the work he did for Shakespeare has not yet become completely obliterated. Directors of wandering companies playing Shakespeare have found extraordinary appreciation in the small Irish towns. The lines of *The Merchant* and *Julius Cæsar*, which villagers learnt at the national school, still echo through their minds. It was from those school-inspecting tours with my father that I derived my craze for leisurely travel in remote places. In 1908, when we motored through Innishowen peninsula in the wild north of Donegal, our Darracq was the first motor the old inhabitants had seen and they looked upon it with wonder. I always remember the expression of awe on the face of a white-bearded old fisherman as he gazed at the car. Finally he said in a slow voice : " What wonderful things God does be givin' to the people, to be sure. Now that I've seen it, I'll be tellin' them all in the next world of what I've seen."

It was on those journeys through Ireland that I got glimpses of the vivid world of poetry and song that exists close to the soil of Ireland, whose peasants, tramps, pedlars, fiddlers, bagpipe players, became the heroes of her literary renaissance. We thought precious little of fiddlers, bagpipe players or Ireland's literary renaissance in that mournful year of 1920. Even my friend the old blind penny-whistle-player of St. Stephen's Green—an optimist if ever there was one—would pull his tousled beard and turn up his sightless eyeballs, saying in a whining tone : " What are we comin' to at all at all ? There's a curse on this country. Tell me, son, where am I standin' now ? "

" You're outside the Shelbourne Hotel."

The old man would then straighten himself and play in shrill quavering tones " God Save the King."

The old man was right : there seemed to be a curse on Ireland.

The murders and the burnings had increased tenfold through 1920 and on the 20th of November of that year came the climax of horror with " Bloody Sunday." On that day fourteen British officers were murdered in their beds by the Sinn Feiners. Early in the morning the " skip " or college servant awoke me with the words : " Oh, sur, there's after been a terrible massacre."

" Massacre ? What do you mean ? "

" I'm after seein' it—too true, I'm tellin' ye. An' I comin' along in the street I seen a gintleman in pyjamas leanin' out of a window wid his hand stretched out as if he was callin' out. When I got up near the house there was n'ere a moan out of him. ' He's as dead as

a door-nail,' said a man who was passin'.   God save us,
sur—what is the country comin' to ?   There's scores
of poor gintlemen lyin' wallowin' in their blood."

When I dressed and went out into College Green I
soon heard the details.   The officers, instead of being
in barracks, were staying in various houses in the city.
They were taken completely by surprise by the gunmen
and some were in bed with their wives.   In one case
a wife threw herself in front of the raiders and tried to
shield her husband, but in vain.   The murderers emptied
their revolvers into him.   She was taken later in the
day to a hospital—a raving lunatic.   Dublin, on that dark
November Sunday, was like a city of the dead : there
were very few in the streets and people talked in whispers
as though they were afraid to call down still greater
calamities.   Two of the fourteen I knew—one with
whom I had been drinking a few days previously in the
bar of Jammet's restaurant.   The other, a young officer,
was engaged to a friend of mine.   A few days later I
watched from my rooms in Trinity the procession of
fourteen coffins covered with Union Jacks pass slowly
through the crowded streets.   Who but Voltaire would
have found the eloquence to cry out against *la bêtise
humaine*—the hideous idiocy of human cruelty?   Sean
O'Casey's heroine might well cry out : " Sacred Heart
of the Crucified Jesus, take away our hearts o' stone an'
give us hearts o' flesh.   Take away this murdherin' hate
an' give us Thine own eternal love."

In the Irish nation, however, there is a weird quality
of grotesque humour which springs up in the most tragic
moments—a spirit of antithesis which arises from the
innate stoicism of the people.   It is this jaunty stoicism
in distress which makes Ireland the most glorious picaresque nation after Spain, for in Dublin there is a philosophy of hunger, a code of knight-errantry among the

poor and destitute which cannot be subdued by horror,
cruelty and injustice. Many a time with medical students
on their rounds I visited those haunts of the picaresque
which would have given Cervantes more copy than ever
he got from Monipodio's school for robbers in Seville.
Among that crowded population of waifs and strays the
Irish revolutionary " on the run " would always find a
hiding-place. No threat of military reprisals, no bribery
would frighten those poor starving wretches into yielding up their secrets. Living in destitution worse than
any I had seen among the sulphur workers of Sicily or
the slum-dwellers of Naples, they yet preserved their
grotesque humour, which at times would swell into
an uproarious symphony of macabre laughter. Becky
Cooper, Dublin's scarfaced Celestina ; the Jesting Whip-
pet—a whore, whose nickname was due to her unlimited
capacity for alcoholic liquors (she was aptly called after
the smaller or female tanks of the British military occupation) ; Mossy Banks, a decrepit street-walker, so-called
by a bibulous poet in a fit of melancholy reminiscence of
green fields. Not one of them would have hesitated to
fight, spy and perjure themselves to protect the boys " on
the run." Characteristic of those days was my experience one night during Curfew hours. The Curfew imposed by the military was a new experience for Dubliners
accustomed to loiter in the streets until the late hours.
At first they paid little attention to the ordinance, but
the fear of being caught by a flying squad of Tans soon
made them dash for their houses before the appointed
hour. Those of us who lived in Trinity College enjoyed
the Curfew period—it gave spice to life to play hide-and-
seek with the police lorries patrolling the dark streets.
It was not by any means easy to dodge those cars, for
they had on the front a powerful searchlight, whose rays
searched out every nook and corner of the street for

fugitives—" for all the world as if we had been bloody Zeppelins," said an irate Gaelic friend to me as he dodged behind a pillar. One night two of us became separated from our companions, and, instead of standing still and merging into the stone-work of a house in Dame Street, we moved and the searchlight caught us. Instantly the lorry halted. " Hands up ! " cried half a dozen harsh voices. " Run across here quick. Hands up ! quick, or you're for it." We ran over and stood timidly in front of the lorry. One was never quite sure with Black and Tans : if they were drunk they would wave their automatics about and occasionally in their fervour they would press the trigger. However, on this occasion they were gruffly good-humoured. " Why were you not in before Curfew?—no excuse—no arguments—get into the lorry." Giving us both a playful kick behind, he pushed us into the lorry. The lorry was already full of people—mostly women. Some of them were lying on the floor in a drunken stupor, others, as soon as the lorry began to move on, became vociferous and cried out : " Up Ireland —up the rebels—wrap me in the green flag ! " The police paid no attention but drove on through the silent streets, switching their sinister flashlight from side to side —our insides were shaken up and down as we jolted— the drunken women fell in a heap, the men cursed, until there was a regular riot of invective and song. Round and round the streets we careered, halting every now and then to pick up a truant Curfew-breaker—generally under the influence of liquor. Finally, we were deposited at the police station. " What's your name ? " said a good-humoured, red-faced sergeant of mammoth size bred specially for the Dublin Metropolitan Police. When we announced that we were Trinity students the sergeant winked at us, saying : " Trinity boys is it—medicals I don't think—well, have yez any money on ye ? " When we replied affirmatively we were separated from the waifs and strays and taken into a snug inner room. The rest of the night was spent playing cards with the police.   I won eightpence, my friend lost sixpence—we drank four bottles of Guinness each and at five in the morning we were conducted by a constable in state to the front gate of the College.   There are many worse places than an Irish police station and there were few men who had much evil to say of the good-natured Metropolitan Police or the Constabulary—as fine a body of men as one could find anywhere in the world.

In December I went out to Italy to visit Italia and make arrangements for our marriage. " What matter if we shall be paupers ? " said she. " We are young and we both can work."   When I arrived at Capo Santa Chiara all the old fishermen and their cronies came up to salute me and congratulate me on my luck in winning Signorina Italia for a bride.   One old woman with a severe face pulled me aside, saying : " What right have you to take a fine Italian girl and carry her off to the other side of the world ?   She should marry one of her own race."   In spite of this declaration, she gave us her hearty blessing.

Everyone on the cape had his own vision of affairs and he hastened to give it.   One exclaimed against the dock-labourers, who in spite of strikes and depressed trades had made so much money that they were able to buy themselves villas in the suburbs of Genoa.   Another talked of Fiume and quoted the saying : " It is not Italy who has annexed Fiume, but Fiume who has annexed Italy."   A third gave a dramatic description of the strike tactics of the Socialists.   " Do you know," said he, " that during this year there have been no fewer than 1,881 strikes ?   Things cannot go on much longer as they are. There will be a huge revolution and we shall all march

back to the trenches again." Everybody spoke of the
Fascist revolution which was preparing itself. One
would mention the name of Mario Sonzini, a labourer
who was one of the first martyrs of the Fascist cause :
another would enlarge on the big part played by the
" plotonisti "—the ex-servicemen who had held non-
commissioned rank and who after the war was over,
formed themselves into units. As for the university
students, they played a preponderating part and were
to be found in every section.

It was then that I made the acquaintance for the first
time with the young student Black Shirts. Many came
to visit Don Alberto and Donna Delfina. Good-
looking, athletic fellows they were, quiet, unassuming,
with a certain solemnity of manner. Many of them were
thin-lipped and fanatical and I mentally compared them
with our revolutionaries at home. The chief organizer
of the movement for Liguria in those days was a certain
Lantini—who to-day occupies the exalted post of Secretary
of State of the Corporations. In those days Lantini was a
tempestuous force in Genoa. Gifted with indefatigable
energy, he spared others no more than he spared himself.
He would walk up and down his room firing off rapid
sentences at one : " The movement is growing—growing
—first of all on aristocracy—the aristocracy of Piazza
San Sepolcro Milan where it was formed—the aristocracy
of the trenches—then the bourgeoisie came in—the little
bourgeoisie, mind you—conservative in the best Italian
tradition—then the movement right from the first included the students, the workers in the city and even the
workers in the country districts." Lantini would then
go on to explain how intricate was the secret service built
up by the organization, and he would question me about
the Sinn Feiners—about Michael Collins especially, about
De Valera and Erskine Childers. I was amazed at his

intimate knowledge of our revolutionary movement until
he explained in a burst of confidence that the Fascist
authorities had copied many of the efficient points in the
Sinn Fein secret service methods.   I felt quite ashamed of
not being a Sinn Feiner when he paid compliments to
Ireland in my name.

" There is one point, however, where we are superior
to you," said another Fascist, " you have not got the
manganello (stick) and castor oil."

" God forbid," said I to myself as I thought of
those brawny black-shirted youths wielding ashplants
in a crowded street.   Castor oil, too, given in large doses
is an uncomfortable medicine, but it leaves no ill-effects.
Thinking things over in my mind, I came to the conclusion
that the stick and castor oil method is kindlier than the
revolver method which was used in our country.   The
Italian method was a combination of brutality and humour and it certainly was effective—a *katharsis* or purifica-
tion of the emotions for those who gave and those who
received.   Nevertheless, the whole question of violence
and reprisals aroused fierce arguments around the family
table.   Donna Delfina was in favour of the *manganello*
and castor oil because it did not do irreparable injury
and it put the fear of God into the Communist agitators.
Don Alberto wavered.   He was all in favour of the
Black Shirts but he belonged to the old school and he did
not like truculence in youth.   Italia was definitely against
the violent side of Fascism and she tried to sway me, but
I thought of ambushes and nightly shootings in Dublin
and I devoutly wished the Black and Tans and Sinn
Feiners could fight one another with shillelaghs and
castor oil instead of revolvers and gelignite.

It was a relief for me to escape from those interminable
discussions on political theories and ideologies and go
for long walks with Italia into the country around Genoa.

Some days we followed the coast road towards Recco and Camogli, two little towns which have given sailors to the navy ever since the old days of the republic, or we would push on to Santa Margherita, Paraggi and Portofino, whence we could gaze entranced at the sweeping curve of the golden riviera as far as Spezia. It was the only time in my life when not a single doubt ruffled the calm surface of my mind. I lived in the glorious present and the future stretched before me like a broad path strewn with rose-petals. I made the most absurd plans which I knew could never be realized. Italia, in spite of her woman's practical sense, encouraged me in my fantasy because it was the one moment in our lives when we could live without a care in the world.

Another day I took my fiddle together and we walked up the road into the mountains. We visited the village of Zoagli, where she knew some peasant women who did the wonderful traditional brocades which the Genoese hang from their windows on feast-days. I played all the Italian and Sicilian tunes I could remember for the old women as they worked and Italia sang the " Canzone del Piave " and the song of Monte Grappa, thus bringing back to my memory the first day I had ever seen and heard her in the Genoese military hospital. " How strangely destiny works," said I. " If I had not been lent by the British Y.M.C.A. to Italian Red Cross to fiddle to your soldiers, I should never have seen your golden hair or heard your sweet voice. I should have departed after demobilization without a memory of Italy and I should probably never have returned."

" You would have married an Irish girl and you would lead a happier life. One should never marry outside one's race—that is what the Fascists say, and they are right. Here am I leaving not only Italy but the Latin world for the Northern, of which I know nothing, not even a word of English. It is as if I were allowing you to snatch me away to fairyland."

"That is not true. You are bringing Italy and the Latin world with you. You will civilize me, the Northern barbarian, and I shall follow the example of so many British poets and writers who added to their nationality of birth the second nationality of art and beauty, which is Italian."

After our marriage in Genoa we set off straight for Spain, where we spent three months roaming about the country. We were equipped with third-class kilometric tickets which enabled us to buy three thousand kilometres of Spain. At the end of our lengthy wandering my wife was a hardened vagabond. The return to England and Ireland was a new experience for me because she had never been in an English-speaking country and to me fell the task of initiating her into all the complexities of Anglo-Saxon life. It is difficult for those who have been brought up according to British conventions to understand what a vast cleavage exists between Anglo-Saxon and Latin civilization. My wife, who was born in South America and had always lived within the orbit of Italian, Spanish or French influences, found herself at first *désorientée* even in London. We arrived there at the beginning of the fogs. The City of Mist seemed to her unreal ; she could not accustom herself to the vague, blurred outlines, the slower rhythm of the people. At first she was amazed at the calm and self-control of the English. It took her a long time to accustom herself to the phlegmatic behaviour of the people. I would remind her that the world makes a great mistake in laying stress on British phlegm. " The English are not cold," I would say : " they are the only people who have achieved equilibrium between contrary forces. If you could gaze into the mind of an Englishman you would find it torn this way and that by powerful passions, but there is always the stern self-control which produces that appearance of serene coldness."

"I know," replied my wife, "but I wish they would let themselves go more and be more spontaneous. If they would only make a scene sometimes and let us see their drama."

"God forbid," said I. "England would then be a country bristling with dramatists, but it would be the most uncomfortable place in Europe to live in."

"All the same, I'm afraid of English people; they don't criticize you openly or blame you, but they give you a mute, sidelong glance which makes you feel more guilty than if you had committed a mortal sin."

One night I brought her to a play by Galsworthy. As luck would have it, there was one minor part, an Italian night-club proprietor, which was acted with all the exaggerated gusto that the English like to put into their portrayal of the stage Italian. My wife was pained. She got the impression that in England, whenever an Italian is brought on the stage, he has to belong to the category of gangster, ice-cream vendor or organ-grinder.

I had painted a very vivid picture of Ireland for her. I had eliminated most references to gunmen, Black and Tans, burnings, and I had described the Emerald Isle as a kind of Mediterranean island which had broken loose and floated into the misty Western ocean—a land where the people, in addition to their Hibernian Celtic qualities, had something Latin about them. I laid stress on the green fields, the delicate sunsets, the melancholy lakes, undulating mountains such as we saw in Galicia. Our arrival, alas, was somewhat of a disillusion to her. The crossing from Holyhead was rough, the rain pattered dismally upon the roofs of the shabby carriages of the suburban train from Kingstown Harbour. The entrance

to Dublin is like what one reads about in the ancient fairy
stories—a squalid vestibule leading to the brilliant scene.
Westland Row may boast that it is the dingiest terminus
in all Europe.   We drove away from it in a decrepit cab,
and the jarvey, instead of taking us by the broad, noble
streets, preferred to jog along through a series of slum
districts until we reached our suburban home.   I could
see that my wife's eager expectancy had vanished.   Her
face showed the chill of disillusion.   Shooting was still
lively in the city, for the first day she went out by herself
a bomb exploded near the tram in which she was travelling.   A few days later, returning from the theatre, our
tram was caught between opposing rifle-fire and we all
lay at the bottom of the vehicle for twenty minutes, listening to the rattle and whistling of bullets.   " This is worse
than Milan," said my wife, " for life seems so normal
here, and then suddenly one finds oneself in the midst of
an inferno."   She, however, soon adapted herself completely to Irish life.   She accepted all the conventions
and she discovered in us many traits which reminded her
of Italy, but as she possessed the remorseless logic of the
Italians, she never could resist poking fun at the irrational
basis of all Anglo-Saxon and even Anglo-Irish society.
  " How I envy the British," she would say.   " They are
the only free people in the world.   They are free because
they all agree among themselves to give up certain liber-
ties for the benefit of all.   In England they are born with
a sense of law.   They organize themselves spontaneously
without anybody telling them that they must do this or
do that.   In our country we are naturally rebellious, we
do not organize our own lives.   Only occasionally when
we create a hero do we follow him and obey his commands, but he has got to dominate us and proclaim long
lists of rules ; whereas the British naturally discipline
themselves.   I am always amused when the British talk

of equality. Is there any country in Europe where there is more inequality than in England, where people seem to fall naturally into different classes ? Look at the Dukes and Lords. In other countries they would be completely unimportant, but in England I see the papers full of details about their lives. A Society marriage draws hundreds of the poorer classes, who watch festivities, not with hatred in their hearts, but with benevolent feelings for those scions of ancient families. Everything in these countries seems to arise by the grace of God. People are not forced by the Government to give charity, but they group together spontaneously and look after poor and sick without any State interference." It took my wife a long time to understand our idea of the family. As an Italian whose whole life was centred in the family, she could not understand the custom in these countries of sending children away to preparatory and public schools.

"People here," she said, "try to weaken the bonds uniting the various members of the family. They try to turn out their sons, and daughters even, according to one gloriously efficient pattern by sending them to boarding-schools which are veritable centres of traditional hierarchy. In Italy it is so different. There the children go to the day school to study and they have their character moulded in the home."

I then made a vigorous defence of the public school, but at first my wife was not convinced and she would say that the most important subjects in those schools were football, cricket and rowing.

"And why not," said I, " if those games develop team spirit, fair play and character ? "

Strange to relate, as time went on our positions became reversed. My wife became a firm advocate of the public-school system. It was she who upheld the notion that

the traditional life in the ancient boarding-schools was
the best education for a pioneer race, whereas I began
to wonder if our hero-worship of the athlete at school
and many other honoured conventions were not unsuited
to life in the modern world.   My wife, however, would
remind me of a visit we had paid to Gibraltar during a
period when Europe seemed to be on the brink of war.
As soon as we left the ship we walked up the town and
all of a sudden we came to a cricket ground.   There on
the greensward a team of British sailors were playing.
My wife gazed entranced at the white-clad figures and
she said :

" Who can deny that the British are the happiest people
in the world ?   Europe may blaze up, revolutionaries
may rave about Communist or Fascist ideologies, but
England calmly goes on with her game of cricket."

" The British," said I, " are always saved by their sense
of humour."

To which she replied :

" What a multitude of sins you all conceal beneath that
phrase ' sense of humour.'   Whenever you British talk
about ' sense of humour ' you catch us Continentals at
a disadvantage.   You disarm us by that strange elusive
quality which we are not supposed to possess.   In Italy,
humour is a strident thing, a spirit of antithesis which
arises in a man's mind.   No sooner does he create a
beautiful image in his mind than he sets to work to
deform it."

" I know," said I.   " He is like the imp of Pirandello
who pulls the mechanism to bits to see how it is made.
Yes, humour is a mixture of elements.   George Mere-
dith tried to define it when he said : ' If you laugh all
round the ridiculous person, tumble him, roll him about,
deal him a smack, and drop a tear on him, own his like-
ness to you, and yours to your neighbour, spare him as

little as you shun, pity him as you expose, it is a spirit of Humour that is moving you.' "

" Whatever it is," said my wife, " Humour is a peerless weapon of the British when dealing with foreign countries. I remember the rage of the Italians at the Genoa conference when Lloyd George brought his golf-clubs. England will always win over us when she uses to the full her batteries of Humour."

CHAPTER XXIII

THE MARCH ON ROME

. . . . .

Noon descends around me now
'Tis the noon of Autumn's glow.
When a soft and purple mist
like a vaporous amethyst,

. . . . .

IN the summer of 1922 my wife and I set out for Italy
after the tragic Irish civil war. It was a relief to
find oneself *en route* for the continent after days and
nights haunted by the sound of rifles and machine-guns.
We went, first of all, to Geneva to stay with some Jewish
friends who had a villa by the lake. Geneva in 1922
certainly justified the wish which its great citizen Jean
Jacques Rousseau made for it nearly 150 years ago.
Rousseau expressed his ideas in a little work called
*Extract of the Project of Perpetual Peace by M. L'Abbé Saint
Pierre*. After a study of the Greek amphictyons, the
German confederation, and the Helvetian league, he
affirmed that a federation of the different European countries, with a permanent assembly, acting as a court of
justice, and making decisions respected by common
military action, would be the best method to secure world
peace. Rousseau's dream became realized in the modern
League of Nations with its beautiful palace on the edge
of Lake Leman. Geneva made one dream of a warless
world. At first I saw nothing but the beauty of the lake

stretching away into the blue misty distance, the waters in their liquid transparency dotted here and there with ships, their triangular white sails making them look like gulls, or else the gaily-bedecked steamers fretting the waters into foam. Under the brilliant sun that makes the white houses stand out in sharp relief against the background of blue and gold one gets the impression that Geneva has only to breathe to live. The landscape, with the peaceful waters, seems to lull and fascinate by its nonchalance.

Have we come to the shore of the lotos-eaters? Yet here stands a queen of industry, a city that has always been connected with struggles both of sword and pen. How many writers came here and found repose after their stormy struggles? Byron, whose soul seemed more completely inspired by the ruthless roaring of the furious ocean, repented of his passion's bitterness, his ear attuned to Leman's suave monotony. George Eliot, with all her active energy, tells us that the beauty of Geneva produces the effect of chloroform. The drowsy numbness it causes makes us even wish to pinch ourselves awake. Yet the beauty of the lake is not monotonous; it changes at the different hours of the day. In the early morning Mont Blanc seems to rise from the mist like Thetis from the foam. The sight of Europe's lonely peak produces very different emotions. It seems out of harmony with the worldly beauty of the sunny lake and happy city. I have to adjust myself, and instead of seeing a happy, rosy-cheeked child playing about in the fragrant gardens on the grass warm with the sun, I see the ice maiden, with her pale face and green hair, and I hear her chilling laugh that resounds through the ravines.

Franz Hodler, the great Swiss painter, when he painted Mont Blanc and the lake, did well to substitute rugged mountains for the smiling villas on the river's edge.

Let us live by this sunny lake and we could dream for ever of world peace. We could dream of goodness and brotherhood :

> What pleasure can we have
> To war with evil ? Is there any peace
> In ever climbing up the climbing wave ?
> All things have rest, and ripen toward the grave
> In silence ; ripen, fall and cease :
> Give us long rest or death, dark death, or dreamful ease.

There is not a single statesman or politician in Europe who, upon arriving here, could refrain from eating of the lotos and sinking with a sigh upon the beds of amaranth and moly. But there is always that towering peak of the ice maiden to rouse us from our slothful ease. Mont Blanc reminds me of the Italian dolomites. And so we pass from the paradise by the lake to Domodossola and the Italian frontier. During the short time that we had been absent from Italy a mighty change had taken place. The Italian nation, like the serpent, had shed its old skin. The country was no longer the same. It was as if some magician had quickened the heart-beat of the people and changed the rhythm of their lives. When I look back over my impressions of Italy ever since 1918 I find that I must divide them into two classes—those before 1922 and those after 1922. Before 1922, events in Italy plodded along in a normal tempo ; a musician would say at the rate of an honest John Trot andante, but after 1922 and ever since, events in Italy have become speeded up and my impressions marshal themselves in sharp outline. I see the Italian scene as a rapid puppet play ; a hurrying to and fro of frenzied workers at the behest of a stern-eyed master. Good-bye, lotos-eating Italy ! These eager little men do not possess the word in their vocabulary. The trumpets blare on all sides the slogan " Marciare non Marcire "—March on, don't

wither away. They always march on, they are galvanized into action. The whizzing and whirling of
their cog-wheels allow no truce in the mad race towards
death that will mean final peace.

Now the prophecy of Marinetti, author of *Le démon
de la vitesse*, had come to pass. Italy had to wake up to
face the new machine age. Was the machine to be master
or slave of humanity, destroyer or constructor ? Was man
to be completely absorbed by the machine, broken into
minute subdivisions to feed the monster ? Would the
man of the future entirely disappear under its dominion ?
Every moment was of importance in this struggle of Man
with the machine. To Hell with all illusions ! Not a
single working day should be wasted for the sake of
illusionary catchwords such as, Liberty, Equality and
Fraternity. Down with Parliament ! Its system might
suit the slower, vital rhythm of a Nordic race, but it was
incapable of making quick decisions or solving immediate
problems. And so Mussolini, the leader and mouthpiece of the nation, exclaimed :

Fascism sprang from my mind and from my heart, but also from
the deep and eternal necessity of the Mediterranean. Fascism is
a living force which has swept a Bolshevik State from the horizon,
and now considers that the time has come finally to settle accounts
with the Liberal State. Our ideal consists in denying completely
and absolutely the Liberalism of 1789. The world is proceeding
towards the Age of the Machine and in this Age, instead of the
reign of the masses there must come the reign of the chosen few.

Who was to be the whipping boy ? Giolitti, the foxy,
expert politician. But Mussolini, with his strange power
of alternately blowing hot and cold, outmanœuvred the
veteran. The latter soon had to admit that his adversary
not only had command of the masses but was as much
of a daredevil as Colleoni, Cesare Borgia, or any of the
great *condottieri*, with the difference that he had in addition

the expert and the ruthless efficiency of an aeroplane or
a machine-gun. Those who would understand the
rhythm which Mussolini implanted in the Italians during
those fateful days of 1922 should read his novel, *The
Battle of the Machines*, wherein he describes the death-
struggle between the three great forces, Intellect, Capital,
Labour. Capital and Labour engage in a contest which
threatens to destroy human society. What will happen
unless those two deathly opponents are conquered by a
third force, Intellect ? With Intellect's victory the result
will be the reign of talent and ultimately the Utopia.
More characteristic still is a story describing a mad
violinist performing on the stage. Like a super Gypsy
Paganini he plays faster and faster, with ever-increasing
fierceness and savagery, until the strings of his fiddle snap
one after another and the tumultuous crowd whom he
has lashed into the frenzy of the dance dashes on to the
stage and tears the virtuoso to pieces when his strings
break and he is unable to satisfy its lust for rhythm. No
wonder that Elizabeth Förster-Nietzsche declared that
Mussolini was the superman himself prophesied by her
brother. But Mussolini, unlike the Nietzschean hero,
has never been blinded by his own triumphs. He was
the first to notice the faults of the Fascist Movement,
and no sooner did public opinion pave the way for his
ascent to power than he determined to moderate his
words and impose a discipline upon his followers. His
speeches in the months preceding the March on Rome
were devoid of rhetoric, but they were full of brutal facts.
" Dante is great," said he, " because he understood that
words are living things." No leader has ever said
harsher things of his followers than Mussolini, and he
lashed his people with his tongue. He pointed out all
their faults, their hereditary failings, and by those methods
he completely transformed the Italian nation. It is

significant to note the foundation of the review " Gerarchia," or hierarchy. This is how he defines the word :

Hierarchy means responsibility, duty and discipline. History records the event of thousands and thousands of régimes which have arisen, lived, declined and passed away under a new régime. Under a new régime one must preserve those qualities of the old which are still capable of development. Upon the old traditions the new shoots must be grafted. Thus we must prepare the way for a new world ; thus we may build a bridge between the past and the future.

In Italy, before the March on Rome, those three words, Responsibility, Duty and Discipline, were answered by the three time-honoured words, Liberty, Equality and Fraternity, like a strophe and anti-strophe of a Greek chorus.

But those chanting the three words, Responsibility, Duty and Discipline, overwhelmed their opponents because they sang in unison together, following the same strict rhythm, and besides, they had added another hymn to the collection of songs marking the successive stages of Italy's advance to complete nationhood. That song we heard in city and in village throughout the summer of 1922 : it has become the symbol of Fascism and its name is " Giovinezza." " Giovinezza " is a song of youth and beauty, but it also signifies duty and discipline, for those who talked of " hierarchy " banded themselves together to fight those who would destroy the ranks which society needs if it is to flourish. Mussolini did not follow the Futurists who had denied what they called " Passéisme," and cried out for the destruction of all that the past had bequeathed.

We do not [said he] want to repudiate the past, for then we should be repudiating ourselves. We are already the past, for we live in the present and face those who are to come. Neither do we mean to cut ourselves off from the life of the future, for our present is a future faced with those who have gone before us. Our philosophical and political position is one of watchful control, of meditative discipline. We are determined to achieve a synthesis or state of equilibrium which will enable us to emerge from the stormy sea of the world crisis.

By such words did the Duce reveal himself as the traditional Italian, always trying to reach that harmony or balance of contrary forces. Those words, too, sprang from that cultured primitiveness which we discover in every manifestation of the Italian genius. Mussolini, even before he had seized power, knew that in spite of all his work for the unification of Italy and the consolidation of its internal power he would find himself overwhelmed by international problems.

Italy [he said] is bottled up in the Adriatic, a little bowl of water one could wash one's face in. Compared with the problems of world politics, that of the Mediterranean is but a small affair, a little overflow from two oceans. Yet I cannot take up the question because I am called to attend to the contest at Peretola, or because there have been blows struck at Gorgonzola or Roccannuccia. Someone has been killed, all Italy can think of nothing else, Fascism is entirely absorbed in the matter.[1]

Thus, from the first, by dint of abusing and spurring on the Italian people he set himself to train up a new generation of men devoid of the narrow regionalism which had been the curse of the country. He wanted men who would consider the Italian problem from a European point of view. They were to be acutely sensitive to Italian prestige and feel the pride of a race called to take part in the destinies of the world. Italy could only become a great nation if her people would preserve their unity at home and show to the world a united front.

In 1922 those words were decried as ranting by the Liberalists and Socialists. They were decried by the

[1] M. G. Sarfatti, *The Life of B. Mussolini*, London, 1925, p. 291.

followers of Don Sturzo, the leader of the people's party, but Mussolini, with that unerring belief in his own star, knew that his hour was at hand. The country was in a parlous condition ; the different parties kept up their eternal haggling, the strikes continued, industry was ruined, the lira had sunk to the nadir, the workers lived in misery, everyone asked : " Who will create order out of chaos ? "

Mussolini prepared his advent to power with the instinct of a great dramatist. He never concealed his motives. He put all his cards on the table. We all knew that the crisis was coming because he marked each stage of his advance by a great meeting and speech. In June he wrote :

To-morrow the conquest of Rome will determine the position of Fascism as opposed to the Italian state. We shall be with the State and for the State whenever it shows itself the jealous guardian and defender of national tradition, of national sentiment, of national will. We shall oppose the State whenever it shows itself incapable of standing out against the disintegrating elements which threaten national solidarity.

Then came the General Strike of August which threatened to engulf the country. There was consternation, and people thought that the end of the world had come. But Mussolini was ready. Instead of giving *carte blanche* to his followers to fire off their rifles and throw their hand-grenades, he prepared a surprise for the general public. The Fascists did not attack the strikers. Instead, they carried out the duties of the workers in the cities ; they drove the engines on the railways, they conducted the trams, they set in motion, in fact, the normal life of Italy, which had stopped, and the strike ended as a miserable failure. It is interesting to note that the procedure was the same as the British employed during the famous General Strike in 1926.

The Strike of August, 1922, was the general rehearsal of the March on Rome. The mass of the people, henceforth, looked upon the Duce as a deliverer. He was no longer the fire-eater; he could triumph over disorder by peaceful methods.

Mussolini's power was increased further by his link with the Nationalists or Blue Shirts. Up to now the Nationalists, under their brilliant leaders Corradini and Federzoni, had worked in separate organizations, but now they joined forces with the Duce. The next step was the great speech at the national festival of the 20th of September in Udine. Thousands gathered to listen to the leader, and they heard the full explanation of the link between Blue Shirts and Black Shirts. Formerly, Mussolini had been republican whereas the Nationalists were Royalists, but at Udine he made the following declaration :

" Our programme is simple. We want to govern Italy, but we have to face a great problem. Can this transformation be achieved without the overthrow of the monarchy ? "

Pausing to allow the question time to sink in the minds of his audience, he then fired a fresh one :

" Why are we Republicans ? Because we see that the king is not king enough."

In this dramatic way he dispelled all the doubts of those who had feared that when he came into power he would make himself president of a republic. Instead, he now showed that he would strengthen the position of the House of Savoy. The Udine speech sounded the clarion, for Mussolini proclaimed that if he did get into power he would initiate gigantic reforms :

" Our Movement is only in its prehistoric stage. It is only now starting to develop, but to-morrow history will begin."

Down in Rome it was said that Prime Minister Facta chuckled, saying :

" What that journalist has said is moonshine, nothing but words. What can he do so long as the army is in my hands ? "

Facta made the same mistake as many others have done since, in dismissing Mussolini as a clever rhetorical bluffer. Such people forget that in the Duce, as in Napoleon and Cæsar, there are two contradictory personalities working in harmony. On the one hand, there is the dynamic personality, gifted with bold imagination—the Nietzschean spirit, dashing onwards ruthlessly. We might compare it to the wild violinist of the story whipping his audience up by his rhythms into the frenzied dance. On the other hand, there is the cold, logical personality of the chess-player who calculates his moves and aims at being a constructor. We might compare such a personality to the architect planning his building. Sometimes the dynamic personality gets the uppermost, sometimes the cool logical one, but the greatness of the man consists in knowing instinctively when to harmonize those two personalities, in order to achieve his end.

The result of the Udine speech was a secret meeting at which the five movements of the March on Rome were drawn up.

First movement—Occupation of the public buildings in the larger towns.

Second movement—Concentration of the Fascist forces round Santa Marinella, Foligno, Tivoli, Volturno.

Third movement—Ultimatum to the king, demanding the surrender of power.

Fourth movement—Sudden attack on Rome and seizure of power.

Fifth movement—The formation of the Fascist

Government in one of the central Italian towns, concentration of the entire force of Black Shirts in a general attack against Rome.

But Rome knew nothing of those revolutionary plans.

The next step was the meeting at Naples on the 24th of October. Forty thousand Fascists appeared from all parts of Italy, an army of Black Shirts. Then, for the first time, Mussolini spoke as a general commanding his troops and, for the first time, he wore over his black shirt a scarf with the colours of Rome. To understand the full significance of that speech we should remember that Mussolini was reminding his followers that their motto was that of Garibaldi : " O Roma, o Morte." In Mussolini at that moment the dramatist and the creator of rhythms was uppermost. Like a great actor, he was able to work on the historical imagery of the Italians who are always, in their fiery patriotism, eager to invoke the past. Just as the Red Shirts of Garibaldi stirred to noble enthusiasm the grandfathers of the present generation and made them welcome the heroes after the " Breccia di Porta Pia," so now in 1922 the youth of Italy, with their minds fixed on the valorous enterprises of the past, in their black shirts, wearing the medals won in the late war, were to begin their march on Rome.

And so the congress broke up as a disciplined army with the fateful cry of destiny—" To Rome ! To Rome ! " Three days later, from Milan at midnight, Mussolini delivered his ultimatum to Italy, in which he announced that he was crossing the Rubicon. Even here his amazing power to spring surprises showed itself. Everyone was expecting an attack on Rome, according to the ancient tradition, whereas he worked from the outer circumference of the country. He concentrated his forces of Black Shirts at Perugia, the centre of Italy. From there his lines converged on Rome.

What could Facta do ? He wanted to declare a state of siege, but the king, who was a patriot and a realist, refused to sign the order. Facta then tried to play the old parliamentary game of temporizing. A share in the government was to be given to the Fascists. The only reply Mussolini gave was to order the legions at Santa Marinella and Tivoli to advance on Rome. He himself, however, had not left Milan. He refused to go to Rome to discuss and compromise with Facta.

"Unless," said he, " I am given an absolute mandate to form a government, I will not leave Milan unless it is to place myself at the head of the legions."

On the 29th of October, the king called Mussolini to Rome to offer him the mandate to form a government.

And so the March on Rome ended. What made the Fascist victory so memorable was that it was produced without the terrible excesses that mar revolutions. Every victorious army that has ever entered Rome, from Sulla to Garibaldi, did so over a heap of corpses.

Actually, on the 30th of October, the day after he had set out from Milan, the Duce had constituted the Government and obtained the sanction of the king. His next step was to order the Black Shirts back to their homes from Rome within twenty-four hours. There was a triumphal march through the Corso, past the tomb of the Unknown Soldier in the Piazza Venezia and up the hill of the Quirinal in front of the Royal Palace. The men dispersed, the cheering ceased, and Mussolini was heard to say : " E adesso, andiamo a lavorare " (And now let us set to work).

CHAPTER XXIV

AFTERMATH

THE opponents of the new régime did not consider themselves routed by the March on Rome. " Reculer pour mieux sauter " was their watchword. The martial rhythm of " Giovinezza " did not sweep them off their feet. They expected that the fire-eating leader of the Fascists would soon moderate his impulses and it would be possible for the old political game to start afresh. If they had paid attention to the writings and speeches of the Duce in the years preceding the March on Rome, they would have understood that this was not a simple *coup d'état* leading to the formation of a government which was a camouflage of old systems, but a new, vital movement, a quickening of national rhythms.

Mussolini's first speech as Prime Minister was moderate in the circumstances :

I could have [said he] driven out the old Parliament and formed a pure Fascist Government, if I had wished. I did not want to do this, at least, not at the present hour of victory. I have thus made a Coalition Government, not because I attach any importance to Parliamentary majorities, but because I want to bring the forces of the nation together for reconstructive work.

There were many stabs at the old régime in the speech :

Now that I am Prime Minister, everyone asks me for a programme. We don't want programmes in Italy, but men to carry

333

them out. Every problem of Italian life has been worked out on paper but the will to transform those plans into realities is wanting. The Government has this firm and decided will.

Those words represented the wish and determination that was uppermost in the minds of all the young Fascists : to initiate practical reforms and carry them through without the delays caused by Parliamentary procedure.

Another stab at Parliament itself :

As long as it is possible I shall not govern against this Chamber but it must recognize that its term of life is, at most, two years, and maybe only two days. I demand plenipotentiary powers, for I wish to take over the complete responsibility.

A final stab at the old-fashioned politicians and orators :

Gentlemen, cease worrying the country with your empty prattle. I am told that fifty-two members want to speak in the debate on the Government programme. Don't you think that number is excessive ? This is not our task, but to work actively at the task of creating a great nation.

Not a single deputy arose to champion the dying Parliament. They all bowed their heads and submitted to the lash. Nitti wrote : " Not a single man in the Parliament protested, and it was deeply sad and humiliating to witness that nobody dared to reply to the disdainful voice."

The one champion of Liberalism who descended into the lists was Senator Albertini, the editor of the *Corriere della Sera*. Albertini possessed great influence through his paper, which was immensely popular, not only in Italy but abroad. His speech was a striking defence of the fundamental tenets of Liberalism, and the courageous attitude of the orator himself was in contrast to the ineffectual spirit of the Parliament. Step by step, he described the dangers inherent in Fascism. He laid stress on the turbulent energy of the youthful movement. He foresaw this restless, ruthless spirit ending in a terrible explosion. With all its faults Liberalism was the only solution. Liberalism did not mean everlasting unrest. Its clearly defined principles would produce order and tranquillity.

Mussolini answered the Senator with the question :

What is pure Liberalism ? If pure Liberalism means that in the name of political freedom we should allow a few ignorant criminals or fanatics to ruin, at their will, a country of forty million people, then I must decline to contemplate the idea of being a pure Liberal.

He then went on to remind Albertini that Liberalism did not spring from peace and tranquillity, but was the result of two great revolutions. Constitutional Government in England and Liberalism in France, in fact, all the principles and ideas included under the name of nineteenth-century Liberalism, started from a great revolutionary movement of the peoples.

" Without that revolutionary movement," said he, " the honourable Senator would not to-day have been able to recite the eulogy of pure Liberalism."

It was instructive to listen to the conversation in the cafés in Milan in those days. My Fascist friends would give me long lectures on national problems :

" We have been too long," they said, " the happy hunting-ground of foreign nations. We have had every kind of Government known to history, but we have never up to the present had a truly national Government. We borrowed our Liberalism from England, our Radical-Democracy from France, our Socialism from Germany, and our Bolshevism from Russia. When we achieved our unity and independence in 1870 we did not weld ourselves into a nation. Look at the World War ! At the beginning, was any country so divided in its allegiance as ours ? To-day, however, for the first time we have a Government supported by the masses of the people."

In the early years of Fascism, that is to say, from 1922–24–25 in spite of the driving force of the Government, there was an undercurrent of opposition in certain quarters. The Socialists, Communists and Republicans were a mass of discordant views and opinions. They capitalized their discontent. Some of them were sincere men, longing for the snows of yesteryear. Others were political opportunists, cynical intriguers and international crooks. Many, too, had grievances against the new forceful Government which had taken drastic action in the Government services.

Looking back on those days, I can sympathize with the dismay felt by those *ronds de cuir* who had for years vegetated in their Government jobs. Here was a young man of 38 tearing asunder the screens which had protected the officials from the inquisitive public gaze. They felt the whole world sinking away from them as they heard the harsh harangues :

" The nation must become industrialized and disciplined, if our aims are to be achieved."

" Order, work and discipline " : the three words seemed to sparkle in huge, red neon signs.

" Any civil servant who arrives late or goes away before his time will be dismissed."

" Get on with the job." That was the motto of those early years, but the murmurs of discontent rose into cries of execration when the tragic Matteotti incident took place. It was the climax of many months of grim struggle. In the beginning of 1924 the mandate of the Chamber terminated. Mussolini, at that time, did not want to proclaim himself dictator, and so he arranged for new elections. He drew up a list of the Conservatives and Liberals of Right tendencies who were to fight the block of Left candidates. As a result of the election the National block triumphed, and the Chamber had a Fascist majority. But then they had to face fierce attacks by the defeated Leftists who accused the Prime Minister of having created a majority by terrorism, and by the bayonets of his militia. But he replied that his party had received five million votes, and in the Parliament he read out the news of the Fascists who had been assassinated by the political opponents. Eighteen Fascists had been killed and fourteen wounded during the electoral campaign. Most of the crimes had been committed by Italian Communists, the ramifications of whose power spread even to France. Mussolini needed the granite strength of his personality to withstand the onslaughts of Parliament. The dialogue was conducted as follows :

Mussolini : You have heard the facts. Can you still say that the Communist danger is over and that the armed militia must be dissolved ?

Opposition : Yes, if the militia disappeared, and if your despotism ceased, there would be no longer any Communist danger.

Mussolini : We all know how you kept the Communists in check when you were in power. Have you forgotten that under your Government the factories were given away to the Communists ?

Such was the atmosphere when the news of Matteotti's murder burst on the world. It was the explosion which had for so long been threatening. Matteotti was one of the younger hopes of the Socialists. He was a vigorous orator and a pitiless opponent of Fascism. Then one night, in the month of June, he disappeared. His assassins had " taken him for a ride," murdered him, and dumped his body in a wood. It was found some time later full of knife-wounds. There was no doubt that the murder had been committed by Fascists.

I was in Milan and Genoa less than a month after the terrible crime and I found some of my Fascist friends in deep despair.

" You know what the Duce said when he heard the news of Matteotti's death," said one :

It's the worst dagger thrust in the back I have ever received. What is going to happen to the Fascist Party if such crimes are committed? Where is the discipline which was the watchword of the movement ? Are we always fated in Italy to destroy our movements by senseless violence ? Look what the foreign press will make out of this crime !

The opposition in Italy were not slow to make the most of their opportunity. After delivering a fierce onslaught on the Government, they seceded from the Parliament just as in ancient times the Roman Plebs had seceded to the Aventine. Looking back on those turbulent days from my secure point of vantage, I find it difficult to understand the motives that prompted some of the thoughtful members of the Opposition to adopt such a course. From their point of view, it was as if they had suddenly determined to commit *hara-kiri*. The only explanation I can find for their secession is that those who professed loyalty to the Constitution and who condemned Mussolini and the Fascists for having violated the laws, allowed themselves in the heat of the moment to be subjugated entirely by Communists, Anarchists, and those who prided themselves on being the servants of the Moscow Government. Nothing could have suited the Fascists better than the Aventine secession. Henceforth, the Duce could carry out his plans unhindered. The secession did not even arouse a great tempest of indignation in the country, for people were weary of wrangling and wanted to settle down under strong government. When some of the Aventine members did try to slip back into the Parliament, the premier insisted that they should declare their allegiance to the Fascist régime and give up their connection with those abroad who were plotting against the Government. Fascism, henceforth, became more totalitarian. Mussolini, by his speech of January 3, 1925, declared that the State must become a Fascist State in complete contrast with the ancient Liberal-Democratic one.

Mussolini had shaken off his enemies and, though they barked at him, it was at a distance. There is no doubt that he suffered deeply on account of Matteotti's crime. Friends say that "for a time after, his life seemed completely wrecked." [1] In Parliament, he expressed his horror in the following words :

Nobody can doubt the sincere horror of the Government in this crime. I can say with truth what Talleyrand said when the Duke of Enghien was executed : "This is not only a crime, it is a blunder." The whole nation recoils with the greatest horror at such an outrage. I can state that twenty-four hours after the 'discovery of the murder all those already suspected had been arrested. The claim of justice is being ruthlessly carried out.

Mussolini's vigour was undaunted. In order to bury the sinister affair, he actually assumed full responsibility for everything, though nobody could sincerely believe that he, or the Fascist Party as a whole, was responsible for the Matteotti murder. As so often happens in new revolutionary régimes, certain criminals had become linked with the movement and had committed the crime for their own purposes. Delcroix, in his book *Un Uomo e un Popolo*, shows that nearly all the men who were involved in the murder have since become anti-Fascist, and have plotted abroad against the régime.

In any case, Mussolini's speech of the 3rd January, 1925, marks the beginning of the second phase of the

[1] M. Sarfatti, op. cit., p. 275.

Fascist revolution. That speech showed that he was heading straight for the totalitarian State. Henceforth, the Duce had no longer any need for the support of the political parties, for he had succeeded in his first steps towards economic reconstruction. Among my anti-Fascist friends, however, I heard bitter criticisms of the régime. Some of them commented sadly on the failure of the Opposition after the Matteotti murder. They had hoped to break Mussolini, as Crispi had been broken after the Italian defeat at Adua in 1896. Actually, a shadow government had been formed, and, according to some well-informed friends, it consisted of Nitti as Prime Minister, Sforza as Foreign Minister and Guglielmo Ferrero as Minister of Education. One evening, after we had argued fruitlessly for many an hour, one of my friends, as he departed, handed me a book saying : " Here is something that will convert you. It is by one of the men who should be in power to-day." The book was called *Democracy in Italy*, and it was by Ferrero himself, the author of that great work *The Greatness and Decadence of Rome*. Ferrero, in his defence of democracy, made a frontal attack on the Fascist dictator. One of his principal points was that the Great War, as regards Italy, was a revolution from top to bottom. When, in 1915, Italy intervened in the War, she destroyed the time-honoured parliamentary dictatorship which could be symbolized in the magician Giolitti.

" In May, 1915," said Ferrero, " old and young broke into the chamber of that magician and robbed his book and his wand. When he came back he was no longer magician. All he had of his art was his innocuous magician's cap."

The War was a revolution because it shook the middle classes and the masses, and hastened universal suffrage. It broke the Triple Alliance ; it overthrew the Mon-

archy ; it destroyed the group which had governed up
to 1914, and it left Italy without a government.

Then Ferrero went on to speak contemptuously of
Mussolini's much-vaunted revolution.

> The Fascist revolution [he says] is a return to the past. Look
> at how elections are done ! First of all, an electoral law is extorted
> with threats from Parliament. The Head of the Government,
> himself, chooses those who are to be the deputies of the majority,
> and thus he shows his contempt for national sovereignty which his
> predecessors pretended at least to respect, even when they tried to
> deceive. This is a proof of alarming frankness, for true anarchy
> arises when the violation of the laws is proclaimed in the market-
> place as a right.

In another place he said

> the Governments of Giolitti, Nitti and Depretis were weak, but
> Mussolini's dictatorship will be much weaker still. He will have
> to take on full responsibility for all that is done by his henchmen,
> high and low. He will have to think of everything, see everything,
> decide everything, for he will have no means of imposing what he
> wants on his followers and seeing that they carry it out. More
> than his predecessors, he will be a slave of dictatorship, chained to
> power. Mussolini might say of his dictatorship what Tiberius said
> when the Empire was offered to him : " lupum se auribus tenere "
> (he had the wolf by the ears).

In another place he said that the revolutionary system
which Mussolini had unleashed to conquer power would
devour him. In former days revolutionary forces could
be tamed by a dictator (Napoleon), by a dynasty (House
of Hohenzollern and House of Savoy), by a minister
(Bismarck), acting as policeman to keep order and
herald adventurous wars. But all that ceased in 1918
with the Armistice.

Ferrero traced the stages of what he calls " Illegality "
from the end of the War onwards. Deliberate lawlessness, according to him, started with the burning of the
offices of the newspaper *Avanti* in 1919, and continued

until the Fascist elections of the 6th of April, 1924, and the murder of Matteotti. The latter, he calls the second great catastrophe of Illegality.

That [he said] should be the last catastrophe, if Italy is not destined to perish like Russia and Austria. The present régime think that if they punish the murderers the people will declare itself satisfied, but it is not enough to avenge the memory of the noble citizens whom the dagger of the assassin has killed : illegality must also disappear. We must immolate this monster on the tomb of Giacomo Matteotti. It is the only funeral sacrifice that is worthy of him.

He then went on to make a comparison between the dictatorship of Julius Cæsar and the present day.

Twenty centuries back, we find the same forces at work. We find the illusion of dictatorship that hides its own impotence beneath its full powers ; a chief who tries to satisfy all, without satisfying anyone ; the continual domination by extremists, the rapid prosperity of favourites, the interference with electoral systems, the suspicions and accusations murmured on all sides when Marcellus, Consul in 51 B.C., was murdered by an unknown hand.

" Events of to-day," said the author, " have copied faithfully the history of ancient times. Is Mussolini a modern Cæsar, or was Cæsar a Mussolini of antiquity ? "

When I had finished reading Ferrero's book I went off to visit a Fascist friend, feeling myself primed with arguments, but he, in a short time, pulverized me. He quoted articles by Ferrero, written at the time of the Abyssinian War in 1896.

" Read," said he, " Croce's Liberal history. Even he felt pity for Crispi who was hounded to death by Ferrero, Nitti, and the rest of them. Think of the tragedy of the 1st of March, 1896, that day of Adua, when the Italian army lost 8,000 men killed and wounded and left 1,800 as prisoners with the Abyssinians. That was a day of weeping and lamentation for every home in Italy except for Ferrero, Nitti, Bissolati and others, who actually exulted in the defeat of Adua because it laid low the hated enemy, Crispi. Remember what the great Carducci thought about Ferrero. ' I am ashamed to think,' said he, ' that the ignorant, insensate, and foul insults of Guglielmo Ferrero against Crispi have been written in Italian.' Ferrero did not limit his insults to Crispi. He actually insulted the Italian officers and soldiers in Adua, whose heroism won the admiration of the whole world."

I longed to take up the cudgels with the anti-Fascist friend who had given me the book, but I did not see him until February, 1936. I then found that he had become an ardent champion of the Duce. He had volunteered for the Abyssinian campaign and his conversation was devoted mainly to the theme of Italy's need for expansion.

The historical parallels drawn by Ferrero are instructive because they explain the wish of the modern Italians to trace the continuity of their race from ancient Roman times. Cæsar and Augustus remind them that a dictator achieves nothing by mere conquest or power unless he changes the character of the people and carries out a social revolution. Cæsar had studied human nature in war, which is an ideal observatory, and he had determined to give the Roman people a will, a conscience, and a sense of responsibility. He planned his reforms, but he left it to Augustus to carry them out. Some years ago, an historical novel on the subject of Cæsar was published in German by Mirko Jelusich and translated into Italian, which illustrates the contrast between Cæsar, the dictator, and Cicero, the Liberal. The following dialogue between the two is instructive, when read in the light of events in Italy since 1925 :

Cicero (as if he was explaining something to a capricious child) :
This is the end of the republic !

Cæsar : Republic ! What does the republic mean to you ? A
commercial association without a single noble thought, with the
word " Equality " written on its banners to deceive the people !

Cicero : Cæsar !

Cæsar : That republic I have liquidated. As a matter of fact,
I really want what you yourselves say you want. I give a meaning
to that word which you always have on the tips of your tongues—
the word " Liberty." I have a task and I want to carry it out, the
task of liberating the people from you. I want to point out your
insufficiency and break down the wall of restrictions which you
have raised in years of secret manœuvring. I want to give men will,
resolution, responsibility. I have smashed the Government of
wooden heads and I have restored justice.[1]

Mussolini calmly and serenely began to build up the
Fascist Totalitarian State on a legal basis. The rhythmic
movement which he had imparted to the Italian nation
began to accelerate still more. All through the peninsula the factories hummed. The country welcomed the
boom and looked forward to an era of prosperity. The
Duce then began his policy of decentralization. So far
from wishing to concentrate everything in its hands, the
Government gave the prefects and high functionaries
of the State full administrative powers, and at the same
time increased their responsibility. The heads of pro-
vincial departments were not obliged to refer perpetually
to the ministries in Rome. Thus was carried out that
policy of Responsibility which had always been one of
the watchwords of the Fascist régime. Very soon a
special type of official was trained full of independence
and self-reliance and ready to adapt himself to the new
accelerated rhythm of economic life. Mussolini did not
slacken his efforts. On the one hand, he educated a
Fascist mentality ; on the other hand, he gave the mass

[1] Mirko Jelusich, *Cæsar* (Italian Trans. by G. Prampolini and
A. Tenca), Milan, 1931, p. 429.

of the people so many surprises that they had no leisure
to ruminate over grievances. Take the question of War
debts. He suddenly sent Count Volpi, the Minister of
Finance, off to America to regulate the debt. When
the latter returned, the Duce stabilized the lira and told
the people that each citizen could contribute to the
repayment of the War debt. " Italy has forty million
inhabitants," said he. " If every man gives the country
a dollar, we have already repaid the first instalment of
the American loan." Within a week the sum required
was oversubscribed. The newspapers published the
names of the subscribers, and every man considered it
his duty to take part in the scheme. Mussolini did not
limit himself to present-day schemes, he also thought
of the past. In every district in Italy archæological
work was encouraged. I remember my surprise when
I met the Mayor of Assisi. I had expected to find a
bloated alderman of the old-fashioned type. Instead,
I found an eager young classical scholar who, in addition to being a most efficient functionary, had a deep
interest in the artistic and archæological remains of his
city. The five years from 1925–30 we might consider
as a preliminary period of solid, reconstructive work,
laying the basis of Italy's power to-day.

CHAPTER XXV

CAPO SANTA CHIARA

MY own life, also, during the years from 1923–6, was passing through a period of reconstruction. Those were years of optimism. It seemed as if Europe had begun to emerge from the disastrous aftermath of the Great War. In my own country the new Government of the Free State set to work with enthusiasm at the task of reconstruction. Most of the ministers were young men devoid of administrative experience, but in a short time they proved themselves more hard-working and efficient than the former rulers of the country. A spirit of comparative tolerance took the place of ancient deep-seated hatred. There was give and take. Many of the Anglo-Irish Unionists, with unexampled patriotism, played their part in assisting the Government in its work of building up a new country. The spirit of tolerance in those days could be symbolized by the relationship that existed between Dublin's two rival universities. Some of us in Trinity College, who were eager to foster the spirit of toleration and good-fellowship, joined with colleagues in the National University and founded an inter-University Society, wherein we could discuss amicably the problems of our country.

Dublin, in those days, became a cosmopolitan city, because the foreign nations sent diplomatic representatives, and visitors from abroad would say with surprise

that our society was delightfully intriguing, owing to
its mixture of English, Celtic and Latin elements. I
remember the visit of my friend, Carlo Placci, to Dublin
in those years. Placci, for many years, had been the
Beau Nash of Florentine society. He was a pure-bred
Tuscan with the wit of Abbé Galiani and the Tuscan
dignity of a Renaissance courtier. Carlo Placci's visit
to Dublin established the city in its niche of fame among
the smaller capitals of Europe. His eagle eye scanned
out the land and discovered in us an individual charm
which, in his articles in the *Corriere della Sera*, he compared with that of Prague, Budapest and Vienna. Those
were the days when the literary *cénacles* flourished in
Dublin because the writers could gather around the two
great leaders of intellectual Ireland, W. B. Yeats and
George Russell (A.E.). They did their best in those
days to encourage their countrymen to study European
problems. A. E.'s room in Plunkett House, with its
walls covered with his imaginative frescoes, became a
rendezvous for all those who came to Ireland from
abroad. His weekly paper *The Irish Statesman* was a
voice preaching a new European spirit. It gave opportunities to writers of every hue, and it discussed every
new revolutionary movement serenely and critically
without taking sides. In the pages of *The Irish Statesman* it was possible to follow a commentary on the new
reconstructive work carried out in Italy.

After my election to Fellowship in Trinity College,
Dublin, I spent most of my long summer vacations in
Italy in Don Alberto's villa on Capo Santa Chiara. My
son was born there in 1923, and we gave him the Chris-
tian name of Landi, after Donna Delfina's father, the
Garibaldian general. It was a sad time for us because
Donna Delfina began to decline in health. She, whom
I had seen so vivacious and fiery a few years before,

was now pale and emaciated. A distressing cough racked her lungs and warned us that she had fallen a victim to consumption. Poor Donna Delfina! She had overtaxed her strength by her untiring exertions during the War. At first, we had every hope of saving her if we could transport her into the mountains, so Don Alberto bought a villa in the village of Masone, in the Ligurian Alps. It was a two-storied house with veranda and wooden balconies, built on a slope of the mountain outside the town. At a distance, its yellow walls stood out, bosomed amidst pines and chestnut trees. During the summer months Masone was a paradise of green; there were fresh breezes to mitigate the heat of the sun. During the winter, however, Masone becomes submerged beneath its thick covering of snow and it is given over entirely to its own small population of hardy mountaineers. During the winter of 1923, Donna Delfina was so ill that she could not be transported back to Capo Santa Chiara, and so Don Alberto and his one unmarried daughter, Tina, resigned themselves to a winter spent among the snows. My wife and I and the rest of the family, when we were able to visit Masone, used to live in rooms in the village below the villa.

Donna Delfina, in spite of her illness, which was wasting her away, had lost none of her courage and energy of mind. Her large, dark eyes burned feverishly; on her pale, emaciated cheek there were hectic spots of red, but she still kept planning for the future. Lying in her bed opposite the window, she could see only the blue sky and distant white peaks. We did not tell her that all round the house the snow had covered the ground to a depth of three feet. We would all the time talk of Spring, and to give her the illusion of a blossoming land, we set vases of fragrant flowers in the window.

She would talk for ever of Spring, of the future, but we felt convinced that she knew that the end was approaching. As so often happens with dying people, her reminiscences turned back to her days of childhood. She would conjure up the vision of her father in the uniform of a *cacciatore alpino* and she would quote for us anecdotes of the Garibaldi period. " Who would mind leaving this world," said she, " when one is certain that the spirit of the Risorgimento has not died in modern Italy? There were many sad years, Alberto, when you and I thought that the old spirit was dying. Do you remember when I said that we should place white roses on the tomb at Caprera to mark the death of an ideal? " She would then say wistfully : " Why do I not hear church bells? It is all so silent here in the country. Not a sound : I can hear nothing but my heart beat. If only I could hear church bells. They would remind me of those years I spent as a child in the mountain villages of Piemonte."

When Christmas was approaching, she called us in one day in great excitement. " There is one thing I long to do. Alberto, you must satisfy my wish. I want to give a big Christmas party for the village. I have organized it in my mind."

She then begged Don Alberto to open the folding doors of her room so that she could see from her bed the large window at the back of the house.

" Look," said she excitedly, " do you see that tall pine tree beyond? It is all covered with snow. How beautiful it is, how silent and deathly it looks in the dim light! That must be my Christmas tree. How deathly it looks! I want to revive it and illuminate it with coloured ribbons and fill its branches with dolls and flowers and countless gifts. Do, Alberto, as I wish. Let it be a magic tree. I know that it stands in full view of the village at the foot of the hill. All the little children will rejoice when they see it. They will come running up here through the snow. It will bring happiness into their lives."

We all set to work in haste. Donna Delfina, from her bed, directed operations. Some of us went to Genoa to buy the coloured lights and ribbons, others went to buy dolls and toys, and Don Alberto, following her express wish, went off to purchase woollen jerseys, stockings, mufflers and all kinds of winter garments, which were to be given as gifts to the poor children. At last Christmas Eve arrived. The mighty tree, which was thirty feet high, was a mass of ribbons and garlands. Nearly every twig, it seemed to me, had some little toy attached to it. Then, when evening fell, we lit up the tree. That tree, blazing with blue, yellow, red, purple, green lights, was a fantastic sight in the midst of the snow. Later that night, as I walked through the village half a mile away, the illuminated tree perched high above seemed to hover like a vaporous garland in the midst of the snowy, desolate immensity between heaven and earth, and it brought to my mind those beautiful lines wherein Calderón describes the Cross of the Redeemer appearing in a sudden ray of light above the ravine with its jagged rocks and gloomy pines :

" Iris de paz, que se puso
Entre las iras del cielo
Y los delitos del mundo."

(" Rainbow of peace which shone between the wrath of Heaven and the sins of the world.")

As I plodded up the narrow path I saw crowds of children making their way towards the villa. They arrived in multitudes, and stood in serried ranks around

the glittering tree. The lights lit up the faces of the
children, and as they moved about restlessly their shadows
flitted across the snow-clad bushes. We had arranged
Donna Delfina's bed close to the open door of her room
so that she could see in the distance the brilliant scene.
Carlin, the *contadino* of the place, from the top of a high
ladder, clipped off the various presents and passed them
down to Don Alberto, who distributed one to each child
in turn. Then the children, after singing and dancing
riotously round the Christmas tree, formed themselves
up into a long procession. Two by two they passed
through the house to Donna Delfina's room, so that
she could see them, and her youngest daughter, Tina,
presented them with the various woollen garments.
Before the children started on their journey home they
gathered in the porch and sang together in their shrill
voices the patriotic songs, and it was my wife, Italia,
who led them. Donna Delfina called out in her sad,
weary voice the titles. First, it had to be the " Hymn
of Garibaldi," followed by the " Song of Oberdan," the
" Hymn of Mameli," the " Song of Monte Grappa,"
ending with the " Bells of San Giusto." When they
had finished, Tina said to her mother in a soft
voice :

" Do not let them go away, Mamma, without singing
some of the songs of Piemonte."

" Ah, yes ! " replied Donna Delfina, " this snow
should make us think of our Piemontesi. Tell them
to sing ' Quel mazzolin di fiori.' "

The children, as they descended the steep path
towards the village, kept up the singing. Their fresh
voices echoed in the distance through the silent night.
Next morning, when she awoke, Donna Delfina looked
from her bed at the tree. Its branches were thickly
covered with snow. " Adesso sì che è veramente la

Morte." Whether the excitement of that Christmas festival was too much for her I know not, but in the early days of the new year she began to fade away rapidly. During the excitement she had been full of mental energy, and it was she who thought of every detail : we merely carried out her wishes. It was the last flickering up of her spirit before the end. At last one evening came when she was in an agony of breathlessness. The doctor had gone back to Genoa earlier, thinking that she was a little better. Then came a sudden turn for the worse. It was late at night, and she had used all the oxygen that the chemist in Genoa had sent. What were we to do ? There was none to be obtained in the mountain villages and there would never be time to make the long journey to Genoa. It was a stormy night with driving snow and some of the roads were blocked. Down in the village I tried to persuade chauffeurs to drive me to Voltri, but they all refused, saying that it was madness to attempt the journey on the perilous winding Alpine road by the Turchino. At last I found one man who was willing to risk the journey. We set out at midnight. The wind drove the snow in our faces and we could hardly see where we were going. The narrow road wound round and round in steep descent. Sometimes we had to dig the car out of the snow. At other times it skidded and slipped perilously near the edge of the precipices on either side. At last we reached Voltri and managed to rouse the sleeping chemist. The journey up the mountain, though difficult, was not so perilous, and we accomplished it in less time. When we arrived at the villa, my wife's sister, Eva, met me.

" She's sinking rapidly," said she, " but the oxygen you have brought will give her her last breath."

She died half an hour later. Two days later we were

setting out towards Genoa, bearing her to her last resting-
place, when our procession was stopped by a large band
of ex-Servicemen.   Most of them were those whom she
had known when they were in No. 1 Red Cross hospital in Genoa and had afterwards befriended.   They
insisted on taking the coffin out of the hearse and they
carried it on their shoulders a mile of the way.   It was
a touching tribute to her memory.   We buried her in
the little rustic cemetery of Apparizione amidst olive
groves on a hill overlooking the Gulf of Genoa.

CHAPTER XXVI

THE LADY FROM THE SEA
ELEANORA DUSE

> Music is liker to encase your essence,
> Yet, you escape, for what you really are
> Hangs to no swiftest flash of evocation,
> But floats in rondure of its perfectness,
> Out of our sight as possible, impossible,
> Peak of a human capability,
> Infinite, spirit with the lightest shadowing
> Of merciful and finite flesh.—AMY LOWELL.

I WAS in Italy when telegrams from the United States announced the death of Eleanora Duse on the 21st of April, 1924, in an hotel in Pittsburg. Her last appearance before the public was on the 5th of April. Immediately afterwards she was stricken down with influenza, followed by pneumonia. All the winter preceding her death she had spent touring America with her Company and passing from one triumphal representation to another. According to friends who had spoken to her on the eve of her departure from Italy, she had an insistent premonition that she would never return, and she had wondered what would happen to her poor actors in a foreign country if she were taken from them. The news of her death produced a deep impression in Italy, where she was looked upon not only as an ethereal spirit whose loveliness was inaccessible to ordinary mortals but a tragic incommunicable queen, carrying the sorrows of the world with her. I had seen her several

354

times on the stage in Turin and Milan when she had
left her retirement at Asolo to give the Italian public
one more vision of her art before departing from this
world.   Once, too, I saw her play in London Ibsen's
The Lady from the Sea.   Even then, she was hovering
between life and death, and people who worked in the
theatre told me that in her dressing-room, during the
intervals of the play, they had to give her oxygen.   My
vision of her will always be a pale, emaciated, grey-haired
lady, walking wearily on the stage, a lonely mask with
great eyes full of sorrow.   She stood like a statue facing
the clamorous audience and her face changed from its
expression of deep sadness to a gracious smile.   She
raised her delicate, white hands with long tapering fingers
in a gesture of welcome to her audience and I thought
of *La Gioconda*, the play which Gabriele D'Annunzio
wrote for those hands.

In this last triumphal appearance of hers she had
nothing to assist her but her unquenchable spirit.   She
was no longer queen of the stage, appearing with a fanfare
of trumpets amidst blazing lights.   She had on this
occasion to combat all the memories of those who remembered her in the past when she was young, full of
vitality, and with that strange fascination which subjugated poets as well as Philistines.   She still had that
marvellous voice with the slow, soft modulations, the
harmonious intonation with its rise and fall, like the
phrasing of a great violinist.   Even before I saw her,
I heard Ellida, the " lady from the sea," speak, and at
once her voice so hypnotized me that when she appeared
upon the stage she became transformed in my eyes.   Her
pale face, as she spoke, was like a mask of alabaster,
behind which a light shone, giving it the varying tones
of gold and amber.   It was her voice and the sad,
languid gestures of those beautiful hands which made me

discover all the tragedy in the enigmatic soul of Ellida, the daughter of the Norwegian lighthouse-keeper. Ellida the sea daughter languishes in the tepid water of the inland fjord. Through the great second act of the drama Eleanora Duse made us feel the growing restlessness of this Valkyrie, the ceaseless torment of her mind. Ellida longs for a peaceful existence beside her husband, who alone can calm her tempestuous spirit, but she cannot resist the sinister attraction of the Stranger. Her monologues, floating through the dark theatre, awoke echoes in our souls. She is alone, gazing fixedly at the lake, and she murmurs the words as if speaking to herself. When the Stranger appears she does not recognize him immediately, but then, all of a sudden she imagines that she sees in his eyes the eyes of the child of hers who died. The eyes of the child used to change their colour according to the caprices of the sea. The Stranger's eyes are the same. " Save me, Wangel, save me if you can," she cries in agony to her husband. Eleanora Duse led us more and more insistently into the depths of Ellida's complex character. The drama of her mind grows in an ever-increasing crescendo of emotion. But it is not emotion torn to tatters but spiritualized, and it is as if we were gazing at that tragic woman through a thin veil which softens the outlines. The scene of Ellida's decision in the last act assumes the value of a symbol. The contrast between the two struggling elements of her character is shown by the smooth, unruffled lake where squalls and hurricanes are unknown and the distant limitless ocean with its sea-horses.

The evening has come and she must make her fateful decision. The Stranger will come at midnight to receive her answer. Wangel now realizes that he has no influence over his wife, and so he renounces her and lets her make the final choice. We hear the ship's bell tolling

in the distance.   All of a sudden, Ellida seems to awaken
from her long dream.   She is no longer restless or
languid, as though subjugated by a force of nature.   In
a firm tone she refuses to follow the Stranger and she
tells Wangel that she is now cured for ever of her
infatuation.   I had seen the *Lady from the Sea* many times
and I had always felt inclined to criticize the great Ibsen
for that sudden, violent metamorphosis of Ellida in the
last act.   Only once did I understand the marvellous
art of the master and that was on the night when I saw
the aged Duse play the part.   She made us feel that such
a sudden change was not impossible in a woman of such
enigmatic nature as the lady from the sea.   She played
the part with such varying " nuance " and such spiritual
power that I felt that Ibsen, in creating the play, had
followed Shakespeare and Calderón in dramatizing the
struggle between Destiny and Man's free will.

"Astra inclinant sed non necessitant," said the
ancients.   And Shakespeare wrote :   " The fault, dear
Brutus, lies not in our stars, but in ourselves, that we
are underlings "—a theme which the intensely religious
Calderón dramatized in *Life is a Dream* and the *Devotion
to the Cross*.

Eleanora Duse herself was a lady from the sea, for
she was born in the Venetian fishing town of Chioggia,
which has been immortalized in Goldoni's sparkling
comedy *Baruffe Chiozzotte*.   The dreaminess of her
temperament and her restlessness, which resembled
Ellida's, sprang from her sailor ancestry.   She was for
ever gazing towards a distant horizon.   Her parents were
wandering actors, and one might even say that she herself
was born in a chariot of Thespis.   Her earliest years
were spent in restless vagabonding from one small Venetian or Lombard town to another.   Hers was the destiny
of the traditional Harlequins, Pulcinellas and Columbines

who had wandered from one end of Europe to another teaching the world to play. At four years of age Duse acted upon the stage, and all her childhood was spent in the theatres of the small towns—a life of grim poverty and hardship. It is interesting to remember that the first occasion when she showed her artistic genius was in Verona, where she played the part of Shakespeare's Juliet. Soon she began her series of triumphs. We imagine her as Electra and Ophelia trailing her robes of tragedy, or else in red melodramas such as *Térèse Raquin* of Zola. Henceforth, her fame spread to Europe. In Paris she played *La Dame aux Camélias* in Sarah Bernhardt's own theatre. Not only in tragedy did she excel, but also in comedy, for it is agreed that no one has ever played Mirandolina, the sprightly heroine of Goldoni, as she did.

But, when I consider the career of Eleanora Duse I visualize a tiny house where she lived next door to D'Annunzio's ornate villa "La Capponcina" at Settignano. The contrast between the two dwellings is instructive. The ascetic simplicity of Duse's character contrasted with the baroque, fanciful nature of the poet. "La Capponcina" was a medley of every style. D'Annunzio had collected a bewildering variety of *bibelots*: panels and lecterns from ancient churches, variegated ornaments, brackets of weird shapes and elaborate decoration were to be found everywhere. It was as full of rarities gathered from all quarters as the sumptuous Venetian palace of Peter Aretine the Divine. But Duse's ascetic little house was called by a Franciscan name, "La Porziuncola." Duse silently and insistently entered into D'Annunzio's thoughts. He said:

" She would enter as a beautiful thought enters the mind."

It was her voice that subjugated the youthful poet. Again and again, he describes through his works the

effect of her voice upon him. He would close his eyes
and listen to her as to music : " The anemones blossom
in her voice as on a woodland meadow in Spring." The
gentle rhythm of her voice would soothe him and give
him peace. " Why pant for the dawn," he wrote, " in
this insomnia of life if the first note from an earthly
voice can bring such melody upon earth." When we
read some of the poet's greatest works, such as the
Laudi, we imagine always in the background the pale,
sylphlike spirit of Duse. She harmonized the tensions
in his wilful nature. When we think of Duse as we read
those poems we understand more clearly the full significance of the Italian Renaissance which was the perfect
expression of Greek as well as Latin civilization. Duse,
with her tranquil power, gave strength to D'Annunzio's
genius. She inspired him to exalt the loveliness of
ancient Greece. After describing the contrast between
the harmony of Greek beauty and modern materialism
he went on in the *Laudi* to sing the pæan of modern Italy,
the land of great individuals. And finally, in a burst of
inspiration, he composed the greatest group of all his
poems, *Alcione*, wherein he fuses together all the contents
of his other works. To D'Annunzio, Duse then
appeared as La Foscarina gliding in a golden gondola
down the great canal of Venice during the Carnival,
saluted by the cheering crowds as a queen. But, in
addition to being a queen, she was also, as he said,
" that lonely wanderer who seemed to carry in the folds
of her robes the frenzy of the multitudes." Her life was
fated to be tragic. It was her destiny to inspire others
by her art and win their love, only to discover that she
was herself remorselessly bound by chains to her stage
life. She realized that she belonged to the public in
body and in soul. Although she craved for love and
affection she had for ever to deny herself and flit through

life storing in her mind a thousand memories of what might have been. The public had the right to fall in love with her, but she could have no secrets from them.

After years of triumph she retired and built herself a house in the classical town of Asolo, immortalized by Pietro Bembo. Some years after her death I visited her house and the local museum containing many of the relics of her career. I saw the robes she wore for her famous parts. The names passed before my mind like a swift vision; La Gioconda, Mirandolina, Francesca da Rimini, Signora Alving, Ellida Wangel. In the museum there were sketches suggesting the scenes in which she had to play her dramas, for Eleanora Duse always insisted upon looking at these pictures when she was studying her part. It was her art always to suggest the surroundings, the background of nature against which the characters played. And so, on one wall I saw a picture of trees shaking in the wind and beside it a photograph of a ship with billowing sails racing over the waves. Those two images, I was told, were for ever before her mind when she was creating her part of Ellida.

The part of Ellida delighted her, but she would always say that the actress playing it should reach, not simply the emotions of the spectator, but his intellect. She would not allow the drama to unfold itself as a mighty symbol, and she would quote the anecdote she had heard of a Norwegian woman whom an English painter had met in a small port in Norway. The woman waited sadly year after year for the return of an English ship in which sailed a man who had promised to return to her.

That is the Lady from the Sea [said Duse]: Ibsen is less symbolical than we think. In the lonely Nordic countries there are women who are waiting for somebody who has promised to return. Everything in this world repeats itself both in the forms of things and in human beings. The greatest and the most humble things resemble one another, just as the eye and the sun have the same shape.[1]

Such a remark was characteristic of her attitude towards the world. All through her life she preserved a tragic sense of her own art : she was for ever seeking despairingly for the ideal expression. On one occasion, during a long conversation I had with the dramatist, Pirandello, he spoke of Duse's art and he quoted a remark of hers where she said :

" Not one, but a thousand women live in me."

" It is no wonder," said the master, " that her face was the mask of tragedy. Every one of her personalities lived its own tragedy in all its intensity."

Other great actresses remain in the memories of men and women as the incarnations of the parts they played. But Eleanora Duse, in the memories of those who saw her, does not appear as Francesca, Ellida or Santuzza. She herself remains the image of one whom the American poetess Amy Lowell called the tragic, incommunicable lady.

Let us then think of her as one of the supreme heroines of Italian drama—one who, in her art, united all the sister arts for the glory of the Theatre. Her voice and her gestures on the stage were the essence of Music and the Dance. But she also understood that music, as D'Annunzio said, is, as it were, the dream of silence, for the essence of music lies not in the sounds but in the silence that precedes the sounds and in the silence which follows them. When she fell under the spell of Gabriele D'Annunzio's poetical and dramatic genius she devoted herself, heart and soul, to the task of interpreting faithfully every " nuance " of his work according to his own wishes. D'Annunzio was a new voice in the world

[1] *Comœdia*, May 1934 (article on Duse, by Bruno Brunelli).

theatre and she was determined to make men hear it in all its beauty. At the end of her life she used often to talk about her ideal theatre. She would not build a mighty structure which would be a blaze of brilliant lights. No, she wished only for a simple white-washed building as ascetic as a refectory of a Franciscan monastery. It would be a meeting-place of artists and lovers of the theatre who would produce upon its stage the great masterpieces.

From her grave beneath the cypress trees on the green hill of Asolo I could see above me the mighty snow-capped peak of Monte Grappa—the altar of the Fatherland.

CHAPTER XXVII

MUSICAL PAGEANT

IN September 1925 I went to Venice for the International Musical Festival. It would be difficult
to imagine a Venice more brilliant or more
festive : all the traditional gaiety had returned to the
city of the lagoons, and those of us who had seen the
grey, deserted canals during the War period could appreciate the transformation that had taken place in the few
preceding years. Venice in the New Italy had become
like Salzburg, a meeting-place of musicians. The whole
festival became a glorious pageant with many attractions
to lead even the austerest contrapuntist to play truant.
The city swarmed with people from every country : the
Piazza San Marco echoed with the babel of different
tongues. It was said that never in her history had she
welcomed so many musicians together. When we think
of music we think of Platonic harmony and of St. Cecilia
pure and undefiled. But harmony, at any rate in the
sense that the saints gave to the word, is not the modern
musician's quest. At any hour of the day if you had
walked down the crowded Piazza, lined on each side
with chairs, outside the cafés, you would have heard
hoarse, raucous voices disputing and vociferating loudly
about some abstruse point of musical art. Nobody got
up very early, though there was a rumour that Schönberg used to marshal his forces for breakfast at 8.30 a.m.
The majority, however, of the celebrities did not rise

much before eleven, and they spent the latter half of
the morning outside the Restaurant Florian sipping
their Vermouth. Florian dates from the early years
of the eighteenth century and has welcomed many
famous men beneath its arcades, including Carlo Gozzi,
Rousseau, Goethe, and Byron. During the festival
it was the great " rendezvous " three times a day, when
people would meet one another :—in the morning for
the " apéritif " ; in the late afternoon for tea ; at night
for coffee when the military band played and the whole
Piazza, with its myriads of candles quivering in the
gentle breeze, became the world's most beautiful drawing-
room. The leaders of the rival factions would gather
their disciples in different groups and pour scorn on
alien worshippers. There was even the tendency to
consider certain hotels as the centres for this or that
composer : thus Schönberg stayed at the " Britannia "
and the disciples and ambassadors from that oracle
hovered round in eager attendance : in the Regina
hotel I discovered Malipiero and his suite : in the
Danieli, Stravinsky and a host of aristocratic admirers
mingled with the fashionable habitués. All those lights
of modern music shed their lustre on Venice, while
out in the Lido's largest hotel loomed the imposing
figure of Richard Strauss, like a flaming cloud on the
horizon. The attractions of the Lido as the week went
on lured away many a music-lover. They were tempted
by the long stretch of velvet strand crowded with men
and women of every nationality burning their bodies
a rich brown in the intervals of swimming in a sea that
was as blue as the sky.

For a music critic, however, there was no slothful
ease. Eager to thread the maze of modern music, he
attended the rehearsals. The rehearsals were held in the
venerable Liceo Benedetto Marcello—the cradle of

music in Venice. In those halls that once resounded to the harmonies of Vivaldi and Marcello I heard an indescribable medley of sound. The passages were thronged with principal geniuses, watchful, and struggling to exercise prior claims on a particular concert-hall. " No wonder," said I to myself, " that they had to make an Englishman president of the International Musical Society, for there is no doubt that it is only an Englishman, and a serene and balanced one of the older generation at that, who can resolve the dissonance of European warring musical factions and produce harmony." E. J. Dent, to-day the Professor of Music in Cambridge, was gifted with infinite patience. It was miraculous to watch the way in which he smoothed over the difficulties, now by subtle tact, now by Saxon firmness and set jaw. I marvelled at the rapidity with which he could pass from Italian to German and then to French in order to explain his meaning to an irate violinist or prima donna.

The International Musical Society was founded in the post-War period in 1922, under the auspices of young Viennese musicians. A festival of modern music was organized at Salzburg in which composers of other nations co-operated. After that meeting it was decided to form an association to carry on festivals and to promote interest in the New Music. In Italy the scheme met with an enthusiastic reception from the modern composers, such as Casella, the organizer of the Venice festival, Malipiero and others. The Italian section had the advantage of the patronage of Gabriele D'Annunzio, Prince of the Snowy Mountain. He, as president, picturesquely baptized the Italian section " Corporazione delle Nuove Musiche." The festivals, with their international juries, served a noble ideal in bringing composers together, but I soon realized the enormous difficulties that had to be surmounted by such

a musical League of Nations. At times I even began
to doubt whether music was, as so many have said,
an international language uniting the world together.
There were so many rivalries, so many jealousies, so
many antipathies between the composers of various
countries that I even wished that a huge printed
notice could have been set above the stage of the theatre
—" Love your neighbour, all you who enter here."

The performances were given in the Teatro Fenice
—by far the most beautiful theatre in Venice. It was
thronged to overflowing every evening with the most
brilliant crowds I had seen since the War. Evidently
the bejewelled loungers of the Lido had sailed across
the intervening lagoon to participate with their humbler
fellow high-brows of the city. Artists are proverbially
renowned for their picturesque unkemptness, but this
was not the case in Venice. The impression as I
gazed down from a box was of a glittering crowd.
There were few who had omitted to put on the conventional dinner jacket, and, speaking generally, the
audience was respectful in its demeanour towards the
performers. But a great distinction must be made
between such a cosmopolitan crowd and the audiences
in England. On the Continent, modern music evokes
passionate conflicting opinions and sometimes we find
brawls of the type that used to rage between Gluckists
and the Piccinists in eighteenth-century Paris. During
the Venetian festival, the theatre resolved itself into
two camps, the applauders and the hissers ; but it was
all very good-humoured bantering. Only occasionally
did the patience of the audience seem exhausted. There
were sonatas which started off in the later Scriabin style
and then became more and more soul-tortured. Crash
followed crash ; dissonance was quadrupled until our
senses reeled and a sickly faintness descended upon us.

I watched the audience : at first there was a trace of humour and an undertone of sniggering, but this gradually gave place to exasperation until someone cried out in a loud voice : " Questo è matto—basta ! " " This is mad—enough of it ! " I need only add that the English listeners were scandalized at the interrupter's bad manners. However, in soul-torturing music the piano was more merciful than the violin. I listened to solo violin sonatas which plunged me into a seething maelstrom. Violin technique, when it is not used for a harmonious purpose, excites the most homicidal tendencies in the listener. On the Continent, before the War, it was common for devotees of the Sevčik violin method to be refused lodgings in towns. Imagine a hurricane of Sevčik passages played up and down by an amazing executant to an accompaniment of escaping gas-jets, shrieks of despair—something phantasmal and weird, as if skeletons were clanging their bones, and one would get some idea of the modernistic solo violin sonata. Never a little section of "cantabile" to show off the beauty of the instrument's tone. Why use a violin for that type of music when howling saxophones, blaring trumpets and clashing cymbals would produce more effect ? It was pathetic to watch the sensitive, golden-voiced creature struggling in vain to shriek its agony. The composers of such works deserved credit for their undoubted sincerity : they were pioneers in an unexplored country but we wished they would reach soon an oasis where they might soothe their tortured genius.

Among the many composers whose works were performed, one personality emerged—Schönberg. Schönberg was a little bald-headed man, affable in manner but fierce in argument. It was not always easy to understand his meaning as his French was as confused as my

German. He gave me the impression of being a Brand in music. His motto might be: "All or Nothing," and throughout his life he has striven valiantly to build his church amid the snows. To those of us who knew him as the composer of the extremely interesting sextet, op. 4, and the string quartet in D minor, op. 7, it was extremely difficult to understand the Schönberg we heard at the festival. There was not much serenity about him: everything was jerky and grotesque, as if he was always making sudden gestures. I heard one unkind critic say: "Schönberg has a sadistic mania for persecuting music." But when I conversed with him I soon realized what an amazing control he possessed over the intellectual resources of music and what a faith he had in his own genius. He seemed to me more of a theorist than an inspired composer, and I could understand why he has been called "Master of those who know" by many of the most celebrated composers in modern Europe. When I broached the subject of Expressionism in music and his own influence on the movement, he replied scornfully that he belonged to no "isms." He had always been independent and individual.

"Music," said he, "must not stand still; it must advance. My views are not those of fifteen years ago when I wrote my manual of harmony. And so I issued a new edition in 1922."

Schönberg is for ever tortured by the fear that his works may be given without sufficient rehearsal. After attending a three-hours' practice of his Serenata, op. 24, I felt inclined to share his anxiety. The Serenata is in seven movements, one of which is a song to the words of a sonnet by Petrarch. The work is scored for the unusual combination of clarinet, bass-clarinet, mandoline, guitar, violin, viola, violoncello, and one voice.

Even after listening patiently to the rehearsal wherein the composer and his players went through the work, bar by bar, it was impossible for me to grasp the significance of such a work. It all seemed to me so weird, apparently so disconnected ; as if it were a book wherein the full-stops and punctuations had been omitted. I felt that it corresponded in music to *Ulysses*, and James Joyce's " interior monologue." I found myself imagining the mentality of the composer in the movement entitled " scena di danza." At first there is just the beginning of waltz rhythm, suddenly dispelled by shrill howls and whistling on the clarinet. The mandoline tinkles fatalistically ; the guitar strums monotonously ; the violin skips spiccato—a jerky little bit of phrase which is broken off by the entrance of the gruff bass-clarinet. We could imagine it in language thus : Jazz dance—nigger minstrels—frilly petticoat—red lips—Guinness corks popping—railway engine—6.30 p.m. train—London Bridge—East Croydon—Bay of Naples—Mandoline serenade—headache—Eno's—nightmare. The love-sonnet of Petrarch with its ethereal beauty, in the mind of this Cagliostro of modernity, resembled the last floating garment lying on the ground of a maiden who has been devoured by a wild beast.

I have often wondered where that music of Schönberg and his disciples will lead us. Can we imagine what the world may be like a hundred years hence, when Mozart, Beethoven and Wagner are relegated to the primitive ages and amateurs play Schönberg as they used to play in our youth Mendelssohn's *Songs without Words*? But will such music satisfy human nature with its romance and soul hunger, or will it not rather symbolize a civilization of Robots who have no nerves ? Schönberg's music, however, shows in its most accentuated form that deep preoccupation with rhythm which is characteristic of modern music. Modern musicians, in fact, would seem to regard melody with the same abhorrence as the Greek mariners regarded the Siren Maidens.

Among the Italian modern composers whose works were performed at the Festival the most popular was Malipiero. Although he would probably have acknowledged a certain Schönberg influence in his works, he was full of Italian traditions, and, in some respects, followed the path abreast of Pizzetti and Casella. Malipiero comes of Venetian ancestry. He had actually two Doges in the family, so his spirit harmonized with " La Serenissima." He was not a melancholy, ascetic dreamer shunning the world, but the very image of the charming, courteous Italian gentleman, still retaining a certain eighteenth-century polish that showed his descent from the vanished society of the Republic of the Doges. My first taste of Malipiero music at that festival led me to study his dramatic music in recent years. His plan was to discover his musical subject first of all, to serve as basis for his scenario. The scenario he patched together from bits of ancient poems. The patchwork quality of these miniature music dramas is characteristic of the modern, incoherent musical mind, but Malipiero's genius imparts a certain baroque unity which links his work up with the eighteenth-century Italian operas. Many of my musical friends in Italy would take me to task for calling Malipiero one of the most Italian of the modern composers. They would say that he had been too deeply influenced by foreign composers such as Stravinsky and Schönberg. But I would call the great authority of Henry Prunières who said that Malipiero's music was attached by deep roots to the ancient Italy of Monteverdi, Vivaldi and Scarlatti.[1] The best proof

[1] H. Prunières. Article in *La Revue Musicale*, March, Paris, 1934.

of Malipiero's modern Italian spirit is to be found in his setting of Pirandello's story *La Favola del Figlio Cambiato* (The Fable of the Changeling).

Pirandello has been the most authentic voice of the modern Italian theatre. His youth was spent in the slumbering Italy of the end of the nineteenth and the beginning of the twentieth century. He was a prophet, but his novel, *The Late Matthew Pascal*, which appeared in 1903, aroused little interest among the public. It was the War that launched Pirandello into world fame and his tortured plays suited the theories of the Grotesque which were dominant in Italian art and literature in those early years after the War.[1] Pirandello's plays achieved European significance, but when we consider his art from an Italian point of view it will be found that his weird visions of Sicilian life which he crystallized in his short stories have a deeper meaning. What Victor Hugo said of Baudelaire's *Les Fleurs du Mal* might be applied to Pirandello's *Novelle per un Anno*— "Il a créé un frisson nouveau." The subject of the opera, " The Fable of the Changeling," with its problem of the double personality and the longing for escape, is not only characteristic of Pirandello but it recalls themes which had been set to music by Malipiero. In construction it resembles that masterpiece of the Grotesque " Così È " (Se vi pare)—" That's the Truth " (If you think so). Up to the last moment the audience are left in doubt. Is the prince, or is he not, the son of the poor woman ? The author, true to his theories of relative reality, leaves each spectator to give his own interpretation. Students of modern Italian music will find it most instructive to study Malipiero's score. It is original in its essence. The musical declamation sets

[1] For Pirandello and the Modern Movement in the Italian theatre see W. Starkie, *Luigi Pirandello*, London, 1937.

the words in sharp relief and, at the same time, recalls the style of the seventeenth-century composers. At one moment we hear echoes of Monteverdi : at another, we follow the rise and fall of a phrase which is unmistakably Gregorian. The musical themes, too, balance the dramatic action and interpret it. There are parodies and burlesques in sound but they are always subservient to the genius of Pirandello the story-teller, and above all floats that most Italian element-melody.

There was one other modern personality of musical Italy whose acquaintance I made during that Venetian festival : Alfredo Casella. He is the most complete musician in Italy to-day. Casella, more than Malipiero, Respighi, Pizzetti, or the other celebrated " Maestri," represents the aspirations of Fascist Italy. There is nothing vague or nebulous about his art. He has mapped out his programme as if he was a man of action. None of his resources has ever been wasted. Step by step he has planned the course his music would take and made it fit into the national Renaissance. It is significant that Casella, strongly nationalist as he is by temperament, should have finished his studies in Paris. Paris has been, for a long time, the Mecca of composers eager to achieve complete expression in national idioms. Manuel de Falla, the celebrated national composer of Spain, has often spoken of deep influences which the Paris of Debussy and Ravel had upon his growing art. The Athenian clarity of French musical thought, so far from turning the composers of other countries into vague cosmopolitans, actually increased their desire to deepen their own race consciousness. Casella, like Falla and others, returned to his native country eager to follow the advice of the great old French master, Gabriel Fauré, the most classical and admirably balanced personality of contemporary music. We have only to listen to that early work of Casella—*Italia* (1909), a rhapsody for orchestra, based upon Southern Italian themes, to discover the nationalist aspirations of the young composer. Mahler, Schönberg, and Stravinsky enriched his personality by giving him formulæ to work upon, as, for instance, in the *Notte di Maggio* (1913), a poem for voice and orchestra which resembles the *Fire Bird*. Some of the works of those years, such as *Pupazzetti* (Little Dolls), with their sketches in miniature worthy of Pirandello and the Teatro Grottesco, introduce a new vein into Italian music. Casella's music is characteristic of the man himself. At one moment he is serious, melancholy, and inclined to pessimism : at another, he flashes repartees and demolishes the arguments of his opponent with his rapier of wit. Casella reached his full development as the most national of the modern Italian composers by his characteristic use and treatment of folk-song. He does not, like many of his predecessors, leave the folk themes in their original state. He transforms them and makes them reflect his various personalities. There is in Casella more unity than in Malipiero. There is the same influence of the eighteenth century that we noted in Malipiero, but Casella has achieved more perfect balance between the ancient and the modern. For this reason critics have called him the spiritual son of Scarlatti and Rossini, and it is around him that many of the vigorous young composers of modern Italy have grouped themselves.

The law-givers of the New Italy have always encouraged musical art. I remember the account given by a French journalist of a visit he paid to Gabriele D'Annunzio during the Fiume campaign. He expected to find the city surrounded with barbed wire, but to his surprise the only barriers he found were oleanders, and when he arrived at the Condottiere's headquarters the poet was unarmed and with a smile greeted him saying : " This evening, if you like, we shall talk of Claude Debussy." D'Annunzio showed his appreciation of the importance of music when as Regent he proclaimed the Constitution of the Carnaro.   Like a modern Lorenzo the Magnificent, he gave greatest importance to the Fine Arts.   By Articles 64 and 65 of the Constitution he gave to music first place in educating the people.

MUSIC

Article LXIV.

Music is a religious and social institution of the Italian Regency of Carnaro.

Every two thousand years a hymn rises from the depths of the people and it perpetuates itself.

A great people is not only one which creates God in its own image, but one which creates also its hymn for its God.

If every Renaissance of a noble race is a lyrical effort, if every unanimous and creative sentiment is lyrical power, if every new order is lyrical order in the vigorous and impetuous sense of the word, then music when considered as the language of ritual exalts the act of life, the work of life.

Is it not true that great music announces to the attentive, anxious multitude the reign of the spirit ?

Just as the cock when it crows excites the dawn, so does music excite the dawn, this dawn : " excitat auroram."

Nevertheless, in the instruments of toil, lucre and play, in the resounding machines which obey an exact rhythm like poetry, music finds its movements and its fulfilment.

From its pauses is formed the silence of the tenth Corporation.

Article LXV.

In all the Communes of the Regency, choral and instrumental companies have been created with State aid.   The college of Aediles has been entrusted with the task of building a Rotunda to hold at least ten thousand listeners, provided with amphitheatres for the people and a vast pit for the orchestra and the choir.

D'Annunzio lived his own dream at Fiume. The dream flashed upon the world for a moment and then disappeared, but some of his ideas were destined to bear fruit in the realistic Italy of Mussolini. Ever since 1922 there has been a sincere attempt to bring the benefit of the great social arts of music and the drama to the masses. Many a traveller who has visited Italy in recent years has borne testimony to the striking performances of operas given in the Roman Amphitheatre of Verona before an audience of thirty thousand people. I myself can never forget the day a few years ago when I saw the drama of Savonarola by Rino Alessi played in the Piazza at Florence. It seemed as if the ghost of the great ascetic preacher had risen from the dead and returned to haunt the very scene where he had trodden his " Via Crucis."

D'Annunzio, too, in Italy, was responsible for leading the music-lovers, and especially the writers and artists, towards Wagner. Music had a double meaning for him : it was both an intimate art leading him into the mood of lonely meditation, and it was also the art that was to dominate the masses. Music came from the people and it was necessary that it should return to the people. The law-givers in Italy have followed D'Annunzio and his hero, Stelio Effrena, in the cult of Bayreuth. The younger Stelios wish to imitate Wagner, and at the back of their minds is always the passionate wish that Italy will eventually create a Latin Wagner, of whom men may say, as they did of Wagner, that his work was the prodigious synthesis of all the aspirations which had wearied the soul of musicians and poets of Germany, from Bach to Beethoven and Wieland to Goethe.

Thus, when we consider the attitude of the New Italy towards arts, especially music, the most social of them, we should recognize the preponderating influence, not only of the prophet Nietzsche, but also of Wagner. D'Annunzio, like Mussolini, followed in his art the theories of Nietzsche when the latter divided all art into two opposing tendencies : the Apollinian tendency towards pure beauty, and the Dionysiac tendency towards something higher than beauty, that is to say, the mystery behind the mask of beauty.

No sooner did I talk of D'Annunzio the music-lover to one of my lively young Venetian friends than he exclaimed sharply :

" Poor old decrepit bard ! I pity him. The youth of Italy has turned away from him. The Futurists have shouted him down and blown their motor-horns at him. Whom has he got on his side except a handful of ' Arditi ' who remember the *Beffa di Buccari* and remain yawning at their posts in the ' Vittoriale ' for old time's sake? He stands pathetically on the shore beckoning to the rising sun, but the boat has put out to sea without him and his voice is lost in the wind."

CHAPTER XXVIII

A VISIT TO CAPRERA

THE TOMB OF THE HERO

I EMBARKED at Città Vecchia for La Maddalena, *en route* for Caprera to make a pilgrimage to the tomb of Garibaldi. At La Maddalena a tiny launch carried me swiftly across the sunlit waters towards the hero's resting-place. Caprera is a massive yellow-grey rock, about three miles long, rising like a fortress in the straits of Bonifacio between Sardinia and Corsica. The neighbouring rocky islands are honeycombed with batteries of artillery and barracks which descend to the water's edge. My launch scudded over the golden waters between battle-cruisers, destroyers, and submarines. Above my head zoomed squadrons of aeroplanes flying in formation. Occasionally, as I passed near the iron-clads, I heard the distant echoes of voices singing in unison. Caprera, strictly speaking, is not an island, for it is linked to the slender line of mainland by a drawbridge. As I sped towards the mausoleum of Italy's greatest hero I tried to drive out of my mind the thoughts of modern mechanical warfare and imagine what this place must have looked like in the early autumn of 1849, when, for the first time, Garibaldi left Rome disillusioned, and retired to live among the fishermen of this deserted isle. I imagined him as he was in those days, a sturdy, bronzed warrior with long, golden hair and a thick tawny beard. He wore a

Calabrian hat with a long black ostrich feather and a red shirt beneath his white South American poncho. On horseback he was as graceful as any knight in ancient chivalry : on foot, he had the slouching walk of a sailor accustomed to balancing on deck in a storm. Behind him followed his faithful servant, the negro giant Anghiar, cloaked in black, with lance and red bandolier. When he came here for the first time, it was to rest for a moment's peace after the tragic events of 1848 succeeding the fall of the Roman Republic. During those terrible months of ceaseless skirmishing he had led his small band through Italy in a fruitless endeavour to stir up his countrymen to resist the Austrians. He was followed by his heroic wife, Anita, the companion of his campaigns in South America. Although she was far advanced in pregnancy she insisted on sharing the dangers of battle with him on this occasion, as so often in the past. Anita, however, was stricken down by fever and could advance no farther. He bade his companions take refuge as best they could, and he hid near the sea in a field of maize with Anita and his dearest companion, Lieutenant Leggiero. Finally, Anita was transported in a cart to a cottage in the neighbourhood where she died. I recalled the words which the hero wrote in his memoirs :

When I placed my wife on the bed I saw that Death had already marked her for his own : I felt for her pulse . . . it had ceased to beat ! Before me, a corpse, lay the mother of my children : directly they see me, I thought, they will ask for their mother. I wept bitterly for the loss of my Anita, for the woman who had been my constant companion in the most adventurous part of my life.

She had been for eighteen years his wife, nurse and companion in battle. Here in Caprera, Garibaldi built his home with the small amount of money that remained

from the days in Montevideo and the inheritance of his
brother Felice.   When he bought a strip of land here
he did not imagine that from the windows of his rustic
house one would see to-day the display of Italy's naval
power.   Caprera, in those days, was for him a hermitage
where he might meditate and dream of what might have
been.

My arrival at the tiny landing-place of the island
made all thoughts of barracks, battleships, and aeroplanes fade from my mind.   Near by was a rough boat-
house where the hero used to store the cutter in which
he sailed across to the mainland.   Here, too, he laid
up the yacht Olga which the English presented to him
in 1864 as a tribute.   A path winds from the seashore
up through the rocks towards the colony.   It is a scene
of wild grandeur, for the crags rise in a jagged maze,
brown, yellow, grey, between which peer occasional
little oases of moss and wild shrubs.   It is a torrential
stream of molten rock, suddenly petrified by the eye of
Medusa ; a storm-swept scene, for even the pine-trees
are bent into queer shapes by the force of the gales that
sweep across these grim expanses.   Occasionally we
come across more tender trees, such as agave or oleander,
planted by the master with the intention of civilizing
the savagery of his surroundings : but their blossoms
and their fleshy leaves only show up by contrast the
austerity of the warrior's home.   There is little shade
on this island, for the pine trees are warped and dwarfed
by huge boulders.   The sea gale has blown them in
such a way that their branches stretch imploringly inland
as though wishing to protect the buildings nestling
beneath.   At last I reached the whitewashed house.
The path had widened into a well-kept road, and around
me I saw a small paradise of hedges, olive-trees, and
flowering shrubs.   I heard birds singing above my head

and, occasionally, the quacking of ducks and the crowing of cocks from the neighbouring farmyard.

First, I visited the tiny wooden hut with its two windows and doors which was the first dwelling that Garibaldi constructed on Caprera. Near by was a larger wooden hut and, beyond, the roomy, comfortable house wherein the hero lived the last years of his life. It has been improved and repaired by the family. My companion on this pilgrimage was my brother-in-law, Mario, of the Italian navy, who was a friend of Donna Clelia, the surviving daughter of Garibaldi. Before we visited her we followed the path towards the tomb which is situated at the back of the house amidst a profusion of red geraniums. Just outside the family graveyard we passed a sentry mounting guard over the dead hero, whose remains lie beneath a mighty mass of granite hewn from a neighbouring cliff. On the stone, in large, black letters, was inscribed the name: GARIBALDI. How I wished that I could lose myself in the contemplation of that noble piece of rock worthy of a Viking's tomb, but, alas, my visions of the hero took to their heels and away, like hey-go-mad, when my eye caught a glimpse of the vulgar, ornate tombs of the family which blatantly proclaimed their relationship. Why did they not lay him to rest beneath the granite on one of the neighbouring wind-swept crags, alone, unapproachable?

My brother-in-law, seeing that I had a disillusioned expression, said to me: "It is always dangerous to visit the relics of the heroes of our dreams, for reality crushes us. You must not think of Garibaldi lying here beneath the heap of moth-eaten laurel crowns, ornaments, trophies which officialdom likes to cast upon a great man once he is dead. Think of Garibaldi's spirit which haunts the places in Italy, France and South

America where he fought. Think of him riding into battle at the head of the Italian legion of Montevideo, or else meeting Carlo Alberto at Roverbella : he lives in the minds of those who fought under him at Velletri, Volturno, and in countless campaigns." We entered the large house where he lived during his later years. It had become a museum, and the walls were covered with crowns of bronze, silver, china and tinfoil. The withered garlands drooped on the walls, the ribbons and rosettes were dusty and mildewed. One felt that life had passed, and it was like visiting the grave of a beloved friend after some years. The wreaths were still there tied up with their bedraggled and discoloured ribbons : the pink and yellow flowers of porcelain already were covered with lichen. All that remained with us was the poignant memory of that day when we laid them on the grave and said a last farewell. Here and there, however, in the midst of this mass of junk and faded photographs accumulated in these rooms, we came across homely objects that were of personal use—a favourite, battered old chair, a big press of the type one still sees in the villages near Genoa for storing the household linen, the carpenter's table and tools with which the hero used to beguile his leisure hours : the invalid chair in which he used to be wheeled from one room to another and out into the garden by his third wife, Francesca Armosino. These simple relics moved me and drove away the oppressive sensation of mustiness and decay.

Mario then introduced me to Donna Clelia, the only surviving daughter of Garibaldi and Francesca Armosino. She resembled her mother, the peasant woman, by her simple austerity, but in her eyes I noted the hawk-like expression of her father. She, herself, insisted on leading us into the room wherein her father had breathed his last. The bed was left exactly as it was when he died, with its pillow and embroidered coverlet. Over it hung the mosquito net, and at one end I noticed a tartan shawl, probably the gift of some Scottish devotee. At the other end of the bed were many naval ribbons placed there as a tribute by sailors who had come there as pilgrims. The room was fragrant, for Donna Clelia had laid a little bunch of white violets upon the sheet. She told me that Donna Francesca until her death forty years later never let a day go by without laying the little sweet-smelling bunch upon the bed.

Donna Clelia led us over to the window from which we could gaze over the great panorama of blue sea and tawny island coastline.

" In the last years of his life," said she, " my father was bedridden with rheumatism, and he lay in a room at the opposite side of the house, but he kept on complaining that he would prefer to die than live without an occasional glimpse at the sea. So my mother secretly got this room ready, for she determined to give him a surprise for his birthday. She had to call in workmen and hew away a great rock outside the window that blocked the view of the sea. When the 4th July came, two years before his death, she wheeled him into the room. The window was wide open and the sun streamed in. When he saw the view of La Maddalena and the blue, sparkling sea he gazed at it for a long time without saying a word and then burst into tears. My mother, to celebrate the occasion, had filled the room with gardenias—they were his favourite bloom—and she had called the fishermen from La Maddalena to play the Hymn of Garibaldi outside the window. Day after day, he sat opposite this window gazing at his beloved sea. How he suffered ! His throat was paralysed and he could hardly swallow even a drop of water. He sat

motionless, gazing out of the window. The sparrows
flew in and perched upon his shoulders. It had been
his custom to feed them off his hand. They chirruped
shrilly and fluttered about him. When I tried to drive
them away he said : ' Do not drive them away. They
are perhaps the souls of my children who have come
to call me.' "

Donna Clelia then spoke of the last orders given by
her father concerning his funeral. He asked that his
body should be cremated, and he gave special instructions
that they were to build a funeral pyre in a spot facing
the Archipelago. There, on a bed of iron, his body
was to be laid and burnt : but the family and the authorities found that this last wish was impossible to fulfil,
and so his body was embalmed and laid to rest beneath
the granite boulder. Donna Clelia led us out of the
house into a pergola which was a mass of flowering
geraniums. Here we sat all through that golden afternoon while she described the deeds of her father and
the heroic companions of his campaigns.

" My father," said she, " deserved the name which
was given to him—' Cavaliere dell' Umanità '—Knight
of Humanity. His sword was always at the disposal
of oppressed peoples. All through his life he combated
injustice. Do you remember the verses he dedicated
to Victor Hugo in which he celebrated his young
militia men :

" Crois-tu qu'ils ont servi, combattu pour des maîtres ?
L'amour de la patrie fut leur seule passion,
Et de l'humanité libre la mission.
Ce n'est pas vrai qu'aux rois nous ayons fait l'aumône :
Nous servions l'Italie, nous ne servions personne.

That is why the great French nation wept for him when
he died, for he had defended France in its hour of
need in 1870. England, too, and America recognized

in him the hero of Liberty. His death, even, was a
bond of friendship uniting the peoples of the world."

" If he had been alive to-day, Donna Clelia," said I,
" he would have used the great influence that he had as
' Cavaliere dell' Umanità,' too, in the cause of peace
and understanding, and he would have welcomed the
New Italy which has risen into the forefront of the
great nations of the world. From his window he
would have seen the blue waters of the Archipelago
dotted with warships, symbols of modern power. I
wonder, Donna Clelia, what he would have thought
of it all."

" He would have told Italy to be strong, united, and
proud of her traditions, and the words which Italy's
great bard dedicated to him may still be chanted :

> " Oggi l'Italia t'adora. Invòcati
> La nuova Roma novello Romolo.
> Tu ascendi, o divino ; di morte
> Lungi i silenzii dal tuo capo.

> " Tu ascendi. E Dante dice a Virgilio :
> Mai non pensammo forma più nobile
> d'eroe."

After we had said farewell to Donna Clelia we roamed
over the rocky island. We visited the nook three
hundred paces on the left of the road which Garibaldi
had chosen for his funeral pyre : we meditated beneath
the favourite fig-tree and the mighty pine with the
double trunk. I thought of the general at various
moments of his life when he appeared in the Archipelago
in his cutter, speeding away from a world at war to find
peace in this secluded island. Here, as he said in a
letter to a friend, he acted like a boy on holiday. No
sooner did he arrive at the little quay than he rambled
through the whole island, set his two horses, Marsala

and Calatafimi, at liberty, and reviewed his donkeys. Then he sowed some wheat, just for the pleasure of casting the seed into the furrows with his own hands.

After his triumphal entry into the eternal city in 1870, when the Government wished to make him a great national gift, he had refused haughtily, asking only for a sack of seeds for his island farm. I imagined him watching over his sheep and cattle : in the cold night when he heard a lamb bleating in the barn he would rise from his bed, go to fetch the tender creature and carry it in his arms into the warm house. I saw him again after the wound in his foot at Aspromonte had stricken him down. Never more could he carry out his daily rural tasks and follow his favourite proverb (the proverb of every Italian peasant), " Chi vuole vada, chi non vuole mandi " (Who wants anything, let him go for it himself : who does not want it, let him give orders). He could no longer roam through the island, jumping from rock to rock like a mountaineer, or else skimming along the water in his small boat in the direction of Sardinia where he used to bivouac with the peasantry in search of game. He was of the same stock as the most characteristic of the ancient Romans, Cincinnatus, and in his eyes a ploughshare was as beautiful an instrument as a sword or gun ; for he knew that all life is a battle and Man is put into the world to fight against the forces of Nature and subdue them, so that out of the jungle he may create a garden. But Cincinnatus on his farm was ever watchful : even when the Government tried to keep him prisoner on Caprera, Garibaldi laid his plans to outwit its squadron of cruisers standing at anchor in the Archipelago. One night at eleven o'clock he put off from his quay in his little row-boat called the *Beccaccino* and with one padded oar he was able to glide between the hostile ships.

They did not see him, for he lay on his side in the boat as he paddled silently through the night across the water to La Maddalena.

When we reached our launch the sun had set and the lights began to twinkle across the water. Soon Caprera loomed behind us like a vast fortress. I could still see the white buildings and the shadowy pines stretching out their gnarled arms towards the tomb.

CHAPTER XXIX

THE DUCE

I SPENT the Summer of 1927 in Rome. I lived in Via Brescia near the Porta Pia, in an apartment lent to me by my friend Luigi Villari. Through the kindness of the Marchese della Torretta, Italian Ambassador in London, an interview with the Duce was arranged for me. My knowledge of Italy's Leader was that possessed by any member of the crowd who had watched his progress from March 1919 when he had launched his movement in Milan. I had stood on innumerable occasions among the masses in Rome, Florence, Venice or Udine, listening to his voice blaring through the loud-speakers of the piazzas : I had watched his gestures of defiance when he was dramatizing a crisis, and I had seen him in the distance winnowing the wheat or ploughing the boundary of yet another Pontine city. My impressions group themselves in two-fold series. I saw him beneath the Italian sky, and his personality swept into my view at repeated intervals when I was beneath the sky of England and Ireland. It was difficult at times to balance my Italian with my British impressions. It is said that distance lends enchantment to the view, but the reverse was true of my memories, for whereas in Italy I would feel myself swept along by the Duce's magnetic personality and his rhythmic mastery of the crowd, when in Dublin, London or Edinburgh my Anglo-Irish caution and watchful

prudence would assert themselves.   In Northern Europe
I was conscious of being outside the wizard's magic
circle and thus beyond his influence.   In my own
country I lived at a slower *tempo* and the characteristic
Mussolinian rhetoric at times jarred upon me because
it was so different to the Anglo-Irish habit of under-
statement.   I used to become irritated with myself when
I read over again in Dublin the glowing speeches which
had so thrilled me in Rome or Florence.   In desperation
I would read them aloud in Italian to my wife, in order
to try and recapture the former spell.   I felt acutely
conscious of this difference existing between the psycho-
logy of Northern Europe and the Mediterranean when
those speeches were translated literally by propagandists
and spread through the English-speaking world.   It
was, of course, necessary to translate accurately the
sharp, cutting phrases of the orator, because only in
this way was it possible to convey an idea of his power,
but as a friend of Italy I longed on many occasions to
soften the asperities, slacken the *tempo*, purge away
superlatives, and blur the outlines, in order that the
Leader's message might arouse sympathy among the
slow-moving, slow-acting Britons who refuse to consider Life as a series of dramatic crises to be overcome.

In Italy it was impossible to walk down a street
without seeing the results of the Duce's work, not only
from a material, but from a spiritual point of view.
His Revolution had completely transformed the Italians
and it was impossible not to be constantly aware of
this fact.   But in England, as a result of the distortion
caused by ceaseless propaganda against the Dictator in
newspapers, books, cinema and radio, his personality,
as seen so clearly under the blue sky of the South, became
in the North obscured, even obliterated by a mass of
excrescences.   It was as if a statue of Carrara marble

had been shipped away from Forte dei Marmi to misty Northern climes and set upon a pedestal in a gloomy deserted garden. The rain pattered upon it, lichen and moss began to creep up its limbs, and damp moisture gradually wore away the clear-cut features. The personality of Mussolini has assumed the proportions of a legend in England. He has become for many harmless citizens a kind of superior bogey-man, a modern counterpart to the Napoleon of 1800, who was called " Boney " by English nursemaids and invoked as a demon to frighten naughty children. The Press photographers have taken infinite pleasure in distributing all over the world distorted likenesses of the Duce. They touched up his pictures before publication, exaggerating the massive jaw, the snarling mouth, the grim frown, and of late, in order to underline grotesqueness, they add rolls of fat to increase the portliness of middle age. The journalists use their ingenuity in writing variations on the Duce's Roman expressions.

" He is a Roman," they say, " therefore he must belong to the purple period when Nero rampaged (' Mussolini fiddles, you know '). He has dredged Lake Nemi—naturally ! That was where the sadistic Emperor Caligula sank Roman galleys with their crews on board to gratify his cruelty. He, too, wished that all the Roman people had but one neck that he might strike it off with a blow."

The so-called Cæsarism of Mussolini gave rise to an immense amount of anecdotes. When an English friend heard that I was to have an interview with the Duce he said : " Mark my words. When he receives you it will be with a light shining behind his head to give the impression of a halo." Another friend, a parson, who has been one of the most idealistic supporters of the League of Nations, told me the following story on

unimpeachable authority, so he said.   An acquaintance
of his, one day, sat waiting in the Duce's ante-room
in the Palazzo Venezia.   The hall was thronged with
diplomats, soldiers, journalists and civil servants, all of
them wondering when their turn would come.   Suddenly the folding doors of the sanctum opened and the
Duce appeared.   " You would hardly believe your ears,"
said the parson, " when I tell you that Mussolini was
dressed in a flowing Roman toga and his head was
wreathed in a crown of bay leaves.   He strode through
the middle of the hall with his jaw stuck out and his
face the image of scornful arrogance.   Without a look
to either side of him he disappeared, leaving the ex-
pectant crowd of diplomats, journalists and civil servants
completely abashed.   You don't believe my story—I
can see by your ironical smile, but I swear that it is true.
I heard it from a man present.   You can't deny that
it is typical.   Mussolini has gone mad with egoism and
vanity."   It was useless to argue with my friend, for
he was a competent classical scholar and he would have
peppered me with epigrammatic tags from Tacitus to
justify his theories of Roman pride, decadence and
devilry.

The night before the interview I received tragic news
from Ireland.   At noon that day (it was Sunday) Kevin
O'Higgins, the Irish patriot and leader, had been brutally
murdered on his way to Mass in Booterstown, Co.
Dublin.   The news overwhelmed me, because, only a
few weeks before, my wife and I had spent a pleasant
day with him and his family.   He had talked then of
his hopes for the future of Ireland, and I, like many of
my countrymen, saw in him the strong leader of the
future, for Kevin O'Higgins was only in his early
thirties.   His short career had been full of promise.
I recalled the incisive qualities of his speeches, his

mordant sarcasm, his moments of passionate seriousness, his flashes of malicious wit. I visualized him standing before the crowd, dominating them by his lucid mind and slow, precise voice. And now he had fallen as yet another victim to the dastardly tradition of assassination which perpetuated itself in Ireland like a curse imposed by the gods long ago.

It was with a heavy heart that I made my way towards the Palazzo Chigi, where the Duce was to receive me. I was ushered into a large hall where many people were waiting. There were ministers and civil servants dressed in black, some ladies, evidently journalists, and various military men in uniform. An usher every now and then would come to the door of the hall and shout out the name in a pompous voice. All of a sudden I heard him cry : " L'Irlanda." " Strange," thought I ; " why should they call out ' Ireland '—surely neither Timothy Healy, the Governor-General, nor President Cosgrave is here." The usher again cried out the name " Ireland," and then catching sight of me, he came over and informed me that it was my turn. He led me along a passage, opened a door, and bowed me into a room brilliantly lighted from the ceiling. At first I thought the room was empty, but then in the far distance, seated behind a diminutive table, I saw a small man gazing at me. As I advanced towards the table I felt myself grow smaller and smaller and the man behind the desk seemed to grow larger and larger, for his eyes gazed straight through me as I walked timidly towards him. Before I reached the table Mussolini rose and came forward and extended his hand, smiling pleasantly and asking me whether I preferred to talk in Italian, French or English. I hastened to say that I preferred to talk in Italian, for my one fear was that he would insist on talking French, English or German, and so I should lose some of the spontaneity of his native expression. His next words to me nearly made me jump, for it was as if he had been able to read my innermost thoughts. " I have heard," said he, " the news about the death of Kevin O'Higgins. I admired him." He then went on to describe in a few words his impressions of the dead Irish leader's personality. As he spoke I marvelled at the uncanny suggestiveness of his remarks on Irish affairs. While he spoke his eyes bored into me like gimlets. I felt that the interview was beginning in a manner entirely different to what I had imagined. Where is the crown of bay leaves—where is the lofty Cæsarism ? I cannot see the halo anywhere. Instead, I meet a man who not only treats me with courteous familiarity but shows a genuine interest in the affairs of my country. I had seen him in public dressed in various uniforms, in black shirt, and in stiff morning coat, striped trousers and butterfly collar. But to-day he was in a navy blue serge suit without any adornment save the tiny badge of the fascio. I could hardly recognize his face when seen at close quarters, so accustomed had I become to the mask of snarling scorn and the massive jaw thrown out. To-day I was hypnotized by his large dark eyes which sparkled when his voice became animated. That voice had still a trace of metallic harshness and the words poured out in jerky, rapid sentences which jabbed my sluggish mind. I should dread being a foreign am- bassador or minister who would have to argue *tête-à-tête* in this lonely room. It has not a shadowy corner in which one might hide from those piercing eyes. To argue with Mussolini would be as hopeless as to fence with him, for he is a past master in word-fencing—no less than with the foil in his hand. Hence the uncom- promising vigour of his speech and those rapid gestures which foreigners think imperious, but which spring from that most Italian necessity of expressing meaning, not only by words but by the language of gesture.

Gradually I began to feel more at my ease. The forbidding mask of unbridled power had disappeared completely. Instead, I found myself gazing into a most lively and winning countenance. His dark, vivacious eyes seemed to light up his face as he spoke. There was harmony in his face and movement, as though the thoughts in his mind set up an unending rhythm which sent numerous tiny electric currents of luminous strength through his frame.

I then realized one of his great powers. He possesses the power of adapting himself to other men. He knows their moods, and being a virtuoso he knows how to play upon them, awaken them, and extract their inner thoughts. It is part of his greatness that he feels an intense interest in other men, no matter how humble they may be. His knowledge of life has not been derived from books but from living personalities, both those with whom he can sympathize and those against whom he can sharpen his tusks in battle. I then recalled the early story which he had written describing the wild violinist who raises his public up to an orgy of excitement—a significant story, when we remember that he himself is a violinist. As I looked at his broad white hands with well-padded fingers I said to myself that he had the touch of the violinist, the natural *vibrato*, which is a source of power when added to his supreme mastery of rhythms. I was afraid, however, to broach the subject of music, at any rate so early in the interview, because he might think the question frivolous. Instead, I spoke of Machiavelli. No sooner had I mentioned the name than he caught up the theme with zest. He told me how he had been familiar with the work of the great Florentine ever since his childhood, for Machiavelli was the gospel of his father. In the evening they used to sit by the kitchen fireside with a volume of Machiavelli's works and read passages aloud to one another. He told me how one day in 1924 the Black Shirt legions of Imola had presented him with a sword engraved with Machiavelli's motto : " It is not by words that States can be maintained." The gift decided his choice of theme for his doctorate in the University of Bologna (it was given to him *honoris causa*, but he insisted upon writing his thesis, which was a commentary on *The Prince*, a book which he called the Statesman's vademecum).

In the Duce's opinion Machiavelli's doctrines are more alive to-day than they were during the Renaissance, for although the externals of life have changed, individuals and races remain the same. From Machiavelli the conversation turned to Nietzsche, whom the Duce seems always to have looked upon as one of his spirits of inspiration. Whereas Machiavelli would seem to appeal to the clear-thinking man of action in him, Nietzsche would seem to appeal to his artistic nature with its unending aspirations. And after Nietzsche, when I mentioned *Reflections on Violence* by Sorel he elaborated the differences between Sorel's theories on Syndicalism and Fascism. As he talked on in his warm, gracious manner I tried mentally to stand back and look upon him from afar. Occasionally when I found myself noting his strong jaw and the slight mannerism of clenching his teeth, I thought of him standing before the populace of Rome or Milan. In 1932 the historian Ludwig has described how one of his interviews had been interrupted when the Duce had to go on to the balcony and address the crowd below. Ludwig, watching him as he stood for a moment gazing down upon the applauding crowd, compared him to a dramatist

who comes to the theatre and finds his actors impatient
to rehearse with him. Then suddenly, when in response
to a gesture by him the shouts of the crowd ceased, his
features became transformed by the effort of tension.
His speech was an attack and the words were hammered
out.[1] To-day, however, as the talk was casual, there
was no feeling of tension in his manner. He was in
an urbane and smiling mood and here and there I noted
traces of humour—a sardonic humour characteristically
Italian, with touches of bitterness in it. He took me
to task for my too narrow conception of the *Risorgimento.* As a matter of fact, I had prepared my question
carefully to draw him. I wanted to lead up to the
great state-religious question. And so I asked him
whether it was not true to say that the *Risorgimento*
had been created for the most part by men who were
atheists and who gloried in their paganism : I quoted
lines from Carducci. But the Duce snapped at me :
" What about Manzoni ? Who was a better Catholic
than he was ? He was a prophet of a united Italy and
a deeply religious one. And what about Mazzini ? He
was also deeply religious."

I then questioned him on his methods of work, his
recreations. He told me that in preparing his speeches
on foreign affairs he sometimes would work far into the
night in order to work out all the details of a particular
question. " But then," he said, " sometimes it happens
that before I deliver the speech I receive news from
abroad which annoys me. I then put away the speech
I have worked at and go down and give the people
twenty minutes of *parole di fuoco*—" words of fire."
Then he said in a softer tone : " But I always act on
the speech I have prepared with infinite care."

Foreigners who have only seen the external mask of

[1] E. Ludwig, Colloqui,

Mussolini the lion-tamer and expert in mass-psychology consider him a bold, dynamic personality dashing onwards ruthlessly. They do not know that his impulsive personality is restrained by another calm one which can balance the former and give a deep, serious serenity to his nature. During the forty minutes that we had been conversing I noticed no traces of the theatrical. But I found it difficult to visualize this man during the different phases of his career as blacksmith, school-teacher, journalist, Socialist agitator who had undergone terms of gaol in several countries, creator of Fascism, dictator and finally Father of his country. A man who has lived through those scenes of turbulence and revolution would naturally reach the stage of blasé serenity after having passed over the whole parabola of human emotions—an attitude of mind which Voltaire described through the medium of Pococurante in *Candide*. But Mussolini after all his battles still possesses a touch of *naïveté* which enables him to enjoy life. Before I left him I had an illustration of this childlike quality. He pulled out plans for the wonderful new town-planning schemes which would transform Rome. He showed how within five years the majestic ruins of Roman antiquity would be delivered from the masses of mean, decrepit buildings which had grown up round them during the centuries and obscured their beauty. As he unfolded his plans his voice rose in tone and he became again the artist constructing his dream. I then thought of him under three aspects—the ancient Roman, full of belief in the mysterious foundation of the city of Romulus : the Catholic, conscious of Rome, the centre of the universal Church : the Condottiere of the Renaissance who could gaze back at the Rome of Michelangelo and harmonize the paganism of classical antiquity with the spirit of Mediæval Christianity. The Duce, meanwhile, was elaborating his vision of a greater Rome which would be the centre of an Empire. He spoke of the problems facing a statesman of the twentieth century—" Problems of necessity," he said, " but also those of grandeur. We must face both kinds to-day. We must house the people adequately and give them schools, hospitals, playgrounds, and improve the communications between one centre and another. But that is not enough : we must inspire the people and make them take pride in the ancient traditions of their race. We must liberate ancient and mediæval Rome from ugly and inadequate surroundings so that a monumental Rome of our own age may rise. Rome must not become a modern city like so many others in the world : it must be a city worthy of its ancient magnificence and its splendours must be constantly renewed so that future generations may admire and respect them." He pointed with emphasis to the plans lying on the table. As he spoke I felt as if, at the bidding of this imperious man, thousands of unseen architects were beginning to construct, stone upon stone, the New Rome out of the soil of the ancient city. I heard in my mind the ceaseless sound of hammering, sawing, and drilling. Through a maze his words came to me : " We must create a new art instead of imitating the ancients. Style is the eternal characteristic of our race : not only does it give the Man of the future rules for the erection of new cities, but it lays down æsthetic laws which are the guides of national harmony."

" Yes," said he at length, " architecture is my favourite art."

Mussolini then turned back to the religious question. " Remember," said he, " that the Latin tradition of Imperial Rome is represented by Catholicism. In my first speech in the Chamber of Deputies in 1921 I stated this clearly. It was Mommsen who said that it was impossible to remain in Rome without a universal idea. Well, I believe that the only universal idea now existing in Rome is that represented by the Vatican. There are in the world over 400,000,000 men who look towards Rome from all parts of the earth. That is a source of pride for us Italians."

It was now time for me to depart and I saw out of the corner of my eye Signor Mameli, the Capo Gabinetto of the Duce, hovering near by with papers for him to sign.

When I left the Palazzo Chigi I went for a long solitary ramble through the streets of Rome, pondering in my mind and recreating my vision of Italy's leader, and calling upon a vast number of memories. No sooner did I conjure him up again before me than I saw him in my mind's eye walking rapidly towards the tomb of the Unknown Soldier on which he was to lay a wreath. Even his rapid, swinging gait explained many things to me. It was the characteristic walk of the popular Leader, the characteristic walk of one accustomed to familiarity with the multitude. His was not the point of view of one who had been cradled a tyrant, but of one who was conscious of having sprung from the masses. The next point that struck me was the Duce's fatalism. No leader in Europe concedes more graciously a private interview. In those days he was less guarded than many a minor politician in other countries. In fact, as the detectives told me on several occasions, they had great difficulty in making him take elementary precautions. I remember on one occasion when I called at the gate-lodge of the Palazzo Torlonia, where the Duce lived, I noticed a typewritten notice posted up on the wall informing the detectives that His Excellency wished on no account to be conscious of their presence. They were to keep out of sight. The Duce, when he gets into his racing car, likes to outstrip all followers. When he drives from the Palazzo Torlonia to the Palazzo Chigi the road is kept clear and he dashes like a bullet through the narrow Porta Pia.

He has the fatalist's trust in his star. Threats of assassination have poured in upon him for close on twenty years but they leave him unmoved. On one occasion he was only saved from death by his strange mannerism of shooting out his jaw when facing the public. It was in 1926 at the opening in Rome of the Surgical Congress. He was walking out of a palace when a mad Irishwoman called Miss Gibson fired at him point-blank from behind a pillar. As a result of the Duce's movement of his jaw the bullet passed through his nose without seriously wounding him. Such was his nerve, however, that a few minutes later we saw him standing on the balcony addressing the crowd and crying out in a thunderous voice that there must be no reprisals. That night he left for Tripoli.

In considering the personality of such a man I have felt all along that we are in the presence of a phenomenon of nature. He has been cast up out of the soil of Italy as a reminder of the eternal, primitive virtues of the Italic race which perpetuate themselves from age to age, as flowers and plants do in the Spring. It is significant that he was the son of a blacksmith born in the land of the Romagna, which was famous in the thirteenth century and gave birth to illustrious families during the Renaissance. The Duce in his autobiography described it thus :

It is a sulphurous land. From it the ripe grapes make a strong wine of fine perfume. There are many springs of iodine waters. And on that plain and on those undulating foothills and mountain spurs the ruins of mediaeval castles and towers thrust up their

grey-yellow walls towards the silent blue sky in testimony of the
virility of centuries now gone. Such was the land, dear to me
because it was my soil. Race and soil hold strong influences upon
us all.

Significant, also, was the fact that he attended school
under the ferule of Valfredo Carducci, the brother of
the civic poet of the *Risorgimento*. After school came
a short period of school-teaching, but in the young
Mussolini there was the wish for a wider world. And
so followed the period of hunger and struggle. In
Switzerland he became labourer, mason, hack translator,
politician ; but in politics he never earned a penny, for,
as he said, " I detest those who live like parasites,
sucking away at the edges of social structures. I hate
men who grow rich in politics." Then came the call
of the army and Mussolini joined a regiment of the
Bersaglieri at Verona : perhaps his swinging gait has
something to do with his training as a bersagliere.

It was the spirit of the army which gave balance to
a mind seething with political revolution. The army
gave him the sense of willing subordination and taught
him the stern, Latin discipline. It also taught him not
to yield to the demagogue spirit and it prevented him
from ever flattering or wheedling the crowd. On many
occasions the Duce has stated that neither his school
friends, his war friends, nor his political friends ever had
the slightest influence upon him. He does not believe
in the influence of books. In the autobiography again
he has said :

> For myself, I have used only one big book.
> For myself, I have had only one great teacher.
> The book is " Life—lived."
> The teacher is day-by-day experience.

There have been, however, certain famous spirits of
the past who have created a background to the Duce.

First of all, we recall Machiavelli, whose genius gave him an acute pessimism in regard to human nature. Some of the sentences of Machiavelli seem to be stamped upon his mind, as, for example, the following, taken from Chapter 17 of *The Prince* :

Men have less scruple in offending a man who makes himself loved than one who makes himself feared, because love is held by the link of obligation, which, because men are of poor stuff, they will break away from as soon as occasion offers : but fear is held by a dread of punishment which is never lost.

Afterwards Mussolini was to explain the doctrines of Machiavelli in terms of modern Italy. The Prince, he held, really personifies the State. The State stood for organization and for restrictions which the individual tried constantly to evade. But it was Nietzsche who added wings to his artistic *condottiere* spirit. The motto which he taught to the young Fascists, " Live dangerously," springs from Nietzsche, and so does the other phrase which I have seen chalked upon walls in cities—" We Fascists hate an easy-going life." From Nietzsche he learned how to be an implacable critic of democratic society, and I can imagine the Duce repeating aloud to himself the following words from Nietzsche's *Birth of Tragedy* :

Yes, friends of mine ; believe as I do in Dionysiac life and in the re-birth of tragedy. The day of Socratic man has passed : crown yourselves with ivy, wave the thyrsus and do not be astonished that the tigers and panthers come up and gently rub themselves against your knees. To-day is the time for daring to be uniquely tragic men.

It is, however, wrong to crowd the literary background of the Duce with aphorisms taken from supermen of the past. He uses them only so long as they suit his purpose. All such thoughts are subordinated to the one great idea which he has inherited from countless

Italian ancestors, we might even say from the soil of
Italy itself, namely, that of recreating Roman power in
the world. At each step of advancement he has had
to call upon his Nietzschean spirit to enable him to take
the risks. Cæsar crossed the Rubicon only once :
Mussolini has crossed it seven times. His genius might
be represented by a two-headed image of Mercury, the
God of Chance. One head is square and Roman with
tenacious jaw and grim frown : the other has sensitive
nose and mouth and its eyes are those of a dreamer.
Each face possesses qualities which the other lacks.

After my long ramble I called to see my friend,
Senator Giovanni Gentile, at his rooms in the Piazza
Paganica. In the early days of the Fascist Government
I was told that Mussolini said of Gentile : " He is my
conscience." Gentile was not only the philosopher of
the Movement, but the great reformer in education. In
contrast to Mussolini he is a calm, peaceful student,
without a trace of the warlike in his constitution. To
talk with him was like continuing my conversation with
the Duce in another key. Gentile is the personification
of philosophic calm. The vastness of his erudition has
not disturbed his tranquil mind, nor has it driven him
to dwell in an ivory tower. As well as being a philosopher and the creator of an idealistic system he is a
great critic. For years he and his former friend, Benedetto Croce, sharpened each other's wits in the past as
if they had been two mighty champions engaging in the
lists. The vigour and swiftness of Gentile's mind have
drawn around him countless disciples, no less than his
benevolence which resembles that of a devout father
confessor. Half an hour's experience of his spiritual
calm made me feel as if I wanted to pour out my own
problems of soul and mind. In slow and measured
sentences he described for me the advent of Fascism

under the inspiration of the Duce. " There were not,"
he said, " the political conditions which produced Italian
decadence in the past. Political slavery is the cause of
many evils but not of the most terrible misfortunes.
Political slavery is only temporary and may be remedied,
but moral slavery is death itself, or, as Gioberti puts it :
' One of those desperate attacks of lethargy and agony
from which mankind cannot be cured save by some
extraordinary force of nature, or, we might say, a
miracle.' And this moral slavery consists in imitating
foreign languages, customs and sentiments. It consists,
in fact, in the absolute loss of national spirit, and Gioberti
said that the national character of a people is its essence,
its soul, and its life. Woe to the nation which has lost
its national genius, for this means losing its own being
and the consciousness of itself." Gentile concluded his
remarks on Gioberti by saying that religious faith and
national vigour depend upon strength of mind which
prevents a nation from being subdued and divided up
by foreigners. Fascist youth to-day draws its strength
from such thinkers as Gioberti, Mazzini and Manzoni,
who shook Italy from its ancient apathy. He then
went on to tell me of his educational reforms, for in
October 1922 Mussolini had appointed him Minister of
Public Instruction and had given him unconditional
powers.

Gentile might be called a peripatetic philosopher, for
he likes to ramble slowly along. The rhythm of walking excites him to expound his views. On one occasion
we mounted to the Pincio Garden, and as we plodded
along the Master poured out his views on Italy, Humanism, and Europe. We sat beneath the trees in that
enchanted spot from which we could gaze down over
the mighty panorama of the eternal city. I questioned
him at length out of his book, *The Reform of Education*,

which had meant more to me than any other book I had read on the subject. He would reply in his soft, mellow voice. Down below in the far distance I could hear the roar of traffic, but up here we were in peace : not a sound, save the gentle twittering of birds and the slight rustle of leaves. In such a scene as this Plato had established his Academy. I wish to take leave of Gentile, the idealist, in the following words, which seem to me to sum up his spirit of humanism :

Each one of us has a different path to follow in this world and each one will have his own education. But all paths converge to one point where we all gather to lead in common that universal life which alone makes us men. And as we meet in this centre we must understand each other and we should be able to speak the same language of the spirit. We are compelled by an irresistible will to live this common life and together to constitute one spirit. But this end we shall never attain if man, who ought to be entire and complete, acts as a mere fragment and if man insists on fencing off his little piece of " this threshing-floor that makes him cruel." Then war will break out, not a disciplined war governed by law, by an idea, by reason—but a war of every man against his blood—the anarchist uprising, the disintegration of the spirit.

I shall for ever remember that calm man seated beneath the trees in that garden above Rome. He became for me a symbol of the spirit of Humanism flitting like a beautiful spirit above our world.

Giovanni Gentile prolonged in one direction the conversation I had held with the Duce. I now prolonged it in another direction by going to visit Edmondo Rossoni, the great authority on the Corporative State. Edmondo Rossoni was one of the authentic Fascists of the original movement. He was associated for many years in socialist activity with Mussolini. He was a great contrast to the philosopher Gentile. A small

man, sharp, energetic, bright-eyed, and full of electrical
energy—" a man accustomed to dominate the turbulent
mob," said I to myself as I studied his grim sharp features.

He was dressed in a black shirt which showed up
by antithesis his bronzed, lined face, making it look like
an ancient cameo.   He started off without any ceremony
to tell me about the virtues of the Fascist Revolution.
" It is a revolution," said he, " not merely of national,
but also of world significance.   You come from England
and you'll probably laugh when I tell you that peace
to-day lies between Rome and Moscow.   You British
keep Moscow at a distance but, so far, you seem unwilling to borrow anything from Rome.   You can't
deny that destructive forces are pressing upon you and
your much-vaunted Democracy must end in Socialism—
that is, in a system more or less similar to that adopted
by Moscow.   Now I want to impress upon you that
you must not follow those who regard Fascism merely
as a Conservative force.   If you do, you will fail to
understand the principles which have sprung from the
Revolution of October 1922.   Our new ideas on the
corporative organization of society will become the basis
for the reorganization of the modern state.   In some
respects we are only following the tendency of the times.
Even in England Trade Unionism has changed its
objective and is turning towards truer and more responsible methods of group action.   Other parties opposed
to Trade Unionism are adopting standpoints which
closely approximate to the principles of Fascist Syndicalism.   Now the aim of Fascist Syndicalism is unity and
collaboration ; it does not oppose, but conforms to the
needs of production ; it does not deny the conscious
aims of Labour, but harmonizes them with the aims
and with the industrial experience of the managers.
This is the true and fundamental difference between

Fascist Syndicalism and Trade Unionism, for the latter is based on class warfare."

Rossoni then went on exposing his Syndicalist doctrine. First of all, he made an attack upon Socialism, showing the great harm that resulted to the other workers. But then he attacked the employers, saying that in their reaction against Socialism they and their supporters tried merely to defend all their own prerogatives and attributes. " Foreign countries," he said, " will not understand the constructive side of Fascism. When they are struggling with Socialism they think they can appeal to Fascism, simply as an anti-Socialist force. In the international circle at Geneva members fire whole broadsides at a puppet which actually has no existence in the Italian system. Political and financial speculators spend their time slandering Fascism, and through Fascism the New Italy. The Mussolini method is to steer clear of polemics with internal and external enemies of Fascism, and instead, to underline all that Fascism is doing to discipline the life of the country and to raise the prestige and dignity of Italy."

When I hazarded some remarks about political parties and groups, Rossoni interrupted impetuously, saying : " Fascism has removed all meaning from the old political jargon of ' Right ' and ' Left.' We shed no tears, I tell you, over the destruction of those innumerable parties which infested the political camps. Our militant Fascists were called cruel tyrants by you, but if you examine the question I am sure you will agree that unification and simplification are elemental necessities to a people that desires good government." The words of Rossoni became linked in my mind with those I had heard from Gentile and from the Duce. " Simplification " and " Unification." Those two words might be taken as the motto of modern Italy in all its phases.

Rossoni continued in detail with his explanation of Fascist Syndicalism, and as I took my leave of him he said : " Do not fall into the mistake of thinking that we Fascists will ever go back to the Parliamentary, Democratic and Liberal forms of Government. We have finished with Parliamentary Democracy which produces instability and disorder, or else absolute tyranny of the party system. We want to form an assembly of Fascios and Corporations which will harmonize with our totalitarian principles. The Fascios and Corporations will represent eventually the whole Italian people. Our ideal is to unify all the forces of the nation, for in this way we shall be strong." With these words he raised his hand, giving me the Fascist-Roman salute, and I departed.

During the years of 1928, '29, and '30 I followed very closely the various stages leading to a solution of the religious problem in Italy. From my interview with the Duce I had gathered that the thought uppermost in his mind in 1927 was the religious question. His last words to me had been an assertion that Fascism was determined to bring about a settlement of a matter which had torn Italian life asunder in the past. So difficult did the whole Roman Question seem that the subject had been shelved in the past by the politicians. The Papacy had kept up a continual fire of protest against the Italian occupation of Rome. For over thirty years the diplomats of the Vatican had kept up the cry of temporal power without ceasing. When the Great War began, many people believed Pope Benedict XV would have tried to solve the Roman Question with the help of Italy's enemies, for it was Benedict who in one of his consistorial allocutions proclaimed that the condition of the Roman Pontiff did not allow him the full use of

that liberty which he needed in the government of the
Church. Pope Benedict, however, was an Italian patriot.
Through Cardinal Gasparri in 1915 he declared that the
Holy See expected the settlement of his situation would
arise not " from foreign arms, but from the sense of
justice of the Italian people, in their own real interests."

When Mussolini came into power he announced that
the Fascist State recognized itself as a Catholic State.
He not only declared on many occasions that the Catholic
religion was the history of Italy, but he also manifested
on many occasions the deep reverence of his Government towards religion. And so on the 11th February,
1929, the Lateran Treaty was signed, regulating the
relations between Italy and the Holy See. By the
political Treaty Mussolini declared that the Roman
Catholic Apostolic religion was the religion of the State.
The Treaty then went on to create the Vatican City
and to declare that the Italian Government had no right
to interfere therein. In fact, the territory of the Vatican
City was always to be considered as a neutral and in-
violable territory. By the terms of the Treaty and the
Concordat the Holy See renounced all claims, even moral
ones, over Rome and gave explicit and solemn recognition
to the Kingdom of Italy under the Monarchy of the
Savoy Dynasty with Rome as the capital of the Italian
State. Permission was given also to other religions to
practise freely. Catholics, Protestants and Jews were
all thus enabled to enjoy equal rights.

There is no doubt that the Lateran Treaty has made
an enormous difference in Italy. In former days I had
been struck by the abyss dividing Catholic from Free
Thinker. Although the Italians have always been a
religious people, there was throughout the country an
immense amount of anti-clericalism. Mussolini, true to
his policy of unity and harmony, has diminished these

dissolvent tendencies. Ever since 1929 there has been a definite expansion of religious feeling in the country. I had many opportunities of observing this, not only in Italy itself, in Sardinia and Sicily, but also in America, which I visited in 1929, '30, and '31. On one occasion when I was on a lecture tour in the Middle Western States I had to speak in a Baptist College in the town of Beloit, in the State of Wisconsin. The subject of my lecture was "Italy and the Vatican Accord." My audience was composed of the Baptist citizens of the town who listened to me with tolerant good-humour. They were interested to hear about Italy and its struggles with Catholicism. In the front row of the hall was a small, fat man dressed in black and wearing a Roman collar. His wild enthusiasm was in contrast to the phlegmatic behaviour of the rest of the audience. He broke into applause at every pause in my lecture. Afterwards he came up to me and introduced himself. He was the priest of the Italian colony in Beloit, a native of South Italy. When I went back to his Presbytery I drank some glasses of the home-made Italian wine he manufactured for himself (it was the Age of Prohibition) and I listened to his rapturous comments on the religious peace which had been made by Pope Pius XI and the Duce. "I am an exile," cried he as he raised his glass, "but I may now cry 'Viva Italia! Viva il Duce.' Up to this we Italians have always been divided. In the past I was a member of Don Sturzo's party, the P.P.I. (Partito Popolare Italiano), and the Fascists were anathema to me. But now we Italians are all united under Church and State." The little priest then brought me down to visit his church, which had been decorated, mostly by the members of his congregation, Sicilian workers every one of them. The chapel with its rustic ornaments reminded me of many I had seen in Sicily. And when

I spoke to the men and women who came there on
Sundays I realized what a great work of reconciliation
had been accomplished by the Lateran Treaty. It had
broken down the last barrier which prevented the complete unity of the Italian people at home and abroad.

During the Summer of 1930 I found myself once more
in Capo Santa Chiara with my wife and children. My
father-in-law, Don Alberto, had been in very poor health
for the past year and we determined to spend the summer
with him. In the month of August we went up to
stay in his villa at Masone in the Ligurian Alps, sacred
to all of us through memories of Donna Delfina.
Masone was a paradise of green : the woods of chestnuts gave relief from the sun, and the rose-bushes which
had been the joy of Donna Delfina were now in flower.
As the 10th August was the anniversary of several
members of the family, Don Alberto arranged a feast
and the long table was set in the shade of the lofty pine-
tree. We were a joyous party and each of us had little
silk tricolours which we waved excitedly. Beside my
wife was seated Mario, who was back on leave from
the Mediterranean where he commanded one of Italy's
newest cruisers. My wife's sister, Eva, was there with
her two sons, Alberto and Orazio, and her little girl,
Nennele. They romped about the garden with my two
children, Landi and Alma. Don Alberto was full of
excitement. In spite of his staunch Garibaldian ideas,
he rejoiced in the peace which had been established by
the Holy Father and the Duce. " Ci vuole per la
massa," said he thoughtfully. " We Garibaldians, in
the past, were too extreme : we did not think enough
of the great masses who must be given spiritual manna
which will enable them to live. Instead, they had been
taught that there was no God, that Heaven and Hell

were in this world, and beyond the grave there was nothing. How foolish we all were! We should have taught men to draw closer to one another and create a religion of pity. Religion may be an illusion, but it is a blessing if it curbs the wild beast within mankind. Let man have religion if it is not used as an instrument of coercion and torture, and if men will not kill one another for the love of God." He said those words in a grave and solemn tone, and I thought of him as a lonely survivor of an ancient heroic age. His sharp features, his grey beard, his furrowed, weather-beaten countenance reminded me of the pioneer and the colonizer. How frail he looked to-day! His face was pale and drawn, but there was a hectic flush in his cheeks. A host of memories seemed to well up in his mind as he spoke to us on the green sunlit lawn beneath that tall pine-tree—" sentinel of death," he called it— which was an ever-present reminder of the snowy days of Christmas 1923 when his wife lay dying. As he continued, his emotion seemed to grow and his sentences became jerky, as though his heart-beat was too swift for his weak body. He drew his hand wearily across his brow. " My toil is now over : I may rest for ever here in Italy in the land where I was born." Smiling sadly at Italia and Eva, he added : " I am proud that my daughters have gone out into the world and settled in distant countries, some in South America and others in North America and Northern Europe. Each one of them carries a tiny particle of that eternal spirit of my country." He paused again and gazed dreamily out into the green valley and the distant mountains. " What we want to-day in the world is the brotherhood of peoples—that will only arise when each nationality achieves its perfect unity. . . . When I was young I was fiercely national . . . I saw my country divided against itself. Now Italy has finally become a united nation. . . . My vision extends farther. I dream of the future when the many nationalities composing that exquisite pattern which we call Europe will extend the hand of friendship towards one another. If that only happens, we shall reach the Millennium." He paused for a long time and his head drooped forward. There was dead silence, for all of us, even the small children, felt a strange fear descending upon us. He then raised his head and said : " It is now the time for me to drink the health of all my dear children." He rose slowly to his feet, holding in his trembling hand the glass of golden wine, saying : " I raise my glass and drink to you who are here and to those who are far away." All of a sudden, we heard him sigh deeply. He tottered an instant and fell forward on the table. We rushed over and carried him into the house. In a few moments he was dead.

CHAPTER XXX

MEDITERRANEAN SEA

FROM 1930 onwards a favourite topic of conversation among Italians was the Expansion of
Italy. The five preceding years had been a
great progressive period at home. Italy strengthened
herself, and instead of the former class struggles there
was co-operation between all members of society. The
institutions of the country harmonized together in their
syndicates, federations, confederations and corporations.
The principle of State supremacy was completed by
that of perfect equality between Capital and Labour
acting in the same legal and political plane. But now
that order had been established in Italy itself, men
began to wake up to the possibilities of the country's
colonies.

I found myself, like many English people, under a
misapprehension as regards Italy's natural wealth. The
artistic beauties of her numerous city-states blinded me
to the truth that Italy is a poor country, half of whose
area is mountainous and cannot be cultivated with
profit. In addition to this, large sections of the fertile
plane have been subject to inundations and to malaria.
The population meanwhile, since the unification in 1870,
increased at a rapid rate, and in 1928 the total was close
on 41,000,000.[1] As the economic development did not
tally with the increasing population, and as Italy in those

[1] L. Villari, *The Expansion of Italy*, London, 1929, pp. 34-5.

413

early days of unity did not possess colonies, her people
began to emigrate in vast numbers to countries which
needed labour to cultivate the land and build their roads
and railways. Italians emigrated to North and South
America where higher wages were paid and new settlers
were welcomed. The great prairies of the Middle
West, the orchards of California, the cotton plantations
of the Mississippi valley, the coffee plantations of Brazil
and the ranches of the Argentine were the scene of
operations of the Italian husbandmen. The Italian
emigrant type whom I had so often met in my journeys
through the United States was, as a rule, a characteristic
product of Calabria or Sicily. Thrifty, hard-working,
and resourceful, he would plod along year after year,
living frugally and putting by his savings, so that
eventually he might return to buy a tiny farm in Southern
Italy.

Villari has described the results of this vast demo-
graphic movement. The countries to which the Italian
emigrated obtained many benefits, for without them
the development of those lands would have been re-
tarded. But for Italy the results were only in part
beneficial. It is true that the emigrants saved and sent
home money : it is true that emigration taught the
chauvinistic Italians what the rest of the world was like.
But there were many drawbacks to emigration on such
a large scale. If the more educated classes had emigrated, bringing with them a system of life and a culture
of their own, the result would have been to increase
the influence of Italy abroad : but instead, only the
unskilled workers, the most ignorant and backward of
the population, became emigrants. And so the notion
spread among the Italian workers and among the
foreigners with whom they lived that the Italian race
was an inferior one, only fit to produce road-makers,

stone-breakers, and donkey-men for the rich foreign capitalists. Many people used to say : " What will happen to Italy if America closes its doors to the Italian emigrants ? " This did take place when, after the War, the United States restricted emigration from Italy practically to nothing at all. It was then that the rise of Fascism completely transformed public opinion in Italy with regard to the whole question.

We are no longer [cried the Duce] willing to be the universal provider of millions of brawny workers to fill up the gaps in countries with a declining birth-rate. One of the fundamental doctrines of Fascism is that the Italians must think of Italy first of all. Employment must be found for them at home, and if they go abroad they must still keep their link with the Mother Country.

The Duce, from the beginning, encouraged his ministers to study the colonial problems. He initiated the wonderful work of draining the marshes and stamping out malaria ; but in spite of the untiring energy of the Italian peasant who possesses all the great traditions of the Roman colonus, Italy's available land did not suffice for her vast population. Her few colonies were too small to absorb more than a fraction of her available colonists. Even Tripolitania and Cyrenaica, when developed to the utmost by such a wise governor as Marshal Balbo, cannot be compared as colonies with those of other great European powers.

Owing to the war in 1896 with Abyssinia, colonization had become very difficult, and the defeat of Adua which rankled in the popular mind put an end to all great schemes of development at that time. The colony of Eritrea came, in fact, to be looked upon in Italy as a white elephant and was not evacuated only on account of the loss of prestige which such a decision would have involved. Public opinion, for many years, had ceased to take any interest in it and almost tried to forget its very existence.[1] But the Libyan war against the Turks in 1911 had given a fillip to Italy's schemes of expansion and encouraged the people to gaze with more kindly eyes at the distant colony, especially as the native Ascari troops of Eritrea proved themselves such loyal and devoted fighters in the War. Italian Somaliland, too, was developed by the Government : roads were built, agriculture improved, and the cotton trade stimulated. But it was impossible for such a colony, separated as it was from Eritrea, to absorb any large quantity of white population.

In the city cafés the conversation would always turn to the Great War, and my Italian friends would point out to me the gains secured by Great Britain and France. " As a result of the War," said they, " Great Britain acquired 989,000 square miles of territory with 9,323,000 inhabitants. France acquired 253,000 square miles and 6,460,000 inhabitants. What did we get—23,726 square miles and 1,672,000 inhabitants."

Whenever I tried to rebut those accusations they would reply immediately : " You can't deny that England and France got the lion's share, and, in addition, those mandates are very rich in minerals and other raw materials, whereas those assigned to us are mostly mountain and nothing else. There would have been a very different story to tell if we had only sent strong delegates to the Peace Conference. They would have shown a stiff upper lip to Clemenceau and Lloyd George, those heads of rival empires who prated loudly of humanitarian doctrines and rattled off stock phrases about Christian virtue and worlds fit for democracy in order to camouflage their greed. Italy deserves to acquire colonies suitable for white settlers, for no other

[1] L. Villari, op. cit., p. 46.

country in the world possesses such quantities of strong, adaptable, hard-working colonists. If the League of Nations hands over any more mandates it will have to be to Italy : the Fascist Government will not be so easily bamboozled as its predecessors."

It was during the five years before 1935 that I noticed how certain authors of the nineteenth century sprang into greater prominence than they had enjoyed during their lifetime. Take, for instance, the case of Alfredo Oriani, who had voiced the aspirations of the imperial-minded Italians in the days of Francesco Crispi. Oriani's book, *L'Ora d'Africa*, written about 1896, had described the ideals of African colonization. He tried to spur on his countrymen to take their share in the African adventure : he paid noble tribute to the heroes who lost their lives at Dogalì in Eritrea : he turned aside from Italy to celebrate the glorious heroism of the Boers in their struggle against British imperialism, and he compared Cecil Rhodes to an Italian condottiere of the Renaissance.

Many of the Italians of my acquaintance read *L'Ora d'Africa* from cover to cover, pondering over its message. Oriani became for them a prophet of the New Fascist Italy. They would have wished to write some of those pages in letters of gold and set them up on a white signpost pointing the way to the Via dell' Impero. Consider the following passage written in the late 'nineties :

The moment of our glorious history changed to a moment of shame. Garibaldi, Mazzini, and all the heroes of the revolution had died ; a commonplace democracy belittled the greatness of our genius and character by giving it a mean interpretation. They wanted no war with Africa, for they insisted that it possessed the same national rights as Italy. They confused the historic period with the pre-historic. They forgot that if the more civilized had not always conquered the more barbarous nations, civilization

would never have grown : if Alexander had not invaded the East
the fusion between East and West would not have taken place :
if Rome had not subjected all the world the Greek spirit would
not have penetrated it and its unity would not have been accomplished : if christianity had not combated all the paganisms it
would not have established itself : if the barbarians had not invaded the Roman Empire the Middle Ages would not have been
confirmed : if Spain and England had respected the nationality
of the American natives, America to-day would not be the equal
of Europe and the discovery of Christopher Columbus would
not have helped her more than the earlier discoveries by Green-
landers, Japanese and Indians. But democracy, nurtured on the
principles of moral and political equality, failed to understand that
its high truths became force when applied outside their own
historic period to barbarous peoples. They failed to understand
that by coming into contact with uncivilized peoples they would
be forced to go to war.

His appeal to Italy after the defeat of Adua in 1896
sounded on deaf ears, but in the years preceding 1936
his words resounded like a clarion :

Italy which has twice been the centre of the world and to-day
has risen to full nationhood cannot withdraw herself from this
work of universal civilization. History follows the same moral
law as nature by securing the triumph of the most perfect form
and the noblest idea.

The words in which he expressed his scorn of the
Italian people who had left their soldiers to die unheeded
at Adua in 1896 sound like speeches of the Duce in
1935–6. He compared the people to the kings of old who
were flattered by courtiers into giving up their power.
The people thus become presumptuous because they
are ignorant, timid because they are deceived in every
victory by false leaders. And so in the end they lie
down in the mud of the street waiting for a new voice
to rouse them from their lethargy. Listen to his stric-
tures against the bourgeoisie of those days :

Italy now is starting afresh. All her organs are in working order; all the old parties have been liquidated; the people want to use the power which the bourgeoisie can no longer exercise because industrialism has degraded them. But Socialism draws its strength from the appetites it unleashes and especially from the cowardice of the bourgeoisie which gives in bit by bit, struggling to trick its way back to power every time it capitulates. Italy is more vital than Spain or France. Something ferments in our race : look how prolific it is ! We can and we must become a great nation.

In those five years, I vagabonded far and wide through the Mediterranean, and a fiddle is a good companion when a man wants to enter the society of the humble folk. A *cantastoria* or a *giullare* hears all the anecdotes, the thoughts and the hopes that run through the mind of the people. On some occasions I revisited Messina, Syracuse and Palermo. On one journey I tramped through Sardinia from Terranova to Cagliari. I visited Tripoli and Benghazi to study the wonderful colonial improvements initiated by the Duce after 1926 and carried on by Marshal Balbo. In every place I found the same spirit of empire which Oriani had prophesied. Men, women and children all over Italy and its possessions had become Mediterranean-minded. A man who is Mediterranean-minded brings certain topics into his conversations with the regularity of Leit-motifs in a Wagnerian opera. He talks of Rome, but not in terms of the Eternal City itself, but rather as a symbol of Mediterranean unity which Rome had created and tenaciously held for centuries. The words *pax Romana* are for ever on his lips. He will describe the Italian city-states of Venice, Genoa, Pisa, in terms of their colonial enterprise, reminding you that their descendants still flourish in all the countries coasting the Mediterranean. Then he will tell you how the discovery of the sea route to the Indies and the navigation of the Atlantic had caused the decline in importance of the Mediterranean and, in consequence, the powerlessness of Italy in the face of foreign invasion. He will finish, saying triumphantly that the opening of the Suez Canal in 1869 gave back to the Mediterranean the importance it had lost in the sixteenth century.

I had many conversations on the subject of the Mediterranean with Frenchmen and Englishmen as well as Italians. Frenchmen of the historic-minded type start off by reflections on the ancient rivalry in the Mediterranean between the French and Spanish monarchies, a rivalry which converged in the Italian peninsula. Then they would pass on to the long period of ceaseless struggle between England and France lasting from the Peace of Utrecht down to the period of the Revolution, and they would not forget to mention the acquisition of Corsica, saying: " Ah, Corsica ! Voilà la clef de la Méditerranée. Yes ! Monsieur, a key of Italy and Barbary, at any rate, in the past." But Frenchmen prefer to skip the past and come to the nineteenth century, when Algeria became the base for France's colonial expansion.

In the early days of the period from 1930–5 it was difficult to find an ordinary Englishman who wished to argue about the Mediterranean. As writers have frequently said, the British are always unprepared for grave emergencies. They do not like to stir themselves out of their pleasant routine and worry their heads over the sudden expansionist ambitions of totalitarian states. Hence the characteristic description of the British which is repeated again and again : " The British, as a general rule, only win one important battle in a war, but it happens fortunately for Great Britain to be usually the last one in the war."

The British, who are naval-minded, do not consider

the Mediterranean problem by itself; it is only an aspect of the problem of imperial defence, for there is not one Mediterranean sea—there is the Sea, the sea is a medium universal in character which both links and separates the British Commonwealth of Nations.[1] Without control of sea communications the existence of all the inhabitants of Great Britain would be imperilled, for the raw material she needs for industrial purposes would be unattainable, and without that control the enemy would be able to command the resources of the world. Commander King-Hall, however, thinks that many people hold an exaggerated idea as to the importance of the Mediterranean to British import trade.

There are, however, political reasons which make it imperative for the English to be concerned with the Mediterranean. We have only to cast our minds back to the wars of the eighteenth century and the struggle between France and England in the days of Napoleon to realize what a decisive part was played by British naval power. The development of British power in the fifteenth century was conditioned by command of the sea routes. Commander King-Hall quotes the instance during the Great War when a mistake on the part of the British Navy allowed the *Goeben* and *Breslau* to escape up the Dardanelles, an event which perhaps more than any other caused Turkey to enter the War on the side of the Central European Powers. He further says that the Great War in its later stages may be regarded as an attempt by the Allied Powers, backed by the resources of the civilized world, to overcome the resistance of a citadel which was in effect Central Europe. The Mediterranean Sea, he calls the southern window

[1] Commander Stephen King-Hall, R.N., *British Policy in the Mediterranean.* International Conciliation, January, 1938, New York.

of Central Europe, and the Allies endeavoured to force their way over the window-ledge.[1]

Thus the political and strategical importance of the Mediterranean during the Great War overshadowed any importance it may have had for Great Britain as an artery of trade. The Mediterranean area, from the British point of view, has become more than a mere link in imperial communications. It is still, as it has so often been since the days of Greece, Carthage and Rome, a centre in which political struggles might lead to the rise and fall of great empires.

Many of those arguments were lost upon the historic-minded Italians with whom I conversed. They would start off by saying that Italy was a purely Mediterranean country and that this Mediterranean character was accentuated by the Alps which separated the peninsula from the rest of Europe.

"All our activity," said they, "has been directed towards the Mediterranean from the dawn of our history. Before Rome had even reached the Alps she had established her colonies in Sicily, in Carthage, and in Spain, as well as in the East. Rome created her great power, simply owing to the fact that she was a Mediterranean people and was able to unify Mediterranean civilization. No other country in Europe is so closely bound to the Mediterranean as Italy, not even Spain, France, or England. We are the only people that may proudly call it 'mare nostrum.'"

They would then quote passages from the thinkers of the Risorgimento, who were all agreed that the future of Italy was in the Mediterranean and that her power should extend beyond that inland sea to Africa and Asia where she might find an outlet for her national activity. "You British," they would say, "have never given us

[1] Commander Stephen King-Hall, R.N., op. cit., p. 8.

full credit for the amazing national spirit of energy
showed by our nation since 1870." The mention of
the Suez Canal would draw from them the remark that
Italian engineers, technicians and labourers had a great
deal to do with its construction. They would say :
" The ' Suez Canal ' is a phrase full of brilliancy in the
modern epoch : it has acquired a title of nobility, almost
of sanctity. That is to say, it is a central point on the
highway of the British Empire. But as time goes on
the international character of the Suez Canal will increase
in importance. We do not want to attack the interests
of any other great power, but we must insist that we
possess more important interests in the Mediterranean
than any other nation because we are the largest nation
which is uniquely Mediterranean. We have no interests
in contradiction to those of England but she should
realize that her vital centres are around the Mediterranean
rather than in that sea. It is for her a passage leading
from one part of her Empire to the other, but for us
it is a question of life and death."

One noticed from 1930 onwards all through Italy
and its islands the rise of a more assertive spirit.
This spirit of Roman pride, not devoid of arrogance,
could be observed among the poorer as well as the
richer classes. It was the consequence of Mussolini's
slogan : " Work to the uttermost." As peoples who
have known the Duce intimately have said, it was
not the particular result which really mattered, for his
true ambition was that his revolution should become a
second Renaissance of the Italian soul. He aimed at
regenerating the entire character of the nation.

Where he showed his magic as a leader was in
imparting to his people a collective, intoxicated rhythm
of ceaseless movement. During those years I watched
the amazing spectacle of a whole nation forswearing

the pleasures of individual life and accepting with enthusiasm, nay with joy, collective creation. The more magnificent the work achieved, the higher the spirits of the people rose. They actually felt themselves growing in stature simultaneously with their country. Hence the solemnity and touch of arrogance of those slim young Italians, who prided themselves on possessing the remorseless efficiency of a perfectly functioning machine of latest design. Can we wonder that the Duce felt himself impelled to give them other worlds to conquer ?

Occasionally he uttered one of his dramatic prophecies, as for instance at the Quinquennial Assembly of Fascists on the 18th March, 1934, when he spoke of " a natural expansion which should lead to a collaboration between Italy and the peoples of Africa and the East." Italy, he added, could, above all, civilize Africa, and her position in the Mediterranean gave her this right and imposed this duty on her. He said that she needed no privileges or monopolies, but she did not want earlier arrivals to block her spiritual, political and economic expansion.

It was in July of that year that Marshal Badoglio visited Eritrea to investigate the colonies' " defences." English Liberal papers, even then, hinted that the purpose of the Marshal's visit was to report on the prospects of a campaign in Abyssinia in 1934. However, as far as the general world was concerned, there was then no rumour of the war to come, but those of us who spent months in Italy noticed the increasing acceleration of national rhythm. There were rumours of economic crises, though this was only to be expected owing to world depression. Mussolini's policy of fixing the value of the lira to a high level imposed an additional burden on the country, for tariffs were raised, international trade restricted, and people were driven to increase their home production.

Then came the Abyssinian frontier incident at Walwal in December 1934 which burst upon an astonished world. Some weeks later, on the 6th and 7th January, 1935, the famous talks took place between Pierre Laval, French Prime Minister, and the Duce—a meeting which to-day reads like the prologue of a big drama. Laval has been bitterly attacked and has been called the villain of the Abyssinian affair. But when he went to visit the Duce in January 1935 he was only following the policy of his predecessor, Barthou, who, at the time of his assassination, had been seeking an alliance with Italy against Germany. Laval wished to make a general European settlement with Italy and dispel that jealous rivalry in the Mediterranean which had existed ever since France, in 1882, had appropriated Tunis.

Italy had turned a covetous eye on Tunis, for that country had always been a fruitful sphere of operations for her Sicilian colonists. The Italians of Tunis were intensely national. They retained their own language, schools and institutions, and afterwards, during the Abyssinian War, actually subscribed one of the largest amounts of gold to the Mother Country. The visit of Laval changed matters. Would it not be possible for France and Italy to become close friends again and co-operate in a Mediterranean policy ? Surely this would be possible, seeing that they were sisters in the Latin world ? Much speculation was rife about the private dinner at the French Embassy in Rome where the two men discussed their differences. The world, however, was not allowed to hear a full report of what transpired. We learnt that a settlement had been reached on all questions concerning the application of Article 13 of the London Agreement of the 26th

April, 1915. Italy was authorized to extend her Libyan frontier and to carve off a small slice of French Somaliland. She was also granted a small amount of French shares in the Gibuti–Addis Abeba railway, and finally the Tunisian question was settled by the Italian residents renouncing their nationality after a certain date. Everyone was astonished that the famous meeting produced so little tangible results. In fact, the terms accepted gave many the impression that Mussolini had given away to the French Prime Minister more than he received. The Duce was quoted later as saying that in the whole area transferred by France to Italy in North Africa his experts had only been able to discover the existence of sixty-nine inhabitants and those had to be searched for like a needle in a haystack.

I had an interesting illustration of the general public's reaction to the meeting when some time afterwards I visited Tunis. In the cafés of the city I talked with many Italians, and almost with one voice they exclaimed : " Ci hanno venduti—We have been sold. Here we are, the most Italian of the Duce's subjects, and yet we are handed over to the French." It was only gradually that the truth was ascertained. Laval had given " carte blanche " to the Duce to go ahead with his expansionist policy in Abyssinia. Mussolini, henceforth, had nothing to fear from France at Geneva, however much Laval might protest that he had said no word to encourage the Italian adventure. When he had said good-bye to his French guest at the station the Duce knew it was safe to go ahead with his great design. Laval, who had now achieved his aims, which were to secure France from any fear of future attack by Italy, left Rome for Geneva, where Abyssinia was waiting to make her appeal to the League.

Italy had won the first round in the diplomatic contest.

CHAPTER XXXI

THE LION OF JUDAH

FOR some years past I had been hearing people in Italy say that 1935 would be the year of destiny. The saying acquired added significance when people would couple it with reflections on " Man of destiny " and " Mussolini's star." Among Italian youths it was common to hear contemptuous phrases about the decadence of the British Empire and England's selfish pacifism.

" England," one would say, " is like an overfed lion. You can twist his tail without fear : he won't raise his paw unless it is to flick away the flies that disturb his slumber." Such remarks used to irritate me because I knew they were the result of the blatant propaganda that was being given to the people in large doses. It sprang from the knowledge that Great Britain had reduced her defences to the minimum, and so left herself in a position of great weakness, should any trouble arise. To people who are militarists the spectacle of neighbouring peace-lovers seems an absurd anomaly. Once the hounds of war are let loose everybody must rouse himself in alarm and cry danger.

England's only fault was that up to the last she believed that a peaceful solution could be achieved in a world which still remembered the greatest cataclysm of history. Officially, at the beginning of 1935, the relations between England and Italy were cordial. At

the court of St. James there was Count Grandi, one
of the most popular Italian ambassadors who ever held
the post, a friend of the Duce, and a realist in politics,
with the additional experience of having held the post
of Foreign Minister in the Fascist Government. Even
when relations became strained, Grandi, with his
consummate tact, smoothed over matters and maintained all through the crisis a dignity which was
wholly admirable. Italy, now that she had the secret
support of France, cautiously approached England.
At this stage it was intimated from Rome that the
Italian Government wished to exchange views with
Great Britain concerning the mutual and harmonious
development of British and Italian interests in Abyssinia. In blunt words, this meant that Italy would
guarantee British interests in Abyssinia if Britain would
follow the example of France and turn a blind eye to
what might happen there. The National Government's
policy at that time might be summed up in the phrase :
" this way and that divided the swift mind." The
Foreign Minister was Sir John Simon, whose brilliant
talents as a lawyer were fully engaged in trying to
interpret the chameleon policy of his colleagues in the
Cabinet. He had to try to conciliate the ideas of
disarmament with Hitler's breaches of the Treaty of
Versailles. He had, in fact, to personify the spirit
of Compromise. Consequently he became a target
for attack by everyone, at home and abroad.

In those early months of 1935 Sir John Simon personi-
fied also the British policy of " Wait and See." He
did not want to encourage Mussolini's expansionist
ideas, but he was unwilling to refuse the offer of Italian
collaboration in Abyssinia. And so a departmental com-
mittee was appointed under Sir John Maffey, which, after
its investigations, declared that there were no vital

British interests in Abyssinia to necessitate British resistance to an Italian conquest of Abyssinia. Italian
control of Abyssinia would on some grounds be
advantageous, on others disadvantageous. From the
standpoint of Imperial defence an independent Abyssinia
would be preferable to an Italian Abyssinia, but the
threat to British interests appeared distant and would
depend only on a war with Italy, which, for the moment,
appeared improbable.[1] This report was significant in
proving that the British Government knew from the
first of the Italian plan. However, the general comment
in those early months of 1935 was that Mussolini was
trying his old game of bluffing England and Europe.
In the London clubs I met many military men and
others who said : " He is blustering like a swashbuckler.
All the same, he can't be idiotic enough to take on
Abyssinia, especially after the lesson of Adua in 1896."

Even on February 15 of that year Sir John Simon
told Parliament that the mobilization of two divisions
by Italy was merely a precautionary measure and would
not prejudice the Italian Government's endeavours
" to seek an amicable settlement of their differences
with Ethiopia." Meanwhile, Italy and Abyssinia were
arguing fiercely about Walwal, and soon matters reached
a deadlock. As we now know from his frank, outspoken book, General De Bono had already set out in
January for East Africa with the title of High Commissioner. He carried the following instructions from
the Duce :

You leave with the olive-branch in your pocket : we shall see
how the Walwal affair turns out. If it suits to accept the con-

---

[1] The Maffey Report, which was presented in June 1935, did
not reach the public until its sensational publication by Virginio
Gayda in the " Giornale d'Italia " of February 20, 1936.

ditions offered us in consequence of the award, you will tell the Emperor that you are sent to collaborate in European friendly relations between the two countries : if no solution of the incident is offered, we shall follow affairs in exclusive accordance with our own standpoint.

De Bono organized an army corps of Ascaris and prepared for the arrival of Italian troops. He constructed roads, barracks, hospitals and aerodromes. Soldiers and workmen began to arrive at Massaua. Note after note came from the Duce, urging him to speed his preparations. None of the sailings of troops from Italy was kept a secret, but how could they have passed unnoticed when everybody in Port Said saw crowded Italian transports passing through the Suez Canal ? In England people were still sceptical. As for the Emperor, Haile Selassie, he bided his time, hoping that the League of Nations would take action. Many of his Rases urged him to attack the Italians, but he knew that he would be in a helpless position if he became the aggressor. And so he bided his time and placed his trust in the League of Nations.

Looking back on those days, it has always seemed to me that the powers in whom he trusted did, as it was said at the time, " lead him up the garden path to his own destruction." Why did the little man prove so stubborn in the face of overwhelming odds ? It is now said that Sir Sidney Barton warned him not to count on British military intervention. Why, in view of opinions, which we now know were set out in the Maffey report, did he not try to make terms with the Italians ? Why later, when England was trying to be a peace-maker, did he not pay heed to her advice to him to sue for peace ? As Martelli says in his excellent account of the events before the War : " The idea, indeed, seems to have been fixed in the Emperor's head all along that anything was better, even his own ruin, than concessions to Italy." [1]

The Emperor, however, received support from the great masses in England which had been mobilized by the League of Nations Union, the Churches and the Left Wing parties. A storm of indignation began to rise against Italy which was to continue unabated for several years. All the hatred and contempt for the Italians which had smouldered for a long time broke out in all its violence. It was a kind of counter-blast to the arrogant attitude taken up by the war-minded Italians towards the British. The storm began to rage in earnest when the result of the Peace Ballot was announced on the 27th of June, 1935. There was, according to the figures of the ballot, a slight majority shown in favour of the military sanctions in the case of one nation attacking another. Martelli, however, in his analysis shows that it could not be held that the majority of votes in the ballot signified a majority of the British public, for the people who filled in the paper were those well disposed to the aims of the organizers who had been canvassing them strenuously for six months. On the other hand, opponents of the League and, in consequence, of the ballot, which was openly boycotted by the biggest party in England, the Conservative, refused to have anything to do with it. He adds : " One can imagine, in fact, the anti-sanctionists drawing up the same questions in a different form, conducting propaganda in the opposite sense and achieving equally satisfactory results." [2]

Nevertheless, the announcement of the result caused a sensation. Up to this the Government had tried to put off the evil day. Prime Minister Baldwin, on

[1] G. Martelli, *Italy Against the World*, London, 1937, pp. 58-9.
[2] G. Martelli, op. cit., pp. 83-4.

November 23, 1934, in a speech at Glasgow, had said:
" Never as an individual will I sanction the British
Navy being used for an armed blockade of any country
in the world until I know what the U.S.A. is going to
do." Abyssinia had made, again and again, piteous
appeals to the League, but the British Government,
even when they were seated around the table in conference at Stresa, had not brought up the question of
Abyssinia or warned the Duce of the dangers of trespassing in Africa. But now the great public opinion of
England had realized that the Government were unwilling to fight for Abyssinia or the League. The
Prime Minister then, with his unerring sense of the veer-
ing wind of politics, contradicted the speech he had made
in November, wherein he had said that a collective
peace system was " perfectly impracticable," and now
described the League of Nations as " the sheet anchor
of British policy."

Meanwhile, the struggle continued. The Abyssinian
question devastated every home in England, Ireland,
Scotland and Wales. Every accusation, fair or unfair,
was dragged up against Italy: all means, fair or
foul, of exciting scorn, indignation or contempt were
exploited. Bishops, clergymen, teachers, politicians,
became fanatical in their fervour: the wrath of Jehovah
was called down upon Italy by the preachers in the
pulpits.

They were sad months for those like myself who had
hoped to see friendship between Italy and England.
I shunned many friends in my clubs because friendly
argument was no longer possible. Where was that
gentle toleration, that sense of humour which had always
been Britain's heritage? Formerly I had always been
struck by the solid good sense and balance of the British
mind. In dealing with foreign affairs the Briton had

generally taken a detached point of view and his humour, which has been defined as the genius of thoughtful laughter, had carried his diplomacy unscathed through Europe, for foreign nations never fail to drop their guard once that genuine British spirit enters into play. The Abyssinian affair, however, showed that England had shed many of her traditional qualities of island nation : she was becoming as highly strung, irritable and nervy as continental nations which are only separated from one another by hedges. She was trying to follow the accelerated Latin rhythm of Europe without realizing that it was completely unsuited to her nation's God-given tempo.

When I was in Italy during that fateful summer of 1935 I had many arguments with Italians and British who still possessed sane, balanced minds. The Italians were frankly nonplussed. They thought that once the French had removed their objections to the Italian affair in Abyssinia there would be no difficulty with England.

" After all," said they, " it was the British who encouraged us to create an empire in Abyssinia and prevent the French getting it. We are doing to-day no more than England did on countless occasions in the past. We have always had the deepest admiration for the British as an imperialist race. We feel reverence for the qualities that enabled the men of your islands to conquer India, the Sudan, and the other British possessions throughout the world. Our most fervent prayer would be that the Italians could follow in the way traced out by those great adventurers."

When I, timidly, for the sake of argument, said that matters had changed since the foundation of the League, I drew down upon my head angry retorts from my friends :

" The British, now that they have satisfied their imperialistic appetite, wish to act like the dog in the manger. They have partitioned the best parts of the world among themselves and now the nations who started later in the race for power must remain empty-handed."

Then an English friend who spends the winters at Rapallo quoted the result of the Peace Ballot, saying :

" England is at present suffering from one of her periodic attacks of conscience which always coincide with an outburst of nationalistic spirit. What a spectacle, this hosanna to the League and peace at the moment when England is starting to build armaments on the biggest scale in her history ! But, mark you, when they do at last strengthen their defences and gird up their sinews to defend the Empire, they will not say that it is for the sake of Britain : no ! it will be for ' Collective Security ' and to strengthen the League. This was the way that we British acted in the nineteenth century during the heyday of our imperialists. We invaded Africa ; we created colonies, but always we had our missionaries to remind us that God blessed our work."

Then a cynical French friend butted into the dialogue with the words :

" You British are absolutely incorrigible with your hypocrisy and your absurd irrational minds. It is impossible for a logical Frenchman to follow you at all. You should have backed us up through thick and thin and then we could, both of us, have strengthened the League. Instead of that you turned to Germany. If you had followed France's warnings ever since the War you would not have driven us to send Barthou to make the pact with Russia, nor would Laval have given Mussolini *carte blanche* in Abyssinia. We were the people who held staunchly to the League : you English never gave it very deep thought. And now you come to us with your hand over your heart saying with your eyes upturned to Heaven: 'I am converted. I want to strengthen the Covenant.' Then you try to drive a wedge between us and Italy at the very moment when Germany has flouted the Treaty of Versailles by imposing conscription. You calmly ask us to break with Italy and expose the Savoy frontier, and yet you offer us nothing in return save a vague promise that in future you will adhere to collective security—a policy that we have been urging on you in vain for years. No, sir! do not prate about British idealism and Christian justice."

Mussolini, in an interview given to the Conservative French paper *Le Matin* voiced the Italian attitude as follows :

We have had a sincere and faithful friendship with the British people for many years, but to-day we find it monstrous that a nation which dominates the world refuses us a wretched plot of ground in the African sun. Many times I have given the assurance to Great Britain that her interests in Abyssinia will be safeguarded. . . . Never from our side will come any hostile act against a European nation : but if one is committed against us, it means war.

Pathetic attempts were made by England to ward off the threatening war by small concessions to Italy. Abyssinia was to be persuaded to hand over portions of Ogaden in return for a strip of territory in British Somaliland with an outlet to the sea at Zeila. But those proposals were refused scornfully by the Duce. They had the additional effect of annoying the French, who had, it appears, not been consulted about them, and were already irritated with England over the Anglo-German naval treaty. In Italy I watched the acceleration of the national rhythm and the growing tension caused by the dramatic speeches of the Duce. The

Press shrieked in headlines. The streets resounded with tramping soldiers. The Piazza Venezia in Rome echoed with the patriotic songs of Italy and Africa. Again the words of Marinetti, creator of the " Le Démon de la Vitesse," surged through my mind : " Holla-hé ! Holla-ho ! Stridionla, stridionla, stridion-laire ! " In Geneva, meeting followed meeting, a solemn conclave of perplexed Europeans set in the midst of Lotosland. The glittering lake was too peaceful, but high above those white sails and those fragrant gardens loomed the summit of Mont Blanc with threatening snows. The telegraph wires buzzed : the telephone bells tinkled : little men ran hither and thither shouting breathlessly the word " Compromise," for the sands of time were running out : Anglo-Africans, with a knowing air, would shake their heads and say : " The rains will soon be over, and then what next ? " In London, old soldiers would say : " The Italian bluffer will find he has bitten off more than he can chew. Wait till his men get into action against the Abyssinians. Italians can't fight. We remember them in Italy in 1918. Besides, what good will his vaunted aeroplanes be to him in Abyssinia, with its rugged passes, its ambas, its caves and jungle where guerilla warriors may hide ?

Carefully I tried to explain to those arm-chair critics that even if they were correct in their sweeping judgment of Italy in 1918, she had changed considerably since that date : but they pooh-poohed my remarks, saying that I was led astray by my affection for Italian singing, art and beauty. When, for curiosity, they listened to the Italian stations on the radio, they used to forget all their British phlegm and become livid with fury ; for, during those months, and during all the Abyssinian War, there was a lady broadcaster in Rome who, in the most perfect English and in a calm, crystalline voice, said the most vitriolic things about English policy, English hypocrisy, English intrigue and English motives. She was called Signorina Sergio, a charming, graceful lady whose English was so perfect that it became a mannerism. Her voice, with its diabolic calmness, distilled subtle poisons over the atmosphere. She enraged the British public by her Olympian superiority. When they had recovered their equanimity late at night, they were roused to a fresh tempest of rage next morning when they read quotations from the leading articles of Virginio Gayda in the *Giornale d'Italia*. Virginio Gayda, whom I also met in Rome, was a pleasant, inoffensive journalist with a flair for the telling phrase. He became, however, one of the bogey-men of England. He was called the mouthpiece of Mussolini, and it was said that the Duce often wrote the articles himself. I, for one, do not believe that story, but I am sure that Virginio Gayda, as editor of the *Giornale d'Italia*, was entrusted by his master with the task of pulling the lion's tail and pricking him incessantly. He made a virtue of the high-sounding phrase of attack laden with superlatives and experimented in methods of annoyance. Every article imputed sinister motives to the British Secret Service, the War Office, and the Liberal and Socialist Members of Parliament. Italians dismissed all their former notions of the good, honest Britisher and conjured up visions of countless British spies and " agents provocateurs," carrying on a network of intrigue in the Mediterranean and the Near East. Even Lawrence of Arabia rose from the dead and schemed and plotted with the Lion of Judah against the Italians. It was said that Great Britain had made a secret agreement with the Emperor, according to which England would give military help to Abyssinia in return for concessions of territory. Very few of the general public in Italy seemed to be aware of the fact that it was the mass of the English people, whipped up by the League of Nations Union and the churches, which was making the Government dance to its tune. Both countries were playing feverishly the game of tit for tat. I heard the chorus of opinion in both countries answering one another like strophe and antistrophe in a Greek tragedy.

The British Government strengthened the Mediterranean fleet. Alexandria became a mass of battleships and aeroplanes.

The French became even more sour and bad-tempered at this useless demonstration which increased the risks of war. The League discussions still continued in the atmosphere of Lotos-land. It was pathetic to see the idealists of the League, those who had moulded their minds in accordance with traditions of world peace, struggling vainly to fight the Dragon of Nationalism. They longed for a champion to enter the lists on their behalf, a pure spirit like Parsifal, who would ride into battle championing an international code of ethics. It was then that they hit upon the immaculate, youthful Anthony Eden. He became the ideal of those who looked upon themselves as the keepers of the world's conscience. Anthony Eden comes of sturdy British stock and he would probably claim to be as staunch a nationalist as any true-dyed Conservative in England. But at Geneva he had to appear to the world crowned with a pale halo of sanctity. He had to be on his guard lest any member of the countless peace societies, anti-war societies, anti-Fascist societies should suspect him of thinking merely of the interests of his own country. And so he stood before all the world like a Prince Charming of the fairy stories, ready to do battle on behalf of Collective Security against the dragon who, in this case, was Benito Mussolini, breathing fire from his lair in Rome.   Anthony Eden was encouraged to persevere by the famous speech delivered by Sir Samuel Hoare on the 11th of September, in which he declared that the British Government and people maintained their support of the League and its ideals as the most effective way of insuring peace.   " The League stands," he said, " and my country stands with it, for the collective maintenance of the Covenant in its entirety, and particularly for steady and collective resistance to all acts of unprovoked aggression."   In England that speech aroused amazing enthusiasm among those who believed that the League's hour had come and that the next step would be the imposition of sanctions on Italy.   It was a case of the wish being father to the thought.   They did not pay attention to the cautious references in the speech to the " collective maintenance " of the Covenant. Sir Samuel Hoare, who knew the French determination not to be dragged into war, had in reality not said any more than that England would act if the other members of the League were prepared to do so also.   The Sanctionists, however, saw in the speech a justification for their hopes.

It is interesting to remember at this juncture the statement made on the 28th of December, 1935, by Laval in the Chamber of Deputies, in which he referred to the conversations he had with Sir Samuel Hoare and Mr. Eden on the 10th of September—that is to say, on the eve of the meeting of the Assembly.

We found ourselves [he said] instantaneously in agreement in ruling out military sanctions, not adopting any measure of naval blockade, never contemplating the closure of the Suez Canal— in a word, ruling out everything that might lead to war.[1]

As a result of Sir Samuel Hoare's speech, the Assembly became galvanized into action and Great Britain led the

[1] G. Martelli, op. cit., p. 150.

League to battle. Even the cautious Pierre Laval proclaimed his loyalty to the League, saying that it was the keynote of French policy. The Italians, however, were engaged in feverish preparations for war. The same scenes that had preceded the March on Rome in 1922 and the entry of Italy into war in 1915 repeated themselves. Baron Aloisi, the pale-faced, melancholy aristocrat, was left standing like a lonely statue at Geneva, pointing the finger of warning. Then came the characteristic dramatic touch by which the Duce marked the moment of crisis. It was announced to the Italian people that on a certain day he would order the general mobilization of all the forces of the country. This general mobilization was to signify to the world that the whole Italian people was sharing in the national enterprise. The order was given in the afternoon of the 2nd of October. All work ceased throughout the length and breadth of Italy; the church bells pealed; the trumpets blared; the drums rolled; there was a scurrying to and fro through every street as men took their places in their phalanxes. The masses filled every square in the country. In Rome the enthusiasm was extraordinary. The centre of all was the Piazza Venezia, where, from the balcony of the historic palace, Mussolini proclaimed to his countrymen and to the whole world that Fascist Italy was going to war. On my radio at home in Dublin I heard the harsh voice haranguing the people.

Black Shirts of the Revolution! Men and women of all Italy! Italians scattered throughout the world and beyond the seas: listen! A solemn hour is about to strike in the history of the Fatherland. Twenty million men fill at this moment the squares of all Italy . . . Twenty million men: one heart alone, one will alone, one decision alone . . . For many months past the wheel of destiny, driven on by our calm, determined purpose, has been moving towards the goal: in these hours its rhythm is more rapid and henceforth its course cannot be checked. Not only is an army marching towards its objective, but forty million Italians are marching in unison with this army. They are united because there is an attempt to commit against them the blackest of all injustices, to rob them of a place in the sun.

Sometimes the sound faded and sometimes it blared on my ear, mingled with atmospherics and the sound of cheering. Then I heard the inexorable voice continue :

After the common victory to which Italy had given its supreme contribution of 670,000 dead, 400,000 mutilated, and one million wounded, around the table of the hateful peace conference Italy received nothing but the scanty scraps of the rich colonial plunder. We have been patient with Ethiopia for forty years. Now, enough !

A roar greeted the orator. The scornful intonation given to the words " scarse briciole del ricco bottino coloniale " burned them into the minds of the people who heard them. I contrasted the speech with its dramatic pauses and interruptions, which sounded as though the Leader was thinking aloud in the presence of his people, with the one I heard on that famous day of St. Mark in 1919 when Gabriele D'Annunzio proclaimed his Fiume campaign. D'Annunzio had distilled his words, syllable by syllable, into the ears of the masses. His slow, precise voice rose and fell like the song of a minstrel and spread over his audience like olive oil on the surface of the sea. The voice of the Duce bit the words and rapped them out at the people. Each sentence was like a prod from a bayonet :

. . . To sanctions of an economic character we will reply with our discipline, our sobriety and our spirit of sacrifice. To military sanctions we will reply with military measures : to acts of war we will reply with acts of war . . . Proletarian and Fascist Italy, Italy of Vittorio Veneto and the Revolution is on its feet. Let the cry of your firm, unshakable decision fill the sky and be a comfort to the soldiers who wait over there in Africa. Let it spur on our friends and warn our enemies in all parts of the world. Let it be a cry of justice and a cry of victory.

Early next morning, on the 3rd of October, I heard the newsboys in the streets of Dublin crying out " Stop Press ! Stop Press ! " I bought a paper and read the announcement that Count Ciano and a squadron of planes had flown over Adua. That morning the Italian troops crossed the frontier river Mareb and began to advance into Abyssinia.

CHAPTER XXXII

PLOUGHING THE BOUNDARY

WHEN I arrived in Italy in December 1935, I imagined that I was back in the days of 1918, with this difference, that now the Italian people were exulting in War which the Futurists described as " the only hygiene in the world." Marinetti, who had now become an Academician and a Classic, defined the African War as follows :

I. The most synthetic way of summing up to-day one's own life by serving the New Italy of Mussolini ;

II. The most exact précis of our spiritual values ;

III. The perfect interpretation of the most African lyrical ardour of our peninsula ;

IV. The cleverest intensifier of all our pleasures ;

V. The integral sport ;

VI. The most powerful inspiration to poetry, painting, architecture, by its exuberant gift of images, colours, volumes and sounds.

When I arrived at Capo Santa Chiara I stayed with my wife's sister Eva and her three children. Mario was away organizing the naval defences on some island. The friends, who came to greet me, immediately started hot discussions on the War and England.

" What has happened ? " said they. " Why has England taken such action against Italy ? The most treacherous blow of all was the dispatch of all those battleships to the Mediterranean. Did they really think that we were going to be intimidated?"

One friend informed me that for every battleship Britain sent there was an Italian aviator ready to pounce down in a plane full of high explosives and destroy it. "Mussolini," said he, "asked for 100 volunteers for this Death Squadron and at once 600 presented themselves. They knew that they were sure to be victims, for the squadron was to be of the same type as the Japanese human torpedo section, devotees of death." I was immensely struck, during my stay in Italy at that time, by the passionate patriotism of men, women and children and their ascetic self-denial. In every household, as a result of sanctions, economies were made and expenses rigidly controlled. Meat became a luxury and people fed mostly on vegetables and macaroni.

"It is not a sacrifice for us," said Eva, "to do without meat two or more days of the week when you think that thirty years ago the majority of Italian families only ate meat once a week, and in certain provinces of the country the poor only ate it on solemn occasions."

She then went on to tell me that the reason for doing without meat was that the Government were determined, now that imports were lacking, to preserve the cattle so that there might be an abundance of milk, cheeses and butter. Milk, especially, had even acquired additional importance now that the Italian scientists had discovered how to make wool out of it. It was amusing to hear Italian friends sing the praises of the vegetable diet.

There was great rivalry among the women of the Cape in the matter of what they called "Sanctions cooking." For butter they substituted olive oil and lard: they used black bread instead of white because the former possessed greater nutritive value than the latter. They prepared the vegetable dishes with scientific care, combining the different varieties of juice in such a way that they might act as a substitute for meat. As far as the women of the Cape were concerned, they came to the villa to ask for Donna Delfina's old book of recipes which she had prepared during the lean days of the Great War. She little thought when she prepared them with scientific accuracy that they would serve again twenty years later in the campaign of Sanctions. Even the children in the schools made their own sacrifices to the cause. They were eager to give up comforts and pleasures and devote hours of the week to helping the poorer children. It was a striking sight to watch the ceremonies of handing over rings and gold ornaments, for it gave me a curious feeling of the continuity of history. Those majestic matrons in black, handing over their gold rings and receiving in return rings of steel, reminded me of the ancient Rome of the Republic. On the Cape, one day, I met an old woman who used to come every evening during the Great War to be fed by Donna Delfina. She said to me :

" In the Great War I gave my husband to Italy : in this war I am ready to give my only son. Our last war was made by the rich. This is our war—the war of the poor."

In Rome I heard many ironic comments on the ill-starred Hoare-Laval Plan. Prime Minister Baldwin and Anthony Eden were singled out for special condemnation : they were accused of every Machiavellian kind of sharp practice. It was useless for me to remind those friends that the British Government had tried its best to avoid war but had been unable to withstand the avalanche of public opinion which cried out that a premium was being put on aggression. " The Hoare-Laval Plan," said I, " was the natural consequence of the Government's determination to avoid war. They were desperately eager to discover a compromise, and when the League of Nations Union and the churches again whipped the English people into fury the Government threw up its hands in surrender. They were like schoolboys caught by an irate farmer stealing apples from his loft. They clambered sheepishly down and stood trembling, waiting for the stick to fall upon their back."

My Roman friends, however, could not understand why England had become so anti-Italian.

" Why," said one of them, a young diplomat who spoke English like a native, " have the British tried every means to discredit us and to magnify the War? First of all, it was a war of Italy versus England; then it became a war by Italy to seize Egypt; then it became a Latin versus a Teutonic war; then it became a war of Catholicism versus Masonry and Protestantism."

What pained those English-speaking Italians more than anything was England's ingratitude.

" Italy has deserved well of England for many reasons," said they. " Have you forgotten the Boer War when we alone on the Continent remained friendly to you? Even with regard to Africa we gave you valuable help in Somaliland, and during the Great War our help was immensely valuable, though you have always under-estimated it."

Then with the remorseless logic of the Latin race they exclaimed against the injustice of the League of Nations which chose the Abyssinian quarrel as a test of its strength, while neglecting to give more than verbal condemnation to the war between Paraguay and Bolivia or the Japanese annexation of part of China.

" We believe," said they, " that the League of Nations is only a convenient pretext with Great Britain, beneath which she hides her own private objections to Italian expansion in Abyssinia. This is all the more incomprehensible to us when the Duce, who always puts his cards on the table, had stated publicly that British interests around Lake Tana and the head-waters of the Nile would be respected. Frankly, we cannot understand the moral admonitions which British statesmen such as Mr. Anthony Eden have seen fit to utter against Italy. They reek of hypocrisy, and we remember the ancient cry of ' perfide Albion.' It was Britain who encouraged us to occupy in 1885 the port of Massaua. In 1891 we obtained from Britain recognition of the Italian's sphere in Abyssinia. If, instead of being defeated at Adua in 1896, Italy had then managed to subdue the whole of Abyssinia, England would not only not have opposed her, but would have encouraged her, and that was at a time when England was under no obligations to Italy. Can you wonder, therefore, that we feel intensely bitter about the whole matter ? "

As a result of a bounteous meal at the classic restaurant " Libotte " the conversation became vaguer and more general. My Italian friends said that we British had never understood the literature of their country.

" You British," they said, " have never read or pondered over such a book as *Mastro Don Gesualdo*, by Verga, which shows the traditional life of the peasant and his rugged determination. You still go on thinking of Italy as the country of tenors and mandolines. Whenever you do come to our country you look upon it as an Arcadia created by the Renaissance. Delenda est Arcadia! Italy is one of the countries in the world which is on the upward grade. She is moving at a rapid rhythm. Her proletariat are all united in an attempt to secure a new outlet for their energy. The Italian worker can no longer find sufficient elbow-room

in Italy.   He cannot emigrate because countries such as
America have already been closed to him.   Yet he wants
his piece of land which he will cultivate and on which he
will build his house and found a family."

Next day my Italian friends carried me off to the
Pontine Marshes to watch the Duce ploughing the
boundary.   As I saw the short, squat figure of Italy's
dictator manœuvring the plough I imagined the foundation of the eternal city by Romulus.

· First of all, when Romulus had cut away the reeds
and brambles and made a clearing he harnessed two
white oxen to a plough and began to make a broad
furrow.   After wreathing his brow with flowers, he
ploughed the furrow north, south, west and east, saying :
" This shall be the sacred boundary of the city."   While
he worked I saw flocks of birds hovering in the red
sky above his head.   Then, suddenly, from one of the
neighbouring hills, there came Remus, the shepherd
dressed in skins, who held converse with the ploughman :

" To-day," said the ploughman, " the gods are propitious : I have seen twelve vultures in the sky : to-day
have I ploughed the boundary of the city."

The shepherd replied : " I have come from the mountains to play you my song.   Stop your ploughing and
listen to me."

Then did he play a wild tune upon Pan-pipes, so
that the birds were stilled and the rocks echoed : but
the ploughman said : " Brother, may the gods deafen
my ears to your tune : you learnt it in the jungle among
the wild ravenous beasts.   Lay aside your pipes of Pan
and join me, your brother, within the boundary of our
city."

" What shall I do within the city ? "

" Live by the law of the gods."

" Who will impose the law ? "

" All of us who share in the city."

" I'll have none of your law, brother ploughman, nor your gods either. I'll go back to my mountains, where my sheep follow the sound of my pipes."

" Brother shepherd, cease roaming like a lost soul."

" To roam is sweet, brother : the trees and wild plants give me sustenance, the rocky spring quenches my thirst ; the surface of the earth supplies my wants."

The ploughman for answer picked up a sod, saying : " Look, brother, at this soil : we in the city seek the earth-mother's gifts beneath the surface, turning them up with yonder plough and fertilizing her womb that she may produce a hundredfold. She is the great mother who will give us wealth and power. Come within the boundary, brother, and help us to build our eternal city."

The shepherd gave no answer, but waving farewell, he turned on his heel and walked rapidly into the dusk. The sounds of his wild piping lingered in distant echoes. For a moment the ploughman stood listening ; then with a sigh he resumed his task. At each of the four corners of the square enclosure, he set a black stone and I saw him sacrificing on a rock near by to Bona Dea, the goddess of fertility, and to Hercules, the god of strength. The smoke from the altar clouded the scene and all that was visible was a slender flame shooting upwards into the sky.

Such was my vision of the ancient ritual over which I had pondered many an evening at sunset when I roamed through the Via Velabro leading from the edge of the River Tiber up to the Palatine. Mussolini's ritualistic gesture in ploughing the boundaries of the new towns which are to arise in the Pontine Marshes was a reminder that what is primordial and natural possesses more decisive power here than in any other country, for Italy is one of the oldest cultures in the world and the phenomenon of decadence is unknown there. As writers have shown, the people in Italy renews itself periodically as plants do from Spring to Spring and its basic character is unequivocally primitive.[1]　I had driven out to the Pontine Marshes by the Via Appia Antica by way of Terracina, which was the ancient Roman city of Anxur. The immense plain, stretching between the Volscian Mountains, the Tyrrhene Sea, and the Alban Hills, used to be the southern part of the Papal States. Even in the days of ancient Rome this region was called the Pontine Marshes, or Pomptinae Paludes, because it was a breeding ground of malaria. In the early history of Rome, however, this territory was the most fertile of all, for Livy described the marshes as : " Locus ille olim trium et viginti urbium fuisse dicitur " (It was said to be the region of twenty-three cities). Virgil, Horace, Ovid, Juvenal, Martial and Lucan sang the fame of that region, whose name was supposed to derive from the Volscian town of Pometia. After the early defeat of the Volscians the land gradually became a fen and the population disappeared. The Romans carried their power through Italy and through the Mediterranean, but they allowed the Pontine Marshes to become a wild, uncultivated spot. Julius Cæsar, alone, attempted to redeem the lands by the construction of a great canal which would drain the soil. But the assassins' daggers cut short the project and the marsh grew still wilder. Horace, in the fifth of the first book of the Satires, describes his journey to Terracina, where he had to wait for his friends Mæcenas, Cocceius Nerva and Fonteius Capito, and he says that it was necessary to cross the marsh in a boat.

Ever since the days of that great Venetian painter

[1] Count H. Keyserling, *Europe*, London, 1928, p. 149.

of the eighteenth century, Piranesi, the Pontine Marshes have attracted the artist by their varied sinister beauties. Painters of romantic temperament such as the Frenchman Ernest Hébert described peasants, yellow-skinned and haggard with malaria, gliding in boats slowly down the river through a desolate landscape. Their eyes were bright with fever and the Angel of Death had touched them with its wing, reminding us of Dante's famous description of fever in the *Divine Comedy*:

> Qual' è colui ch'ha sì presso il ribrezzo.
> della quartana ch'ha già l'ugne smorte.
> e triema tutto, pur guardando il rezzo?

Alfredo Oriani, who, in his writing, has foreshadowed so much of the present-day greatness of Italy, has described the desolation of the Agro Romano:

> It is a mournful spectacle! Wherever I turn my eyes I see naked expansions of meadow, ravaged and unending. At rare intervals a few twisted oak trees stand up like the survivors of some catastrophe, spared as a refuge for ravens and crows by these spirits of destruction.

It was, however, the hero Garibaldi who gave the most striking prophecy of the reclamation of the marshes by Mussolini. He described a dream which he had at the age of 18 in Rome, a dream which in a flash inspired him to fight for the emancipation of his country. It was sunrise and he found himself mounting the marble steps to the Belvedere whence he could see over the vast deserted panorama of the Roman Campagna. To his amazement there appeared before his eyes, instead of the dreaded Pontine Marshes, fertile fields under cultivation which reminded him of the enchanting vegetation of the Valley of the Po. Instead of jungle he saw flowering gardens and trees laden with every kind of fruit, and an immense plain billowing with golden wheat. What amazed him most of all was to see the great mass of husbandmen toiling in the fields.

Garibaldi's dream had come to pass. And so the Pontine Marshes have become a vast territory of settlers. They have become the new province of Littoria inaugurated in 1934 by Mussolini. The new province has an extension of 201,170 hectares and a population of 215,000.

Nearly every year since 1932 the Duce has ploughed the boundary of a new city. First of all came Littoria. In his inaugural speech the Duce described the event thus :

We have inaugurated the ninety-third province of the kingdom. In order to realize the importance of the event it suffices to reflect for one single minute that here in this square, only three years ago, lingered the deadly marsh-land. We have pledged ourselves to a stern campaign. We had against us Nature, material conditions, and—even worse—the scepticism, the mental inertia and the moral cowardice of those who, before beginning the battle, wished to be certain of victory ; while for us Fascists the conflict is even more important than the victory ; for when the battle is undertaken with resolute firmness victory is infallibly its crown.

Those were significant words and recalled to my mind the vision I had seen of Romulus ploughing the boundary of Rome with the white oxen and laying the black stone at the four corners. Here, at any rate, we may no longer catch the sound of Pan-pipes of Remus, for Remus is dead. Remus the shepherd, in search of unbridled freedom, had followed the adage : " The Lord will provide." He had hunted in the jungle here and laid traps for the wild birds. Even the gaunt yellow goddess of Fever, for ever stalking his movements, had not dismayed him, for he preferred his freedom, even at the risk of imminent death. He followed his lonely way, for he was an anarchist and unwilling to live within the boundary marked by the four black stones.

I visited four or five farms in the plain. They are all worked by ex-Service men, most of whom come from the Venetian province and Lombardy, for it is there that men know the great secrets of the soil. The "podere" consists of some 15–25 hectares of land with two-storeyed farmhouse, stables, bakery and dairy. Each settlement must consist of not less than six members. Most of the families consist of 13–14, that is to say, in addition to the man and his wife and children there are grandmother, grandfather, sisters, and even occasionally cousins. This is characteristic of Italy, where farming is a family co-operative enterprise. One "podere" was run by a young man from Padua with his wife, sisters, brother and children. He had a bull, five cows and two donkeys in the stables, and his poultry yard was full of hens and ducks. I sat in the parlour telling stories to the children and listening to tales of the war in the Alps, narrated in a strong Venetian dialect by the owner and his brother. They told me that the farmers in the Pontine Marshes worked co-operatively and are very friendly with one another. When I visited Sabaudia in the middle of the day I found it empty. The streets were deserted, for all the people were out working in the plain. But towards evening I saw hosts of men and women on bicycles approaching. Soon the town was full of excited people : the broad, roomy cafés were thronged and it was soon time for the theatrical and cinema performances to begin. After the people have enjoyed their hours of leisure they drive their cars and ride their bicycles back to their farms. I was interested to observe the methods employed to make rural life more attractive for the modern worker. The town with the broad piazza acts as the assembly and the place of enjoyment of the settlers. In the town, too, they may obtain advice on agricultural methods, for every two hundred "poderi" has a group of offices, where experts work and supervise the methods used in farming. The town, too, supplies the hospitals, schools, and play-grounds for the children. Finally, the town is a place of beauty. It has been perfectly planned and its buildings have plenty of marble and travertine in their construction.

There is no doubt that this system of land reclamation which Italy has carried out, not only in these Pontine Marshes, but also in other parts of Italy, Sicily and Sardinia, is the noblest work that the Duce has inspired. In a sense this work of land reclamation is a history of the Italian people. It reminds us that ever since the most ancient times the population from generation to generation have had to wrest the soil, metre by metre, from the devastating fury of water, marshes, malaria and drought.

As I returned towards Rome the deep, golden afternoon sun gave a strange glow to the scene. On my right I saw stretching the long line of the Claudian aqueduct, a reminder of the Republic of Cincinnatus. Before we entered the eternal city the sky had become a deep red and the streets sank suddenly into the dusk.

CHAPTER XXXIII

MY ABYSSINIAN DIARY

BY a stroke of good fortune I obtained from the Italian authorities permission to visit the Abyssinian front. No sooner did I receive my passes, including an attractive armlet of red with the words " Servizio stampa " in yellow on it, than I was packed off to Naples to await the troop-ship. When I arrived there I thought the festival of Piedigrotta must be on, for the people were in holiday mood and the streets resounded with singing. It was the same old melody-conscious Naples that I had known in 1919, but in those days it was a city of ragged Pulcinellas. It was as much as a man could do to walk a few steps down the crowded Via Toledo without being accosted every moment by beggars. Fascist Italy cleaned up Naples, and for some years I missed the intoxicating gaiety of the people. It was as if Pulcinella, the most famous spirit of the Neapolitan people, had died. But now Naples seemed again to have returned to its pristine gaiety and Pulcinella appeared in his white shirt, white cap, and baggy breeches. I met him again and again as I walked up and down the Riva del Chiatamone ; but instead of singing " Funiculì, funiculà " and " O Sole Mio " he sang the latest war songs, for Naples was throbbing with excitement, as it was the port of embarkation for distant Abyssinia.

I had asked an Italian friend to give me the name

of a really cheap pension. He told me to go to the
" Pensione Palumbo " in the Via Chiaia. I drove up
to it in an open carriage, thinking it was an ordinary
boarding-house. I was surprised, however, to find it
full of officers, and I saw various highly painted girls
lolling about.

" What are your terms ? " said I to the old landlady.

" That depends how long you stay," said she winking.

" If I like it I might stay three days," said I.

" God forbid," answered the old Celestina ; " you
would be dead ! "

" This seems to be a mighty queer place," said I to
myself as I followed her upstairs. She called in a stentorian voice the name Laura la Goriziana—the girl from
Gorizia. Laura, who was tall and big-breasted, made
herself very agreeable to me. She asked me a series of
breathless questions about—my age, my profession, my
bank balance, my health, my appetite.

" Where are you off to ? " said she.

" I'm off to Asmara," said I.

" Why ? " said she.

" Active service," said I.

" So am I," said she.

" How ? " said I.

" Active service too," said she with a roguish side-
glance. " Fifty of us girls are sailing in a few weeks
for Massaua."

We had several rounds of red Barbera wine which
she ordered and I paid for. As she poured some into
my glass she murmured the refrain :

> " Il Barbera
> riscalda meglio
> del carbone inglese."
>
> (Barbera warms us
> better than English coal.)

She gave me a holy picture of " Our Lady of Pompeii "
—the luckiest image in Naples, saying : " Two thousand years ago Pompeii was a centre of fashion and full
of high society. There were crowds of lovely ladies
but they did all kinds of ' porcherie.' Then one day
Our Lady sent thunderbolts and eruptions and covered
up the sight of the whole city for its sins." The image
represented Our Lady of Pompeii sitting on a well.

Next day, while I was waiting for the boat, I spent
some hours in the taverns of Via Spotero and listened
to conversations about the War and home affairs. One
man—a *ragioniere*—told me that things were very bad
in Italy. " We have no tourists," said he, " and business with England is closed down. And yet Naples
used to live on the British. I wonder when all these
politics and diplomacy will let the people make friends
again with them. We have nothing really against them
and they have nothing against us." Then he went on
to speak of the War and the victory, and his whole
manner changed. " We shall be at Harrar next : you'll
see, signore, for Graziani is the greatest general in the
world. This war is a revenge for him. He has it hot
for the Abyssinians."

Naples has become a modern city, but it still clings
to some of its superstitions. The tavern where I drank
the parting glass with friends had two horns on the
wall as a protection against the " evil eye," and before
I embarked a girl presented me with the lucky coral
charm.

Our ship, *Sardegna*, carried 3,500 troops drawn from
all regions of Italy. As I walked about the deck I heard
Neapolitan, Sicilian, Genoese, and Milanese dialects
jumbled up together. There were enormous crowds
on the jetty singing patriotic songs, to which the troops
on board replied. Just as we glided out to sea the

crowd let off pink and white fireworks, and the harbour became a mass of fairy lights. The sea was like glass in the Bay of Naples, and in the distance we could still hear the faint sounds of singing in chorus.

Ours was a singing ship. From early morning to late night the troops kept up continuous singing. The repertory of those soldiers was endless. This Italian war has had its special songs, and the men have long memories. Some hardened Colonials take up the refrain of " A Tripoli," a song composed in 1911 at the time of the Libyan War : an old sergeant hums in a quavering voice for me an old song of 1894 about " Africanella." Those who fought in the Great War sang " The Song of Monte Grappa." But the whole ship roars at the refrain of " Faccetta Nera " (Black Face), which is the song of the present war. This they follow by another which starts :

> " Dear Virginia,
> I'm off to Abyssinia."

I was told that nearly all the " fiancées " of the Colonial troops have changed their names to Virginia to suit the rhyme.

As for myself, I had included in my extremely light luggage (handbag, music-case, violin) an old copy of the songs I used to play for the mountain troops in the North of Italy during the Great War. At the first notes I played of " The Song of the Alpino " and " The Bridge of Bassano," the whole crowd of " Alpini " came running towards me as if I had been the Pied Piper of Hamelin. For our ship was full of " Alpini "—some of them tough young mountaineers from the Northern frontiers of Italy, others grey-haired men who had fought through the Great War.

At Port Said the ship was surrounded by little boats

full of Italians, who sang songs to which our troops
on board added their chorus.   There was one woman
called Maria Uva, who had become a heroine for the
Italian troops travelling to Abyssinia.   For the past ten
months she had not missed a single boat that passed
through the canal.

She follows every ship in her car from Port Said as
far as Ismailia.   Every few minutes she halts the car,
descends and sings to us.   Her voice is very clear, and
we can hear all that she says as she carries on a dialogue
with the ship's crew.   She stands in front of the car's
headlamps and I see that she has wrapped an Italian
flag around her.   She sings one verse ; the soldiers on
board sing another in response.   It is said that Maria
Uva gets thousands of post cards from soldiers who
pass through the Suez Canal.

When we entered the Red Sea the awnings were put
over the decks, the troops put on their pith helmets,
and one by one the officers appeared with heads shaved.
When we finally reached Massaua the heat became
sweltering, for Massaua has the reputation of being the
hottest place in the world—a damp, suffocating heat
which saps a man's energy and fills him with depression.

We arrived at Massaua at nightfall, and the troops,
after receiving their emergency rations, disembarked,
and were marched over to lorries, which took them up
to Asmara.

Massaua is crammed with oil-ships, coal-ships, troop-
ships, hospital-ships.   The small town has long ago
given up trying to cope with the enormous crowds that
throng the cafés and restaurants.   At night, as the
troops pour out of the ships, it is a fantastic sight,
for all the scene is illuminated by flares and brilliant
lights.   There are some attractive buildings in colonial
style, but the majority are shacks of wood.   It is like

the setting of an Eastern play by an ultra-modern scenic artist. Moorish arches, between which one can see masts and the funnels of destroyers; Arabs in turbans languidly lolling beside sweating Italian navvies, naked to the waist; balconies lit in a blaze of electric lights, with gramophones and loud-speakers playing away. Shouts, honks of cars, sirens, words of command, snorting engines. And over all a strange indefinable smell of burnt spice and paprika.

"That is *berberè*," said my friend, Colonel De Meo from Libya, a poet and friend of Gabriele D'Annunzio.

Massaua, on this sweltering night, caused me acute discomfort as I mopped my brow and cursed my folly in coming out East in winter clothing. But my friend the D'Annunzian colonel exulted.

"I cannot sleep, I am so excited," said he, as he walked up and down through the crowds of Eritreans and Arabs from the Yemen. "Can't you smell Africa? Here am I again—back in a colonial war after twenty years. O the joy of it!"

My friend the colonel was like a war-horse pawing the ground before battle. He was to command a battalion of Ascari troops, and he longed to be out in Abyssinian jungle with them. He was full of the exaltation of war.

"War," said he, "is the reason for life. It is war that brings man to his full stature. It is in war that all egoism and meanness disappear. It is in war that we meet with the virtues of sacrifice to an ideal. People become sluggish without the spirit of war to quicken their blood."

My friend the colonel was certainly a personality— a disturbing one to an unwarlike vagabond like myself!

In the early morning I was escorted to a little motor-train called "La Littorina," and we started off for

Asmara. For three hours our train climbed up through the most amazing mountain scenery. Ethiopia is not kind to the stranger. Along the coast from Massaua stretches the torrid Dancalian desert, and when the traveller tries to reach the interior he has to scale a chain of rugged mountain ranges.

With reason has this land been called the African Switzerland—a country full of every kind of vegetation. From the sweltering tropical valleys low down, full of malaria, which the Abyssinians call *quolla*, we rise to the highlands full of sycamores and the strange Euphorbia trees, with their arms outstretched like candelabra.

With me was an Italian missionary who had spent many years in Abyssinia.

" Do you see that Euphorbia tree ? " says he. " From that tree the natives make a subtle slow poison. That poison was used by those princesses called the poisoners. When an Emperor was jealous of a Ras, he married him off to one of those royal princesses and she would poison him in a year by the sap from the Euphorbia."

Near the village of Nefasit we saw a vast regiment of big monkeys scrambling up the rocks above our train. When I arrived at Asmara I started to walk rapidly down the street, but hardly had I walked a few steps when I collapsed. The air at Asmara, which stands at an altitude of about 8,000 feet, is so rare that one's heart takes time to acclimatize itself.

At Asmara you wake up in the morning full of energy ; the sun is shining, the air is cool. But as soon as you hurry down the street you feel all of a sudden as if your next breath would never come. This is the reason why so many people have what are called " Asmara nerves."

Asmara itself is an attractive colonial town, with its fine modern church, cinema, Fascist headquarters, hotel, and a few streets of up-to-date shops and cafés. But all of a sudden it has become the base for a huge army. Consequently Asmara has turned into what looks like a town of Louisiana during a rush of pioneers. The traffic of motor-lorries and cars is as thick as the Great North Road out of London. The streets are crammed with soldiers wandering aimlessly about. If you go to a shop it is necessary to stand in a queue that stretches down the street.

There are very few white women to be seen in Asmara, and if a pretty girl walks down the street she becomes as much the cynosure of neighbouring eyes as if she had been a princess out of the *Arabian Nights*. As a compensation, there are hosts of Eritrean women dressed in the white *shamma*, with their hair combed into the most fantastic fashion of tiny curls. These women at a distance smell of incense and spices, but when you go near you catch a whiff of the rancid butter which they put in their hair.

The native quarter consists of hovels and *tuculs*. The *tucul*, which is the characteristic Abyssinian dwelling, is a cylindrical hut made of manure and earth, and roofed with thatch. A village of *tuculs* looks like a collection of monster beehives.

Here and there in the native streets are little *tetch* shops—dark, sinister holes where you see women squatting by charcoal fires. *Tetch* is the national intoxicant of Abyssinia, and consists of a mixture of fermented honey and water. When I tasted it I felt inclined to vomit, but I was told that it drives Ethiopians into a wild state of Bacchic frenzy if indulged in unwisely. The *tetch* shop, however, is a place of ritual.

One day I received the much-coveted permission to go to the Front south of Makallè. It was couched in formal language, inviting me to be the guest of G.H.Q.,

and informing me that I should be given the opportunity of flying over the Front in a military 'plane.

Next morning I got up at 5.30 and was driven to
the airport, which is miles out of Asmara. It is no
easy task to penetrate to the landing-field, as it is guarded
by many Ascari sentries, who are coldly resolute, and
unsparing in the use of their rifles.

It was a weird sight to stand in the dark near our
'plane, deafened by the roar of its engines, and watch
its three motors spitting blue fire. Each of those
bombing 'planes holds five or six people—two pilots,
an observer, two machine-gunners and a wireless
operator. The machine-gun works on a swivel and
can fire through the side windows, and (as is now usual)
it can shoot downwards through a large opening in the
floor between the two pilots.

" Where shall I sit ? " said I timidly, seeing that there
was not much space for me to squeeze into.

" Squat on that wooden case in the middle," said
one of the pilots gruffly.

" What is inside ? " said I nervously.

" Bombs or letters," said the wireless operator,
grinning.

Most of my view of the country was through the
big opening in the floor of the 'plane. A most fantastic land to fly over—a desolate land. Not a dwelling-
place to be seen anywhere, no signs of cultivation,
nothing but one jagged mountain after another. Ethiopia shows Nature in her most freakish and whimsical
mood. At one moment I see gorges reminding me of
the Grand Canyon, Colorado ; at another there are
mesetas of Spain or the sea of stone of Montenegro.
The earth in many places is blood-red, and then it turns
to purple, and then golden brown, and here and there
are spots of chalky white. A volcanic land, whittled

and carved into spectral shapes by the constant, ever-lasting process of erosion. Spiky mountain-tops, coni-cal hills, innocent-looking plateau lands ending abruptly in a terrifying sheer drop of thousands of feet.

At last below I see a multitude of tiny huts, like bugs on a red and yellow carpet, and we fly on towards a grim table-mountain. This is Makallè, and the table-mountain is Amba Aradam, whose summit is bristling with Abyssinians. South of Makallè is the old fort of Enda Jesus, where are the tents of G.H.Q.

My problem was to discover the tent assigned to me. Press people, who are hardened war correspondents, bring their own tents and equipment, map, spirit-lamp and torch. I had no equipment except handbag, music-case and violin, but I was given a tent and camp-bed.

I thanked my stars I had not been tropical-minded, for the nights at Enda Jesus were as cold and windy as March in Dublin. In the morning and afternoon I shed waistcoat and vest, but after sundown I was glad to have a fur coat.

My first day at the Front was a Sunday, and I was driven over a new road to Maidolò, where Mass was said just behind the lines for a division of Blackshirt Militia. The little altar was set on a rock in open country. Three soldiers with fixed bayonets stood on each side of the priest. There was a choir and a band of brass instruments. The voices floated into the clear air on that sunny morning : a scene of peace, yet we were only about ten minutes from the front line.

To my amazement I recognized the bearded priest who officiated. He was Father Garaventa, whom I had heard say Mass on the Italian front at the end of the Great War. Afterwards I talked to him of the old days of 1918–19. He then told me of a mutual friend

—poor Father Giuliani, who had been killed a few days before in battle. He was kneeling by a dying Italian soldier administering the Last Sacraments when he was shot by an Abyssinian soldier.

Father Giuliani was one of the most valiant chaplains I have ever known. He had three silver medals for valour, and in addition was one of the famous preachers in Italy. I shall never forget the sermon I heard him preach in January 1919, in a church in North Italy that had been bombed. He stood in front of the altar and preached to us, and around his feet were many tiny children who had been put by their mothers within the altar-rails.

My visit to the Front in Abyssinia awakened countless slumbering memories. I met many friends whose lives had never crossed mine since those days of 1918. Many of those militia men, whose tents I visited at Maidolò, had fought in the Great War side by side with British and French troops.

After Mass I drank coffee with them, and countless glasses of Maraschino, which brought every sentimental thought in my mind to the surface. Some would say : " To Hell with the British," and then in the next breath : " Do you remember Captain Radcliffe, or Lieutenant Smith, or Sergeant Turner—what splendid fellows they were ? "

I spent many hours discussing the war freely with those soldiers. One of the battalions from Palermo was called the married men's battalion. Not one of them had less than four children at home, and yet they had all volunteered for active service in East Africa.

Many of them who had fought in the Great War had renounced grades and officer's rank to join the Blackshirt militia battalions.

" Why did you volunteer ? " said I to several.

" Because we were unemployed," said they. " Where can we emigrate ? America is closed to us, and so is Australia. What can we do ? It is better to be out here where we get a bit of money which we can send home, and, besides, there is the adventure."

Then one soldier stooped down, picked up a sod, broke it between his fingers, with the air of a connoisseur, saying : " Look at that : it is good earth. A mighty fine crop could come out of that."

I then remembered what the old fish-woman at Genoa had said to me a few weeks before : " This, signore, is a war of the poor. We are all with the Duce, because he knows that Italy is a poor country. I lost my husband in the war of 1915–18, and I've sent my only son out to Abyssinia. It was better than having him unemployed at home wondering where the next meal would come from."

As I wandered from one battalion to another, I could only marvel at the transformation which had taken place in the Italian nation since those stirring days of Vittorio Veneto. I well remember the regional differences of Italy in those days—how the Piemontese, or Milanese, used to scorn the Neapolitan, a Sicilian. Italy was a country of individualist regions and city states. To-day there is unity. On the front line in Abyssinia, just below Amba Aradam, I found the militia of Catania and Syracuse next those from Forlì and Pisa.

I arrived at Makallè some days after the fierce Battle of the Caverns in the sinister valley of the Calaminò, near where the River Gabbat joins the River Ghevà and in the neighbourhood of that famous landmark, the " Solitary Tree." Driving from the camp of Enda Jesus, we passed through wild, monotonous country

consisting of hills, plateau land, and gorges, full of
a riot of rank vegetation.

After passing through the small village of Debri,
whose burnt *tuculs* were a grim reminder of battle, we
finally reached the valley of the Calaminò.

It was here that the Division of Blackshirts had their
baptism of fire in the battles from January 19 to 23.
Opposing fire from all sides, the Division had to advance
against the Abyssinian troops of Ras Mulugeta posted
on Amba Aradam, or Ship Mountain, so-called because
it resembles the prow of a ship.   From the summit of
the table-mountain Amba Aradam, the Abyssinians were
able to threaten the movements of the Italian troops in
the valley beneath.

It was a ferocious battle : step by step the Blackshirts
advanced, carrying machine-guns on their shoulders.   It
was necessary to fight on the edges of precipices, all
the time clinging desperately to jagged rocks with dizzy
drops beneath.   It was a battle of bayonet charges and
hand-grenades.   Soldiers whom I saw in advance posts
gave me epic descriptions of the amazing powers possessed by Abyssinian soldiers of camouflaging their positions.   Branches of trees, leaves, and rocks were used
by them to conceal their whereabouts.   They often
rubbed earth over their faces and dressed their heads
in leaves to avoid being seen, and they remained motionless for hours until darkness.   Then they would creep
forward like cats and make their sudden attack.

On one occasion some of their troops advanced
against a tiny *fortino* and managed to arrive within eight
metres of the Italians without being seen by the watchful
machine-gunners—and this was in the early afternoon !
The courage of the Abyssinian fighters was remarkable ;
they rushed *en masse* upon the machine-guns.

The battle conditions in those cavern-riddled fastnesses of Amba Aradam, and the savage peaks of the Tembien, were admirably suited to troops like the Alpini, who could scale precipices and fight engagements in country that would give the ordinary soldier an attack of vertigo. I then remembered my Alpini friends on the *Sardegna*—hardened fellows from Piemonte and the Venetian Province, whose epic in the Great War was written by Paolo Monelli in his book, *Scarpe Al Sole*.

When I saw him in the Press tent at Enda Jesus I said to him: " Now I know why you were sent out here as war correspondent. The Alpini must be going to do some more of their hair-raising, night-climbing attacks."

When we came to the end of the road through the Calaminò valley we halted the car, and walked along a track by the river. The river flowed peacefully through a luxuriant wealth of vegetation. The birds sang sweetly in the bushes and overhanging trees. On each side were grim mountain heights. We came to a lonely little outpost of about twelve soldiers guarding one section of the valley. The men were behind a roughly walled fort of loose stones. I can imagine few more dismal spots in the world than that *fortino* in the Calaminò valley—a handful of men dumped down in a hostile territory a few steps away from the mobile enemy.

Even in sunlight, every one of those men had to keep his eyes skinned. He had to be for ever ready to face sudden attack, for the enemy could so easily creep up to them under cover of those rocks and twining undergrowth. At night I could imagine no grimmer task than to keep watch with machine-gun behind the tiny wall of loose stones. Sounds at night become magnified, and the rustling of bushes or a falling stone creates terrors. To add to these terrors there were the hyænas and jackals, which were particularly active after the big battle.

The long-drawn moan of the hyænas, which the Abyssinians call vampires, and the baby laughter of the carrion-scenting jackals, were heard by night. For days after the battle the wind blew over from beyond the lines the terrible odour of unburied corpses.

It does not pay to take short cuts on the Abyssinian front. One of my friends, a well-known war correspondent, who was visiting the scene of the caverns with other journalists, tried to make a short cut and lost his way. In his ignorance he went on walking towards the Abyssinian lines. Suddenly he saw an Abyssinian warrior between two rocks of the mountain, staring, with gun pointed straight at him. He raised his hands and was sure that his last moment had come. But the Abyssinian did not move. Then the wind blew, and a terrible stench assailed the American's nostrils. He then found that the Abyssinian was dead. He had been killed five days before, but his body was wedged in between two rocks. After that warning he turned back, and the rest of the company soon rescued him.

At Makallè I witnessed the state entry of Marshal Badoglio, and his review of the native troops of Ras Gugsa.

Makallè is an important town on account of its market, which takes place every week and is thronged by natives from this part of Abyssinia. When Marshal Badoglio arrived the women, dressed in white, stood in groups and performed the " Ellelta," a cry of joyful welcome. It is a shrill trilling sound made at the back of their throat, and in the distance it sounded like a choir of birds.

This cry of joy was in honour of the Marshal, but it is the ritual performed by the women when their

warriors return from battle. They stand on the cliffs
and gaze out over the country, waiting for the arrival
of husband or son. When they see them approach
they all trill loudly in their honour. After Marshal
Badoglio had reviewed the troops of Ras Gugsa, he
received the homage of the various chieftains and made
a formal speech. Each sentence was translated by a
very tall Abyssinian interpreter for their benefit. In
the speech the Marshal informed the chieftains that Italy
would give the people of the Tigrè justice and would
compensate them for the losses they had sustained in war.

" Gold is tested by fire," he said, " and friendship
is tested in hard times. Italy will see how loyal the
Tigreans will prove as friends, and she will never forget them." He then concluded with the characteristic
phrase : " We, Italians, are men of war ; we do not
love words, we love deeds."

From such a speech I realized that in dealing with
the Ras and chieftains, the Italian generals must employ
a solemn and ceremonious language. After the review,
I was presented to Ras Gugsa and was allowed to visit
his castle—an imposing building on an eminence outside the town. In every window there were machine-
gunners from the Ras's army ensconced behind sandbags.

Ras Gugsa did not impress me by his military appearance. Perhaps this was due to the fact that he was
not dressed in the Abyssinian warrior's costume but in
khaki. His body was rather soft and flabby and lacked
that sinewy elegance I so much admired in the Ascari
troops. He was good-looking, but rather languid, and
did not look like a fighter. I was, however, impressed
by the smart appearance of his troops, who had been
equipped by the Italians.

I was honoured by an invitation to lunch at G.H.Q.,
and had the opportunity of making the acquaintance of

Marshal Badoglio. Meals in G.H.Q. tent are a formidable business for a mere civilian. When I walked to my place amid all the " brass-hats " and " red tabs " I felt like a frightened hero of one of H. M. Bateman's drawings. It was the most solemn lunch I ever attended, because hardly anyone opened his lips in speech.

" They are silent and as ascetic-looking as a community of Carthusian monks," I said to myself, as I plodded away through my spaghetti and swallowed copious draughts of Chianti wine.

Just then I caught sight of a naval officer at the opposite side of the tent—he smiled and winked roguishly at me. Afterwards he said to me : " You should dine with the Navy and you would hear plenty of talk."

" What ? " I said. " Do the modern Italian headquarters make such a practice of taciturnity ? "

" Yes," he replied. " The military slogan is—deeds, not words. Modern generals don't talk, they act. Besides, the Marshal is a Piemontese and, so, more silent and hard-bitten than a Scotsman."

I smiled, because I remembered a certain Italian general—a Ferrarese—whose *bons mots* were the theme of Roman society.

Marshal Badoglio is an imposing figure—characteristically Piemontese, thick-set, firm and resolute, with an obstinate chin and a smile that makes you correct your first impression.

" Calm, cold-blooded, mathematical," you say to yourself, but when he smiles he resembles a good-natured father of a family.

I was lucky enough to witness the submission of 3,000 warriors of the Azebò Galla tribe, who lived in the neighbourhood of Lake Ashangi, beyond the mountain fastness of Amba Alagi. When the Gallas arrived at the Italian lines they were weary and famished. They had trekked for days and days, subsisting as best they could on herbs and what loot they could *razz*. They had fought two fierce battles with Abyssinian foes, and had lost 107 men.

As for their wives and children, they had left them in their own country, telling them to take to the mountains and to fend for themselves as best they could in the caves and lairs. " We submit to you," said they to the Italian commander, " but Italy must come to our aid and send machines through the air over there to save our families."

A languid, worn-out crew they were when they arrived, but as soon as they had been given flour and water, and had made their bread, they began at once to execute a war-dance. I saw them descending a hill at noon, dancing as they went, and brandishing long spears, while their curved swords flashed in the sun. Tall, thin, swarthy warriors, dressed in dirty white *shammas*, with bare feet and legs.

As soon as they saw us they cried out, " Kerbit— Kerbit ! " which, I was told, meant " matches " (the Gallas generally make fire by rubbing pieces of wood together, so matches were a luxury). After a great deal of bargaining, with the help of our Ascari boy servant, Tessariam, I managed to emerge triumphant with one of the scimitars after paying two thalers. The Gallas, when I offered Italian lire in coins and notes, shook their heads, made a sound with their lips, and shouted out : " Karshi—Karshi," which means " thalers." The Abyssinian thaler is a large, beautiful silver coin with the head of Maria Theresa upon it and the date 1780. No other money satisfied the natives, and when one gave it to them they bit the coin and tested it carefully. A thaler cost anything from 10 to 15 lire.

The Galla warrior from whom I purchased the curved sword was a tall, strapping fellow with fine features and a head of tousled black hair. With the aid of the bright-eyed youth Tessariam I managed to carry on a brisk conversation, and when words failed it was possible to use a wealth of gesture.

He was fully armed, for he had spear, curved sword, rifle (very old pattern) and a sinister little curved knife in a scabbard fitted to his cartridge-belt.

" What is that little knife for ? " said I to Tessariam.

" That is for mutilating," answered the boy with a sardonic grin. He then went on to enlighten me on the subject of the barbarous practice of castration which the warriors in the heat of battle often carry out on the persons of their enemies. The Galla warrior when he was questioned concerning the functions of the little knife replied that it was only used on the enemy after death. The trophies are dried and used as ornaments.

In the evening, when I was in the Galla camp a new big batch arrived and began at once to establish themselves in their new surroundings. As they had come from a low-lying district near Lake Ashangi, they found the atmosphere of the hills very cold, and they wrapped their voluminous *shammas* around their heads.

To anyone who is interested in the ways of the nomadic Gypsies it was fascinating to watch the primitive Gallas. First they spied out the land, and some saw that down by a stream there were thick rushes. With a wild whoop a body of them rushed down and tore up the reeds. Then they began to build rapidly strange structures of reeds as protection against the wind which always rises in the late afternoon. They set little heaps of loose stones to strengthen the walls of the reed tents. Then they lit fires and heated round stones, while others took a mass of flour, moistened it and

rolled it into a big white ball. Next they put a very
hot round stone inside the moist ball and set the mass
to cook by the fire. By these means the *berguttà*, or
bread, is cooked all the way through.

From being a chaotic band of nomads, wearied and
hungry, they had become an efficient tribe. All around
me were the little green reed structures with their heaps
of stones and fires burning merrily. Then someone said
that it was time for them to dance another " Fantasia,"
and a sudden ripple of excitement passed through the
serried bands. Here and there men jumped to their
feet and brandished their swords and spears. They
formed up into bands of twenty or thirty. Each band
made a circle and encouraged the principal dancers to
face one another in mock battle. Two would begin to
jerk their bodies about and prance and wriggle, waving
their swords and making passes at each other. With
cat-like agility they would advance and retreat, and all
the time the chorus of the rest would sway their bodies
and chant in a monotonous sing-song the following
wild tune, which I was able to transcribe:

Again and again they repeated the sing-song, swaying
their bodies, beating their hands, and one leader blew
martially on a little brass trumpet, which I was told
was the instrument of war. It was all a performance
of mad excitement, and I watched the two dancers roll
their eyes and lurch towards each other.

The sweat poured down their swarthy cheeks and
necks, the curved scimitars flashed in the setting sun.

Then I heard the word " Anta ! " (Listen), and one
of their minstrels began to recite a long rigmarole—a

narrative ballad it was—and he mimed it with appro-
priate gestures, advancing three paces and then retreat-
ing three paces, while all his companions kept up a
continual buzzing comment.

I should have continued for hours listening to his
fascinating performance had my attention not been
diverted by the Ascari boy Tessariam, who led a band
of the Gallas over to our motor. Their joy was to
get into the car and blow the horn—a noise which
made them laugh uproariously.

One of the Gallas attached himself to me. He was
a man of about 40, very black-skinned, with hair just
beginning to turn grey. A fine noble figure of a man,
with something wistful about his expression. He did
not join in the dancing or in the antics of the others
in the car. He just stood by me and gazed at me.
Then he handed me his long, heavy spear, saying,
" Zubu," which means " Good."

" What does he want me to do with the spear ? "
said I to Tessariam.

" He wants to give it to you as a gift," was the reply.

I took the spear and I offered him two thalers in
return, but he shook his head.

" He won't take money from you because he says he
wants you to be his *Ghetanà* (master)."

The Galla then came up and spoke excitedly to
Tessariam, who said :

" The Galla wants to become your son."

" My son ? " said I incredulously.

" Yes ; he says he wants to become your son and
go far away with you for ever."

" But why should he want to go away with me ? "

" Because you are white and have blue eyes. The
white man has all the graces of God."

The Galla then looked at me imploringly in the hope

that I would take him under my wing. He pointed to the motor-car lamps which had been turned on, saying (as Tessariam told me) that the light was the eye of God.

When he saw me depart he bowed his head and sat apart from the rest—the picture of unrelieved sorrow. I felt sad to leave him, and I shall long remember his eager face and quiet dignity of manner.

Some days later at Adua I came across the famous " Phantom Band," which was led by a splendid personality called Ligg Tuclu. Ligg Tuclu submitted when the Italians captured Adua. He was an Abyssinian noble, and a relation, I was told, of King John's family. He turned against the Abyssinians when Ras Seyum took his lands and property and exiled him.

Ligg Tuclu and his band of 300 used to go out of the lines at night and not return for three or four days. When they did return they would bring back rifles of the enemy instead of scalps. Rifles they cherished as the most precious of possessions. Even in hospital I saw wounded Abyssinian warriors lying in the bed with their rifles beside them.

Out of such fighters Italy created her bands of Ascari troops whose heroism and loyalty were one of the great features of this war. There were few finer sights out there than to watch a regiment of Ascaris marching past. They are the most elegant soldiers imaginable, for when they walk they swing their lean sinewy bodies with as much rhythmic grace as if they had been trained dancers. They march barefooted and they can accomplish prodigious distances in a short time. I was told that they can easily march 200 kilometres in two days. It would, however, be more correct to say that they skip and run rather than march, for no white troops can keep up with them.

The commanding officer, for this reason, always rides
a mule. Unlike white troops, they carry no weighty
pack, for their food is of the simplest. Yet it was a
fascinating sight to see them in the camp cutting the
raw meat in strips with the knife held between their
toes. The strips of raw meat they hang over their
tents to dry and they eat it raw. Raw meat, I was
told, is responsible for the prevalence of tape-worm in
the Abyssinian population. Their one delicacy is *berberè*, or paprika. I was told by Italian officers that a
troop of Ascaris on the march can never resist the
temptation of *berberè*. Whenever they observe a field
of it in the distance they rush off with a wild whoop
to *razz* it.

The wives of the Ascaris walk about as proudly as
their husbands, and they wear scarfs of the same colour
as the regimental colours of their husbands.

On several occasions I had the opportunity at Adua
and Amba Galliano of visiting the Ascari *tuculs* and
tasting the *berguttà* and drinking *suà*, a beer of very
smoky taste with the colour of dirty milk. In those
tuculs I met seasoned old Ascari shumbashis, who had
fought for the Italians in the disastrous war of 1896.
Those old men lived on full of memories of those terrible days when Baratieri's force was cut to pieces by
the Abyssinian warriors in the mountain pass.

I left the camp at the foot of Amba Aradam a few
days before the big advance which was to culminate in
the capture of the summit, the defeat of Ras Mulugeta's
army, and the victorious advance on Amba Alagi. We
set out at dawn to drive back to Asmara—a magic
dawn of peace. Not a sound anywhere; a grey-green
light in the sky; tiny lights in the distance from the
isolated camps. Above us towered the gigantic, threatening mass of Amba Aradam.

My purpose in my motor journey was to visit the various colonies of road-workers who enable the Italian army to advance into the heart of this fierce country. In traditional Roman fashion the conquest of North Abyssinia has been a conquest by roads. I can now understand why the ancient Romans called their priests Pontifices, or bridge-makers. Their influence sprang from the immense importance which the emigrants attached to bridges, for the rivers barred the way of the advancing bands.

Imagine great tracts of wild country where the natives have never seen wheeled vehicles, and where transport has only been by mule over mule-track. As a result of the heroic work of the road-workers, there are now roads capable of bringing civilization and progress to a people sunk in squalor and misery. Here and there in the deserted country we came across colonies of road-workers—fine, bronzed fellows working indefatigably under the broiling sun.

Before I visited Abyssinia I believed the reports which said that the roads would collapse when the rains came. But now I have seen for myself that the long road from Massaua to Makallè is as permanent as the roads in North Italy. The foundations are of stone and the surface is asphalted. Three services of road-workers were co-ordinated. First the military engineers, who opened up roads at the Front according as the army advanced. I had seen them at work in the Tembien, with their rifles piled beside them, ready for any surprise attack. Then came the Ordnance troops and " centuries " of workers, who consolidated what had been done by the military engineers. Finally came the private industrial enterprises from Italy, who brought asphalt from the Abruzzi province.

We halted at colonies between Maimakden and

Adigrat. Here were tents, hospital, shop and recreation hut. The first place I visited was the hospital, but in most of the colonies it was closed as there were no patients. It has often been stated that climatic conditions are terrible in Abyssinia and that the Italian army would be a prey to every disease under the sun. As a result of the medical organization created by that great expert in tropical diseases, Sir Aldo Castellani, there were no epidemics among the Italian soldiers, and in some places I saw the orderlies of the medical units working on the roads.

In spite, however, of the wonderful roads, motor travelling in Northern Abyssinia was a grim experience at times for a nervy person. After four or five hours of rapid driving up and down dizzy, corkscrew roads, skirting the edges of precipices, diving down into deep valleys in an interminable switchback course, I ceased to have any body—I felt my head soar through a cloud of dust.

After days of driving up seemingly inaccessible mountains I began to realize the true value of the Italian motor-drivers, who deserve the title of Knights of the Road. Abroad we often think of the Italians as an excitable, nervy, temperamental race. But consider the chauffeur in Ethiopia—he is more imperturbable than any Scotsman I have ever met.

He drives ahead from dawn to dusk through the blinding cloud of yellow dust, over boulders, through streams, round corkscrew bends, without saying a word. Sometimes he misses an oncoming lumbering lorry by inches as he negotiates a hairpin bend on the edge of a precipice that drops a sheer 2,000 feet.

When I arrived at Asmara in the evening, I met at dinner a big concourse of officers back from the Front. Among them Marinetti, the founder of the Italian

Futurist movement in art and literature. He had only just come out of action with his troops in the mountains of the Tembien, and he gave us all a graphic description of the fighting qualities of the Blackshirts.

As I watched him relating his experiences with a wealth of gesture, I thought of the art movement which he launched years ago. He was one of the first to protest against effeminacy in literature, music, painting and architecture. Once in Venice he declared to his excited followers : " Burn the gondolas, those swings for fools, and erect up to the sky the rigid geometry of large metallic bridges and factories with waving train of smoke ; abolish everywhere the languishing curve of the old architecture."

The Great War stifled the movement of Marinetti for a time, but afterwards in Italy the followers of the master continued their task of destroying the last vestiges of the worn-out Romanticism. As an Italian officer, friend of Marinetti, said to me : " We need to shout twice as loud and exaggerate our theories in order to kill that accursed Arcadian idea which the Anglo-Saxon world has always had of us."

" What do you mean by Arcadia ? " I asked.

" I mean the Renaissance," he replied, scornfully. " Confess : you were drugged in your youth in England into thinking of Italy as a stage for pastoral drama, where rural shepherds flirted with rural shepherdesses. God save my country from Arcadia, tenors, and mandolines. Plague on those sentimental travellers who visit Florence with a guide-book to the antiquities, and look upon Italy as a fair tomb."

Strange to relate, Marinetti himself was not so ultra in his views as I expected. Middle age and fame had changed him from a fierce revolutionary into a conservative. Besides, out here he was full of thoughts of action and enterprise—but he added under his breath : " Those ideas of mine were necessary once. The youth of the country needed to be jerked into a life of action."

From Asmara I made my next expedition by car to Adua, the scene of the culminating disaster of the campaign of 1896, when the Italian force was outnumbered by the troops of Menelik and beaten after a gallant fight. The capture of Adua at the beginning of this war was a necessary prelude—a vindication of the past. Outside the town on a height the Italian soldiers have set up a monument to the heroes who perished in the battle of 1896.

I had always thought of Adua as a big town—the capital of the kingdom of Ras Seyum. It is, however, a squalid collection of thatched cylindrical *tuculs*, made of earth and dung. The only imposing building of stone is the Italian Consulate. The day after my arrival at Adua I asked permission to visit the palace of Ras Seyum, which is surrounded by a wall and overlooks the beehive town.

In the courtyard I came across a large band of native children marshalled by an Ascari boy, who was schooling them in the Italian alphabet. Inside the dilapidated castle I heard the sound of merry voices of women. It had been turned into a hospital for natives, where they could receive free medical attendance. On an operating table in the middle of the room lay a native with bare back exposed.

A doctor from Rome was operating on him for a tubercular wound. Around the walls and in the courtyard were many Abyssinian girls waiting their turn to see the doctor. Such a crowd of chattering, laughing women I have rarely seen. All of them dressed in white *shammas* with their black hair crimped and curled, and glistening with butter.

The doctor treated them like children, and took great pains to explain his meaning. He had an oldish native woman to help him in his task of marshalling the women. One by one he called them by name and made notes about them on a chart.

Their names were strange and hard to pronounce : Damalò Lette Haimanot ; Busunesc Boggalè ; Roman Iman. The name I liked best belonged to a beautiful girl with refined, sensitive profile and skin that was the colour of honey. She was called Ghera Mascal, which means " Slave of the Cross."

The people are completely primitive in their ideas. They have always trusted to the exorcisms of priests or to the ministrations of witch-doctors, who peddle amulets in the villages and fill their simple minds with notions of strange ritual. One of these witch cures was to cut the head off a dog and carry it three times round the house of the sick. In some places the people believe in driving hysteria out of women by blows on the back with a whip. The whipping, they think, expels the evil spirit. When the patient recovers from the drubbing she is said to be cured.

One of the most pathetic sights is to see the lepers crowding round the porch leading to the famous church of Enda Mariam at Axum. Not being accustomed to travel in the East, the thought of lepers filled me with horror.

I thought that they rang a bell to warn people of their approach. But the lepers at Axum held out their withered hands for alms, pawed me, and breathed in my face until I felt sure I was polluted by the miasma of the foul disease. Some of them lay under a sheet and stuck out a withered hand, others seemed to be literally crumbling away as they stood before me like a column of porous stone.

There are two entrance porches to the holy of holies —the church of Enda Mariam, also called the church of Holy Mary of Zion. After passing through the first porch I found myself in a large enclosure in which were very ancient slabs which must have belonged to altars in the fourth or fifth centuries—the same period as the two great monoliths of Axum. The stone slabs had channels cut in them, and were probably used to collect the blood of the sacrificed victim.

At the second porch I saw a venerable old priest squatting on one of the steps and keeping guard. In the enclosure were huts where the hermits live their ascetic life of fasting and penance. The church, standing at the top of stone steps, is a fine building erected by the Portuguese in the sixteenth century. It is surrounded by thick woods full of birds which sang sweetly.

Here and there I came across more Coptic priests dressed in white with white head-dress. They walked up and down under the shady avenues muttering to themselves and flicking away the myriad flies with white horsehair whisks. One of them, an old man with skin like feathered mahogany and a white beard, read to himself out of an ancient yellow vellum book.

The church was a sad place—the buildings were crumbling away, the enclosure was overgrown with weeds. The priests walked slowly and languidly up and down in this retreat. It was hard to believe that this church and enclosure was the centre of the Abyssinian religion—a place hallowed by centuries of tradition.

Christianity was introduced into Abyssinia about the year 340. The majority of the inhabitants of the country belonged to the Agau race, who were heathen animists. Their gods were Astar (Heaven); Meder (Mother Earth); Beher (god of the sea); Mahrem (god of war). It was the two brothers Edetius and Frumentius who established Christianity in Axum. The king of the country, Ezana, who had preferred the idolatry of Mahrem, as we can see for ourselves from an extant inscription, forswore paganism, and became converted to the worship of the God of Heaven (that is to say, Christianity).

After a century of orthodoxy the Abyssinian Christians, influenced by the Byzantine Church, accepted the monophysite heresy. They denied to Jesus Christ the two natures, human and divine, and held that they were united in one person. The monks who spread this doctrine in Ethiopia were the famous " Nine Saints," Syrian monks who founded monasteries and translated the Scriptures into Ge'ez—the ancient language of Abyssinia—which is still used by the priests at Axum. The Arabic conquests in Egypt separated the Christian Church of Abyssinia from the Eastern Church until the thirteenth century, when the dynasty of Salomonidi (so called because, according to the popular Abyssinian legend, they descended from Menelik, the supposed son of Solomon and the Queen of Sheba) established relations with the Patriarch of Alexandria.

Then in the sixteenth century the Jesuits from Portugal sent missions to the country, and even converted the King to the Catholic faith. But the natives, led by the monks of the Coptic Church, rebelled against the Jesuit teaching, they were driven out of Abyssinia and their books burnt.

In modern days a great deal of influence has been introduced into the country by missionaries, such as my friend, Monsignor Santa, who had spent thirty years of his life in religious and educational work.

The religious question will be no easy one in Abyssinia, where there are so many cults. Already the Italians have won the support of the Moslems, such as the Gallas, by their determination to build a mosque at Axum. At Massaua, some days after my visit to Enda Mariam, there was a solemn ceremony at which the Sherif Morgani, the leader of the Moslems who claims to be a descendant of the Prophet, made great donations of gold to the Italian cause.

At Adua I spent a day with Alberto Pollera, the most celebrated authority and writer on Abyssinian subjects. He has spent close upon fifty years out there and has written many books on the thirty races who inhabit Ethiopia. He emphasized the complex character of the Abyssinians.

They are a mass of contradictions. An Abyssinian is very attached to life and sometimes even cowardly, but yet he is able, when led, to fight with extraordinary ferocity, and die like a hero.

He is humble and servile, and I have seen him kiss the feet of Italian soldiers, but he can at times be haughty and unbending. He despises woman and thinks her of no account, and yet he is capable of fighting to death for her.

According to Pollera, the country of North Abyssinia offers great possibility for agricultural development on account of the rich valleys whose soil has never been fully developed. It is possible to gather two harvests a year from such lands. Water there is everywhere, but it will be necessary to sink wells to a depth of fifteen metres.

But the difficulty of the Northern country is that the rains are not great enough to fertilize the earth sufficiently. Northern Abyssinia is not as suitable for the European colonist as the rich land in the south of the country which has been captured by the troops of General Graziani. Up to the present the natives have only scratched the surface of that country, whether in the north or south.

It is a country inhabited by isolated bands of nomads. I saw here and there nomad shepherds following their flocks. All of them had curved sticks which they held horizontally at the back of their neck. The stick was curved so that it would be an efficient weapon to kill the snakes that infest the jungle. Those nomad bands live in huts of dried leaves and straw until the flocks have eaten up the pasture and then they move on elsewhere. The natives when they do plant a crop have the pernicious habit of setting fire to the jungle just to frighten away the birds who peck at the ears of corn.

It is common to see at harvest-time great forest fires which spread far and wide.

While I was at Adua I was the guest of the Ordnance Command in the camp outside the town. In the troops of this sector I came across an extraordinary variety of Italian types. As at Makallè, the regions of the country were all represented. Sardinian side by side with Sicilian, Genoese with Calabrian. None of those soldiers had any thoughts for Europe. Their minds were all full of the adventure of conquering a new piece of the world for their country.

I was more than ever convinced that the Italian army was an army of colonists. Some of them said with pride : " The Government has sent out a thousand ploughs by the last boat." The rank and file cannot understand the point of view of those European nations who try to prevent them from conquering that empty, backward land. " Is it not better for the world," they say, " if we civilize and enrich this land by our toil ? We who came from a country that is poor and over-populated, only ask to be allowed to work by the sweat of our brow." A young officer before I left said the following words, which have remained in my mind : " There are some countries in Europe who want the ruin and destruction of Italy. In the end they may succeed. But we shall fight to the last with the courage of despair. And Italy will become a cemetery which people will visit with flowers in their hands to cast upon the graves of dead ideals."

It was an interesting experience for me to spend pleasant hours conversing with the young officers of the aerial squadrons. My friend and mentor, Count Bosdari, introduced me to the members of the Mess in the airport. One of the most attractive personalities I met was Alessandro Pavolini, son of an old friend of mine in Florence, Professor Pavolini. Alessandro, though only 33 years of age, is a member for Florence, head of the Corporation of Arts for that city and high up in the hierarchy of Fascism. Like so many of those young rulers of present-day Italy, he is a man of action as well and had acted as observer in Count Ciano's 'plane which led the squadron called " La Disperata." As for Count Ciano, he struck me as the true young Fascist, belonging to that aristocracy of youth which it has been Fascist Italy's intention to create. He is an intellectual and an art-lover, full of a sensitive appreciation of beautiful things. But those qualities are balanced by others belonging to the man of action and sportsman.

Ever since the march on Rome in 1922, Italy has turned out many of those brilliant young leaders who constitute a new body of men in Europe. They are not class-conscious, for classes, in the old-fashioned sense, have been abolished. Some of them come from noble or wealthy families ; others, by dint of talent and hard work, have raised themselves to positions of deep responsibility in the hierarchy of their country. Count Bosdari quoted to me instances of millionaires from Rome joining the rank and file of the Blackshirt divi-

sions because they could not endure doing nothing in
Italy. They are all aristocrats in the sense that Professor
Camillo Pellizzi, himself one of them, gives to the word
in his epoch-making book, *Fascismo-Aristocrazia*. And
the Abyssinian campaign gave them all an opportunity,
for it was the first national Fascist expedition.

As a contrast to the young Fascist type I met many
of the older generation. There was, for instance,
Colonel Bertolini, the famous aviator of war days, who,
alas, was to crash with his machine on one of the *ambas*
shortly after. Tuscan born and bred, with the most
delightfully malicious humour I have ever heard, he
told us stories which Boccaccio might have whispered
in his ear. He enjoyed pulling the legs of solemn
Fascists and mocking their gravity by his astonishing
repertory of Rabelaisian yarns. At one moment he
would use the crest of the Colleoni family—" tre segni
della maschia possa," as D'Annunzio called it—as the
underlying motif of his anecdote. At another moment
he would quote proverbs about the native city-states
of his companions as follows:

> " Venetians, grandees all of them,
> Paduans, great doctors,
> Vicentines, mean as be-damned,
> Veronese, mad, the lot of them."

Sometimes I was the target of his sprightly Renaissance
wit, coming as I did from the British world. He made
fun of our national hypocrisy, our Puritanism, our
dowdy spinsters, and above all, our sexual repressions.

" Whenever I think of Hell," said he, " I cannot
visualize it as a place of eternal fire, but as one of
your English industrial towns on a day when the rain
is pattering on the slate roofs and the wind is moaning
up the street; a place whose horizon is bounded by
dark factory chimneys, with crowds of women muffled

up in waterproofs slipping in the puddles in their goloshes, with red noses peering out of heavy mufflers."

Bertolini, unlike many of the modern Italians, could always see a joke against himself or his country. Whenever I attacked Italy he would screw his face up and shoot a humorous glance at me as a warning that he held some weapon of satire up his sleeve to use against me. With all that he was proud of his profession, not for the honours he had won as pilot, but for the influence he had wielded as instructor to the youthful airmen. "I have created," said he, "so many pilots of the Italian army in the last eight years that I may call myself an aerial midwife delivering Mother Italy of a fertile brood of pilots."

Then there were the chaplains and missionaries whom I came to regard as the most valuable mentors, on account of the information they were able to give me about Abyssinian life. There was Monsignor Santa who had spent thirty years of his life in Abyssinia, part of the time at Addis Abeba. Monsignor Santa looked upon the Abyssinians with affection. "They are," said he, "very thin-skinned—just like children. One must always take them smiling and not be annoyed." He then told me that in Abyssinia the word of Menelik was like the Gospel. Everything he had ever said was supposed to be divinely inspired. He was not so much a warrior as a clever ruler who knew the mentality of his country.

"The Abyssinians," said the Monsignor, "love tribunals above anything. They love long arguments full of fierceness and rhetoric. That is why you will find a special arbitration judge in the market-place at Makallè whose job is to settle the arguments between two irate sellers. As soon as he gives his decision the two litigants embrace and wait for the next opportunity to start another quarrel. Even the children here play at tribunals with judge, accuser and defendant."

He told me of one case where a man fell off a tree and killed another. The family of the victim immediately, following the national system of vendetta, demanded the execution of the fellow who had fallen off the tree, even though the killing of the man had been accidental. Menelik, however, astutely gave to the family his decision, as follows : " Yes," said he, " the killer shall be executed, but it will be in the same way as he killed the other man. He must stand under the tree and one of you must fall on top of him." The family gave up pursuing the matter any further. This method recalled to my mind Arab justice in Morocco which was enforced on the principle of an eye for an eye and a tooth for a tooth.

I must say I felt inclined to agree with Monsignor Santa's description of the Abyssinians as naïve when I saw the behaviour of the men and women of Adua. They received the benefits of modern civilization from their Italian conquerors in a spirit of uproarious mirth. The new methods of hygiene became a game in which old and young participated. On one occasion in a secluded spot I passed a long row of brand-new latrines constructed by the troops for the natives. Those using them had stones in their hands which they beat together loudly and shouted at the top of their voices. The din was deafening, and the walls echoed and re-echoed to the symphony of roaring laughter as they wriggled about on their seats banging the stones.

As a grand finale to my stay in Asmara I visited with a few companions a *tetch* shop in the native quarter to test the ritual. We walked up the hill towards the line of beehive *tuculs*, followed narrow winding paths and stumbled over sharp stones. Some of them were open, and within I could see charcoal fires with figures squatting round in a circle. Occasionally we passed doors across which were stretched red and yellow curtains. Here and there mahogany-coloured Ascaris plodding bare-foot over the muddy ground slipped into the *tetch* shops, which could be distinguished from the other *tuculs* by the trade sign of the two empty bottles. We mounted the street to a large *tucul* belonging to a girl called Mulunesc Tesemmà. She received us gravely in the hut and shut the door. The smell of charcoal fumes, aloes and *berberè* was overpowering. The girl took up a can of oil and poured it on the fire. The flames illuminated her dusky face and gave her the appearance of a sinister witch. Her skin was very dark, smoky and smooth : it glistened in the quivering flames. She was a tall majestic girl of slender figure, and her flowing white *shamma* was closely moulded to the upper part of her figure.

She took off her *shamma*, and underneath she wore a red silk robe. Her necklace of gold coins, her gold ear rings and Coptic cross shone in the firelight. In the deep shadows I saw the canopied bed behind a coloured curtain. At the opposite side was a shelf crowded with bottles. On stools lay a profusion of coloured silk garments. Without saying a word the girl began to prepare the *tetch*, and when she had served it to us she took up an Abyssinian lyre-banjo and squatted down by the glowing fire. She put one hand lightly over the four strings and with the other she played lower down over the sound-box near the bridge. As she thrummed she sang in a low, monotonous nasal voice. The light of the fire cast her shadow across the floor. When we entered the *tucul* we were full of animal spirits and eager for a spree, but the influence of this solemn woman chilled our light-heartedness. When she paused

in her chanting we were plunged in a shadowy silence.
Not a sound save the faint clink of the gold bracelets
on her arms. Through the medium of an Ascari interpreter whom we had with us, we tried to start a bantering conversation with her, but she did not unbend.
She was languid and cold and did not make any attempt
to seduce. " And yet she is a *sciarmutta* (prostitute),"
said one of my companions meditatively. " What a
difference to the Arab girls one sees in the cafés in
Morocco ! " One Italian friend who had lived years in
Abyssinia then enlightened us. He told us that it is
the custom for the Abyssinians to perform a certain
operation on the female sex which takes away sexual
desire from them—a salutary custom, he added, in
this climate which acts as a constant irritant to erotic
impulses. As a consequence of the operation, which
is carried out when the girl is very young, Abyssinian
women become submissive to their husbands. " A
woman in this country," said he, " must slave from
morning to night for her husband : she is little better
than a beast of burden." My friend added that the
operation is performed in the villages by old women,
who go through the streets crying out their trade. They
are called *tagliatrici di farfalle* (butterfly-cutters). In
Abyssinia it is not considered a disgrace for a woman
to become a *sciarmutta*. In fact it is true to say that
men seek her as a wife, for she has managed to amass
a dowry by her trade. Year by year she saves thalers
and buys gold ornaments. Hence the profusion of gold
ear-rings, coins and bracelets I had admired on Mulunesc
Tesemmà. The *sciarmutta* has her own code of morals.
She is puritanical in her objection to nudity : Mulunesc,
for instance, was completely covered and she would on
no account have disrobed to please an Ascari lover.
It is strange to think that this *tetch* that we drank—

a mixture of fermented honey, water and perfumed spices—drives the Abyssinians into wild intoxication. Its effect upon me was to make me dismally bilious. The girl, after she had served us, poured some more oil on the charcoal fire and started again her weird chanting. The *tetch* and the mixture of potent smells drove us all into a state of dreamy somnolence. The girl's voice hypnotized me and the shadows seemed to deepen. She had become a witch wife, a Hecate weaving spells in a magic cell. The ceaseless repetition of the chanted rhythm released my mind from everyday reality and made me float away in a dream-land under the spell of the sorceress with her glistening black hair curled like an Egyptian goddess, her deep brown complexion and her eyes flashing in the firelight. After a time the song ceased and I awoke to the squalor of the scene. The *tucul* had become sultry and oppressive, and I was glad when we stood up to take our leave. She dismissed us with a solemn and even haughty expression, and as I saw her standing in the doorway in her red silk robe with her golden bracelets and ornaments, I thought of her as the priestess of some Oriental rite— Maya, the goddess of Illusion, bewitching men by her enigmatic smile and raising her arms towards the moon.

Outside in the dark streets there was silence. Here and there Ascaris slipped noiselessly past us like phantoms. In the distance I heard a faint chorus of insistent moaning : they were the hyænas which haunt the countryside at night-time. The Abyssinian, when he wants to express his loathing for anyone, compares him to the sinister hyæna. For that reason he calls the metal-workers, who are despised and feared in the country, " hyæna men." There is the same prejudice against the metal-worker in Abyssinia as in Europe where the Gypsy copper-smiths have been for centuries credited with

vampirism. In Abyssinia the "hyæna men" are supposed to practise their evil witchcraft by night like
werwolves. They are said to be descended from devils,
and they haunt graveyards under the light of the moon,
in search of corpses newly buried. They have the same
reputation for cowardice as the Gypsy and make very
bad soldiers. I was astonished, however, to hear in
Abyssinia stories of a mysterious race called the Roms,
which had disappeared centuries ago, leaving after them
a host of songs and legends. Alberto Pollera told me
that they were nomad shepherds, fierce in character, and
irresistible in battle. They were tall warriors armed
with long spears which they wielded with mighty power.
The songs describe how the Roms became so proud of
their military prowess that they even raised their spears
against Heaven, and God, to punish them, turned part
of their skin the colour of raw meat, wherefore the
birds of prey attacked them and tried to eat their brains.
The Roms then declined. It was said that their women-
folk only brought forth male offspring and their cows
only female, so that the sons could not find wives and
the cows could not find bulls. In desperation they
constructed huge tombs in which they buried themselves, their beasts and their wealth. In various parts
of the country one may see those huge tombs, which
resemble the prehistoric "houses of the witches" in
Sardinia. Portuguese travellers in the seventeenth
century called the nomads, whom they had met near the
River Tacazzè, by the name "Rumos" and referred
to their warlike qualities.

I left Abyssinia in February at the beginning of the
Great Push which was to terminate with the capture of
Addis Abeba, and made my way down from the tem-
porate climate of Asmara to the infernal heat of Massaua.
I sat on my bag on the pier for a whole sweltering night

waiting to embark on the ship. There was hardly room to move, for dense crowds of soldiers were disembarking. Beside me a crowd of Arabs from the Yemen lay huddled together under blankets like a monstrous rag ball. Eventually I managed to force my way up on to a balcony from which I could gaze over the scene. Below me was a wriggling mass of soldiers waiting wearily ; some curled up ; others stretched out full length ; some lying on their backs ; others standing up—a medley of shaven heads, faces, legs, thighs, hands at every angle, and above, a brilliant arc lamp shone upon the crowd, showing up in relief here and there sweating faces, topees and kit. Only an artist with the power of Picasso could paint that astonishing symphony of rhythmic tones with its light and shade, its movement, and the background of masts, booms, funnels and big guns.

The ship that brought me back to Naples was an Italian luxury liner, the *Victoria* from Shanghai. My companions were General Ugo Sani, a well-known soldier, commander of an army corps in the battle of the Piave ; Senator Tournon and Luigi Turco, both of them experts on agriculture and land development. The General had been staying at G.H.Q. as the guest of Marshal Badoglio, and he forecast the speedy advance of the Italian troops. " The Marshal," said he, " has the tenacity, modesty, and kindly good nature of a Piemontese villager. His whole career has been a steady, rapid progression from honour to honour, but it has never made him forget the rural scene in which he spent his youth." I told the General how I had once passed through the Marshal's native village of Grazzano di Monferrato in the province of Asti. Some of the inhabitants, showing me the house where the soldier was born, told me more about his campaigns than I could have read in books. The village butcher described how, when the Marshal returned from active service, he would spend his time with the men of the village playing bowls, or else chatting with his friend the parish priest. " Even in Abyssinia," said the General, " he never forgets to send a telegram from time to time to the village."

Soon the streets of Italy were to resound with the cries of triumph, celebrating the return of the Marshal's victorious troops. His message announcing the capture of Addis Abeba was celebrated in Rome in characteristic fashion and a huge crowd thronged the Piazza Venezia to hear the Duce announce the foundation of the Italian Empire. When the Marshal returned to Italy he published an account of his military operations in Abyssinia which is a model of what a commentary should be. True to his practical military genius, he did not once indulge through its pages in high-soaring flights of rhetoric. One quality which endears his book to readers is the noble tribute he paid here and there to the Abyssinian soldiers. Again and again he praised the rank and file and pointed out that their insuperable courage failed, owing to the incompetence of their leaders. In the end he gave general comments on modern warfare which are significant when read in the light of modern events. " War to-day," he says, " can only be visualized as a harmoniously co-ordinated use of all the armed forces— knit into a single fascio by powerful and consciously felt bonds of comradeship—under the orders of a single commander whose mind is fixed on the attainment of a single hope of victory." Those words have remained fixed in my mind, for they explain the whole development of the Italian modern State with its unity and harmony. My visit to Abyssinia had been made, not so much for the purpose of visiting that strange, Oriental country, as for studying the task achieved by 14 years of Fascist Rome. The month spent with the troops on foreign service was enough to convince me that the unity of Italy which had been sketched out by Cavour and Garibaldi in the nineteenth century and developed by the Great War had only now in 1935–6 been completely achieved. As an Italian friend said to me : " Cavour made Italy ; Mussolini made the Italians ; sanctions united them."

As I was writing the above lines on Marshal Badoglio I heard the news of the death of Gabriele D'Annunzio. My thoughts flitted away to the distant Vittoriale : I saw the tiny death-room with its walls covered with ash-coloured leather and the bed shaped like a bier on which the poet lay covered with medals, daggers, and pistols, the mementoes of his former triumphs. I thought of his Secret Book which he had given to the world two years previously with the words : " Here is a fistful of my ashes, I cast over you my own ashes. Begone ! " For years Europe's greatest craftsman of words had been chiselling his mausoleum with the ardour of a Benvenuto Cellini. Even the architecture of Vathek's castle had assumed a funereal aspect and the white stones with their inscriptions commemorating the heroes of the poet's world emerged from the green foliage of the garden with the precision of sepulchral monuments. To-morrow he will be laid beside the bodies of his legionaries in the little hillside cemetery within a short distance from the frontier of the Fatherland. That spot will be for ever haunted by the ghost of one who in his writing followed the dictum of St. Augustine : " Scribere est ars bene movendi." Lying there he is assured of immortality, for any invader of the Fatherland must march across that cemetery where the ghost stands sentinel.

EPILOGUE

Noon descends, and after noon
Autumn's evening meets me soon,
Leading the infantine moon,
And that one star, which to her
Almost seems to minister
Half the crimson light she brings
From the sunset's radiant springs.

ROME, September, 1937. I found myself at sunset by Saint Sebastian's Gate. Before me stretched the ancient Via Appia, the queen of all roads, leading from the eternal city to Capua, Benevento and Brindisi in the heel of Italy. I trudged wearily along the dusty road, descending the Slope of Mars. On my left I passed the small church " Domine quo vadis " which took its name from a legend of St. Peter. At this point the Apostle, fleeing from prison, met Our Saviour carrying the cross. St. Peter uttered the words : " Master, whither goest thou ? " To which the Lord answered : " I am going to Rome to be crucified again." Upon which St. Peter repented of his flight and returned to Rome to suffer martyrdom. A little distance down the road I came to a great round tower resting on square foundations—the tomb of Caecilia Metella, the daughter of Metellus Creticus, and the wife of the younger Crassus, Cæsar's legate in Gaul. By that majestic fortress I lay down to rest and collected my thoughts. It had been a long day of ceaseless plodding. I had begun my journey at sunrise on the Capitoline Hill, and from morn till eve had followed the whims of my mind which led me from one historical spot to another. Now, in the cool of the evening a great chaotic mass of impressions crowded upon my inner eye which I tried to marshal into a semblance of order. In twelve hours I had wandered and lived through the successive stages of Rome's immense history, and my mind was overwhelmed by the bewildering succession of personalities and stones. Gazing from the Capitol upon the Forum I had imagined it as it was some centuries ago when its desolated area was the haunt of oxen and buffaloes. It was then known as the Campo Vaccino : only a few isolated pillars protruded from the jungle. Such must have been its desolation when Romulus ploughed the boundary on the Palatine and fought the Sabines in the marshy valley below. Then " Roma quadrata " began its historic process of incorporation. First of all, Rome of the Palatine mountain : then that commune united with another commune on the neighbouring hill of the Quirinal and there were two Romes, the Rome of the mountain and the Rome of the hill—two distinct collectivities combining together in a superior unity. From my point of vantage I could follow in my mind the various stages of the process. First one hostile tribe and then another made peace with the central state until all the seven hills were included : and then the Comitium at the foot of the Capitol became the peaceful meeting-place and soon the valley between the Seven Hills became the Forum, or central point of the new community.

Occasionally a column or a piece of wall brought vividly before me some great personality, whose life and deeds floated to my ears as a *motif* in that vast symphony. A piece of stylobate and three columns of Parian marble brought echoes of the victory at Lake Regillus in 496 B.C.,

when the Romans won, through the intercession of the
Heavenly Twins, Castor and Pollux : a heap of sub-
structures reminded me of Julius Cæsar, for on that spot,
where he had erected an oratorical tribune, Mark Antony
pronounced the famous oration in March 44 B.C. at the
funeral of the murdered dictator. In those huddled
monuments of the Forum the drama of centuries may
to-day be re-enacted in a moment. When I raised my
eyes from the remains of the Temple of Divus Julius
I saw the Triumphal Arch of Septimius Severus, commemorating the victories of that cosmopolitan tyrant,
whose son, Caracalla, aped the airs of Alexander the
Great and fulfilled the prophecy of Juvenal that the
Syrian Orontes would overflow into the Tiber. And
the conical Black Stone of Baal was set by the Emperor
Elagabalus, the priest of the unconquered sun-god, in
the Forum amidst the sacred symbols of the rustic gods
of Italy.

Walking slowly along the Via Sacra I had conjured
up in my mind the vision of those later emperors :
Antoninus Pius, whose domestic virtues and colourless
character reminded his contemporaries of " Pius
Æneas " : he still lives in our minds to-day through the
columns of Eubœan marble of the temple he dedicated
to his wife Faustina. He had stood by the death-bed of
his adoptive father Hadrian, who, before breathing his last,
addressed his own soul in lines which pierce through the
chaos of those declining years of the Empire like a star.

> " Tell me, swift flitting soul, I pray,
> Guest and companion of my clay,
> Whither away, whither away,
> So pale, so stiff, so bare to-day,
> Never to play, never to play ? "

The Arch of Constantine had brought before me the
strong personality of that emperor who had marched on

Rome, after he had seen the vision of the Cross with the legend " By this Conquer " written upon it. Again I had mounted the Capitoline Hill towards the lofty church of Santa Maria in Araceli, for it is the one spot in the eternal city where Paganism and Christianity met together in perfect harmony. Even to-day the name Ara Cæli—the Altar of Heaven—suggests the name given by Augustus to commemorate Apollo's words uttered by the Cumæan sibyl in answer to the question put by him as to his successor. Apollo's words were : " A Hebrew Child, Himself God, stronger than all the gods, orders me from Heaven to give him place "—words that reminded me of those given by the oracle at Delphi to the Emperor Julian the Apostate when he questioned it as to the success of his struggle for the pagan gods against Christ. The church at the summit of those 124 steps is the fairest watch-tower in Rome. It is perched in the clear air above the city and its steps are always thronged with cripples, blind men, itinerant minstrels and ragged children. To all those humble worshippers Santa Maria in Araceli is an everlasting kindly presence. As they climb up the steep steps they feel as if they were rising out of the mirk and misery of the world into golden, sunlit spaces. From the top of the steps I looked down upon the bustling life of mankind below. I had watched the cars dashing through the streets and heard the distant roar of traffic and the faint honk of motor-horns. The world below with the scurrying multitudes seemed to be a gigantic ant-hill.

Then I had descended into the maze of streets, turning aside here and there as my whim guided me, towards the countless churches rising up to commemorate the successive stages of the evolution of the Universal Faith. At San Clemente, with its remains of a fourth-century basilica, I halted to visit its subterranean Temple of

Mithras. The altar was decorated with reliefs of the god sacrificing a bull, assisted by two figures representing the rising and setting sun. As I stood before the cavity which served as a receptacle for the blood of the sacrificed bulls I pondered over those days in the third century A.D. when Sol Invictus—the Unconquered Sun, of whom the ruler of the Empire became the earthly emanation—was exalted by Aurelian above all the gods of Rome. The gods of Italy and Greece had become pale, colourless phantoms without even power to symbolize Imperial unity. Divinity had been cheapened by the motley herd of emperors upon whom it had been conferred. For a moment in the world's history the absolute rulers debated which of the two universal religions they would impose upon mankind—Sun-worship or Christianity.

From the Lateran I passed to St. Lorenzo Fuori le Mura and thence on to Santa Pudenziana and by successive stages to St. Peter's, whose dome soars above Rome like a mirage in the sky seen by the lonely pilgrim plodding his way through the Campagna towards the city.

From the crowded Piazza Venezia, where lies the Unknown Soldier, I had followed the broad Via dell' Impero through the Forum of Trajan. The palace of the Lictors, rising like a giant in the majestic highway, was a fitting symbol of the modern idea which must harmonize with its ancient surroundings. The palace reminded me of the twenty years I had known Italy. Those twenty years became twenty leagues of wandering through Time, and I felt like Tom Thumb with the magic boots which enabled him to hop a league at a time and dash through the world like hey-go-mad. Melancholy Rome—the city of oppressive dreams, I had seen at the end of the War had made way for the Rome of modern youthful energy. As I walked on I had passed bands of young men and young girls singing songs as they tramped in step along the Via dei Trionfi. From the large avenues I could see over the Palatine and Aventine Hills. The new roads formed a girdle around the Imperial city and the girdle was a link between the sea, the city, and the Roman hill towns. Then I conjured up in my mind the vision of Italy's leader, Benito Mussolini. He had conceived the mighty plan of making this city express the aspirations of the Italians who, though bearing in their bones the most ancient traditions of Europe, yet are, at the same time, one of the vigorous, youthful nations with only a few years of national unity to their credit. I imagined I heard those young men and women crying out : " We are Roman citizens, and proud of our heritage, but we are determined to use to the full the benefits of modern civilization which we have won by our efforts."

As I heard them I thought of Nietzsche's words in *Zarathustra* : " It was from the sun they learnt their message —from the Sun, who, when he sets, is so rich : out of his inexhaustible riches he flings gold into the sea so that the poorest fishermen row with golden oars."

As I linger by this ruin at dusk I hear the distant sound of church bells of the eternal city. They remind me of the Italian destiny in the world to-day. Italy with the spirit of Catholicism rules from Rome a great part of the world, and by her example she may enable mankind to win new unity by combining the ancient religious spirit, the hunger for immortality, with modern mass-ideals. By pursuing such ideals Italy will draw men away from the modern Satanic impulses which would deny the spiritual peace, and call up the demons of

Hatred and Discord in every country. For the venerable stones of Rome teach us that Christianity triumphed
because it drew the enslaved and oppressed peoples
together in loving brotherhood.   The Romans of to-day
must weave their great and ancient civilization into
the general European pattern.   They must bestow their
qualities upon the neighbouring nations and receive
from the latter their gifts in return.   From France, the
natural ally and partner in the Mediterranean, they may
draw inspiration, for France since the eighteenth century
has been the fairest garden of culture in the world ; from
Germany with its North and South Teutonic tensions
they will draw the Germanic ideas of a natural hierarchy
of nations ; and above all, from friendly relations with
England and the British Commonwealth of Nations they
may derive that spirit of human toleration and frank
individualism which may be summed up in the two
phrases : " Live and let live " and " The Englishman's
home is his castle."   From England's island empire
they may learn that instinctive spiritual quality of happiness which caused the idea of imperial unity to bloom
into the Commonwealth of free nations combining as
members of the same family in the defence of their
common heritage.

When I rose to return to Rome the night had fallen in
the shadowy spaces under the old walls.   It was pitch-
dark, but the moon shone upon the Via Appia, touching
the cypresses and the ruined walls with silver.   Not a
soul was about, but the stillness of the night awakened
countless ghosts along this white, unending road lined
with tombstones.

DUBLIN,
  St. Patrick's Day, 1938.

INDEX

INDEX